GOLDEN DONORS

GOLDEN DONORS

A New Anatomy of the Great Foundations

Waldemar A. Nielsen

With a new introduction by the author

Transaction Publishers
New Brunswick (U.S.A.) and London (U.K.)

Third printing 2008

New material this edition copyright © 2002 by Transaction Publishers, New Brunswick, New Jersey. Originally published in 1985 by Truman Talley Books/E. P. Dutton

This book is printed on acid-free paper that meets the American National Standard for Permanence of Paper for Printed Library Materials.

Library of Congress Catalog Number: 2001047646
ISBN: 978-0-7658-0912-4
Printed in the United States of America

Library of Congress Cataloging-in-Publication Data

Nielsen, Waldemar A.
    Golden donors : a new anatomy of the great foundations / Waldemar A. Nielsen ; with a new introduction by the author.
        p. cm.
    Originally published: New York : Truman Talley Books : E. P. Dutton, c1985.
    Includes bibliographical references and index.
    ISBN 0-7658-0912-5 (pbk. : alk. paper)
    1. Philanthropists—United States—Biography. 2. Endowments—United States—History. 3. Charitable uses, trusts, and foundations—United States—History. I. Title.

HV27 .N53 2001
361.7'632'0973—dc21   2001047646

To Signe and Marina

Contents

PART III—PATTERNS AND PROSPECTS

Introduction to the Transaction Edition

When *The Golden Donors* was published in 1985, my preface spoke to the profound and complex changes affecting American philanthropy that had taken place since the publication of my 1972 study, *The Big Foundations*. In fact, what I imagined would be a six-month update of the first book turned out to be a three-year project. Today, as I look back over the past decade and a half, I realize that equally profound changes affecting American philanthropy occurred in those years.

For example, national prosperity assured that philanthropy entered the twenty-first century with the establishment of several new "mega-foundations" and unprecedented growth in the assets of many others. It is estimated that $41 trillion to $136 trillion dollars will change hands in the intergenerational transfer of wealth over the next fifty years, and more and more of the estimated 276 deca-millionaires and 350,000 millionaires will formalize their giving. The ranking of the big foundations has and will continue to change as will the number and kinds of vehicles wealthy donors choose to use. The trends are already visible.

IRS records report that 54,000 private family foundations filed 990 forms in 1997—an increase from 37,000 in 1989. Community Foundations have grown by leaps and bounds across the nation. In addition, for-profit financial institutions have entered the field. Over the last ten years, commercial donor-advised funds have become an extremely successful giving model. The first of its kind, The Fidelity Charitable Gift Fund, has grown to 22,000 donors and holds assets of $2.3 billion. The new young millionaires, most of whom succeeded as entrepreneurs in the high tech industries, have developed a new form of grant making they call "venture philanthropy," while philanthropy as a whole has embraced the concept that its initiatives should be strategic and outcomes-based. The best philanthropy always was based on achieving specific goals, but wider acceptance of these principles is to be applauded.

In the middle of all this change, it is important to note one that stands out above all others. In 1972, philanthropy was as much a man's world as professional baseball. Few women played significant roles, and the vast majority of these were widows and the daughters of the foundation founders. Even then, with some notable exceptions, it was male lawyers and advisors who controlled foundation direction. By 1985, that was beginning to change. Today, women are a powerful force in the field. They lead major foundations and overall they share board seats and staff positions equally with men. It can truly be said that there has been a "feminization" of philanthropy, and it remains to be seen if or how this will change patterns of giving.

Charitable giving at the turn of the century deserves the serious research and study that critics and scholars younger than I can bring to it. I leave it to them to update *The Golden Donors*, and I urge them to write the new books that will illuminate this most remarkable American phenomenon: institutional philanthropy.

Waldemar A. Nielsen
February 2001

Preface

Some books are the fruit of deep inspiration. This one is more the result of a miscalculation. By the early 1980s I had come to feel that my earlier study of the big American foundations published in 1972 was in need of updating. At that vulnerable moment the new Mac-Arthur Foundation of Chicago, in a revealing demonstration of its inexperience, offered me a grant for that very purpose. Astonished by this unprecedented act of support for my work by a foundation under study, I, in a revealing demonstration of my inexperience, accepted the offer. Shortly thereafter I began what I thought would be about a six-month task.

Now, three years of hard work later, this entirely new study is the outcome. The delay has not been due to uncooperativeness on the part of the foundations under examination. Indeed, this time around they have with only a few exceptions been quite helpful, and I should like to acknowledge the efforts of James Joseph, president of the Council on Foundations, in bringing this about.

Rather, the problem has been simply that far more changes, and more profound and complex changes, affecting American philanthropy have taken place over the past few years than I had realized. Not only is the list and the ranking of the largest foundations greatly different from what it was in the early 1970s but the nonprofit sector as a whole and the environment in which it functions have gone through a historic shift. In the intervening years, the hundreds of thousands of private educational institutions, hospitals, and cultural and charitable agencies have suffered a punishing ordeal of inflation. Public support for the expansion of governmental social programs of various kinds passed its high-water mark and has begun to recede. A mood of conservatism has spread over the country, and a new administration in Washington reflecting that mood has swept into power.

The developments of the past fifteen years have posed more problems and possibly opened more major opportunities for service by the large American foundations than any similar period in half a century. So the writing of this book has been for me a fascinating and ultimately encouraging voyage of discovery, in the course of which I have received much valuable help and for which I am most grateful.

First of all I want to thank the MacArthur Foundation not only for its help but also for the terms on which it was given. In the words of President John Corbally, "In making you this grant the MacArthur Foundation wants to be clear that you have the same freedom and the same responsibility for its use as our Prize Award recipients. The fact of MacArthur Foundation financing for your study should not in any way affect your analysis and evaluation of this Foundation. We hope and trust that you will deal with our institution in precisely the same way you deal with the others in your study. If you should praise us in certain respects, we will, of course, be pleased; and if you criticize us, we shall consider your criticisms carefully. Our purpose in financing your work was to get the benefit of an objective appraisal of our efforts and see our activities in the broader context of the general evolution of the larger American Foundations."

Second, I should like to express my appreciation to the Aspen Institute and its president, Joseph E. Slater, for their assistance and to the great number of foundation trustees, staff members, and grantees who have provided me with essential and sometimes rather sensitive information. It would have been helpful if more of them had been willing to be identified and quoted, but I understand their reasons for insisting on anonymity.

I should like to thank the capable and cooperative staff of the Foundation Center in assisting me in my research, Virginia Hodgkinson and Murray Weitzman of the research staff of Independent Sector, and in addition Kathleen Levin, Susan Levy, Nancy Lea-Mond, Wendy Sprintz, and Lorraine Blumberg, all of whom were most helpful in gathering information and the preparation of the manuscript.

PART
I

The Backdrop

The Money
and the Men

The industrialization and immense development of the American economy in the 120 years since the Civil War have produced a few million millionaires (as of 1980 it is estimated that some 700,000 were alive and prospering), several hundred centimillionaires, and a dozen or two billionaires. Many of these fortunes subsequently evaporated in the vicissitudes of business cycles or business failure, and others, though they were preserved, disappeared from public view, having been divided among numerous heirs of the founders.

However, in a development of American capitalism not foreseen by Karl Marx, a significant fraction have been converted over the decades into private grant-making foundations. More than twenty-two thousand of varying size are now in operation, with total resources of $50 billion and annual grants of nearly $4 billion.

No other nation in the world has such an array of aggregations of private wealth devoted to public purposes; no other nation has been so encouraging to donors to create such philanthropic institutions; no other has given them, once created, such freedom of action; and in no other have foundations played such a significant role in the nation's life.

Among these thousands of foundations are thirty-six, each of which has assets in excess of $250 million. This book is about this small and powerful group—about the men who created them and why they did it, and about the magnificent accomplishments of some, the mediocrity of others, and the miserable failure of a few—and about the changing social, economic, and political context in which they now operate.

Each has its own special story: its own origins, peculiarities, faults, and virtues. As a group, they are institutions like no others, operating in their own unique degree of abstraction from external pressures and controls, according to their own largely self-imposed rules. They are private, and yet their activities cut across a broad spectrum of public concerns and public issues. They are the only important power centers in American life not controlled by market forces, electoral constituencies, bodies of members, or even formally established canons of conduct, all of which give them their extraordinary flexibility and potential influence.

Yet they remain little known and even less understood, shrouded in mystery, inspiring in some the highest hopes and expectations and in others dark fears and resentments. By some they are seen as the Hope of the Future, our Secret Weapon for progress; by others as our Fifth Column; and by still others as our invisible Fourth Branch of Government. They are as distinctively American, for better or worse, as the flag or the eagle.

The Big Benefactories

The list of these foundations and their assets as of late 1984 follows:

Name	Headquarters	Date Estab-lished	Assets
Ford Foundation	New York, N.Y.	1936	$3.4 billion
The John D. and Catherine T. MacArthur Foundation	Chicago, Ill.	1970	$1.5 billion

Name	Headquarters	Date Estab- lished	Assets
Robert Wood Johnson Foundation	Princeton, N.J.	1953	$1.25 billion
W. K. Kellogg Foundation	Battle Creek, Mich.	1930	$1.2 billion
Pew Memorial Trust	Philadelphia, Pa.	1957	$1.2 billion
Andrew W. Mellon Foundation	New York, N.Y.	1954	$1.1 billion
Rockefeller Foundation	New York, N.Y.	1913	$1 billion
Lilly Endowment, Inc.	Indianapolis, Ind.	1937	$800 million
Kresge Foundation	Troy, Mich.	1924	$790 million
William and Flora Hewlett Foundation	Menlo Park, Calif.	1966	$575 million
Charles Stewart Mott Foundation	Flint, Mich.	1926	$540 million
Carnegie Corporation of New York	New York, N.Y.	1911	$500 million
Duke Endowment	Charlotte, N.C.	1924	$500 million
San Francisco Foundation (including the Buck Trust)	San Francisco, Calif.	1947	$490 million
W. M. Keck Foundation	Los Angeles, Calif.	1954	$490 million
Richard King Mellon Foundation	Pittsburgh, Pa.	1947	$490 million
McKnight Foundation	Minneapolis, Minn.	1953	$450 million
J. E. and L. E. Mabee Foundation	Tulsa, Okla.	1948	$375 million
New York Community Trust	New York, N.Y.	1923	$370 million
Alfred P. Sloan Foundation	New York, N.Y.	1934	$360 million

Name	Headquarters	Date Estab- lished	Assets
Samuel Roberts Noble Foundation	Ardmore, Okla.	1945	$340 million
The Gannett Foundation, Inc.	Rochester, N.Y.	1935	$330 million
Cleveland Foundation	Cleveland, Ohio	1914	$310 million
James Irvine Foundation	Newport Beach, Calif.	1937	$300 million
J. Howard Pew Freedom Trust	Philadelphia, Pa.	1957	$300 million
Conrad N. Hilton Foundation	Beverly Hills, Calif.	1944	$300 million (anticipated)
Houston Endowment	Houston, Texas	1937	$300 million
Edna McConnell Clark Foundation	New York, N.Y.	1950	$280 million
Weingart Foundation	Los Angeles, Calif.	1951	$275 million
William Penn Foundation	Philadelphia, Pa.	1945	$275 million
Henry J. Kaiser Family Foundation	Menlo Park, Calif.	1948	$275 million
Moody Foundation	Galveston, Texas	1942	$270 million
Bush Foundation	St. Paul, Minn.	1953	$265 million
Surdna Foundation, Inc.	New York, N.Y.	1917	$260 million
Brown Foundation, Inc.	Houston, Texas	1951	$250 million
William Randolph Hearst Foundation	New York, N.Y.	1949	$250 million

(By mid-1985, as a result of a surge in the securities markets, these portfolio values had increased on average about 12 percent.)

These thirty-six comprise only an insignificant fraction of the total number of existing American foundations, but they represent a very high concentration of wealth, holding almost half of the assets of all of them. In addition, because of other special qualities, they have a significance even larger than their huge resources alone might suggest. Because they are closely associated with rich donor families and prominent corporate and other leaders, they lie at or near the center of gravity of the American establishment. Their position in the intricate web of personal and institutional influence gives them a power that less strategically located institutions do not have.

Their activities bring them into regular contact with leading individuals from academia, science, medicine, the arts, and charitable agencies of every kind. They are marketplaces and nodal points for the exchange of information about trends, problems, and emerging ideas in the vast nonprofit sector of society.

By the fact that they are grant-making foundations whose funds are not tied to the maintenance of a particular hospital, school, or laboratory, their resources are maneuverable. By their selective assistance they can affect the character of other institutions, whole fields of research, and the vigor of particular art forms or new social movements. They can therefore be instruments of innovation and social adaptation, as well as of general sustenance to established nonprofit institutions.

Most important of all, they can assemble the specialized competencies needed to deal with major and complex issues of public policy. The Flexner report on American medical schools, the Myrdal report on the predicament of American blacks, and the work of the Carnegie Council on Policy Studies in Higher Education, all financed by the Carnegie Foundation in its long career, are examples of the broad impact that such foundation initiatives can have.

In short, the largest foundations not only are larger than the others, but they are different in their possibilities. They have critical mass, and their funds have leverage. Their potential to shape and alter the course of affairs is thus enormous, which is not to suggest that all of them, or even most of them, are able to take advantage of it. But the possibilities are there. That this is sensed even if not clearly understood by politicians, the press, and the public is reflected in the extravagant expectations as well as the outbursts of fear, resentment, and denunciation periodically directed at them.

Mirrors and Windows

The establishment of the very large American foundations, which began in the late nineteenth century, represented the beginning of a whole new phase in the American tradition of charity and altruism. Up until roughly the time of the Civil War "benevolence" and "good works" were interpreted by the wealthy both in the East and the Middle West to involve an obligation of personal service and civic stewardship. The notion was that successful citizens owed a dual obligation of both time and money to the communities in which they had prospered. Many upper-crust New Yorkers, Philadelphians, and Bostonians at the time spent a good part of their free time in charitable work. Kathleen McCarthy in her excellent study of the evolution of charity in Chicago, *Noblesse Oblige*, gives the example of William B. Ogden, a New Yorker who came to that city, amassed a fortune, and served as its first mayor. Despite his far-flung business activities Ogden "never forgot in his busiest days to visit the suffering," and he spent not less than six hours a week in making personal visits to the poor.

But after the Civil War this idea of an obligation of personal involvement was transformed into monetized and eventually bureaucratized philanthropy. As McCarthy describes the process in Chicago, socially prominent men and women in the 1870s and 1880s moved further and further from the personal service ethic and became more involved in such activities as sponsoring operas or concerts in the name of charity. As one indignant cleric wrote at the time, "Jesus never instituted a charity ball where, amid the voluptuous swell of the dance, the rustle of silks, the sparkle of diamonds, and the stimulus of wine and women dressed decolleté, he could dissipate his love for the lowly."

Out of this changing concept of benevolence, from the giving of service to the giving of money, institutionalized philanthropy in the United States emerged. Altruism is now to a great extent organized, professionalized, programmed—perhaps even industrialized. As a result some would say the heart has gone out of it; others believe that the change has made possible some of the most important advances in education, science, health, and other fields in recent history and has produced human benefits infinitely beyond anything that old-style charity could ever have brought about. In any event the existing big foundations are the ultimate and most obvious manifestation of the transformation in the concept of the charitable obligation of the wealthy that has taken place over the past century.

Money and the Men

A closer look at the list of the largest foundations makes several points apparent: Some of the most formidable figures in American economic history are there: Rockefeller, Carnegie, Ford, and the Mellons. But some others conspicuously are missing: Where are such names as J. P. Morgan; H. L. Hunt, the Texas oil billionaire; Thomas Watson, creator of IBM; and the du Ponts? And who are these unknowns such as Irvine, MacArthur, Bush, Mabee, and Buck?

The answers to some such questions are available: There are so many du Ponts now, and their massive fortune has been split so many ways and into so many foundations, that no single one any longer ranks among the topmost. Hunt managed to make at least four of the many children he sired billionaires, but he was too stingy to give much of his fortune to charity. (Hunt was married to three women, two of them apparently in parallel, and by the time of his death in 1974 he left seventy direct living descendants. According to his biographer, Harry Hurt, Hunt thought he "carried a genius gene. He believed that by fathering children he was doing the world a favor, providing the human race with its future leaders, even as he provided himself with an ever-increasing flock of self-images.") Morgan may have been less wealthy at the end of his life than is generally supposed. And where the Watson money will eventually surface philanthropically is not yet known.

But the larger fact is that no one, not even the U.S. Treasury, knows just who the richest Americans are at any given date, where they may have sequestered their wealth, and where it goes when they die. (The extensive use of legal trusts of various kinds is one of the major obfuscatory factors. As the British writer Anthony Sampson said of these devices in his *The New Anatomy of Britain*, "The great family trusts are like underground rivers in a barren countryside, the only signs of whose existence are the green fields they make fertile in unexpected places." In the United States, *Forbes* magazine now makes the most serious attempt to map the location of American wealth, to the great annoyance of the individuals listed. The gaps and inaccuracies, however, are necessarily very large, given the inaccessibility of the basic information.) So it is not possible to make a precise evaluation with any confidence of just how kindly American capitalists are, and whether they are on the whole more charitably inclined than their wealthy counterparts in Western Europe, or the Middle East, or Asia.

But it does appear that Christian and Jewish religious precepts about charity and good works, a population with many immigrants from impoverished backgrounds, the immense opportunities for wealth accumulation provided by the expansion of the American economy in the past 150 years, and a political and tax system encouraging to such giving have all helped produce a wealthy class somewhat more inclined to philanthropy than is the case in many other societies. At least one conclusion can definitely be drawn, namely that at the present time the United States has far more private philanthropic foundations, and they dispose of far greater wealth, than any of the other developed, democratic countries. Not included in the foregoing list, it should be noted, are great foundations of the past that deliberately spent themselves out of existence, such as the Julius Rosenwald Fund. Nor are "operating foundations," which use their funds for their own activities rather than making grants to others, such as the huge Hawaiian trust, Bishop's Estate, founded by a native princess, which owns about 10 percent of the land of the islands but is classified now as an educational institution; and the Alfred I. du Pont–de Nemours Foundation, which has now removed its blemished record from public view by retreating into the status of a "hospital." Neither are the names of a few generous and major donors like Walter Annenberg, the Philadelphia publisher and former ambassador to Great Britain, who makes most of his gifts on a personal basis without channeling them through a foundation, included.

Examination of the dates when the various foundations were established, the industries on which the donors' fortunes were based, and the geographical location of their headquarters provides a recapitulation of American economic history. The earliest ones were based on Eastern fortunes gained from basic industries and natural resources: oil, steel, and coal. In the first decades of the twentieth century, fortunes derived from mass production and mass merchandising (automobiles, cornflakes, tobacco, and chain stores) were put into philanthropy, most of them out of the Middle West. Somewhat later, pharmaceutical, construction, real estate, and mass-media fortunes gave birth to other large foundations. Still later, the Southwest and the West Coast, through fortunes based on real estate, oil, electronics, and hotels, became strongly represented. Great wealth gathering has thus migrated from the East to the Mid- and Southwest and then to the Far West over the decades, along with population.

These successive waves of industrial and economic development are reflected in the birthrate and distribution of big foundations. New England no longer has, and the Rocky Mountain region, the Northwest, and Alaska do not yet have, any of the very largest foundations, although all now have some foundations of size and substance. (The distribution of major foundations across the country on the whole, but not precisely, reflects the distribution of millionaires. According to the United States Trust Company, which studies this subject, New York led the list in 1980 with 56,000; it was followed by California with 38,000; Illinois with 35,000; Ohio with 31,000; Florida with 29,000; and New Jersey with 28,000. Somewhat surprisingly Minnesota ranked ninth, ahead of Texas, in tenth place. Even more surprisingly the state of Idaho ranked ahead of both, in eighth place, with 26,000. And in density of millionaires per thousand, Idaho was more than three times as rich in this respect as any other state.)

The Donors

Foundations, even the largest, are typically the lengthened shadows of a few individuals, and the study of them has to begin with a study of their creators. By definition the donors of the foundations included in this study have been the richest of the rich. Some were colorful figures, including the eccentric Andrew Carnegie, the flamboyant William Randolph Hearst, and the theatrical Conrad Hilton. Some were more remote, even aloof, including the elder John D. Rockefeller, Andrew W. Mellon, and Alfred Sloan of General Motors. Some were remarkably obscure, given their wealth, such as Ben Weingart, who probably died of syphilis, and shy, withdrawn Will Kellogg, who according to his doctor "was deeply unhappy and frustrated. In my long practice of psychiatry I don't know of a more lonely, isolated individual."

Some were simply colorless, like Bush, McKnight, and Gannett. A few were downright nasty: MacArthur, Moody, and Henry Ford.

But apart from the wide range of personalities among these giant acquisitors, what kind of people were they? As a group, what do they tell us about the structure and characteristics of American society?

First, without exception, all of the builders of the fortunes on which these huge foundations are based were men. In the several phases of American history in which these fortunes were amassed, and down to the present day, women have not been the tycoons and economic empire builders. (The great disparity in income between men and women is not just a historical fact. In 1981 the U.S. Census Bureau reported that 669,000 men, but only 22,000 women, earned seventy-five thousand dollars or more, a ratio of thirty to one.) Their role in philanthropy derives from their being the wives or in some instances the daughters of tycoons.

In several cases, however, through marriage or inheritance, the donors of these foundations have been women. Ailsa Mellon, daughter of Andrew W. Mellon, created her own foundation with her inheritance, which after her death was merged with that of her brother Paul to form the present A. W. Mellon Foundation. In some instances the designation of the wife as codonor of a foundation was simply an act of courtesy by her husband. But sometimes the wife or daughter of the donor has played a powerful role in the formation and activities of the foundation. Edna McConnell Clark was a strong personality with strong philanthropic interests, and the foundation that bears her name is in a real sense her creation. Mary Moody Northen, daughter of the donor of the Moody Foundation, has been the single most stable and constructive factor in the troubled career of that Texas foundation. Mrs. Helen A. Benedict, daughter of John Andrus, donor of the Surdna Foundation (his name spelled backward), ran it single-handedly for thirty years after his death. Mrs. Virginia Binger, daughter of the donor of the McKnight Foundation, is the most active and influential heiress in any of the very large foundations today. Together with its executive director, whom she selected, she has provided that foundation with its guiding spirit and has been responsible for many of its best accomplishments. (Among smaller foundations outside the scope of this study there have been a number of brilliant examples of leadership by women: Mrs. Marshall Field has in large part been responsible for the remarkable achievements of the Field Foundation, and Mrs.

Mary Lasker has personally led the influential work of the Albert and Mary Lasker Foundation. Mrs. Brooke Astor has given extraordinarily effective leadership to the work of the foundation established by her late husband, Vincent Astor.)

In few instances women have been prominent essentially as troublemakers and gadflys. Mrs. Archibald Bush, Zsa Zsa Gabor, one-time wife of Conrad Hilton, and Laura Winston, common-law wife of the donor of the Weingart Foundation, through litigation tried to divert foundation assets to themselves. Jane Irvine Smith and Willametta Keck laid heavy legal siege against the Irvine and Keck foundations to try to force the trustees to manage their assets in a more productive fashion.

On the whole, however, large-scale philanthropy is made up of male-dominated institutions. With few exceptions, men have been the decisive factors in creating the foundations; they have been responsible, as in the case of Rockefeller, Carnegie, and Robert Wood Johnson, for some of philanthropy's greatest achievements; and in other instances—Irvine, Moody, Keck, and others—they have been responsible for some of its worst fiascoes. Males, white males, have likewise generally controlled the boards and have monopolized the senior executive and professional staff positions. This has now begun slowly to change as the legal, economic, professional, and social status of women in American society generally has improved.

Second, there are no blacks, Hispanics, or Asians among the donors of the largest foundations; there are no Italians or Poles. One was a Catholic (Hilton), and one, Ben Weingart, of Jewish background, but he was not a religious man and took no part in the affairs of the Jewish community. Individuals of northern European and Protestant background have been predominant in the American economy and in American philanthropy and possibly remain so at the present time, although any listing of the large foundations tends to reflect the large fortunes accumulated at least twenty or thirty years previously.

From a social-class perspective, the big money that has gone into philanthropy has not been aristocratic or "old" money on the whole but has come from the fruits of entrepreneurship and the efforts of mostly "self-made" men. (This is consistent with the findings of current research on America's affluent. In 1892, 84 percent of the country's millionaires were self-made men; in the 1980s, 80 percent of Americans with a net worth of $1 million or more received little or none of their wealth by inheritance.) The A. W.

Mellon Foundation is based on the inherited wealth of Ailsa and Paul Mellon; William Randolph Hearst was a millionaire's son; the donor of the Irvine Foundation inherited the ranch from which its assets derive; and the donors of the Pew, Lilly, and Johnson foundations came from families already moderately wealthy. But all the other donors rose from more modest circumstances. A number were the sons of poor, in some instances extremely impoverished, families: Rockefeller, Carnegie, Kellogg, Kresge, Jones, Mabee, Noble, Bush, McKnight, and MacArthur. Of the remainder, most came from middle-class families who could give them a good education and a start in business but not large resources or powerful support. This group would include William Hewlett, Conrad Hilton, Charles Stewart Mott, and James Buchanan Duke.

In their business activities, the donors were, with the exception of Beryl Buck and possibly James Irvine II, all builders of major corporations over a period of many years, not mere lucky speculators or "wheeler-dealers." And even Irvine spent a good part of his life assembling and improving his vast ranch. Although several of them became involved in finance, none of these great fortunes, with the arguable exception of the Mellons', derived from banking. Likewise, it is to be noted that none of the donors made his fortune out of armaments.

Why They Did It: The Mixture of Motives

Establishing a foundation is an act like no other. It has obvious legal, tax, and financial aspects. It confronts the donor with the need to make final decisions about future control of the company and about the role to be given to heirs. But the most daunting aspects arise from the fact that it is done often in the face of death. And because the purpose of the creation is not profit making but the advancement of human welfare, it obliges the donor to hold a mirror up to himself and to his most profound religious, social, ethical, and philosophical convictions—or if he has none, to confront that terrible realization.

Moreover, these choices and decisions tend to come late in life when other demands and obligations are the most pressing and when a donor's sheer physical and psychic energy is often in sharp decline.

For anyone who would attempt to describe the motivation of donors in these circumstances, another difficulty arises because they tend not to be the kind of men who leave behind them a written record of their thoughts on such personal matters. What may have been their deeper psychological impulses cannot therefore be known, and it is fruitless to speculate about them in the absence of information. Social scientists have exhaustively explored the possible motives behind acts of altruism—guilt, the desire to be loved, the hope of eternal redemption, social competitiveness, even social hostility—to the point where acts that at one time were seen as virtuous and noble are now often made to seem mere manifestations of a psychopathic disorder. Nor have charity and philanthropy always been seen by philosophers and writers in a kindly light. Thoreau in the nineteenth century wrote that "he who bestows the largest amount of time and money on the needy may be doing the most by his mode of life to produce the misery which he strives in vain to relieve." John Steinbeck, the novelist, writing in the twentieth century, was even more caustic:

> Perhaps the most overrated virtue in our list of shoddy virtues is that of giving. Giving builds up the ego of the giver, makes him superior and higher and larger than the receiver. Nearly always, giving is selfish pleasure, and in many cases is a downright destructive and evil thing. One has only to remember some of the wolfish financiers who spend two thirds of their lives clawing a fortune out of the guts of society and the latter third pushing it back. It is not enough to suppose that their philanthropy is a kind of frightened restitution, or that their natures change when they have enough. Such a nature never has enough and natures do not change that readily. I think that the impulse is the same in both cases. For giving can bring the same sense of superiority as getting does, and philanthropy may be another kind of spiritual avarice.

Another writer, Louis Auchincloss, has a less caustic but still skeptical view. He begins by recalling Thorstein Veblen's theory of the leisure class and the concept of conspicuous consumption. But Auchincloss, a close observer of the habits of the upper classes, concludes that the flaunting of wealth to demonstrate the virility of the accumulator to the tribe is no longer the solution it used to be. He then reviews the other possibilities of what a tycoon can do with his wealth: hoard it, try to establish a family dynasty, collect art, go into politics (himself, or via his sons, as Joe Kennedy did), or give it away. In the end, he writes, "One keeps coming back to the conclusion that the only present practical, dignified alternative to conspicuous consumption seems to be plain charity. Would Veblen have called that the most conspicuous consumption of all? I am afraid he would."

Without attempting to plumb such murky depths, an examination of the available fragmentary evidence makes it possible on a more modest basis to identify some of the factors that led the donors of the large foundations to establish them. Clearly, tax and legal considerations are normally important and in a few cases at least were of primary importance in causing foundations to be established. Such considerations were not significant, of course, for those few created before passage of the federal income tax before World War I.

The desire to keep the donor's major creation, his company, in family or familiar hands was a rather frequent concern: Ford, Kaiser, Clark, Kellogg, Lilly, Haas (of the William Penn Foundation), and Noble. Irvine, Keck, Moody, Hearst, Gannett, and Duke, in fact, went to extraordinary lengths to attempt to assure this. Childlessness may have been an impelling factor in several cases: Weingart, the Pews, Kellogg, Jesse Jones, Mabee, Bush, and Sloan.

Apart from material considerations, it appears that a general sense of social obligation was often operative: gratitude to the country for the opportunities it had provided, sometimes remembrance of childhood hardships and poverty, or a feeling of the "duty" of the rich to share their good fortune. Traces of religious influence are apparent in the motivation of about a third of these donors, although only a few were active churchmen: Duke, Lilly, Pew, Hilton, and Rockefeller.

Only about half of them demonstrated any serious interest in philanthropy and "good works" during their lifetime: Rockefeller, Carnegie, Duke, the Pews, Kellogg, Mott, Lilly, and the Mellon heirs, outstandingly. On the other hand, several had little or no interest: Sloan, Hearst, Moody, Irvine, Keck, MacArthur, and Weingart. MacArthur thought the whole idea of giving money away was nonsense if not pernicious, and Weingart expressed the view that when he died, if he could, he would "just order a larger shroud and take it with him."

Thus, overall, about half of the large foundations were created in part out of a strong charitable motivation and sense of civic or social responsibility. But in half the cases or more the donors endowed their foundations simply because they were running out of time, were drowning in money, and were unable to think of anything better to do with it. This is not surprising, and not necessarily even too derogatory. They were primarily men of practical affairs, not saints, social philosophers, or reformers, and they behaved accordingly until the end of their lives.

The Purposes Intended

In looking over the biographies and trust indentures of many of the donors there is a quality of resignation, of vagueness, sometimes virtually of abandonment of their fortune, in arranging their affairs as they approached the end of their life. This is reflected in the common use of legal boiler plate in stating the purposes of their philanthropic creations and the absence of substantive guidance or stated convictions about the purposes the funds might best serve.

A few—such as Henry Ford and John MacArthur—had no identifiable charitable purpose in mind whatever. MacArthur refused even to discuss the question. "I'll make the money," he told his trustees, "you guys will have to figure out how to spend it."

Only about a third of them had specific objectives in mind: Kaiser in prepaid health plans, Richard King Mellon in urban redevelopment, Paul Mellon in the humanities, Mott in the "community school" concept, Kellogg in the welfare of children, and Robert Wood Johnson in the health-care system.

Most had only a local and parochial horizon of interests: Duke in the Carolinas; Jesse Jones in Houston, Texas; Moody in Galveston, Texas; Mott in Flint, Michigan; and Richard King Mellon in Pittsburgh. Some were sectarian in their outlook (Lilly and the Episcopalians, Moody and the Baptists, Pew and the Presbyterians, Hilton and the Catholics).

A tiny number of the big donors had in mind a concept of *scientific philanthropy:* that is, of getting at the causes of social ills rather than simply ameliorating the symptoms. The elder Rockefeller and Carnegie also had a highly developed sense of leveraging philanthropic gifts by influencing the pattern of government outlays. But such sophisticated thinking about philanthropic giving has been rare. Most of the big donors seem to have had no method in mind for their foundations other than to supply money to "worthy" institutions, such as their alma mater, or a hospital.

Likewise the fields of interest reflected in their directives were relatively limited: overwhelmingly, higher education, health, and medical care. Almost none had any serious concern with social problems, from mental health to minorities or the physically handicapped. Scientific research has been of interest only to a handful. International matters have been beyond the ken of all but a few.

In just two cases was the donor strongly motivated by ideological rather than social concerns, Alfred Sloan and Joe Pew, although a number of them were generally of ultraconservative and antigovernment viewpoint.

On the whole, therefore, what the donors gave their foundations was a mass of resources and little else. Far from being wise, farsighted, public-spirited, purposeful benefactors, many of the big donors set up their foundations if not in a fit of absentmindedness then simply as part of tidying up their affairs at the end of a lifetime devoted to business and the acquisition of wealth.

All of which may seem most peculiar, for it conforms neither to the myths that have been spun about the major philanthropic donors by their admirers nor to the fears and accusations that have been directed against "the ruling circles of American capitalism" by Marxist detractors.

In contrast to charges of sinister purpose behind their charity and of intentions to poison and propagandize society for the benefit of the wealthy class, the donors on the whole seem to have been little more than vaguely benign in their objectives, with a most rudimentary, even primitive, concept of the role their foundations might play.

The resulting social costs may have been heavy in a number of cases by delaying the development of effective foundation programs. But there have been some benefits. Had a large proportion of foundation donors been highly sophisticated in constructing and launching their foundations to carry out programs of social, educational, and economic change in accordance with their values and their business interests—in other words, if they had in fact behaved as Marxist critics have long alleged—then philanthropy in the United States would surely not have survived the political backlash that would have followed. It is only their muddleheadedness combined with generally good intentions that has made it possible for the elitist institution of private philanthropy to survive in a populistic and democratic society like the American.

Organizational Arrangements

If the donors were sometimes indifferent in their interest in philanthropy and amateurish in defining the role of their foundations, that may not be commendable but it is at least understandable. In dealing with such matters, they were not on familiar ground. But all of them in the course of their business careers had had vast and successful experience in setting up new organizations. They had accumulated great wisdom about how to structure a governing board and to include on it individuals of relevant experience. They were well aware of the dangers of conflicts of interest and personality clashes and how to avoid them. They knew, too, the importance of assembling qualified, specialized, motivated staff.

Odd then that as foundation creators it is precisely in designing the organizations to spend their endowments that the donors have been at their sentimental, innocent, and injudicious worst.

In moving from the profit-making to the not-for-profit sphere, they with few exceptions forgot their accumulated organizational skills entirely. Characteristically they went for advice mostly to their lawyers and accountants. On the substance of what the foundation might do and how it might be best structured to accomplish it, they either consulted no one; or turned to their minister, or wife, or child; or relied on friends and associates as ignorant about philanthropic matters as they themselves.

In choosing trustees, they most frequently named family members, when they were in some rapport with the family, or old business colleagues.

Staffing was most often an afterthought, frequently with the result that the directorship fell to someone—a failed but amiable executive of the donor's company or the retired head of a local college—with credentials that were at best coincidental.

In such board and staff selections, the process may not have been as utterly mindless as appears. The real intention of the donor may often have been primarily to serve some family purpose, or to maintain links between his company and foundation, rather than to meet the needs of the foundation itself. Or he may simply have turned to familiar and friendly figures in dealing with an amorphous and unfamiliar, and perhaps quite intimidating, set of problems.

Whatever the reasons, the results were often unfortunate and sometimes catastrophic. A number of the big foundations were distracted, even paralyzed, for years because of family quarrels, litigation, and disputes among the trustees: the Irvine Foundation was long a spectacle of such difficulties; the Keck Foundation has floundered for a considerable period in a similar stew, spiced by charges that some of the trustees were milking the assets; the MacArthur Foundation was still, six years after the donor's death, almost immobilized by battles among the donor's son, officers of his company, and the "outside" members of the board; the Moody Foundation got into such family warfare that the attorney general of Texas had to step in and reorganize the board; the Bush Foundation in Minnesota had a similar experience; the Edna McConnell Clark Foundation was racked for several years by differences among the donors' children.

Even among some of the better arranged foundations, considerable time had to pass, because of the donor's arrangements, before they were able to become fully effective: Andrew Carnegie at his death left his principal foundation so burdened with an overhang of future commitments and with a board so conflicted that it required twenty years to extricate itself. The Pew foundations were mediocre at best for a long period until able leadership took over and led them to higher ground.

Indeed, only about one-fourth of the largest foundations—Rockefeller, Kellogg, Duke, Kresge, A. W. Mellon, R. K. Mellon, Hewlett, McKnight, and William Penn—can be said to have been organized by their donors so that they were able to get off to a clean start and develop without undue delay into fully functioning institutions. This is not an exceptionally impressive batting average for some thirty of the all-time heavy hitters of American business.

Donor Demise

Foundations at the start mirror their donors and are a composite of their strengths and weaknesses as philanthropists. In a few instances, the donor has been a living presence for a good number of years after his foundation was activated: Rockefeller, Carnegie,

Mott, Kellogg, and Paul and Richard King Mellon, for example. But most often, even if his foundation is legally incorporated well before his death, it does not receive substantial funds until he is gone. As long as he lives—and a good fraction of the major donors have lived extraordinarily long lives—he can and typically does exercise complete control. (JDR lived to ninety-nine, S. S. Kresge to ninety-nine, C. S. Mott to ninety-eight, W. K. Kellogg to ninety-one, William McKnight to ninety, and William Moody to eighty-nine.) But eventually, sooner or later, he dies.

At that point the institution passes into other hands: family members and old business associates for a time, and ultimately strangers and professionals. The rate at which the influence of the donor and his family declines and that of individuals unrelated to him and his company becomes predominant varies greatly. Some donors have left a strong and enduring mark on their foundations. More often, their imprint is faint and temporary, usually because their personal interest and involvement were never great and their foundations were never fully operative while they were alive.

Very seldom does it last more than a few years. Likewise, it is rare for the influence of his family and descendants to remain strong for more than one or two generations. Although donor families in most cases have only a passing interest in philanthropy, there are a few notable exceptions: the Rockefellers, who have sustained a tradition of philanthropic interest over five generations; the Mellons; the du Ponts; the Pews, and a few others. But even these dynasties are beginning to become frayed. The current generation of Rockefellers are now quite divided in their philanthropic interests and degree of commitment. The Mellon tradition continues for the present but has split in its directions and may suffer sharp decline in the not too distant future. The du Ponts have never had an interest in social, scientific, or educational philanthropy but only in philanthropy as a form of baronial self-indulgence; and the Pew family, insofar as can be discerned through the heavy screening that is maintained around their foundations, is a disappearing factor.

As the process of transformation proceeds, the institution comes under the control of a self-selected board of trustees with no personal links to the donor and, to some degree, of the professional staff. It has then achieved its "mature" character, adhering to some extent to the traditions and patterns it has acquired but also reshaped by the changing social and political context within which it operates.

Only two of the foundations in this study are strongly influenced at the present time by a living donor: Hewlett and A. W. Mellon. About a dozen are still controlled by members of his family and others who personally knew him. Ten more are under considerable influence of family and old friends but balanced by the presence of a number of "independent" trustees. About a dozen, or one third, including the three community foundations in this study, are essentially free of, or without benefit of, direct influence by the donor, his family, or his old business friends.

The past fifteen years have been a time of profound change in the whole context and atmosphere in which these and all foundations have had to operate. It is necessary therefore to sketch in this background before attempting to paint the individual portraits of these sometimes wonderful and sometimes disappointing philanthropic giants.

Reform, Rejuvenation, and a New Dilemma

Foundations in the United States for a long time lived in the shadows of secrecy, which in turn spawned great suspicion. This produced periodic attacks by various critics, usually in highly ideological terms, which sometimes had a temporarily intimidating effect but did not significantly impede the great achievements of a few, or the abuse of their privileges by a good many. Their public standing reached its low point in the late 1960s. But since then, cleansed and forced into the daylight, American philanthropy has experienced a great reinvigoration and regained much of its lost public trust.

Almost as soon as the first of the large foundations were established by Andrew Carnegie and John D. Rockefeller they were denounced as instruments of capitalist manipulation. The staff director of the U.S. Commission on Industrial Relations, Basil Manly, in 1915 charged:

The domination by the men in whose hands the final control of a large part of American industry rests is not limited to their employees, but is being rapidly extended to control the education and social survival of the Nation.

This control is being extended largely through the creation of enormous privately managed funds for indefinite purposes, hereafter designated "foundations," by the endowment of colleges and universities . . . as well as through controlling or influencing the public press. . . .

As regards the foundations created for unlimited general purposes and endowed with enormous resources, their ultimate possibilities are so grave a menace, not only as regards their own activities and influence but also the benumbing effect which they have on private citizens and public bodies, that if they could be clearly differentiated from other forms of voluntary altruistic effort, it would be desirable to recommend their abolition.

In the 1950s the attack came not from the old Left, but from the extreme Right. René Wormser, a lawyer and fervid anticommunist who served as counsel to the Reece Committee of the House of Representatives that investigated foundations, said:

The grant-making [foundation] can exercise enormous power through the direct use of its funds. Moreover, it materially increases its power and influence by building collateral alliances which serve greatly to insulate it against criticism. . . . These dangers (to our society) relate chiefly to the use of foundation funds for political ends; they arise out of the accumulation of substantial economic power and of cultural influence in the hands of a class of administrators of tax exempt funds established in perpetuity. An "elite" has thus emerged, in control of gigantic financial resources operating outside of our democratic processes, which is willing and able to shape the future of this nation of mankind in the image of its own values and concepts.

The New Left, in the 1960s, borrowing freely from both ends of the ideological spectrum, saw the origins of foundations in the greed and corruption of the corporate establishment. The political power of foundations, according to this view, derives only in part from the volume of their assets. Even more pernicious is the concept of *strategic philanthropy* by which they:

> ... sustain the complex nerve centers and guidance mechanism for a whole system of institutional power. ... The Foundations ... are the base of the network of organizations through which the nerve centers of wealth impress their will on Washington. This network, the ganglia of foundation intelligence, is composed of a panoply of "independent" research and policy organizations, jointly financed and staffed by the foundations and the corporate community, which as a group set the terms and define the horizon of choice for the long-range policies of the United States Government. ... [They have] been nothing less than a means of shifting the balance of political thinking and political power in the United States consistently in the direction of the moderates and those supporting the *status quo* and against those advocating more revolutionary change.

The reality through the 1960s had remarkably little resemblance to these extravagant fears. From the period of World War I through World War II, there were a few examples of foundation funds being used for the propagandizing of the conservative viewpoint, but they were inconsequential. In the McCarthy period the great furor generated by right-wing columnists such as George Sokolsky and Fulton Lewis, Jr., about subversiveness and radicalism in foundations was without substance; and for anyone familiar with the boards, staffs, and activities of foundations in that period, the general charge that they operated in a highly coordinated and politically sophisticated way to shift the balance of political thinking and political power in the country to the left, or indeed in any direction, was impossible to take seriously.

In any event, such broadsides had little practical effect, and no restrictive legislation or regulation of foundations resulted. But beginning in the early 1960s a different kind of assault on them was begun that in time put them in bad odor with both the Congress and the public and eventually led to sweeping reforms being enacted.

This remarkable train of events all began with a bumbling but persistent campaign by a maverick old Texas congressman, Wright Patman.

For many years he had carried on a personal crusade in Congress against Wall Street, chain stores, monopolies, and "greedy millionaires" in general. He began his attack on foundations in 1961 with a speech praising their "wonderful work" but questioning the motives of some of their donors. The following year the House authorized him to hire a staff, conduct studies, and hold hearings. Over the next several years he published a series of reports charging foundations with various kinds of security manipulations and the use of their assets to seize control of business corporations. Through numerous stories in the press, the public became aware of these accusations and the Congress, both House and Senate, became sensitized to the problem of foundation abuses. In 1964, as a result, the Senate Finance Committee asked the Treasury Department to look into the problem. The Treasury report that was issued in 1965 turned out to be the most penetrating analysis and the most constructive set of recommendations concerning the faults of foundations and what could be done to correct them ever produced. Upon its issuance a number of the big foundations immediately dispatched their lawyers to Washington to try to block any legislation on the basis of the recommendations, and, for a time, they succeeded. But in 1968 a wave of taxpayer protest against the burdens and inequities of the tax laws led the House Ways and Means Committee under Chairman Wilbur Mills of Arkansas to begin major hearings on questions of "tax reform."

The first witness called was Patman, who got matters off to a lively start:

> Today I shall introduce a bill to end a gross inequity which this country and its citizens can no longer afford: the tax-exempt status of the so-called privately controlled charitable foundations, and their propensity for domination of business and accumulation of wealth.
>
> Put most bluntly, philanthropy—one of mankind's more noble instincts—has been perverted into a vehicle for institutionalized, deliberate evasion of fiscal and moral responsibility to the nation. . . .

On the second day of the hearings, Congressman John Rooney, a Democrat from Brooklyn, New York, told a story to agitate any politician's heart. He charged that in his previous election campaign his opponent had used his private tax-exempt foundation as his secret weapon, as a political machine "oiled" by charity dollars. Rooney concluded his testimony in these words:

"This time, Mr. Chairman, it happened in my district. It can—and probably will—happen in your districts. In fact the appeal of this political gimmick is a threat to every officeholder, in Congress or elsewhere, who does not have access to a fat bankroll or to a business or to a tax-exempt foundation."

On the third day McGeorge Bundy, then president of the Ford Foundation, made a bad situation worse by an extraordinarily offensive demonstration of arrogance before the committee.

In the following weeks the foundations tried to dig out of the debris by muzzling Bundy and by bringing forth some of their most imposing defenders from business and public life to testify on their behalf, with mixed results.

In the end the Congress passed the most elaborate set of new rules and restrictions ever placed on foundations, covering everything from public reporting to diversification of assets and the lessening of interlocking relationships among foundations, donor companies, and donor families.

The first reactions by some foundation leaders were gloomy in the extreme. The head of the Carnegie Corporation, Alan Pifer, said darkly, "From what I have witnessed in Washington in recent months, it is my sad conclusion that the role played by free private institutions as a bulwark of the American democratic system may be in jeopardy." About the new law he concluded that "its broad, sweeping provisions, the fallacious concepts which inform it, and the ignorance and myths on which it is based add up to nothing less than a vast disservice to the nation."

As events have now shown, Pifer in his assessment could not have been more wrong. The Tax Reform Act of 1969, although it contained some elements of overkill, was on the whole a most effective piece of reform legislation. It corrected the worst of the abuses of the foundation device by donors and their associated companies, particularly the use of foundations to avoid taxes without commensurate benefits to charity (the so-called payout problem) and as a device to maintain financial control of a family company. The result is that general confidence in the value of foundations both in Congress and across the nation has not only been restored but has now probably reached its highest point in history.

This transformation in the climate of opinion was most clearly demonstrated during the hearings held in Washington in late 1983, when the House Ways and Means Committee made its first major review of the needs and problems of foundations following the landmark legislation of 1969.

The tone of the hearings was generally respectful, even friendly, in sharp contrast to the situation in 1969. If Wright Patman epitomized the attitude of the earlier period, Barber Conable, a Republican from New York, epitomized the mood in 1983. In his opening statement at the hearings, he expressed the hope that they would "help the committee to help foundations continue their important philanthropic work with a minimum of hindrance from unnecessary or discriminatory rules. . . ."

The friendly atmosphere prevailed despite the fact that the occasion for the hearings was another display of foundation self-seeking. More than a dozen of them in the preceding months had lined up at the legislative trough, seeking special exemption from the requirement of the 1969 law that they divest themselves of very large holdings of the shares of associated companies. As Representative Fortney Stark, a Democrat from California, noted in criticizing these efforts, the provisions had been enacted "to prevent foundations from being a guise for the operation of a business and to ensure that foundation investment decisions were based on sound investment policy rather than a tie to the donor's original company. . . . The ferocity with which these foundations cling to these specific assets proves the wisdom of the underlying rule." The hearings had been scheduled initially as a means of dealing with this multiplicity of appeals for special treatment.

At another time, such provocation might well have produced a blast of congressional denunciation and further restrictions. But because of the beneficial effects of the earlier legislation and the good work of a number of sensible people in Congress and in philanthropy, the result was that basic reforms were not compromised, some needed adjustments in the law were enacted, and the usefulness of foundations was endorsed.

Patman, the Inadvertent Benefactor

The events of 1969 and what led up to them were not a credit to philanthropy. In previous years a few of the large foundations had made a record of magnificent accomplishment. But along with their good work there had developed serious abuses and habits that foundation leaders had consistently ignored or denied, deficiencies that the 1965 Treasury report had identified and documented.

The field of philanthropy was ignorant of the facts about itself—about its own faults and failures of performance, about comparative investment performance, and even about the needs, problems, and attitudes of its clientele. As a result, it was intellectually moribund. There was little communication among foundations on philanthropic issues. There did not exist a recognized forum or publication for the candid discussion of problems. There was only the most rudimentary base of research data and analysis on philanthropy because foundations had never been willing to spend money on such possibly embarrassing activity. In lieu of any effort to measure and examine the role of the huge private nonprofit sector in American life, a few paragraphs from Alexis de Tocqueville on the subject were endlessly repeated. And instead of a hard examination of the performance, possibilities, and limitations of foundations, ritual references to the Carnegie public libraries and the Rockefeller Foundation's work in controlling hookworm and yellow fever were substituted.

Individualism and encapsulation generally prevailed, along with a tendency to dismiss any criticism from the outside as irrelevant or malicious. As a result, the hearings of 1969 and the subsequent legislation left most of the prominent figures in philanthropy in a state of panic, almost terror, that in the event has proved most fortunate, because it succeeded in stirring them out of their complacency, as perhaps nothing less could have done, to address realistically some of their problems. One set of helpful side effects was organizational. Almost immediately informal groups sprang up across the country where foundation executives gathered to discuss the requirements and implications of the Tax Reform Act of 1969. Later, as the groups continued to function, their discussions began to range over all kinds of professional problems and emerging issues. Now known as Regional Associations of Grantmakers (RAGs), they have become an important and invigorating feature of the national philanthropic apparatus. Also what are called *affinity groups:* that is, foundations with a common interest in certain fields or problems, have been formed, and they have begun to play an important role in the exchange of program ideas. An example is the group calling itself Grantmakers in Health.

As a means of helping foundations to defend themselves

against Rep. Patman's attacks, John D. Rockefeller III had taken the lead in forming a Commission on Private Philanthropy and Public Needs to develop some organized information about foundations and to make some independent recommendations for improving their performance. Headed by John Filer, an insurance executive, the commission had to work in haste, and its results were uneven. But some of them proved to have unexpectedly useful long-term benefits. One such was the formation of a "donee group" to give voice to the complaints of smaller and less established nonprofits that felt discriminated against by foundation grant procedures and policies. This ad hoc body subsequently evolved into the National Committee for Responsive Philanthropy, which under the direction of Robert Bothwell has become a useful gadfly on the foundation rump.

On the West Coast, at the initiative of a brave young entrepreneur, Norton Kiritz, a Grantsmanship Center was launched, which through its lively publications and training seminars sought to serve the needs of that same excluded "underclass" of organizations. It has become another stimulating source of ideas from the nonprofit "counterculture."

Following an earlier set of congressional investigations of foundations in the mid-1950s, a Foundation Library Center had been created by a small group led by John Gardner and James Perkins of the Carnegie Corporation to try to break down the wall of self-imposed secrecy surrounding philanthropy. After the Patman hearings, this little agency, since renamed the Foundation Center, suddenly won much greater support. It became a more vigorous and creative factor in gathering information about foundations and in making it conveniently accessible to grant-seekers and to others with a more general interest. It has now established several of its own libraries around the country and has developed a network of 150 reference collections in public libraries, with at least one in every state in the union. It publishes a national *Foundation Directory,* "profiles" of the major foundations, a *National Data Book* of information about all twenty-two thousand foundations, an annual *Foundation Grants Index,* and computer-produced guides for grant-seekers to those foundations that make grants in various subject-matter fields. The center has become the primary source of information about foundations and, more than any other single factor, has finally made information about foundations generally accessible.

As more information has become available and as serious discussion of issues has begun, more useful books, free of the platitudinous quality of most earlier writings, such as John Nason's study of the problems of foundation boards of trustees and the valuable *Handbook for Community Foundations* by Eugene Struckhoff, have begun to appear. Of special significance have been the speeches and articles of a few knowledgeable individuals, most notably Pablo Eisenberg, head of the nonprofit Center for Community Change, and James Douglas, a British scholar, raising fundamental issues of the role of foundations and of equity and social responsibility in regard to their performance.

The Council on Foundations, which for many years had been little more than a third-rate trade association, also was transformed by the impact of the Patman hearings, but much more slowly, reflecting the continuing heavy drag on its development of its many backward-looking members. Its publication, *Foundation News*, responded to the new atmosphere by gradually becoming less of an uncritical house organ and more of a professional journal. During the 1970s the council itself had a succession of better and poorer leaders, but the better ones after a short stay tended to move on to more interesting assignments. As late as 1981 John Coleman, in announcing the withdrawal of the Edna McConnell Clark Foundation from council membership, wrote an explanatory letter that annoyed the old guard greatly but summarized the organization's weaknesses at the time. Among the hopes he expressed for what the council should become were these:

1. A president who is a powerful, inspiring and courageous spokesman for the philanthropic community.
2. A back-up staff that is so alert, imaginative and bright that we feel we have to run fast to keep up with them.
3. A legislative/administrative presence in Washington that is alert and aggressive, but that avoids the self-righteousness and narrowness characteristic of so much that we've said on our own behalf to date.
4. A set of standards for membership with so much bite to them that not all the current members can, or would want to, meet them and that would stretch that majority of us who chose to stay to act more openly, accountably, and professionally.
5. A magazine that has both more appeal and more guts than

Foundation News now has, so that a monthly ho-hum will be replaced with a hurrah most months and a vigorous dissent in others.
6. An annual meeting that is at once more selective, more profound and more worthwhile.

(Enough of these hopes have since been realized that the Clark Foundation in 1983 renewed its membership.)

As of 1985, the council has finally and fully come alive with an able and energetic new head, James Joseph, a man with distinguished credentials in business, philanthropy, and public service.

These organizational developments and the gradual emergence of a functioning, interactive philanthropic community have been more important to the vitality of this field than they might have been to many others. By their nature, foundations tend to exist in a cocoon, shielded from external stimuli. Without active information exchange and professional debate within the field, it would remain stultified. But with the shock of the Patman experience, invigoration has now come.

A further contributing factor has been the hiring of professional staff by more foundations in recent years. The increase in the number of women in senior staff positions has been beneficial. Among the more prominent examples are Margaret Mahoney, now head of the Commonwealth Fund; Anna Faith Jones, head of the Boston Foundation, a black; Terry Saario, head of the Northwest Area Foundation; Elizabeth McCormack, principal philanthropic advisor to the Rockefeller family; and Susan Berresford, second-in-command at the Ford Foundation. There has also been some increase in the number of blacks and a slight increase in Asians and Hispanics in executive positions. Blacks now hold four of the preeminent posts in the field: James Joseph, head of the Council on Foundations; Franklin Thomas, president of the Ford Foundation; Clifton Wharton, chairman of the Board of Trustees of the Rockefeller Foundation; and Steven Minter, director of the Cleveland Foundation, the oldest and most prestigious of the community foundations.

The result of all this has been to throw open some windows, expose philanthropy to greater public scrutiny, and develop for the first time some real internal debate on issues and ideas. Philanthropy is not yet by any measure a hotbed of intellectual ferment, but it is a far cry from the dull, homogeneous, and smug little enclave it was only a few years ago.

New Knowledge, New Awareness

If the first beneficial effect of the Patman attack was the cleansing of the foundation field of abuses, and the second the stimulation of greater openness and interaction, the third was the development for the first time of serious and substantial research activity on philanthropy and the whole nonprofit sector. The Filer Commission as its principal achievement set this process in motion by financing a considerable body of research on philanthropy during its brief two-year existence. In addition to its final report, the commission, as it disbanded, published a shelf of volumes of research papers that it had commissioned. Nothing comparable to this body of data and analysis had ever existed before. One volume dealt with measurements of the sources of private giving, the extent of volunteering, and the impacts of tax incentives on giving patterns. Another contained studies of foundation activity in various fields: higher education, science, the arts, and so forth. One volume dealt with corporate and community foundations, another with legal studies of the tax code, and still another with federal and state regulation of foundations.

Some of the papers were of much better quality than others, as might have been expected, given the time pressures under which they were done. But some were highly relevant, first-rate pieces of work: for example, Gabriel Rudney's study of the scope and size of the private voluntary sector; the analyses of Martin Feldstein on the impact of tax policies on charitable giving; Sarah Carey's paper on philanthropy and minorities, the poor, and other powerless groups; and the examination of the role of philanthropy in the public policy process by Paul Ylvisaker. Had such landmark studies not been sponsored and published by the Filer Commission, it is unlikely they would ever have been produced or published at all.

Although the report of the Filer Commission made little impact and was soon forgotten, the legacy of its research has been of enormous value. In the years since, dozens of important new studies have followed its pathbreaking efforts.

Little by little and study by study, awareness has grown that foundations are but one element of a vast, amorphous, and hitherto largely invisible "third sector" in American life made up of hundreds of thousands of private colleges and hospitals, museums and cultural centers, laboratories, publications, churches, advocacy groups, and many others. That sector has now been measured and mapped, and its functions and needs identified in ways and to a degree unknown previously. (Some partial studies had been made in the past: Carnegie's work on the funding and problems of higher education, for example, and Kellogg's on the needs of hospitals. But it has only been since the Patman hearings and the work of the Filer Commission that a sustained interest has developed in data gathering and research about the nonprofit sector as a whole.)

Likewise the funding of this huge aggregation of institutions has been traced, and the contribution of the various tributaries measured: individual giving, grants from foundations, earned income, and income received from government. It is now understood also that the money from different sources tends to go to different kinds of recipients: more than half of individual giving goes to churches, for example, but almost none of foundation giving. The varying "mixes" of individual, corporate, and private foundation gifts, along with public funding on which different kinds of nonprofit institutions depend, also now begins to be grasped.

For the first time the common problems of diverse nonprofit organizations are being identified and addressed. An important new organization, Independent Sector, has recently been established precisely to deal with these matters. Under superb leadership, it has quickly become a powerful force on the national scene. One of its major interests is to further extend research on the sector.

As a result of the new understanding that has been gained, it will never again be possible automatically to applaud a grant to build a new hospital wing, or to set up a scholarship program for the high schools of a particular city, or to create yet another center for biomedical research, or to spend large sums of philanthropic funds for the downtown redevelopment of a particular city, as has been the habit of the press and the public in the past.

This does not mean that an exact "science" of philanthropic giving has begun to emerge. Foundation choices in distributing their funds still have to be made in terms of their own purposes, values, insights—and sometimes courage. But it does mean that such choices can now be made with far greater knowledge and awareness of their larger context and broader implications.

Not all foundations have yet responded to the challenges and pressures upon them produced by this new knowledge. Although several have now begun to make some grants "to strengthen the nonprofit sector," none has so far made this a central and ongoing objective of its program. Nonetheless, for philanthropy, by 1980 the Dark Ages had ended, and the Enlightenment had begun.

The advent of the Reagan administration the following year paradoxically gave the trend an important further boost. The times were already difficult for nonprofits, which had been battered by both inflation and the sluggish economy, and when its program of proposed cuts in social programs became known, a wave of apprehension swept through the sector. One result was that a group of foundations jointly financed an emergency study directed by Lester Salamon under the auspices of the Urban Institute to appraise the prospective impacts of the cuts on various categories of nonprofit agencies. Because the estimates that were developed were necessarily based on certain assumptions regarding future government behavior as well as on more factual information, the results of the study were inevitably debatable and were vigorously debated. But its technical quality and the high competence of Salamon and his research team were unassailable, and when the storm had subsided, there remained a clearer understanding than ever before of the immense impact of government policies and funding on nearly all nonprofit institutions other than religious congregations and a reinforced recognition of the necessity and value of such research on a sustained basis.

The initial study was therefore followed by a three-year project financed by some forty foundations to examine in greater detail the scope, structure, and roles of the private nonprofit sector, changes in government policy affecting the sector, and its response to those changes. The first results, issued in mid-1984, made vividly clear what some observers had sensed but had never fully understood in the absence of such data: namely the scope and complexity of the interrelationships between the nonprofit sector and government, the huge and decisive role of government funding in the support of nonprofit agencies, and the ominous dangers of the shift of government policy under President Reagan for the future of the sector.

Among the more startling and significant of the findings were these: Government is now the largest single source of nonprofit income, and even such wealthy and prestigious private institutions as

Harvard, Stanford, and MIT as well as the major Catholic and Protestant charities and the Federation of Jewish Philanthropies are heavily dependent on government funding. A close partnership in which government raises the funds and determines how they should be used and then turns over much of the actual service delivery to private nonprofit institutions has developed. The money to pay for this is delivered in the form of direct grants, purchase-of-service contracts, and third party payments like Medicare. In New York, for example, 68 percent of the government's social service dollars go to support nonprofit providers of social services. As the Defense Department relies on the aerospace industry to produce its airplanes, so many federal departments rely on the nonprofit sector to carry out their programs, and this long-established pattern of collaboration has become the backbone of the human-service delivery system of the United States.

A number of other countries in recent years have been moving toward the American model in order to control the growth of official bureaucracies as well as to gain other advantages. But ironically, since 1980, the United States now seems to be pulling back from it. Medicare and Medicaid spending has continued to increase, boosting support for private hospitals. But federal support for other types of nonprofits has drastically declined. Outside the health field, the federal government is in the process of stripping down if not gutting its partnership with the nonprofit sector. Moreover, the budget proposals of the administration submitted to the Congress in 1984 made it clear that these trends would continue.

For foundations, whose funds go mostly to the same nonprofit institutions and largely for the same purposes as those of government, the implications of the situation so graphically documented in the Salamon findings were enormous. Any major shrinkage or shifts in the $40 billion of annual government funding could virtually destroy the effect of the $4 billion of funding that foundations provide to that same clientele.

That change in the financial context of their operations was one horn of the dilemma on which they are now, and for at least the coming four years will continue to be, impaled.

The other is the transformation of the political environment in which they and other nonprofit organizations now and henceforth must operate, a development with even more profound implications that will be examined in the following chapter.

The Changing
Political Context

Foundations are nonpolitical institutions that, by the nature of their work, live on the edge of politics and in the shadow of, even the embrace of, the programs of government.

They are therefore inevitably affected by the political environment of the times. With the election of President Reagan in 1980 and his reelection in 1984, that political environment has now undergone a deep and perhaps lasting change.

Working with and influencing government programs in certain fields, particularly health, education, and scientific research, has long been a practice of the larger and more energetic foundations. Andrew Carnegie, beginning in the late nineteenth century, by means of his gifts of public libraries, made the long-term support of such educational services an accepted obligation of local governments throughout the country. The General Education Board created by John D. Rockefeller in the early twentieth century

placed advisers in the education departments of a number of southern states who were then able to encourage the improvement of
public schooling for blacks. Immediately after World War II, the
successful and long-established fellowship programs of the Rockefeller Foundation for the advanced training of scientists were copied and greatly enlarged by the newly created National Science
Foundation.

The exercise of this kind of influence on government was generally accepted, even admired. Foundations prided themselves on
their ability to launch and test new kinds of programs that, if successful, would be adopted and funded on a far larger scale by government. Such initiative taking, and the accomplishment of such
"leverage" through government action, became the recognized
mark of the modern, "scientific" foundation.

In the 1950s and 1960s and part of the 1970s, as the American
welfare state expanded and proliferated, the methods by which
foundations sought to stimulate changes in government programs
and policy evolved greatly, as did the range of matters in which
they took an active interest. By the early 1960s, and especially during the Kennedy administration, foundation specialists were in
close communication with their counterparts in the federal government, and the influence of their ideas was not only felt on educational, scientific, and health matters but extended to such areas as
civil rights, urban renewal, foreign economic assistance, international cultural exchanges, and national security.

Under the leadership of such "liberal" foundations as Ford and
Carnegie, philanthropic funds were used to assist organizations
such as the Brookings Institution to prepare "national agendas" of
policy proposals to the federal government; to identify and provide
leadership training for disadvantaged groups such as Hispanics and
native Americans as well as blacks; to develop legal services for the
poor; to open up cultural and scientific exchanges with the countries of Eastern Europe; and to strengthen U.S. participation in the
United Nations. Slightly later, as new movements developed in behalf of environmental protection, consumer's rights, and women's
liberation, foundation funds in some degree were made available to
support those efforts and to encourage related changes in public
policy. Voter registration drives were funded in various parts of the
country; the establishment of a publicly financed system of non-
commercial broadcasting was proposed, and changes in the criminal justice system were recommended. At least a few of the larger

foundations, it seemed, were involved at least indirectly in almost all the major issues of that very turbulent period.

The influence then exerted by this activist minority of foundations was due only in part to the grants they made. In at least equal degree it derived from the ideas and persuasiveness of some of their able staff professionals and from the personal links between them and many leading figures in academia and the media as well as in government. Movement of a number of key individuals back and forth between foundation and government posts in the Kennedy, Johnson, and later the Carter administrations was also noticeable. So although it could not fairly be charged that foundations were doing anything "subversive" or illegal, a few of them at least were playing a much more visible and powerful role across a broad range of public policy questions than ever before.

During this time the politically conservative foundations were on the whole far less enterprising and influential. The only intellectually creditable conservative institution in that period that received their support was the Hoover Institution for War and Peace at Stanford University. But it was the more liberal foundations that were riding high and that felt, sometimes rather arrogantly, that they constituted the vanguard. In fact, however, they were riding for a fall.

New Left and New Right

The factors that led to the shift in political mood in the United States by the end of the 1970s were of course many: from the psychological aftermath of Vietnam to concern about taxes and from the spread of radical egalitarianism at home to increased anxiety about the international situation.

But two were of special relevance to the question of foundations and politics. The first was the revulsion of a key group of intellectuals, many of them formerly of left and liberal tendency, against the excesses of the New Left. The second was a resurgence of concern among traditionalists, including the millions of members of evangelical churches, against what they saw as a general breakdown of conventions and standards in personal, family, and civic life. The first developed into a movement known as *neoconservatism*, the second into the grouping known as the *Moral Majority*.

THE NEOCONSERVATIVES

For those intellectuals who formed the core of the neoconservative movement, many of whom were academics, the triggering event in their political migration to the Right was the student rebellion that erupted on American campuses beginning in the mid-1960s. The evolution toward extremism of the so-called New Left is best exemplified in the history of Students for a Democratic Society (SDS), which was founded in the spring of 1960. It became the largest student organization ever known in the United States and the flamboyant symbol of the American Left during the ensuing decade: a decade of sit-ins and pickets, teach-ins and mass marches, student uprisings and building takeovers, ghetto rebellions, and ultimately the destruction of property by arson and bombs. Until 1965, SDS, according to its leaders at the time, was trying "to make American institutions live up to American ideals." It then moved into a phase of resistance, spreading its activities from coast to coast with open confrontations against these institutions. In its last and revolutionary period SDS set itself consciously on the course of seeking a thorough, and if necessary violent, overthrow of the American system.

Both the force represented by SDS and its turn toward revolutionary action evoked a strong reaction from a number of circles on the democratic Left. A crucially important one centered on a political intellectual, Irving Kristol, who has come to be known as the godfather of the neoconservative movement. Kristol was one of a group, many of whom had been socialists, Trotskyists, and social democrats in an earlier period, who had become actively anticommunist after World War II. Kristol in that period associated himself with the CIA-financed Congress for Cultural Freedom, went to Europe and became editor of one of its publications, the journal *Encounter,* published in London. Under his hand it became within a few years the most influential political-intellectual publication in the English language.

In the early 1960s he returned to New York, bringing with him a network of personal friends and admirers that included a good part of the most prominent anticommunist intellectuals of the Western world. His experience in the ideological wars of Europe had given him an extraordinary education in modern political movements and had honed his polemical style to a keen cutting edge. Deeply disturbed at the chaotic political situation he found on his return, he established a new journal called *The Public Interest*, in company with the prominent sociologist Daniel Bell. Its articles were provocative, they addressed neglected issues, and they struck a responsive chord among a growing body of influential readers because they were free of the kind of liberal cant that at the time had become the conventional academic wisdom.

Within a remarkably short period of time *The Public Interest* won the active support of an outstanding group of academics and public figures, and it became the hub of a nascent intellectual-political movement.

The group was bound together by the intensity of their concern about the condition of the nation: the aggressive destructiveness of the New Left, condoned and aided, in their view, by the liberal establishment; the excessive intrusion of government into the society and the economy; and the decline of public concern about the dangers of communism. Not only were they able and highly motivated, but they were strategically placed in the marketplace of ideas with good connections to politics, business, labor, academia, and the media. Their style was formal, literary, learned, and serious. They were also militant and they gave conservatism a combat capability that was a match in every respect for the big guns of liberalism at the time such as John Kenneth Galbraith and Arthur Schlesinger, Jr.

The *Public Interest* group were of course not alone: *Commentary* magazine, edited by Norman Podhoretz; the American Enterprise Institute under the astute leadership of the Baroodys, father and son; the long-established Hoover Institution; and a growing number of other newer centers and publications were also at work in behalf of the new and invigorated conservatism. But the Kristol group was the core of the movement.

As in any such amorphous aggregation of intellectuals, there are quite a number who consider themselves the true leader. One of these is Podhoretz, who is less of a scholar than a political brawler with a taste for blood. Some sense of the egotism and intensity of feeling in this little elite can be gained from his remarks to a conference, "Our Country and Our Culture," organized by his magazine in early 1983. Speaking of the political situation at the time, Podhoretz said, "We are surrounded by lynch mobs, just barely restrained. . . . But our work has not been in vain. We are a political community now. The resonance of what we do is greater than ever. . . . We are the dominant faction within the world of ideas—

the most influential—the most powerful. . . . By now the liberal culture has to appease *us*. . . . People like us made Reagan's victory, which had been considered impossible." These remarks moved one member of the audience, literary critic Alfred Kazin, on hearing him to recall a couplet of T. S. Eliot in *The Waste Land:* "One of the low on whom assurance sits/As a silk hat on a Bradford millionaire."

THE MONEY COMES

As late as the mid-1960s, corporate philanthropic and "public affairs" money, normally disposed to bet on proven winners, was more directed to liberal institutions like Brookings, especially in support of their international work, than to their less known and less regarded conservative counterparts. A very few foundations, most notably Smith Richardson in North Carolina, were supporting serious ideological and political studies. But most of the conservative donors, such as Pew, were giving to primitive pro–free enterprise and anticommunist propaganda mills such as Harding College in Arkansas or to fundamentalist churches. Most did not give to public policy work at all. As one fund raiser for right-wing causes complained at the time, "H. L. Hunt would invite you to lunch and give you a ham sandwich out of his desk."

By the early 1970s all that had begun to change. Adolph Coor, the Colorado brewer, had begun to fund a wider range of organizations, and as the number of conservative study centers developed they began to attract increasing support. The most important new sources were the Scaife Foundation and other trusts controlled by Richard Scaife of the Mellon family in Pittsburgh. Since 1973 he has poured some $100 million into conservative think tanks, litigation groups, and media projects. Currently his giving is at a level of about $10 million a year, making him the largest single funder of such activities in the country. He is not himself an articulate intellectual and his coarse style is in sharp contrast to the elegance of his uncle, Paul Mellon, horseman, art collector, and bibliophile. But he is purposeful and pragmatic, and his gifts have gone to individuals and institutions with influence. The Noble Foundation in Oklahoma has also given on this same basis, but on a smaller scale.

As significant in the field as Scaife, but working with more limited resources, is the Olin Foundation in New York. For a good many years, it had given regularly to conservative causes, but somewhat randomly. In the late 1970s, the donor, John Olin, brought in William Simon, secretary of the Treasury under President Nixon, to head the board. Simon in turn brought in a bright young neoconservative, Michael Joyce, a protégé of Irving Kristol, to head the staff. Since then the grants of the foundation have been made with a sharp focus on maximizing their impact on government policy and on public opinion.

The funds go not to charitable purposes but strictly for "public policy research" and only to the most outstanding and respected scholars and centers of compatible viewpoint. Among these have been individuals such as Milton Friedman and George Stigler, free-market economists and Nobel laureates; Murray Weidenbaum and Martin Feldstein, economists who have chaired President Reagan's Council of Economic Advisors; and institutions like the American Enterprise Institute, Harvard, Yale, and even the old liberal bastion, the Brookings Institution. The foundation's interests are primarily in the field of domestic economic policy, but it has also supported some work on defense and strategic issues.

The operational theory underlying its grants is taken directly from Kristol's ideas about how political trends are shaped in a modern democracy. In the words of Joyce in an interview with the author:

> People of conservative persuasion have now begun to understand how public policy is percolated. They used to think that the need was to persuade people at the grass-roots level, that economics education would solve the problem. Now it is recognized that public policy initiatives originate in a very small circle and that public policy flows from the apex of a pyramid with a very narrow top to a very wide bottom. In this process ideas and intellectuals count enormously. They are crucial, and the best and most influential ones are especially crucial. . . . The things the Reagan Administration is doing now were perked in a small circle of intellectuals. It would be very mistaken, for example, to believe that supply side economics and all that came from successful car salesmen. The liberal Establishment has always understood the process. It's only now that the conservatives have come to realize it and act upon it.

With the rise of influence and respectability of the conservative intellectuals, and with the growth in number of competent conservative research and policy centers, corporate funds in quantity have also become available. American corporations in the 1960s and 1970s were under increasing pressure from social critics and public advocacy groups to meet new expectations of "social responsibility." As a result they built up their public affairs staffs as well as the budgets of their foundations. By the 1970s, a significant part of this increase began to flow into conservative tax-exempt organizations. Such contributions were felt to be more useful than outright lobbying and political gifts and also less likely to get the company into trouble. To help steer such funds into the right places on the Right, Simon and Kristol in 1979 set up an Institute for Educational Affairs to counsel corporate givers so that their gifts would go to their "friends" and not their "enemies" in the academic community.

With this increased corporate and foundation help, American conservatism by the late 1970s for the first time had begun to develop a greatly broadened intellectual base. It had become a source of new and interesting policy ideas and was attracting the interest of able and idealistic younger people on campuses and elsewhere throughout the country. Through its own publications and personal networks it had also begun to exercise important influence on the professionals in the media.

THE NEW POPULISM

While the neoconservatives were flourishing in these years, a parallel development of equal political importance, and of equivalent involvement with nonprofit institutions and charitable funding, was also under way. There has always existed as part of the mix of American politics a considerable populistic element, alienated and frustrated, hostile to various tendencies in the society, and not usually a part of the regular two-party system. William Jennings Bryan, Huey Long, Father Coughlin, and George Wallace have been among those who have spoken for this constituency.

Their causes have often taken negative form: anti-Catholic, anti-Jewish, antiblack, anti-immigrant, antiunion, anti-Eastern, and so on. More recently they have risen in opposition to abortion, family planning, the women's movement, homosexual rights, and a broad range of other trends in government policy, the media, and international affairs, which they see as threatening or incompatible with their view of life.

The remarkable development that has occurred in recent years is the mobilization of the sentiments and the exploitation of the funding potentialities of these groups, each often with a single-issue concentration, through the most creative and skillful use of modern techniques of mass marketing and new communication technologies. On the whole it appears that the conservatives and fundamentalists have been more alert and more skillful in employing these methods than have been the liberals and the Left.

The impressive examples of their success are many. Several evangelical "radio" and now "television" preachers, including Billy Graham, Oral Roberts, and Jerry Falwell, have built huge followings and in turn financed various nonprofit institutions. Senator Jesse Helms's Congressional Club has also been effective. *The Wall Street Journal* has described it as "a unique political conglomerate, the best known and possibly the largest political fund-raiser on the national scale." It has produced such offshoots as the American Family Institute, the Institute on Money and Inflation, and the Institution on Religion and Democracy, all tax exempt and charitable in legal status. Another important innovator has been the National Rifle Association, which early adopted computerized techniques to capitalize on the strong sentiment among hundreds of thousands of gun owners across the country against gun control legislation to generate contributions on a large scale and to mobilize political action.

Most potent of all has been Richard Viguerie, a direct-mail genius who operates from a suburb of Washington, D.C. He now commands a whole empire of publications, committees, and institutions serving the cause of extreme conservatism and populism. He owns what is widely regarded as probably the single most valuable asset of any political organization, Left or Right, in the United States: namely a battery of computer tapes containing the names and addresses of some 20 million individuals who steadily give money in ten- to twenty-five-dollar amounts to his causes and campaigns. The tapes are kept under lock and key in the basement of his headquarters building. His machines run twenty-four hours a day, distributing some 120 million pieces of personalized mail a year. In the view of James Ridgeway, writing in *The Village Voice* in early 1983, "Without Viguerie and his names, the New Right today would be just another group of funky little magazines and hole-in-the-wall foundations without any overall political purpose or organization." Be that as it may, Viguerie and his main publication, *Conservative Digest,* are now a powerful political force—militant and relentless—that can bring about as much political heat to bear on a specific issue before Congress, or on the White House, or on a state governor or legislature, as any institution in the country.

What is particularly noteworthy is that this massive fund raising and the related political groupings are uncommitted to either political party and not dependent on any small group of wealthy foundations or individual patrons. They therefore are more independent, unpredictable, and unmanageable than other major political factors. Viguerie sees great political significance in the technique of direct mail, which in his view has enabled conservatives for the first time to go over the heads of the establishment and reach the people directly. He in fact takes the position that his populist movement is neither Republican nor Democrat, neither conservative nor liberal, but essentially anti-establishment: anti–big business, big unions, and big government. With the Reagan administration his followers have had great influence, but not to the degree they would like. As a result, they feel free to criticize the president and his administration in the harshest terms, while at the same time generally associating themselves with his conservative approach.

In Viguerie's view,

> The White House is a political basket case as far as I'm concerned. People down there are basically big-business, Establishment types who don't have the foggiest idea about politics. They're listening to Tip O'Neill and Teddy Kennedy, and they're saying the issues are Social Security and unemployment and jobs. . . . The dummies are talking about the other guy's issues, not their own—which should be abortion, busing, sex and violence on television, crime and drugs in schools. . . .

THE NEW CONSERVATIVE NETWORK

As a result of the efforts of the neoconservatives and their corporate and philanthropic supporters, and the neopopulists and their immense capacity to generate individual charitable and political contributions, a whole new political apparatus in the country has now been brought into existence. In the words of Richard Reeves, the syndicated columnist, the capital of the United States is now surrounded, figuratively and literally, "by dozens of conservative institutes, foundations and centers staffed with aggressive scholars and pamphleteers. . . ."

These include think tanks and public policy research institutes of many kinds: centers for studies of national security and foreign policy issues; centers for the study of big government and the reduction of regulation; centers for the study of crime and law enforcement; centers for the study of economic issues, domestic and international; centers for the study and preservation of conservative and traditional values; centers for the study of media issues; and still other centers dealing with issues affecting blacks and other minorities, the advancement of libertarian ideas, educational issues, and labor issues. The network also includes political action committees of every description and a set of legal advocacy groups. There is a major campus outreach operation to involve young educated Americans in the movement. A wide range of publications from *The Public Interest* to *National Review, Conservative Digest, Commentary, Human Events*, and dozens of smaller ones are supported, and links to the media are carefully maintained. The Heritage Foundation, for example, with substantial Scaife help, carries on an editorial briefing series and distributes "distinguished journalist" fellowships. It produces a twice-monthly column, "Heritage Foundation Forum," which is used by more than four hundred newspapers. The education of journalists is also part of the work of another Scaife-backed group, the Media Institute in Washington, D.C. Its newest project is the Economic Communications Center, which provides journalists with quick analyses of current economic issues from a conservative perspective and easy access to experts in the field.

If American conservatism and populism in the 1950s and 1960s had a weak intellectual and research base, weak ties with business and philanthropy, little institutional fund-raising capacity, little appeal to the young and idealistic, and little influence in academia and the media, today that situation has been drastically transformed. This has been done not at the initiative of organized philanthropy but with the substantial strategic support of a few foundations and with the reinforcement of individual charitable and political contributions in vast quantity.

Reaganthropy

The Reagan administration came into office in 1981 with more awareness of, and more feelings and ideas about, the nonprofit sector of American life than any previous one. (Herbert Hoover, as a cabinet officer and later as president, had a strong interest in and ambitious plans for collaboration between government and the nonprofit sector and for increased reliance by government on its services. But he was unable at the time to win much support for his ideas.) In its approach were reflected the concerns of the major elements—neoconservatives, old conservatives, and neopopulists—in the president's victorious coalition.

In his inaugural address, and in a series of major speeches in the early part of his first term, President Reagan gave unprecedented emphasis to the idea of voluntarism. "Isn't it time," he asked,

> to take a fresh look at the ways we provide social services? Not just because they cost so much and waste so much, but because so many of them just don't work. . . . Before government was the principal vehicle of social change, it was understood that the real source of our progress as a people was the private sector. . . . The private sector still offers creative, less expensive, and more efficient alternatives to solving our social problems. . . . Voluntarism is a means of delivering social services more effectively and of preserving our freedoms.

His views and those of his party stood in sharp contrast to the attitudes of previous liberal Democratic administrations. The 1980 Republican platform, for example, had called voluntarism "an essential part of our plan to return government to the people." But it did not rate even a mention in the Democratic platform.

Liberals in general have remained indifferent and silent on the subject for a number of obvious reasons: their alliance with the 14 million people who work for state, local, and federal government, 6 million of whom belong to public employees unions and see voluntarism as a threat to their jobs; the opposition of the women's movement, at least in its earlier phase, which saw voluntarism as exploitative and demeaning; the general liberal preference for professionals with academic credentials rather than "amateurs" in administering to human needs; and more fundamentally, a belief that dates at least from New Deal days that it is inherently better and more democratic to help the needy through government programs than through what is disparagingly called "private charity."

Whatever the reasons that the liberals abandoned voluntarism to Reagan, he seized on it, perceiving that it was in harmony with the values of traditional conservatives; that it directly served the interests of some significant elements of his constituency, especially the churches; and that it fitted his strategy of reducing the government's role and cutting the costs of social programs. Most important, it evoked a positive response from broad segments of the nation.

To promote the concept further, he created a President's Task Force on Private Sector Initiatives in October 1981, headed by a prominent businessman, William K. Verity, and composed of a wide variety of individuals from politics, business, labor, churches, and foundations. The committee went actively about its task, but as it proceeded, even the president seemed to back off from it, successively downgrading the level of its linkage to the White House. (Eventually the liaison responsibility fell to a young man named Rosebush, which led one close observer to remark, "I know the President never promised us a Rose Garden. But we surely had reason to expect more than a Rosebush.") In the end it not only accomplished little but aroused much questioning about the president's motivation in creating it. Richard Cornuelle, a well-known conservative and former executive vice-president of the National Association of Manufacturers, concluded that it had done little more than compile a data bank on successful volunteer efforts: "at least the sixth such data bank . . . I know of." Richard Lyman, president of the Rockefeller Foundation, who was an uneasy member of the Task Force, came to the judgment that the exercise had been "essentially promotional." A staff member put it more bluntly, describing the proceedings as "all ballyhoo and no substance."

Skepticism about the sincerity of the administration's support for voluntarism turned to cynicism after the substance of its policies in the social services area became clear: budget cuts that fell most heavily on the poor; the effort to abolish VISTA, the federal government's domestic volunteer program; and the targeted demolition of neighborhood groups and community development organizations all over the country that were dependent in some degree on government funding. By 1983, the rhetoric had been turned off and the whole subject seemingly dropped.

Ephemeral though the crusade for voluntarism may have been, a second element of the administration's policy toward the nonprofit sector has been much more sustained and serious: namely, a systematic effort to demolish the pretensions of the liberal foundations and the activist nonprofit agencies to a morally superior position on various social issues. Neoconservative intellectuals have been the principal operatives in accomplishing this objective. Just as they played an important role in defining the initial Reagan political agenda, so some of them, once appointed to high official positions, have been able to bring their ideology effectively to bear in the shaping and implementation of government policies toward foundations and other kinds of nonprofit organizations.

The neoconservative view toward foundations in particular was fully formulated well before the administration took office. It consisted of the following principal beliefs and feelings:

1. Foundations are very powerful factors in shaping public attitudes and political trends. This includes foundations of both the Left and the Right.
2. The liberal foundations, which have had predominant influence until recent years, generally were neglectful of the private institutions, "which are at the heart of the American experiment," including the needs of the private economy for investment funds, productivity, and competitiveness.
3. On the other hand, they contributed greatly to the explosive growth of government, the "universalization of benefits," and the attendant waste, cost, and injury to the national well-being.
4. They have directly through their own funds and indirectly through the encouragement of the use of government funds stirred up social hostility by creating all kinds of litigious and agitational groups.
5. They have undermined national security by their neglect of military needs and their equivocal view of the dangers of communism.

In all this, many leading neoconservatives feel, the liberal foundations have been characteristically arrogant, and now that the policies they have promoted "have so manifestly and catastrophically failed," they are still unwilling to admit their failure.

These harsh judgments are not expressed in the crude language of the John Birch Society or McCarthyism but rather in the most sophisticated terms, drawing from the values and symbols of both traditional liberalism and conservatism.

Michael J. Horowitz, counsel to David Stockman, director of the Office of Management and Budget (OMB) in the Reagan White House, is a good example of the kind of articulate political activist from the neoconservative movement who joined the Reagan administration. He is a graduate of Yale University Law School and taught civil-rights law at the University of Mississippi in the mid-1960s. In a remarkably candid interview with Kathleen Teltsch of *The New York Times* in late 1981, he expressed his strong views in these words:

On the rationale of the Reagan reductions in social program budgets:

> The cuts we have made . . . are literally for the purpose of preserving the governement's ability to make payments to people who have no alternative other than . . . government assistance. . . . The hallmark of the New Deal was direct cash aid to the poor . . . on the premise that they had the intelligence and ability to make their own judgments as to how to spend those monies. The benefits of the generic Great Society programs . . . have in many cases not gone to the poor and have really enriched a whole class of business and consultant professionals.

On the controversial CETA program:

> There is nothing more critical that those poor [minority] kids are facing than a decline in private sector productivity and the lack of capital investment. We have the lowest level of savings in Western society. And the idea that failed—that CETA programs can do anything but put cosmetic solutions to what are profound problems of unemployment and a lack of industrial productivity—is a moral outrage. . . . There is nothing more obscene than a number of government tribunes—indifferent to inflation, indifferent to private sector productivity—superseding private sector power and at the same time monopolizing in public discourse all the moral virtues, while the alleged beneficiaries of their efforts have never been more bereft of hope.

On the consequences of liberal foundation policies in the past:

> I think much of what the foundation community did over the
> 1960s and 70s—and they were quite self-righteous about it—
> was to set in motion forces through a whole variety of very
> artful mechanisms that would involve the government in a
> more direct, profound way in financing social welfare pro-
> grams and income redistribution programs and the like . . .
> [with the result that] we have got programs which have been
> animated by an ideology that has victimized the poor most of
> all. . . . When the President talked in his NAACP speech about
> not ceding the moral highground to spokesmen for those pro-
> grams, I think that's what he was talking about.

In these remarks are combined the idealism, the moral fervor,
the combativeness, and the polemical abilities of the intellectual
émigrés from the Left who in the 1960s joined the neoconservative
movement.

Conservative Coalition

At a number of points, but by no means all, the concerns felt by
Horowitz and his colleagues were shared by another element of the
Reagan coalition, the neopopulists, including resentment of the superior attitude of the liberal foundations, opposition to the idea of
feeding government money to advocacy groups (or at least to those
speaking for the poor, minorities, women, and the elderly), and hostility to those agencies of the federal government that were felt to
have become "hotbeds of subversion" under the Carter administration.

The priorities of these two powerful elements in the Reagan
coalition have coincided on what they both regard as three crucial
matters: first, cleaning out the Community Services Administration,
the Legal Services Corporation, and VISTA by eliminating them if
possible and if not, then totally redirecting them; second, "defunding the Left" by cutting off the flow of government money through
grants and contracts to "objectionable political organizations
operating in the guise of nonprofit agencies" (such as the Legal Defense Fund of the National Organization of Women, the Federation

of Southern Cooperatives, and many others), and third, fundamentally crippling, by executive order if possible and by legislation otherwise, the capacity of foundations and other nonprofit organizations to attempt to influence government policy and lobby the Congress.

As a result of the first effort, the Community Services Administration has disappeared, VISTA is now little more than a shell, and the battle over the Legal Services Corporation continues, but the administration has not prevailed because of strong Democratic opposition in the Congress.

Responding to conservative pressures, the Reagan administration has taken savage measures in "defunding the Left." When it came into office, "hit lists" of the liberal organizations that during the Kennedy and Johnson years, and especially during the Carter period, had been favored with government grants and contracts were developed. A great many of these have now suffered substantial, often drastic, reductions in their federal funding. This effort is one on which the neopopulists have particularly vehement feelings. Marshall Breger of the Heritage Foundation states their basic attitude: "If an organization does advocacy it shouldn't get government funding for providing services." Richard Viguerie says, "There are few things we consider more important. . . . We just think it is immoral for taxpayers to fund Planned Parenthood . . . or Cesar Chavez or Acorn. . . . We won't take federal funds and we don't want the Left to have them. It's just scandalous that Jesse Jackson gets federal money." Howard Phillips, chairman of the Conservative Caucus, says, "Many of the groups with innocent-sounding names, whose purpose is to redistribute America's wealth under a campaign of 'economic democracy,' have received funding from not just one but many federal agencies. . . . It's not enough just to document the government funding of these radical groups. Facts about these individuals and organizations must be so thoroughly reported that they never again are eligible to conduct their activities with our hard-earned money."

In its third objective, the crippling of the power of foundations and other nonprofits to influence government policy, the administration's major move has been an attempt to broaden greatly the definition of *political advocacy* by nonprofit organizations receiving funds from government and to cut off any reimbursement for activities that could possibly be construed to be of that nature. The specific action was issuance by OMB in January 1983 of a draft circular, A-122, innocuously titled "Cost Principles for Non-Profit Organizations."

Immediately letters and telegrams by the tens of thousands began to pour into the White House from outraged nonprofit organizations and their members protesting it and from conservatives applauding its restrictions. Brian O'Connell, head of Independent Sector, speaking for its broad membership of nonprofit organizations of every kind, wrote to President Reagan "that the proposed regulation would effectively prevent voluntary organizations from making a variety of necessary and desirable contacts with government officials which do not constitute political advocacy and would prevent these organizations from engaging in political advocacy even when such activities were a small part of their work and were paid for with non-federal funds."

The uproar was such that OMB had to withdraw the proposed document and make some softening changes. The revised version was also generally attacked, but the White House was determined to deprive them of any government funding for any purpose so long as they persisted in their advocacy role. In late April 1984, therefore, OMB issued a final and still greatly restrictive version of the regulations. The affected organizations in response announced plans to continue their fight against what they regard as an infringement of their basic rights.

Reelection and Reconfirmation

Following the president's sweeping election victory in November 1984, the general lines of his policy toward the nonprofits were reaffirmed. His earlier brief crusade in behalf of voluntarism had long since been dropped and been forgotten.

But the drive to "defund the Left" would continue. This was a matter of passionate importance to single-issue and right-wing extremists who sought not only to cripple but to destroy the targeted organizations. Indeed this effort seemed capable, with the tacit endorsement of the administration, of turning into a witch hunt, including not only infringement of constitutional rights but actual violence. The rapidly increasing number of bombings and burnings of Planned Parenthood clinics around the country in 1984, against which the administration raised only belated and halfhearted protest, was an ugly indication of where the unrestrained ardor of this faction might lead.

Likewise, the efforts to strengthen further the public policy apparatus of the conservatives and counter that of the liberals would continue. The Heritage Foundation exemplifies the high degree of development and influence that conservative think tanks have already achieved. Its director has repeatedly claimed that the Reagan administration in its first four years accepted and acted on 60 percent of the many recommendations Heritage had presented to them.

Immediately upon Reagan's reelection, it gave another extraordinary demonstration of its energy and its assumptions about the status it had reached. Before the president had presented his own legislative program to the Congress in his inaugural and state of the union addresses, Heritage in a daring preemptive first strike at presidential prerogative published and widely publicized its program for the second Reagan administration, with policy recommendations on every subject from overhaul of Social Security and the air traffic control system to relations with the Soviet Union. Even in the heyday of the access of the Brookings Institution to the policy councils of Presidents Kennedy and Johnson nothing of equivalent presumptuousness had ever been seen.

Nevertheless, the feeling that the public policy apparatus of the liberals had to be immobilized and weakened remained very strong among key elements of the Reagan coalition. The antagonism of the populist Right toward the activist liberal foundations that in the past have funded programs of affirmative action, population control, "empowerment" of the poor, public interest litigation, and so on, rests on their conviction that such actions have weakened family ties, destroyed traditional values, and produced social disorder. The neoconservative hostility also rests partly on their feeling that the large liberal foundations have provoked some of the most dangerous and destructive tendencies in American life, such as the student disorders of the 1960s. But an even more powerful motivation is their belief that such foundations, through their grants and networks of collaborating think tanks, have powerfully shaped political trends in the past and if not checked and countered will do so again.

Interestingly enough, liberal and Democratic political experts now agree with the neoconservatives about the growing importance of ideas in contemporary politics and therefore of the hatcheries that produce them. This is due, in their common view, to the diminished value in electoral campaigns of old-style political organizations, the decline in party discipline, the rapid growth in the number of independent voters, and the rising importance of television in the campaign process.

William Galston, "issues director" for the Mondale campaign in 1984, speaking of the new "ideas industry" organized by the Republicans over the past twenty years, has said, "It's almost impossible to overrate the importance of ideas in politics. . . . Ronald Reagan won last time on the strength of ideas."

Senator Daniel Patrick Moynihan, Democrat of New York, speaking of the 1980 campaign, agrees: "The Republicans simply left us behind. They became the party of ideas and we were left, in Lord Macaulay's phrase, 'the stupid party.' "

Edward Feulner, head of the Heritage Foundation, the most effective tactical weapon in the new Republican arsenal of nonprofits and a key adviser to the Reagan political strategists, said in the course of the 1984 campaign, "The years in the wilderness (after the Goldwater debacle in 1964) gave us the time to work out challenges to the prevailing orthodoxy. . . . Now we are in the mainstream, and we will suffer for that like the liberals before us." Looking to the future, he added, "The intellectual ferment has already begun on the Left. The foundations in New York—Ford, the Rockefeller Brothers Fund, Carnegie—are beginning to finance study on nuclear issues. On arms control. The freeze. It takes years for ideas to break out, but they will. In a few years we'll be struggling against those ideas."

Summation

Since the advent of Ronald Reagan to the presidency in 1981, a new degree of attention, and tension, has been brought to the rapidly evolving relationships between government and the nonprofit sector, including foundations.

The new features are several. That the Reagan Administration assembled its own preferred group of nonprofit agencies to advise on programs and policies and gave them special access, as well as funding, did not establish a precedent. Previous (Democratic) administrations had set the pattern of extending the spoils system to nonprofit advisory and policy research groups. What was new, however, was that the Republicans were now able to draw on an array of competent organizations of this kind that were of compatible viewpoint. For the first time a kind of balance had been achieved between the two major political parties and political tendencies in their available intellectual and advisory resources. This was on the whole a healthy development, providing a greater competition of ideas and contributing to a higher level of national debate on political and policy issues.

The net effect has been to fix more firmly in national affairs at the federal level the practice of placing certain key nonprofit organizations, including some foundations, in a strategic position in the processes of policy formulation. This is now established practice for Republican as well as Democratic regimes.

The drive of the Reagan administration to deprive private agencies that are considered to be of "unfriendly" viewpoint of access to government contract income and grants is different in its intensity but is not a new Republican invention. ACTION, the federal agency in charge of volunteer programs, gave clear preferment to certain nonprofit agencies and totally excluded others from its favors, for example, during the Carter administration. But the Reagan administration has employed more rigorous ideological criteria and has applied them more brutally than any of its predecessors. And it has gone much further in using, and perhaps misusing, the full powers of government to stifle their influence on policy. This in a sense has been a compliment to the nonprofit sector: no previous administration has ever taken its power so seriously. But the Reagan approach has raised Constitutional questions; it has produced strong resentments; and it has highlighted the potential frictions between government and the nonprofit sector in their increasingly close and extensive relationships as never before.

The effect of these several developments is to add new complexity, new conflict, and new visibility to the relationships among government, politics, and the nonprofits, including their bankers, the foundations. Just as the Reagan presidency marks a watershed in the evolution of the American welfare state, so it represents a pivotal point of change in this sphere.

This background—the blemished beginnings of a number of the largest foundations, the transforming trauma of the field of ph:-

lanthropy at the end of the 1960s at the hands of Congress, its subsequent cleansing and invigoration, and the deep changes set in motion since 1980 in its relationships with government—provides the context within which the following individual portraits of the thirty-six largest grant-making foundations must be interpreted.

PART
II

A Gallery
of Portraits

4

THE PROTOTYPES:
Ford and Rockefeller

Ford Foundation: Ruckus and Recovery

McGeorge Bundy was always considered by the Ivy League–Council on Foreign Relations crowd to have had the Right Stuff, and in 1966, after his high-altitude adventures in Washington in foreign and military affairs, they brought him down to a very soft landing in the Ford Foundation.

The foundation was ready for a change, and, given the impending collapse of the escalation policies he had backed in Vietnam, so was Bundy. His predecessor in the foundation, Henry Heald, an uptight, taciturn engineer and educator, had run it on a businesslike basis for nine uninspired years, and the Board of Trustees had become increasingly restless. As one trustee put it, "This has become the most middle-aged young foundation in the business.

In the next few years I'd like to see it become the youngest middle-aged one around."

Announcement of his appointment gave the staff a lift because he still carried a little of the stardust and glamour of the early Kennedy years. There was apprehension, however, on the part of some of the staff that he might begin by conducting a purge and by sharply restricting their authority. There were also a few very troubled by the role he had played in Washington. One conversation between two senior program officers reportedly went as follows:

"What are the doves going to do now?"
"Stop cooing, I guess."
"They'll become mourning doves, more likely."

Bundy had been a highly successful and popular dean at Harvard University before he went to Washington, and he brought the same easy academic administrative style to the foundation. He left most of the old staff in place and quickly won their support by his nimbleness of mind as well as his receptivity to new ideas. He made it clear that he was prepared to have them take chances in their grant making, even suffer failures, and that he would be supportive. This collegial, communicative, trustful approach was in such contrast to Heald's method that spirits soared. They were boosted even further when David Bell, who had acquired a fine reputation as head of the foreign aid program in Washington, arrived to take charge of the foundation's international activities.

Beneath the smooth, soft surface of Bundy's style, however, was a hard, sharp edge of purpose. He came to the foundation determined to put as much distance as possible between himself and the horror in the Far East and, improbable as the undertaking might seem for a Back Bay Bostonian Republican, to achieve high visibility for himself as a liberal domestic reformer. In this regard he inherited a major asset and at the same time, in terms of his ambition, something of a problem in the person of Paul Ylvisaker. During the Heald regime, Ylvisaker's work in the poverty enclaves of the big cities was considered by many, including Bundy, to be its most brilliant accomplishment. Bundy's first impulse therefore was to make Ylvisaker his vice-president, and he offered him the job. But on second thought he evidently decided that Ylvisaker would cast too large a shadow, so in an awkward and revealing move, he suddenly reversed himself and withdrew the offer. Ylvisaker promptly left.

To replace him Bundy brought in Mitchell (Mike) Sviridoff, a former trade union leader who had made a reputation in running outstanding human-services programs first in New Haven, Connecticut, and then in New York City. The choice proved a happy one, and Sviridoff, building on the strong base laid by his predecessor, developed the foundation's powerful National Affairs program, which became the trademark and the finest achievement of the Bundy presidency.

With his course set, his team in place, and his board solidly behind him, Bundy came roaring out of the chute. He wasted no time with organizational tinkering or the usual ritual of a long, dragged-out program review. He laid down some broad program directions and then left his senior lieutenants largely free to pursue them. His personal efforts were concentrated on issuing declarations on various public issues and on pursuing certain program initiatives that interested him.

In his first year, he announced that the foundation would not hesitate to take positions on public issues such as equal opportunity for minorities. The following year he emphasized the importance of action on problems of voter education and voter participation. A year later, in 1969, he focused on the need to break down overly centralized authority in urban school systems so as to involve parents and local communities to a greater degree in the educational process.

Some of these brave declarations were to come back to haunt him later. But all of them and more were translated into a dramatic series of major program actions.

The times, it must be recalled, were extremely tense. The year before Bundy came to Ford, the Voting Rights Act had been passed, and the Watts riots had occurred. The year after, race riots exploded in more than one hundred cities. In early 1968, President Johnson's Kerner Commission reported that "Our nation is moving toward two societies, one black, one white—separate and unequal."

Bundy after his arrival promptly doubled the budget of the National Affairs program, and many of its new initiatives were sharp, reformist interventions into sensitive matters. Over the next four years, 1966–1970, grants were made to stimulate direct action by minority groups in behalf of better housing, employment, and education programs. There were grants to provide legal aid to the poor and to reform police practices. Some grants were given to established minority organizations such as the NAACP and the Urban League, but others went to new and inexperienced groups, even to street gangs. Reinforced with Ford money, a number of them promptly became more strident in their demands and more involved in local politics.

Grants were made for voter education and registration in both the South and the North. The Center for Community Change was brought into being in Washington "to enhance the voice of the poor in their own destiny" by forming community organizations throughout the country. Support for a number of "public interest" law centers was begun, to make use of the courts to protect consumers, the environment, and minorities. Grants were made to finance changes in the structure of public education, specifically the decentralization of the New York City school system. Also in New York City a $35 million grant was made to Columbia University, which had been a center of student and racial disturbances, to enable it "to relate itself better" to the surrounding black community.

A less controversial but nonetheless highly innovative series of other actions was taken. A commitment of $50 million was made to a new program for "program related investments," by which the foundation would use a portion of its investment portfolio for high-risk loans to minority businesses and real estate projects, for example, thus at the same time advancing the purposes of its grants program. Huge grants were made to strengthen local public television stations throughout the country and to improve the programming capacity of the Corporation for Public Broadcasting. A $13 million grant was made to share with the Rockefeller Foundation the costs of operating an International Maize and Wheat Improvement Center in Mexico.

But it was the foundation's activism on social and racial issues that attracted the greatest public attention. Never in the history of American philanthropy had anything comparable in scale and aggressiveness to the Ford Foundation's assault on problems of race and poverty been seen. The effect was to raise the hopes and expectations of disadvantaged groups all over the country and also to generate a storm of criticism.

In New York City, the push for school decentralization detonated an explosion of black, Jewish, and teacher's union tensions, much of the blame for which was put on Bundy and the foundation for the role they had played. In Cleveland, the foundation's voter registration project, concentrated on black neighborhoods, was seen as a direct philanthropic intrusion into a local election—and one that was felt to have altered the outcome, again arousing bitter controversy. Some of its grants to Mexican-American organizations in the Southwest also were seen as threats by local political establishments and provoked angry backlash.

In Washington, where Congressman Wright Patman was then assembling a catalog of charges against foundations, he asked accusingly on the floor of the House, "Does the Ford Foundation have a grandiose design to bring vast political, economic and social changes to the nation in the 1970s?"

Bundy was undeterred by these reactions; indeed, he seemed to be enjoying himself in the spotlight of national attention and in the role of champion of domestic social reform. His board, however, was becoming nervous, largely because of the notoriety and growing political pressures, but partly because the rate of misfires of even some of the less controversial grants was becoming rather high. The millions given to Columbia University, for example, had little effect in inspiring the great majority of its faculties to turn from their teaching and research preoccupations and to become more involved with the local black community. Several of the initial "program related investments" produced fiascoes, such as a fish farm that failed because of a lack of available water and a cattle feedlot in Colorado that failed because the location was too cold for cattle feeding. There was also some worry that although the foundation had cut back on its extravagant overspending of the final Heald period, it was still living well beyond its income and that Bundy had not made a vigorous effort to bring the budget into better balance.

During 1969, Bundy perhaps for the first time in his life had to confront the fact of significant personal failure. In the background was the fact that the full ugliness and incompetence of the Vietnam adventure and of his role in it had become public, a development that could not have left a man of his ego and intelligence, however skilled in dissembling, unaffected. In the foreground were two lesser but still personally painful matters. On February 12, 1969, *The New York Times* reported that the Ford Foundation had made eight grants, personally approved by Bundy, to prominent members of the staff of the recently assassinated Senator Robert F. Kennedy. The stated purpose was "to ease the transition of the recipients from public to private life," and the grants provided "up to a year of leisure and freedom from immediate financial concern." Some of the winners, such as Joseph Califano, about to return to a $500,000 a year law practice, were hardly needy cases. But the grants, coming after a long series of Ford and Bundy actions skirting the edges of partisan politics, were extremely inflammatory.

Just a week later, Bundy was called to testify on the foundation's behalf before the House Ways and Means Committee. The committee was in a critical mood, and Bundy was contentious. Both Republican and Democratic members considered his attitude to be one of "sneering contempt," and their reaction was to insert into the new legislation specific "Bundy provisions" flatly prohibiting "political and propagandistic grants" and imposing complex restrictions on voter registration projects of the kind Ford had financed in Cleveland.

These various events apparently left Bundy seriously troubled for a time and, according to many visitors in his office, affected his performance of his duties. But during this distressed period his vice-presidents, particularly his old friend Harold (Doc) Howe, who had been brought in to head the Education Division, provided him with needed moral support and made it possible for the thrust of the foundation's programs to continue. In the period 1970–1975 it made a $100 million commitment to increase minority opportunities for higher education, a good part in the form of support for black colleges, and the remainder for scholarships and fellowships. It put some $15 million into a program of research, training, and advocacy for the reform of public school financing in the United States. This was a fundamental effort to redress the general inequity in educational opportunity because of underlying differences in wealth of various school districts and therefore of their expenditures per pupil on education. The program in its rippling effects has had great impact throughout the country.

The foundation continued its pioneering effort to address in a substantial way the special needs of the growing Hispanic population of the United States. It strengthened some existing Hispanic organizations and created new ones. It was instrumental in helping Hispanics enforce their legal rights, improve their political participation, and increase their educational opportunities. It helped bring a whole new generation of trained leadership into existence.

To a degree, similar achievements were made with respect to the needs of native Americans.

Some $30 million was committed during the period to the further rapid growth of Community Development Corporations, which sought not only to improve social services in decayed urban areas but to rehabilitate them physically, to promote a variety of economic development efforts, and to develop minority leadership for these self-help efforts. In the Bedford Stuyvesant area of Brooklyn, New York, a very heavy investment was made partly because of the high regard in which its director, Franklin Thomas, was held by the foundation and by Mike Sviridoff.

Likewise, the foundation's support for public interest law was greatly increased, reaching a total of more than $20 million, making Ford by far the leading financier of this new, influential, and controversial activity. Another field in which the foundation took strong leadership was women's issues, including advocacy activities on behalf of women's rights and programs in employment, family planning, maternal care, child care, and education.

There of course were some misfires and mistakes, in some of which Bundy's personal involvement was prominent. The emergence of the energy problem after the first oil embargo in the early 1970s attracted his interest, and in 1974 an Energy Policy Project was set in motion at a cost of more than $4 million. An interesting feature of this effort was that the director, at the press conference announcing its launching, laid out what its findings and recommendations would be. The study aroused much criticism by some members of the commission as well as various economists and industry leaders as inaccurate, naïve, and demogogic. In 1979, in an effort to counterbalance the biases of the first study, the foundation commissioned a second by a pro-industry body, which neither aroused controversy nor made any discernible contribution to the public debate on energy issues that by then had developed.

The Energy Policy Project reconfirmed the impression that Bundy as a philanthropic gardener personally had rather a brown thumb. Moreover, the characteristics of his ineptitude had by then become identifiable: he had a good perception of major emerging issues and a readiness to charge into them. But he had no awareness of, or a reckless indifference to, the larger forces that might be involved (race hatred and trade union politics in the case of school decentralization in New York, public sensitivity about the political use of philanthropic money in the case of voter registration in

Cleveland and the "Kennedy Boy grants") and no grasp of the kind of self-restraint that the biggest factor in any field has sometimes to impose on itself. There were of course those who did not hesitate to draw some obvious parallels with the misjudgments on larger issues that he had made in Washington a few years earlier.

Nonetheless, by the end of 1975, Bundy had achieved a number of his objectives: He had developed a staff of high morale and outstanding ability; he had transformed the foundation board from an all-white and male group of big names into one of much greater diversity of background; and he had put himself and the foundation at the leading edge of efforts to do something about the nation's most urgent racial and social problems. In so doing, he had positioned the foundation precisely at the intersection of philanthropic and political interests. "It makes no sense," he said, "to suppose an arbitrary division between what is done publicly and what is done privately. One of the obligations of the private organization . . . is to concern itself with the relationship between the problem it is attacking and that part of the problem which . . . is the responsibility of political institutions and political forces."

On the basis of that philosophy, he made the foundation overwhelmingly the most "politically" activist of any of the large foundations. This was carefully documented in a 1980 dissertation by Mary Anna Colwell, a California social scientist. She reviewed the "public policy grants" of all the $100 million and larger foundations and of a sample of those in the $10 to $100 million range of assets, defining such grants as those relating directly to the structure and problems of the U. S. economic and political system. She found that about two hundred to three hundred of the existing twenty-two thousand foundations do this kind of giving and that about 25 percent of the $10 million and larger foundations make some such public policy grants.

The Ford Foundation by her definition devoted about 7 percent of its outlays to these purposes, or about $15 to $17 million a year during the early 1970s. Its impact as a result was predominant in a number of key fields.

For two test years, 1972 and 1975, she tallied in detail these "public policy grants" of the biggest givers and found that Ford alone gave over 50 percent of the total. On some issues it gave nearly all. In 1972, for example, it gave 78 percent of all such grants to monitor and provide planning and advisory services to federal, state, and local governments. It gave 86 percent of the grants in the field of public interest law, 83 percent in civil rights, 77 percent of those to organize citizen political action, and 93 percent of the grants on communications policy and public issues reporting.

In the other sample year, 1975, Ford gave 84 percent of all public policy grants relating to the criminal justice system and 87 percent of those relating to environmental protection and litigation. (For both test years Ford made almost no policy grants relating to the strengthening of the U.S. economy, however.)

She also found that in the style of its grant making, Ford was identified by the heads of a number of recipient organizations as the most forceful in trying to exercise control over them. Several cited attempts by Ford to force changes in their programs; one commented that he had had to be concerned about political considerations as well as competence in hiring staff because of pressures by the foundation.

A TIME OF REASSESSMENT

After ten years of Bundy's leadership, the board in 1975 decided the time had come "to canvass the Foundation's experience, successes and failures . . . focused on the broad objectives sought, the means used to achieve them, and the results."

This review was brought about partly because of some program failures and controversies, partly because of the concerns of some of the business members about the general direction of the foundation's program, and partly by concern about Bundy's loose control over expenditures. Indeed, concern about finances had become acute, and for good reason.

Most foundation heads leave investment management to their board or to outside experts. Bundy, however, took an active and opinionated interest in these matters. From his time at Harvard in the 1950s, he had become aware that ultraconservative and risk-avoiding policies in the handling of endowment funds had, during a decade of buoyant share prices, cost nonprofit institutions considerable income that a more venturesome policy might have produced. In his first annual report in 1966, therefore, in explaining the decision of the foundation to cut back on the large lump-sum grants to universities that had been favored by his predecessor, he suggested that university heads could more than replace the loss by taking a more aggressive stance in the investment of their endowment funds. This advice, because of the collapse of the securities markets in the early 1970s, was to bear bitter fruit for those that followed it.

Bundy urged the same policy on his own trustees and the foundation's finance committee, of which he was a member, with the same results. Between 1966 and 1974, shocking losses were suffered. At the time of his arrival, its portfolio had a value of some $3.7 billion, down somewhat from an earlier high point of $4.1 billion. By 1970 that had slumped to $2.8 billion and then fell further to $1.7 billion in 1974, well over a 50 percent loss in value, taking inflation into account, in some eight years.

This gigantic bath was the result in part of inept investment management, a process that until very recently Ford has always carried out on its own premises with its own staff. In equally large part it was due to failures in what could be called financial management.

In 1967, the year after Bundy's arrival, the foundation overspent its income by $100 million, in 1968 by $60 million, 1969 by $90 million, 1970 by $100 million, 1971 by $100 million, 1972 by $110 million, 1973 by $135 million, and 1974 by $150 million. When the trustees finally acted in 1975 to try seriously to bring outlays into line with income, they cut expenditures back sharply. But although the hemorrhaging was checked, another five years passed before a balance was reached.

There have been several foundations that have deliberately spent themselves out of existence. Ford is unique in that inadvertently and by dint of bad financial and investment management it has dissipated almost three fourths of the real value of its assets over the past fifteen years, a loss of something on the order of $6 billion of philanthropic resources measured in current dollars. No disaster of comparable magnitude has ever been recorded. More precisely, after the strong but belated measures taken in 1975, the value of the foundation's portfolio had gradually recovered to a value of some $3.6 billion in 1984. But if the standard gross national product (GNP) deflator is used to adjust for the deteriorating value of the dollar, the real value of the foundation's assets had dropped in the period 1966 to 1984 by three fourths. Expressed differently, if the portfolio had simply kept up with inflation, its 1984 value would have had to be more than $9 billion to be equal in real terms to what it was worth in the late 1960s.

There was a time when the vast difference in size between

Ford and all the other large foundations generated concern that by its sheer mass it distorted public understanding of philanthropy and created unnecessary fears of "thought control" by foundations. That problem at least has now largely been resolved by the foundation's financial performance.

THE FINAL YEARS

The last years of the Bundy regime were certainly less dramatic, and in some respects less happy, than the first ten. He had fewer dollars and fewer staff to work with. In 1970 the total staff of the foundation had numbered more than fifteen hundred; by 1979, when he left, the number had been reduced to just over seven hundred. This large reduction was accomplished in a skillful and dignified way with no upheaval or staff outcry, under the direction of vice-president Howe.

His problems with his board were accumulating, and David Bell, in a significant board action, had been advanced to the position of "executive vice-president," presumably to play a monitoring role in the foundation's affairs. (Bundy referred to Bell thereafter as "my nursemaid.") But it was nonetheless a period of some valuable initiatives, most notably in connection with nuclear issues. A grant of $4 million, for example, was made for arms-control study and training, a subject in which Bundy had become increasingly interested. The foundation also commissioned a study of public policy issues related to the development of nuclear power.

The international affairs program continued its useful but unspectacular research and training activities in Third World countries and toward the end of the decade developed a limited interest in international human rights issues.

On the other hand, the work in humanities and arts, which had been long and capably directed by W. McNeill Lowry, was phased down, as were programs in law and justice, including public interest law, civil rights, and public television.

By the late 1970s Bundy's accumulated problems with the board had become more troublesome, a major moment being the resignation of Henry Ford II as a trustee in early 1977 after thirty-four years of service. The first announcement by the foundation was all hearts and flowers and fond farewells. But when portions of Ford's letter of resignation became public shortly thereafter, the tone sharply changed. The central point of his letter was that the foundation in its activities had shown no interest in the health of the American economy that made its benefactions possible.

"I'm not playing the role of the hard-headed tycoon who thinks all philanthropoids are socialists and all university professors are communists," he wrote, "I'm just suggesting to the trustees and the staff that the system that makes the Foundation possible very probably is worth preserving. . . ."

He also expressed concern that the foundation had seemed to turn more and more inward in its thinking process and that this was a danger sign. "We have a lot to learn from many sources. We shouldn't tolerate a fortress mentality." His letter was a deeply discouraged, but courteous, statement by a man who had been a source of strength and good sense on the board from the foundation's first years.

Bundy in his reply was polite, but unmoved: "He has a right to expect people to read the letter carefully but I don't think one letter from anyone is going to change the foundation's course." In thus dismissing Mr. Ford's concerns, Bundy only added to the feeling of a number of other members of the board that their views simply had no impact on the foundation's programs.

The following year the Board of Trustees named a committee to find a successor to Bundy, who was scheduled to retire in 1979.

Bundy during his tenure had made mistakes, including some serious ones, in management, program, and politics. (In his intelligence and penchant for getting the foundation into trouble, he reminded some of the older hands very much of Robert Maynard Hutchins, who had been the foundation's enfant terrible in the 1950s.) But he had done two things exceedingly well: He had thrown the resources of the foundation into the breach in a moment of national crisis and danger. He also gave the staff, or at least the senior staff who were members of his inner circle, a strong sense of mission and full opportunity to use their talents in achieving it. He had given them both dignity and excitement, and by the end he had become a beloved figure to most of them.

On the other hand there was a certain nostalgia in the air. Much had changed between 1966 and 1979: In U.S. domestic life, a national readiness to support large and idealistic efforts to deal with social grievances had characterized the beginning; at the end, there were fatigue and disappointment with social experiments, the economy was in serious trouble, national security was a growing concern, and a conservative mood was spreading over the country.

In the new atmosphere neoconservative critics attacked Bundy and the Ford Foundation sharply for having worsened the nation's problems, undermined its unity, and endangered its security by their activities. But those who remembered the circumstances of the 1960s, including many who had been severe critics of geostrategist Bundy, generally felt that after he left Washington, the new domestic Bundy by his leadership of the foundation had rendered a major, indeed historic, service in a very disturbed and dangerous period to the country's self-respect, morale, and perhaps even its capacity to function as a united nation. He was, therefore, able to leave the foundation phase of his career with honor.

THE STUMBLING ADVENT OF FRANK THOMAS

The Ford board conducted an extensive search for Bundy's successor and after appraising the qualifications of a number of first-rate candidates chose one of its own members, Franklin Thomas. He was a black lawyer who had once served as an assistant U.S. Attorney in New York and then ably headed a large neighborhood redevelopment project in the Bedford Stuyvesant area of Brooklyn. His rise to prominence came after he had been "adopted" in the early 1960s by some prominent New York corporate leaders concerned about the city's decay and disorders as a sensible, nonpolitical, nonideological black they could work with.

The news of the appointment was electric in its effect. For the first time leadership of a major mainstream private institution had been accorded to a black. Vernon Jordan of the Urban League called the event more important than the appointment of Thurgood Marshall to the Supreme Court because Thomas "on pure merit and in open competition had been selected over a field of the best people in the country." *The New York Times* said that "when corporate America can hand such power to a black citizen, there is truly hope that race will one day be irrelevant."

In many of the favorable reactions, Bundy was given credit for having created the circumstances by which Thomas's choice had become possible. But Mike Sviridoff, who had directed Bundy's centerpiece National Affairs program, also deserved mention. He had known and worked with Thomas for many years, had been instrumental in his election to the Ford board, and had lobbied actively for him to become the new president.

Within the foundation, reactions were jubilant, and everyone awaited the arrival of their new leader with great expectations.

But then occurred one of the most puzzling, protracted, and damaging transitions of authority any major foundation has ever suffered. Precisely where the truth may lie about what happened is impossible to establish because, as in the Japanese tale of Rashomon, very different perceptions exist.

To the majority of the foundation's staff, the following seems to have occurred:

Thomas arrived in June 1979 and then disappeared into his office for nearly two years, emerging only occasionally for brief, unsatisfactory staff meetings. The contrasts with his predecessor were glaring and increasingly discouraging. Bundy had been interested primarily in programs and only indifferently in administration. Thomas seemed preoccupied with every small detail of structure and procedure.

Bundy was communicative and full of ideas; Thomas, sphinx-like, seemed to have none. Bundy was collegial and trustful of staff; Thomas seemed distrustful and often accusatory. And they, who had been so enthusiastic about Thomas's coming, soon began to ask, "When did we become the enemy?"

They then spent long months writing papers, going to meetings, and writing more papers, all without any sense of direction and without feedback from Thomas. One of them, Robert Schrank, an expert on employment policy, was frustrated and indiscreet enough to describe the internal atmosphere at the time to a newspaper reporter as "Sleepy Hollow, with all the gaiety of a funeral parlor."

Insofar as anything that could seriously be called program planning was done, it happened only after the board put the gun to Thomas's head, and then it was done in haste, almost panic. The product was essentially a repackaging, not a rethinking of the program.

In the words of one senior staffer: "Remember the nursery rhyme, The Three Blind Mice? That's the perfect summary of Thomas's first two and a half years: The mice were all running around blind, and they finally got their tails—and more—cut off."

However, to the small inner circle of staffers with whom Thomas worked closely, the situation appeared totally different. To them, whereas Bundy had had only a casual and limited interest in the foundation's programs except the very few that personally excited him, Thomas had dug deeply into every facet of every program and made his recommendations for changes only after the most thorough reflection. At his general meetings with the staff they contend he listened carefully, probed, and raised fundamental questions. The program-review process, as these staff members saw it, was also systematic and logical: first, reviews of existing programs; then the development of a set of program options for the future; and after that the establishment of a set of broad new areas of program interest, called *themes*, around which the elements of a proposed new program were assembled and presented to the board for decision.

Each group, the outer circle and the inner circle, to this day cannot imagine how the other received the impression it did.

Without question, one seriously aggravating and confusing element in Thomas's relationship with the staff in his first years was that for most of them their principal contact was not with Thomas himself but with an academic management expert he had brought aboard who combined qualities of almost comic ineptitude with an ugly brutality of manner. For a period of many months he kept the staff busy drawing organizational diagrams and rewriting their job descriptions. To aid them in carrying out this assignment he provided a glossary of the active verbs to be used in describing their duties. It contained such helpful clarification of esoteric terms as the following: *attends*, "is present"; *copies*, "duplicates an original"; and *participation*, "takes part." (It is possible that some such tutoring may have been needed, because in a survey of staff opinion about the lunchroom, several complained that the steak tartare on the menu was consistently undercooked.) Among the cost-cutting measures he introduced was the elimination of the desk for logging-in and routing the huge flow of mail the foundation normally receives. As a result, for a considerable period, until the order was reversed, it was impossible to carry on normal program work because the necessary papers were frequently impossible to find.

In any event, and despite the differences of perception within the foundation, many signs became visible to outside observers that something obviously was seriously wrong. Even the board, with glacial alacrity, by late 1980 began to be concerned. At their December meeting they goaded Thomas with sharp questioning to get moving. A few outspokenly wondered whether his heavy outside commitments, including six corporate directorships and chairmanship of a Rockefeller Foundation study on Southern Africa, might be part of the problem. A couple of them with good Washington connections even wondered whether, if he was "frozen at the wheel," they should begin to look for some high government position to which he could be "promoted."

Under pressure, Thomas within a three-month period had a set of new program proposals prepared. After some revisions by the board at a discordant meeting, these became the foundation's "New Agenda for the 1980s," which was unveiled in April with considerable public fanfare. Once that was done, Thomas proceeded in a most peculiar way to complete his overhaul. In what came to be known as the "Mother's Day Massacre," he delegated to his administrative aide and a few chosen staff members the task of selecting the program officers to be removed. More than twenty-five individuals were then summarily fired. In the National Affairs Division, for example, the victims were summoned one by one to a Kafkaesque series of fifteen-minute, back-to-back "interviews" at which they were read a written statement informing them that they no longer "fitted in" and should vacate the premises by a fixed date. Throughout, the vice-president for administration sat silently with a yellow pad, presumably to bear witness that they had received their notification. One described the experience in military terms: "I felt like they were going to tear off my epaulettes and throw them in my face. Or that a voice from somewhere would shout, 'ready, aim, fire.' "

The consequent uproar was considerable, as were the costs to the foundation. Several lawsuits were filed, which were quashed only by large payments to the plaintiffs, and substantial settlements were made with a good number of other individuals on explicit condition that they not take legal action.

At its following meeting in June 1981, the board gave one of its less distinguished performances. The chairman, Alexander Heard, and other members had repeatedly been warned of the calamity that was brewing, but they did nothing. Through the tense preceding months they had shown the most fastidious respect for Thomas's executive prerogatives, but they had shown not the slightest regard for the dignity and self-respect of staff professionals who had given long and honorable service to the foundation.

But after the damage had been done, the board indulged in some ex post facto handwringing, and a couple of members expressed the wish "that the firings might have been handled differently." A warning was also given to Thomas "not to pull this stuff again." One trustee, Irving Shapiro, former head of du Pont, went so far as to say that "Thomas's problem is that he has had no depth of experience in managing a large institution."

Shortly thereafter Thomas, to complete the drama of his takeover, announced his two major staff appointments. To head all domestic and international affairs programs, he chose a young woman of relatively limited foundation experience. To head the overseas offices, he reached well down into the ranks of David Bell's old international staff and selected a man who had been informed only a few months earlier that he should look for a position outside the foundation. These choices seemed to confirm a common impression at the time that he was deeply insecure and felt comfortable only with young or weak subordinates.

In two years of clumsy effort, Thomas had reduced the headquarters professional staff by 75 percent and had reduced its ablest members by an even greater percentage. Quite clearly, Thomas, having been instructed to do a job of housecleaning, had not only removed the accumulated dust and clutter but had also bulldozed out the plumbing, wiring, and most of the load-bearing walls of the foundation.

This was disheartening enough to the many observers who wanted very much for him to be a success in his new role. But even more so was the fact that he had decapitated the most sizable concentration of experience and expertise in the private sector on national social programs and problems precisely at the time when social needs were intensifying after years of inflation and economic decline and when the new Reagan administration had just come upon the scene.

His performance and that of the Ford board over the thirty-month transition added nothing to the luster of philanthropy or to public confidence in the continued effectiveness of what had theretofore been one of the most vigorous and productive of the largest foundations. Neither were the omens for the period to follow promising. Indeed, the very high hopes that had been aroused by his appointment had turned into dark apprehensions.

SECOND-HALF RECOVERY

These apprehensions, however, proved fortunately to be wrong. After the June 1981 board meeting, a nadir having been reached, things began to improve. Thomas had long personal conversations with all of the trustees, stabilized his relationship with them, and listened to their advice. He got rid of his top-sergeant administrative vice-president. He also was able, in the judgment of some of his closest friends, to overcome his personal crisis of self-confidence and to begin to give some leadership to the institution.

In 1979 and 1980, the foundation was still running on the Bundy program and momentum. But by the second half of 1981, Thomas and his appointees were in charge, and some changes in emphasis and operating methods could be noted: expenditures for projects dealing with urban and rural poverty were boosted, for example, and concern for the problems of women was changed from a separate and isolated program to an integral element in all programs. But it was too early to judge how much was substance and how much only rhetoric.

The foundation was also handicapped by the fact that its remaining program staff was very thin in experience in a number of areas. Not only had the Bundy vice-presidents, the "barons," disappeared, but a number of the most outstanding and respected authorities in several of the very fields in which his program would concentrate had been ejected, among them Sol Chafkin in community development, Siobhan Oppenheimer-Nicolau in Hispanic and native American affairs, and Michael Teitelbaum in refugee and immigration policies.

On the other hand, the young woman Thomas had named as his second-in-command, Susan Berresford, proved to be a remarkably hardworking and capable program organizer. As a result, with the help of the remaining older staff and some of the young recruits, ongoing activities were maintained and a few new projects mounted. The major single beneficiary was the Local Initiatives Support Corporation (LISC), which Mike Sviridoff had organized before Thomas's arrival and which he left the foundation in 1980 to direct. LISC offers technical and other assistance to the best of the neighborhood economic development corporations in cities throughout the country. A cooperative venture with a number of major corporations and other foundations, it received nearly $5 million of its initial capital from Ford, and $10 million more in the following two years. By the end of 1984, LISC had received a total of more than $20 million from Ford and had raised an additional $50 million from 250 other donors, mainly corporations.

By 1982, Thomas's own hand could for the first time be clearly discerned in the foundation's actions, and the results were impressive:

A joint venture with fifteen community foundations was formed to tackle the growing problem of teen-age pregnancy by a series of new experimental projects.

A new organization, the Refugee Policy Group, was created in Washington, D.C., to carry out policy research on domestic and international migration issues.

A $2 million grant went to the Manpower Demonstration Research Corporation for a program to test more effective ways of moving welfare recipients off public assistance and into regular jobs.

Especially significant were two nonconfrontational but powerful challenges to the thrust of the social policies of the Reagan administration, namely a $3.5 million grant to the Urban Institute to monitor the impact of the president's budget cuts on local communities across the country and a series of grants to the seventeen "back-up centers" that provide the hundreds of local legal services offices throughout the country with specialized research and guidance on specific problems such as housing and welfare rights. This latter program might well have been seen by the White House as direct opposition to its effort to extinguish the federal Legal Services Corporation.

In 1983 and 1984 more major initiatives were taken:

Together with the Richard King Mellon Foundation, Ford created a new Public Education Fund (PEF) to strengthen inner-city schools serving disadvantaged children. PEF provides technical assistance and in some cases matching grants to some fifty communities to help their schools carry out experimental projects to improve the quality of teaching.

A national program to increase the opportunities for students in community colleges to transfer to accredited four-year institutions was launched. The program was intended to check the serious leakage of minority students from the higher education pipeline. By focusing on the growing network of junior colleges, which now enroll nearly 5 million students, many of them members of minority groups, the foundation made a marked departure from its earlier concentration of assistance on black colleges.

In late 1983, $1.5 million was given to create an International Irrigation Management Institute. It would carry out training and research to improve the capacity of developing countries for better use and more equitable distribution of their water resources, a basic problem in attempting to alleviate rural poverty.

In the spring of 1984 sixteen institutions in the United States and abroad received $3.7 million in grants for "fresh approaches" to dealing with problems of international peace and security.

What was emerging was a clear and important new profile of priorities and philanthropic approach, distinctively different from the Bundy legacy. Its elements were several:

First, in the foundation's domestic social programs, which continue to be the center of gravity of its work, Thomas has taken the foundation beyond the problems of poverty as defined in the Great Society period to "the problem of the underclass." As he sees it, the unwed young mother, with the attendant problems of welfare dependency, child abuse and so on, may be at the heart of it. But other crucial elements are young ghetto street gangs who are responsible for much of the urban violence in the country, and the homeless and others who have permanently dropped out of society. These are among the deepest, most impacted, and ultimately dangerous of the nation's urban problems, and no other foundation has made them its particular niche.

Second, he stresses a collaborative approach with other institutions, especially business, in his words "the economic engine of our society." Such collaboration will not only leverage additional grants but also far more massive "social investments" by corporations. These constitute what he calls *balance-sheet philanthropy:* the billions of dollars of loans for business and housing development that appear on corporate balance sheets as assets rather than on operating statements as contributions. Within the foundation itself he has also given a strong push to *program-related investments:* money that will "do good" but will be repaid in whole or in large part, rather than outright grants.

Third, Thomas brings a *grantee mentality* to the foundation's approach, namely a firm belief that the best and most workable ideas for grants are more likely to come from organizations outside, working directly with people and problems, than from within the foundation and its own staff. He has thus confronted a problem that has long bedeviled Ford, namely, its own imperiousness.

By 1985, the foundation had largely overcome the damage inflicted during the transition from Bundy, and Thomas insists that it is now a much stronger institution on the basis of three critical measurements: When he took over, Ford had some 800 staff members worldwide. It now has 530, and administrative expenses have been reduced accordingly. Its portfolio was then worth $2.1 billion; it has now risen to $3.6 billion. Its annual program budget then was $100 million; it is now $140 million, and the total of grants plus administrative expenses is within the foundation's income.

These gains are impressive. But even though the foundation has largely overcome the damage inflicted during the period of transition from Bundy, it continues to have serious management problems. Many organizations dealing with the foundation, both successful grantees and unsuccessful applicants, feel that its staff is generally weak, that there are serious bottlenecks in the decision-making process, and that its procedures are confused and confusing. There are also some who feel that the old imperiousness is beginning to reappear. Staff morale is still a problem, many feeling that Thomas remains remote and his management methods mysterious.

In the substance of its programs, however, Ford has now regained much of its momentum and is pressing forward in the exploration of new issues relevant to the 1980s and beyond.

One of the most significant of these will be a comprehensive reexamination of American social insurance and welfare policies. The United States, like most of the other industrialized democracies, is confronted with growing demands for social services despite continuing financial stringency. The project will ultimately produce recommendations for alternative more efficient, more equitable, and more acceptable ways of providing such services under these circumstances.

For American philanthropy in general this rebound and recovery of the Ford Foundation is of the greatest importance. Throughout most of its history, Ford has been the dominant liberal force among the large foundations not only because of its massive size but also because of the vigor and effectiveness of several of its leaders, Paul Hoffman and McGeorge Bundy most notably. The mood of the country in the 1980s has become cautious and conservative in many ways, and these tendencies are increasingly reflected in the policies and programs of a good many of the biggest foundations. That Ford will continue to be a force representing the liberal approach and liberal values is therefore even more important than it might otherwise be.

A STUDY IN BLACK AND WHITE

There could not be greater contrasts in the backgrounds and personalities of the two men who have directed the Ford Foundation's affairs since the 1960s, and those contrasts help explain the basic differences in what they have done and how they have done it. They present a fascinating and possibly quite significant study of "top down" and "bottom up" liberalism in contemporary America.

Bundy was the son of wealthy, aristocratic Bostonians; Thomas's father died when he was a boy, and his mother, an immigrant from Barbados, worked as a waitress to raise her six children until she qualified, by going to night school, as a machinist. Bundy spent his adolescence at Groton; Thomas spent his in a black ghetto of Brooklyn. Bundy was a brilliant student and debater; Thomas was a mediocre student but a good basketball player.

For Bundy, everything came easy; for Thomas it came by hard work and the discipline instilled by a remarkably strong mother. Bundy's military service, for example, was as an aide to an admiral who was a friend of the family; Thomas enlisted in the Air Force and earned his commission. For Bundy, who had matured in the Harvard environment, work was a game played with words and concepts; Thomas, as a prosecuting attorney, deputy police commissioner, and head of an organization to rehabilitate a slum, spent his early working years in direct contact with very harsh realities.

Very importantly, Bundy's reference group as he pursued his ambitions was made up of academics and intellectuals; Thomas, as he worked his way up, rung by rung, built his base of strength on his relationships with neighborhood, municipal, and corporate leaders. Bundy, at least until his period of government service, knew only success, which gave him an exaggerated self-confidence. This, in addition to his strongly fortified social and financial position, led him to calculate casually the costs of risk taking and encouraged recklessness. Thomas, in the course of his personal struggles, had acquired an acute awareness of the costs of failure, which encouraged both modesty and caution.

In both cases, the two men have strong personal commitment to alleviating the plight of the poor and disadvantaged. But in one case, this was expressed in a highly conceptualized, interventionist, sometimes confrontational, and accident-prone foundation program. In the other, it is being expressed in a more down-to-earth, responsive, cost-conscious, collaborative, careful approach.

Thomas has finally exorcised the specter of Bundy, which had haunted him, and has assumed full command. He has even begun carefully to speak out on a few public issues—he does everything carefully, even drinking his coffee carefully so as not to spatter his necktie—but nonetheless is for the first time feeling sure enough of himself to assert his views.

If Thomas can combine his pragmatism and strong sense of social purpose with improved skills as a manager and leader, it is possible that he may achieve even greater results than Bundy did. And in the more prudent present mood of the country, fatigued with many failures and extravagances in past approaches to dealing with its social problems, Thomas may be precisely the man for the coming season.

Rockefeller Foundation: Fading Factor

Rockefeller on the basis of its record of sustained major achievements through most of its seventy-year history has been without question the preeminent large American foundation. From the beginning it was the embodiment of the modern, "scientific" approach to philanthropy: attacking root causes rather than alleviating symptoms of human problems, advancing basic knowledge, training leaders, and creating needed new scientific and educational institutions. Moreover its goal was nothing less than to "advance the well being of mankind" on a worldwide basis, and in pursuit of this heroic objective it stationed its people and operated programs in nearly every part of the globe.

But the character of this noble institution has also long been flawed. For the past fifty years it has attempted to carry out, along with its scientific programs, which were its strength, parallel activities in the arts, humanities, and the social sciences. These latter have never prospered in the particular internal atmosphere of the foundation, and the combination has resulted in continuing stresses and contradictions.

Despite this tension at the core of the foundation, its major achievements in science continued for a considerable period, so that despite the middling quality of its other activities it could be regarded overall as a vigorous and productive institution. But within the past fifteen years increasing indications of senescence have appeared. One remedy after another has been tried without great success. Most recently, under a new president, another attempt at institutional rejuvenation is being made. But whether it will work remains to be seen. In the words of one eminent trustee, after five years, "the jury is still out."

ORIGINS AND EVOLUTION

It is a paradox deserving of some reflection that the donor, John D. Rockefeller, Sr., the most generous, creative, and effective philanthropist in American history, was also the most notorious of the great nineteenth-century "robber barons." From the late 1870s through World War I his name was associated with greed, rapacity, cruelty, hypocrisy, and corruption. Ida Tarbell in her landmark book *The History of the Standard Oil Company* published in 1904 saw him as "the supreme villain of his age." Many years later, after the violent passions of the time had cooled, other historians, though they have not vindicated his methods, have at least argued that his record was not worse than that of a number of others and have stressed that the important innovations he brought to large-scale corporate management and organization have gone largely unrecognized.

Whatever the judgment of history may be on Rockefeller as a business tycoon, his tremendous and constructive impact on philanthropy is indisputable. During the 1870s and 1880s he gave progressively greater amounts to various causes, most of them related to his church interests, for he was a man of strict religious upbringing. But it was haphazard giving. In 1892, to correct that, he hired Frederick T. Gates, a former Baptist minister, to advise him. That Gates proved to be an entrepreneurial genius was only another of many proofs of Mr. Rockefeller's acumen in organizing large undertakings in philanthropy as well as in business.

Over the next third of a century, they largely wrote the history of the emergence of modern, large-scale philanthropy. Their first major venture was to transform the University of Chicago from a third-rate school of Baptist origins into one of the nation's great centers of learning with $35 million of gifts. By 1900 the elder

Rockefeller gave up active management of his oil empire to devote more of his energies to philanthropy, and he made his son, JDR, Jr., his general assistant. The talents of father and son, combined with the fervor and flair of Gates, resulted in a veritable explosion of philanthropic creativity. In 1901 a new enterprise, the Rockefeller Institute for Medical Research, was launched. In 1903 they set up the General Education Board to improve educational opportunities for blacks in the South. In 1909 they created the Rockefeller Sanitary Commission to eradicate hookworm in the southern states. Within a short time all of them had been staffed with outstanding men and achieved notable successes.

But Gates was pressing Rockefeller to go still further. He warned him that his wealth was accumulating at such a rate that it would "inundate and destroy him and his family" if he did not channel it into a series of "great corporate philanthropies" to advance scientific agriculture, encourage "civic virtue," and accomplish various other purposes. Persuaded, Rockefeller earmarked $50 million of Standard Oil shares as a starting fund for a new "Rockefeller Foundation" to promote "any and all of the elements of human progress."

He originally wanted the U.S. Senate to charter the institution, and he offered to have a majority of its trustees appointed by high government officials and a group of leading university presidents. But the hatred and suspicion of him at the time were so intense that the offer was rejected. (In that same period the Supreme Court ordered the dissolution of the Standard Oil Company for monopolistic practices and the corruption of public officials.) Finally, with a New York charter, the foundation got under way in 1913. It absorbed the Sanitary Commission, redesignating it the International Health Board, and in the next decade extended its attack on hookworm to sixty-two countries on every continent. That program was followed by a boldly conceived worldwide campaign to control malaria. Funds were provided to build the Peking Union Medical College, which became a place of great intellectual ferment and produced the first generation of Chinese graduates trained in the techniques of Western medicine.

Within the United States, following Abraham Flexner's famous report on the deficiencies of American medical schools, a major effort was made to upgrade the best of them.

The one stinging failure of the foundation in its first decade was a study project in the field of industrial relations headed by

W. L. Mackenzie King of Canada. While it was under way, a strike erupted in a Rockefeller-controlled company, the Colorado Fuel and Iron Company, which turned into one of the most savage in the history of American industry, culminating in the tragic Ludlow Massacre. A federal commission that investigated the incident made headlines for weeks by focusing on the ties of the foundation to Rockefeller business interests. One result was to make the trustees very hesitant about becoming involved again in social and economic issues.

By the end of the 1920s, externally the foundation had acquired worldwide prestige, and internally the scientists and doctors on its staff had become dominant. The governing assumption underlying its program was that science, especially medicine, was the surest—and safest—means of advancing the welfare of humankind.

In the late 1920s, in a process of organizational tidying up, a number of separate Rockefeller philanthropies were reorganized or folded into the foundation, one of which was the Laura Spellman Rockefeller Memorial. It had been the one outstandingly successful Rockefeller project dealing with contemporary social and economic problems. After its absorption, however, its brilliant head, Beardsley Ruml, resigned, and it was converted into an academic operation and lost its vigor. Through the 1930s and until World War II, the International Health Division and the Medical Sciences Division went on with their great work, and the Division of Natural Sciences developed a highly productive program in biology and in those border zones where the physical sciences and biology overlap.

But even during the Great Depression the foundation was unable to make a significant contribution to alleviating the social and economic distress in the country. At the same time, its work in the arts and humanities was so dreary that the director himself said that its main effect had been to buttress "scholasticism and antiquarianism in our universities."

During World War II, largely as a result of the personal efforts of an outstanding president, Raymond Fosdick, it made a notable contribution to the rescue of leading scientists and intellectuals from the Continent. But otherwise the work of the foundation continued on its well-established course: superb achievements in science and medicine and mediocre performance in the social sciences, arts, and humanities.

In the immediate postwar period, two developments disturbed the foundation's program and style of operation. A number of new governmental organizations, based on Rockefeller models, began to take over and enlarge on the foundation's pioneering work in various fields. The United Nations established the World Health Organization, which then began to move into most of the fields theretofore occupied by the International Health Division. The U.S. government established the National Science Foundation, whose program was closely patterned on the Rockefeller Foundation's support of research, scholarship, and institutional development. Gratifying as these activities may have been to the foundation, they left it with redundant facilities and specialized personnel.

Another set of stresses resulted from the retirement of both Fosdick and JDR, Jr., from active leadership of the foundation and the election of JDR 3rd as chairman in late 1952. Fosdick and JDR, Jr., were strong, self-confident men who worked together in close harmony. They were able as a result to maintain cohesion on the board and some balance of influence over the powerful scientific and medical potentates of the staff. JDR 3rd was a less commanding personality than his father, and at the same time he was more disposed to press new program ideas on the staff, particularly the need to address the problem of world population increase. For the next fifteen years, a quiet but determined power struggle was carried on between the staff and a rather divided board. In 1960, the president of the foundation, Dean Rusk, whom JDR 3rd had brought aboard, was called to Washington to become President-elect Kennedy's secretary of state, leaving behind him an organization that still had not yet found its new program bearings, and with an accumulation of unresolved internal management problems.

At this point the trustees took two actions to try to check the institution's decay and to give it a clearer sense of direction. First, they broke precedent by selecting a person from within the staff to become a new president. He was George Harrar, head of its agricultural program in Mexico. A plainspoken man, he took over control in 1961 with very definite, and limited, ideas about how the foundation should be run. He believed it should be reorganized to emphasize fieldwork and the application of already existing knowledge to the needs of the less-developed countries. His aim was to move the foundation "from the library and the laboratory into the fields and streets." Expenditures for academic research correspondingly would be greatly reduced.

Needless to say his strong and specific ideas made a number of people on the staff uneasy, but he was, in contrast to the ambiguity of Rusk, at least a known and respected quantity.

The second move of the trustees was to establish a special committee to develop guidelines for future programs. Unlike most such efforts this one resulted in a report that actually said something. The committee identified five priority problems for future action: the conquest of hunger, control of world population, strengthening selected universities and research centers in the underdeveloped countries, achieving equal opportunity for all Americans, and aiding cultural development. Subsequently, almost at the end of Harrar's term, a sixth program, directed toward the improvement of the quality of the environment, was added.

This "problem approach" clashed totally with what had become the foundation's predominantly academic character. Its various divisions—Medical and Natural Sciences, Humanities, Social Sciences, Agricultural Sciences—were structured along academic lines, and each enjoyed great autonomy. The divisional officers, all highly trained specialists, by and large saw their function as advancing the state of knowledge in their own disciplines, not as working together in interdisciplinary teams and certainly not as practical problem solvers.

Harrar had his work cut out for him. He was going to have to bring a rigid, segmented organization into collaboration with itself to deal with issues of an immediate and interdisciplinary kind, which had never been its forte. His problems were not made easier by the fact that the 1960s were to be one of the most turbulent decades in the social history of the United States, one effect of which was to give the trustees a good many second thoughts about the wisdom of their choice of priorities, especially in domestic matters.

Over the next nine years Harrar in his blunt and hands-on fashion worked diligently at his task, more diligently and effectively on some parts of it than on others.

His main interest and greatest success was in the "conquest of hunger" program. The work on new plant varieties begun in Mexico led to similar successful undertakings in other parts of the world and became a movement now known as the Green Revolution. The International Rice Research Institute (IRRI) in the Philippines, which the foundation in the late 1950s had established in cooperation with the Ford Foundation, succeeded in developing new varieties of much greater yield, with benefits to hundreds of millions of people, mostly in tropical and subtropical areas, for whom rice is the principal food. The success of IRRI encouraged the establishment of additional agricultural research institutes in Nigeria and Colombia and a Maize and Wheat Improvement Center in Mexico. The foundation then capped these developments by taking the lead in organizing a group of twenty-eight organizations from various countries to help spread modern techniques of agriculture throughout the developing world. This remarkable set of achievements is the principal monument to Harrar's service in the foundation.

On problems of population the foundation had been late and timid in getting into the field. But once in, it did very useful work, particularly in research and training. In the long, difficult task of assisting in building stronger universities in developing countries, the foundation in the 1960s gave support to some ten institutions, five of which eventually showed some progress but several of which did not, often because of local political tensions and sometimes outbreaks of civil war. To support its programs in the developing countries the foundation maintained a farflung network of local office and staff representatives at heavy expense. In this respect it was partly an operating, partly a grant-making institution.

In the areas of the arts and of equal opportunity, the kind of nonscientific fields in which the foundation had a long record of ineptitude and ineffectiveness, it was able in the 1960s under Harrar to achieve at least mixed results. Its projects in behalf of ethnic minorities and the rural poor were useful but largely peripheral, and its general distaste for social activism led it to concentrate mostly on risk-free training efforts. In the field of the arts, however, in which JDR 3rd had a very strong interest, the foundation was able to develop a creditable effort to support creative individuals.

The program to improve the quality of the environment was launched late and hesitantly, and by the time of Harrar's departure it had done little more than make a few grants, all of which had a strong scientific or training component.

All in all, Harrar's presidency was a productive one: generally rather stolid and down-to-earth in style but with some aspects of excellence. Staff relationships in the Rockefeller tradition were still faction-ridden and quarrelsome, but Harrar was able despite the segmentation of the foundation by academic disciplines to bring about a degree of teamwork on common problems. And because of an effective partnership that developed between himself and JDR 3rd, relationships between the staff and board remained reasonably workable.

Despite these positive factors, a kind of low-level malaise seemed to pervade the foundation as the 1970s began. The board decided that the institution was suffering from tired blood and needed a strong tonic.

JDR 3rd stepped down as chairman in mid-1971 to be succeeded by Douglas Dillon, a wealthy Wall Street banker and former secretary of the U.S. Treasury. Harrar retired a year later, and the trustees' chosen tonic, John Knowles, took office immediately thereafter. (Jay Rockefeller, JDR 3rd's son, later governor of West Virginia and now senator, was then a member of the foundation's board and is said to have been the chief proponent of Knowles's selection.)

THE CRACK-UP

Dr. John H. Knowles had been head of Massachusetts General Hospital and had gained a considerable public reputation as an outspoken liberal on social as well as specifically medical issues. In 1969 he was a highly controversial nominee for the top health post in the Department of Health, Education and Welfare. His name was eventually withdrawn by the Nixon administration in the face of strong opposition by conservative Republicans and the American Medical Association.

He was a man of warmth, enthusiasm, and eloquence, and initial reaction to his appointment both by the foundation staff and by outside observers was favorable. But he turned out to be less a tonic than a torpedo shot into the flank of a venerable and fragile institution. He began to administer his shock treatment as soon as he arrived. He first startled the staff by distributing a memorandum announcing the formation of a new committee on "intellectual rejuvenation," whose very name conveyed something of a reproach to the organization. His first presidential essay in the 1973 annual report was equally brash. He refused to pay even lip service to the usual sacred cows, including his predecessor and the trustees, and in the tone of his remarks, if not in plain English, he accepted and affirmed the picture of the foundation as a moribund institution.

The same report announced the formation of a special trustee committee to review the foundation's programs, headed by a man who had hoped and expected to be named to the post Knowles held, Princeton president Robert Goheen. The report, issued a year later, titled "The Course Ahead," was a bland document that did not criticize any of the existing programs and made two recommendations for further work to be undertaken, namely renewed emphasis on the arts and humanities and a new program on "conflict in international relations." It was, however, soon outdated by events. The oil embargo, recession, and the collapse of the stock market combined to make it obvious that "the course ahead" had to be one of restricted, not expanded activity.

The Goheen report did not do a great deal to clarify the foundation's program strategy, but Knowles actively confused matters during the same period by issuing declarations and taking program actions that seemed contradictory to the commitee's views. He announced, for example, that the foundation in the future would reduce its heavy traditional emphasis on international programs and increase its attention to domestic issues, including such social questions as welfare, employment and the needs of the aged and the poor.

Even when Knowles tried to carry out board directives, he managed to get into trouble. To revive the work in the humanities, which had languished under Harrar, he brought in an unorthodox younger man, Michael Novak, to chart a new program. Disquiet immediately spread among the staff and trustees. Novak was a Catholic, almost a professional Catholic, in an organization that had always been extremely WASP. He was a militant neoconservative in an organization whose social outlook was generally liberal. He was a champion of Slavic and other white ethnic groups in an organization whose tradition had been concern for racial minorities, especially blacks. Unlike the usual foundation professional, Novak through his writings and political activities was a prominent and controversial factor on the national scene.

Knowles gave him strong backing, and Novak had considerable impact in changing the direction of the foundation's subsequent activity in the humanities. But he began to feel like an embattled outsider, and when the board blocked his appointment as director of the program, he left.

Another of Knowles's appointees, Mason Willrich, who was recruited to head the program in international relations, also made waves. He was brought in to resuscitate the sagging international relations program, and he accepted the appointment on the basis of an explicit understanding with Knowles and the chairman of the board that he would take an activist approach emphasizing policy studies. The reports on energy, arms control, and other issues that were subsequently published were generally well regarded, but some members of the board felt they went too far in committing the foundation to controversial positions. Willrich also brought into being a group of leading economists from various countries, called the Group of Thirty, to meet periodically to discuss international economic trends and issues, a highly praised enterprise that is still in operation. But Willrich was caught somehow in the crossfire between Knowles and the board and was forced to resign.

The Novak and Willrich incidents, plus a good number of other misfires in Knowles's efforts to alter operating procedures and programs, gradually created a general impression that for all his energy and enthusiasm, he was in fact impulsive and erratic as an administrator. His style and some of his public statements, with expletives left undeleted, also came to be regarded by a good portion of the trustees as undignified and inappropriate for the head of the Rockefeller Foundation.

Under the increasingly disorderly circumstances, certain individual members of the board became sharp and persistent critics of specific programs. Trustee Goheen was particularly incensed about what Knowles had done with the humanities program; trustee Nevin Scrimshaw, a physician himself, followed the program in medicine with a critical eye; and Maurice Strong, a Canadian who had served with distinction as the first head of the United Nations program for the environment, watched the foundation's work in that field closely and did not like most of what he saw. Evidently most of the board agreed with him, for in 1978, after a fiasco in its major project, the Hudson River Basin Study, they decided to shut the program down.

When Cyrus Vance began his brief tenure as chairman of the board in 1975 before being called to Washington as President Carter's secretary of state, he attempted to deal with the board's complaints and its increasing factionalism by involving the trustees more directly in the oversight of programs. After Vance, Father Theodore Hesburgh, president of Notre Dame, became chairman, and through his skillful conciliatory efforts, relationships between Knowles and the trustees improved slightly. But the problems of the foundation remained many and serious. Of these, perhaps the most fundamental was the incoherence of the board iteself. In previous years, in response to public demands for greater diversity and "representativeness" in its membership, new trustees of various backgrounds were elected, who in a number of cases had very specific program or constituency interests and sometimes had little experience in performing the general role of policy direction of a complex institution. By the late 1970s, the board in the words of one leading member had become "a mélange, an assemblage of interest cliques, not a responsible mechanism of governance." Among its factions or fragments were the "aggies," the equal opportunity group, the health group, and others. With revolving and sometimes weak leadership the board became so demoralized and indifferent that a degree of absenteeism developed that would have been inconceivable in earlier times. Of those trustees who did attend meetings, a good many came only when there was an item "of special interest" on the docket, an ominous symptom of the extent to which the disease of nonresponsibility for the overall governance of the foundation had taken hold.

In these unhappy circumstances, John Knowles in 1979 was suddenly stricken with cancer and died. Thus came to an end a calamitous presidency, probably the worst interval in the foundation's history since the ill-fated consolidation of the Rockefeller philanthropies in the late 1920s. At that moment the great old flagship of the fleet of American philanthropy—although useful work was going on in some of the compartments below decks—was a rudderless hulk.

THE ADVENT OF RICHARD LYMAN

In August 1980, nine months after Knowles's death, Richard W. Lyman was elected president of the foundation. As head of Stanford University he had acquired a good reputation as an academic administrator, and he had for the preceding four years been a member of the Rockefeller board.

Presumably he was selected because of his managerial and diplomatic abilities, given the severe internal problems of the foundation. In any event, he interpreted his mandate in managerial terms, and he began immediately to try to fix some of the conditions that urgently needed attention, of which there were many: faulty administrative procedures, staffing problems, defects in specific programs, a lack of coordination and collaboration among programs, difficulties involving portfolio management, and of course, problems with the board itself.

He brought in a new and sensible vice-president for personnel to reduce the organizational disorder and restore staff morale. He introduced a number of measures to reduce the excessively hierarchical and compartmentalized style of operation. He began carefully and quietly to replace weaker staff members with new appointees. In so doing, he successfully avoided the kind of internal and external backlash that Frank Thomas's mayhem at the Ford Foundation had produced.

On another front he undertook a vigorous effort to reduce both staff costs and program expenditures. As a trustee, and undoubtedly influenced by his experience as a university administrator, he had been concerned for some time that because of inflation of expenses plus poor investment results the foundation was in danger of "spending itself out of existence." He therefore cut back on some redundant staff positions in New York and trimmed various staff perquisites. By 1983 he had also slashed the number of overseas offices of the foundation from ten to two and the overseas staff from fifty-four to nine. By those actions he reduced operating expenses by more than $3.5 million a year. But he at the same time necessarily changed the foundation's method of operation, if it intended to continue its agricultural work, for example, from one of staff research and direct operations to one of grant making and thereby of dependence on other institutions.

By 1984, the financial situation of the foundation had been brought into substantial balance partly by Lyman's cost cutting, partly by a reduction of $3 million in the foundation's grants budget made promptly after the Congress in 1983 reduced the minimum payout requirement, and partly because the investment committee of the board, under the leadership of a prominent investment banker, trustee James Wolfensohn, was able to achieve extraordinary improvement in the value and returns of the portfolio.

In parallel with these administrative and budgetary changes, Lyman also began a long series of reviews of each of the foundation's programs. This tedious and traditionally incestuous process involved much assembling of information on past grants, consultations with advisers (selected by the program heads themselves), and preparation of staff evaluations and recommendations regarding their own programs. The voluminous papers produced were then submitted to the trustees for their consideration.

Some degree of impatience and frustration on the part of the trustees with this approach to program review can be inferred from the board's decision in 1981, just as the long march of program-by-program reviews was being started, to pass a special $1.5 million appropriation to force the foundation to do more, and to do some new things, on behalf of equal opportunity for minorities. That same year the board also substantially increased the appropriation for "special interests and explorations," a fund intended to enable the staff to have freedom and flexibility in taking advantage of new opportunities and experimenting with new ideas.

That little progress was being made after more than two years of effort in reviewing the foundation's programs, and that little in the way of interesting new ideas had been generated, was implied in Lyman's "president's review" for the 1982 Annual Report written in April 1983. In it he affirmed that with the "tremendous forces for change at work all around us," foundations should be able to find ample problems at home and abroad "to challenge them out of the ruts of routine grant making." But he gave no clue to what the response of the Rockefeller Foundation, if any, to those challenges might be.

By 1984, four years after Lyman's arrival, the slog of the program-review process had been completed, and the results, to a good many members of the board at least, were not uplifting. Some "refinements" and "new approaches" had been added, but no major changes had been made. Indeed it could be said that the only real new feature of the foundation's program over the period was one that resulted not from staff initiative or leadership but from the trustees, namely the special appropriation and directives imposed by the board on a clearly skeptical and reluctant staff in 1981 to invigorate the equal opportunity program. Out of this board mandate has come a multimillion-dollar, multiyear effort to assist single minority-group women who are heads of households.

Another indication of the sluggishness and lack of creativity of the staff under Lyman could be read in the fact that funding for "special interests and explorations" was substantially reduced in 1983 and that the principal grant made from the fund before the cutback was nearly a million dollars to help pay the operating costs of the Rockefeller archives, a rather large collection of family and foundation papers housed in an inconveniently located mansion on the outskirts of New York City.

In its basic and long-established programs, however, the foundation's performance remained uneven. One, that focusing on population, was generally judged excellent. The related program on global health problems is praised for the quality of its scientific work, especially in clinical epidemiology, but it operates in a spirit of almost paranoid competitiveness with other organizations, such as the World Health Organization, working in the same fields, and even with other divisions of the foundation itself.

The program in international relations similarly received mixed reviews by the trustees and outside observers. Its work on world energy problems has been shelved. Its principal project in the area of "regional conflict and international security" was a long and expensive commission on southern Africa, which produced a sensible report but made no perceptible impact. Its work on international economic issues, especially through the Group of Thirty, is felt to have been useful. But there has been a quality of overreaching and underfunding in this as in a number of the other programs of the foundation. In 1982, for example, its objectives were described as follows: "to improve the international monetary system, encourage trade expansion, increase the flow of private capital to developing countries, improve the functioning of commodity and energy markets, and facilitate the coordination of national economic policies." To carry out these monumental purposes, the foundation that year made a total of seven grants totaling $500,000.

The arts and humanities work, long troubled, was still wallowing in unctuous verbiage such as the following statement of purposes: "Humanistic thinkers are encouraged to deepen understanding of the past, assess current ideals and goals, explore ethical issues, and preserve and revitalize America's heritage by studying neglected areas of social and cultural activity." A number of past and present trustees call the effort "mediocre" and "disappointing." A present officer has gone so far as to say, "Mellon's work in this area is ten times as valuable as ours." In 1983, the two programs were merged and a new director brought in to try to rescue the situation.

The huge program to strengthen universities in Third World countries, called Education for Development, which had cost some $125 million over nearly twenty years, had by 1984 been wound down, judged by some to be a victim of turbulent circumstances and by others to be largely a costly white elephant. The great agriculture program, once the centerpiece, was in transition, having been stripped of its overseas apparatus.

And, as virtually foreordained by the foundation's history, the programs in "equal opportunity for all Americans" and on behalf of single female heads of families were in serious trouble. The standard approaches of Rockefeller—research, strengthening of established operating institutions, and advanced training for individuals—did not fit such tasks, and yet the foundation seemed incapable of adapting itself to their special and very different requirements.

In late 1984, nearly five years after Lyman's arrival as president, the foundation announced a $1.5 million, three-year program to encourage better teaching of foreign languages in American high schools. It was the most recent in a series of actions in the humanities program, a strong interest of Lyman, to attempt to improve teaching in those subjects. The program, one of the few new staff initiatives in recent years, provides a reading of the state of the foundation's programming capabilities at the present time. Given the nation's notorious linguistic deficiencies and the degraded status of teaching in the humanities, the action was without question benign and useful. But because dozens of projects with similar objectives have been launched in the years since Word War II by various foundations, school systems, and government agencies, it was hardly groundbreaking. It required selection of an objective and of a grantee, but no creative input of any consequence. Completely uncontroversial, it required no courage or risk taking. It was of a scale that did not require the resources of a major foundation. It was thus in all essential respects the kind of grant that any ordinary, middle-sized, minimally staffed, and essentially reactive foundation might have made.

SLOUCHING TOWARD SENILITY

Linus, the American philosopher, has wisely observed, in the comic strip *Peanuts*, that there is no heavier burden than a great potential. It is equally true, as the Rockefeller Foundation demonstrates, that there is no greater burden than a great past. (It leads, as in the present analysis, to being judged by different standards from those applicable to ordinary institutions. In this appraisal the harsh judgment rendered is therefore not to be interpreted as meaning that Rockefeller today is a poor foundation in the sense that Keck, Brown, and Mabee are poor foundations. By that measure it is a fine foundation. But in relation to its own past standards and in terms of its present potentialities, it is performing very badly.) For at least the last twenty years, the foundation has been struggling to adjust to the consequences of its extraordinary earlier achievements, to changing times, and to its reduced means. Some obvious sets of questions arise from a review of these efforts: First, to solve its persistent and fundamental programming problems, should the foundation in its present circumstances concentrate its efforts and resources on a few priority programs and not only cut back but cut out some others? But with the present makeup of the board, which includes built-in constituencies for every existing program, would any such surgical solution be possible?

Second, given the foundation's generally uneven performance over many years, should it now concentrate its efforts on those fields in which it has been notably successful and drop those in which its results have been more modest, even mediocre? Or, alternatively, can the internal ethos of the institution, which has not been conducive to excellence and achievement in nonscientific activities, be changed in some fundamental and corrective way?

Lewis Thomas, head of the Sloan-Kettering Institute for Cancer Research and a widely admired essayist, has stressed the importance of the "air" of an institution to its accomplishments. What is essential, in his view, if a scientific institution, for example, is to be vibrant and creative, is "for the air to be made right. If you want a bee to make honey, you do not issue protocols on solar navigation or carbohydrate chemistry, you put him together with other bees. . . . And you do what you can to arrange the general environment around the hive. If the air is right, the science will come in its own season, like pure honey."

What is unmistakably clear about the Rockefeller Foundation over the course of nearly half a century is that its air has been "right" in the physical and life sciences, but it has rarely and only intermittently been "right" for dealing with social issues and nonscientific matters. Any well-managed private business would long since have cut its losses in its unproductive lines in order to concentrate its resources and special skills in its areas of strengths and achievement. The Rockefeller Foundation at present, however, seems to be moving precisely in the opposite direction by dismantling its overseas agricultural facilities and scientific staff.

A third line of questioning relates to the appropriate and necessary presidential role if the Rockefeller Foundation is to break out of its descending slow spiral into senility. Lyman came to the foundation without any grand vision in terms of which he hoped to shape its activities. Rather, in dealing with programming as in administrative problems, he has been a "fixer," not a visionary: in his word, an *incrementalist*. To date that approach has not produced any large or exciting changes, although a number of small improvements can be seen.

As a result, the board's restlessness has once again become considerable. As one trustee has said, "To date, Lyman's main contribution has simply been to give the aging process more dignity." At a board retreat in early 1984, its discontents about the program led to long and vigorous discussion and the creation of a committee. That trustee/staff group, in an intriguing exercise in retroactive planning, was devoting its time in early 1985 to examining how the foundation could deal with problems of poverty and development in Third World countries in the future, having dismantled its overseas field staff and offices two years earlier. How useful the trustees can be, even in their state of frustration, in rousing the foundation's program out of its present doldrums remains to be seen. Indeed, whether this can ever be done without strong executive thrust, without leadership that has a broad and compelling image of the institution's future, has to be considered doubtful.

It remains possible, however unlikely, that the foundation's long slide downward has now bottomed out and that some major, exciting new initiatives that will coalesce its fragmented board and inspire its staff will be forthcoming. That is most devoutly to be hoped, for if the Rockefeller Foundation continues to do no better in the years ahead than to muddle and bumble along, the implications for all of philanthropy are very great. This field like every other needs leaders and standard setters. For many years the Rockefeller Foundation provided such leadership. It does no longer. If it cannot somehow reverse the long process of decline that it is now in, a very great loss to philanthropy and even to the nation itself will have been suffered.

5

THE BIG NEWCOMERS:

MacArthur and Robert Wood Johnson

MacArthur Foundation

INTRODUCTION

The John D. and Catherine MacArthur Foundation of Chicago is a new wonderment on the philanthropic scene: the biggest, most bizarre, riotously quarrelsome, disorganized, in some respects even dubious, of the new and very large American foundations. Yet, despite the disorder and all the broken crockery lying about, it has done some interesting things, and it may now be at the point of settling down to some serious development.

Like the Chicago Carl Sandburg described—"City of the big shoulders, hog butcher to the world"—the MacArthur Foundation is rude and rough and bursting with vitality. Its organization, or disorganization, has been indescribable. Its board, ridden with conflicts of interest, has not been a board at all but a collection of disparate, strong-minded, and warring individuals. The donor, John MacArthur, had most of the features of "the unacceptable face of capitalism," and his son, Roderick, who until his death in late 1984 was probably the most powerful single factor in the situation, was like his father a maverick and a "born nose-thumber at society." If the style of most foundation trustees is to deny they have any dirty laundry and to close ranks and maintain a public pretense of perfect harmony regardless of the rows going on in the back room, the style of the MacArthur trustees has been quite the reverse: to threaten each other with lawsuits, denounce each other in the press, and vilify each other in private. After the wave of public and press applause for the foundation's launching of its now famous MacArthur Fellows Program in 1980, one trustee remarked, "What this proves is that roses can grow even out of a manure pile."

THE DONOR

John D. MacArthur, who died at the age of eighty in 1978, was the youngest of seven children. His mother died when he was a boy. His father was a small farmer who became a wandering evangelist. MacArthur's education ended with grade school. From this impoverished beginning he became perhaps the richest man in the United States at the time of his death. (His brothers were strivers too. One became the head of a prosperous Chicago newspaper chain; another, a millionaire insurance company executive; a third, Charles, coauthored the popular play, *The Front Page*, and married actress Helen Hayes.)

His early life was turbulent, and he failed at almost everything he tried: as a student (he quit in the eighth grade), as a Royal Canadian Air Force pilot (he crashed three planes in training), and even as a stowaway (he was discovered before his Europe-bound freighter dropped its New York harbor pilot). But in 1935 he bought a bankrupt Chicago insurance company, Bankers Life and Casualty, for twenty-five hundred dollars. After a couple of years of struggle he got it on its feet, and as the Depression deepened he was able to sweep up a large share of the market for low-cost insurance relinquished by companies that had failed. Then, with cash from the insurance company, he began investing in Florida real estate at the start of the land boom of the 1950s, eventually acquiring tens of thousands of acres of prime properties for its portfolio. By the time of his death he owned all of the stock of Bankers Life and of a dozen other insurance companies. *Forbes* magazine, in the 1970s, called him one of the country's only two billionaires, the other being Daniel K. Ludwig, the shipping magnate.

MacArthur was a tough, tight Scotsman, and the stories of his frugality were many. At one time, when he first became wealthy, he indulged himself briefly in high living. But he soon gave it up. "Too much comfort softens the brain," he decided.

He had no friends. He did not get along with his family. His consuming interest was making money, a game he loved winning, no matter what the stakes. "You know," he explained, "if I play poker for matches . . . hell, I want the matches. I'm a competitor."

In the mid-1960s he and his second wife, Catherine, who had lived in a small house in Chicago, moved to a second-rate hotel he owned in Palm Beach, The Colonnades. There they and two poodles occupied a modest two-bedroom apartment with junky furniture, falling plaster, and a view of the parking lot, where his five-year-old Cadillac rested. His office was a table in the hotel coffee shop, appropriate for a man who drank more than twenty cups a day. There, from six in the morning until late in the evening, in clothes grubby enough for a maintenance worker, he chain-smoked and talked deals with all comers. Much of the time he was picking up parcels of real estate from owners who found themselves in desperate need of money. "There were tears and blood on that table as well as coffee stains," another resident of the hotel once said. "He ran the meanest pawn shop in Florida."

Neither were the business practices of his insurance company generally admired; it was constantly pursued by state and federal regulatory agencies for various kinds of alleged malpractice. Although he was never convicted of criminal conduct, his brother Alfred, president of his own insurance company, once observed: "The darkest day in insurance history was when my brother, John, entered the business." John's view was that the whole history of the insurance industry was pretty dark. When asked once why none of the six cars or two planes in his transport fleet was insured, he replied, "Because the insurance companies are thieves."

In social outlook, he was the classic "rugged individualist." He loathed government waste, bureaucratic paperwork, and every force in American society that tended to deaden individuality. "The only thing that will save this country," he once said, "is a paper shortage."

MacArthur died in January 1978. There were no funeral services. In his will he asked that such ritual be forgone "because most people attend funerals only as a matter of duty."

ACTIVATION OF THE FOUNDATION

The directors MacArthur chose for his foundation, except for his wife, Catherine, and son, J. Roderick, were all old business associates. They included three senior officers of Bankers Life: Paul Doolen, vice-chairman, William Kirby, general counsel, and Robert Ewing, president and board chairman. Paul Harvey, a radio commentator whose program had been sponsored by Bankers Life for more than twenty-five years, was also named. Catherine MacArthur never attended a board meeting. In fact, she thought the whole idea of the foundation was nonsense and suggested that the money simply be turned over to some charity and be done with it.

At the start, the three company men and Paul Harvey, led by William Kirby, were in the dominant position. Rod MacArthur was a minority of one. Matters quickly became spirited because he disagreed fundamentally and militantly with the majority.

The donor left no instructions about how the foundation should be organized or what it should do. The initial board therefore had to try to enunciate the aims of the foundation and, as the magnitude of its responsibilities and of the resources at its command became more evident—and as Rod MacArthur pressed the matter—they also had to confront the question of what kind of individuals should be added to the board.

The first signals of future directions were a little confused. In an early statement Ewing, speaking for the Bankers Life officers on the board, said, "We're mostly a bunch of midwestern businessmen devoted to free enterprise and opposed to more government controls. That's the way we operate our businesses, and that's the way we'll run our foundation." Another company member of the board said that they were "determined to avoid the internationalist, liberal-oriented pattern of philanthropy established by such big Eastern foundations as Ford, Rockefeller and Carnegie."

But at the same time Rod MacArthur declared that foundations had to be on the cutting edge of social change, that they should lead government "as its social conscience," and that he would like to see the MacArthur Foundation concentrate heavily on funding "maverick geniuses" to pursue their own ideas and make their own discoveries. "It's very much in the old man's style, you know," he said. "The idea behind the MacArthur Fellows program is that Albert Einstein could not have written a grant application saying he was going to discover the theory of relativity. . . . My father was a firm believer in the individual. He spent his whole life sneering at stuffed shirts and pooh-poohing institutions."

There was greater consensus among the directors about the style of the foundation's operation. All were agreed that the trustees should play an active and controlling role and that the foundation should carefully avoid putting itself into the hands of the experts, the professionals, and the philanthropic establishment. A favorite anecdote that was repeated frequently among them concerned the experience of one director who consulted an eminent Chicago judge with much philanthropic experience about whether he should agree to serve on the board. The judge's advice was "Sure, do it. For a year it will be interesting and enjoyable. After that you'll have a staff and you won't know what the hell is going on."

As the trustees got down to work in early 1979, it quickly became clear that there were great differences in degree of interest in the foundation among them. Paul Doolen, the chairman, was quoted as saying, "I can't get off this board fast enough." At the other extreme, Rod MacArthur had an intense, consuming interest in the foundation's affairs.

Likewise there was a vast difference in the certainty with which they addressed the problem of the foundation's program focus. William Kirby said, "You never met people who know less about foundations than we know." But Rod MacArthur was determined from the start that the foundation should use most of its money specifically to subsidize "500 to 1,000 of the greatest minds of our time, working on our society's greatest problems."

As a result, for more than a year there was no agreement either on the foundation's purposes or on the hiring of staff. In that period MacArthur lost a great many 4–1 votes, and the company-connected directors would very much have liked to have gotten rid of him.

At that point the wrangling turned into warfare. The major specific issues were the proportion of the foundation's income that should be given to the "geniuses program," the expansion of the

board, and the manner of diversification of the foundation's holdings in Bankers Life.

MacArthur correctly sensed the intense concern of the company-connected directors with any decisions about the sale of the
insurance company, which could potentially mean millions of dollars of personal gain or loss to them; their distaste for public brawl-
ing and name-calling; and their vulnerability to the charge of
conflicts of interest. So by bludgeoning them with the threat of
lawsuits, he gained some key victories, first, a formal decision in
early 1979 that the "MacArthur Fellows Program" would be the
foundation's first major enterprise and would be developed as rapidly as possible. Then in May of that year the board was expanded
to thirteen members by adding John Corbally, a former president of
the University of Illinois; Gaylord Freeman, a prominent Chicago
banker; Nobel Prize scientist Murray Gell-Mann; Jonas Salk, devel-
oper of the polio vaccine; former head of the University of Chicago
and U.S. Attorney General, Edward Levi; president emeritus of the
Massachusetts Institute of Technology Jerome Wiesner; and former
U.S. Secretary of the Treasury William E. Simon. In relation to the
power struggle going on within the foundation, the list of new
directors represented a triumph for MacArthur. All were individuals of high standing, and only a couple of them, most notably Simon,
shared the archconservatism of the company-connected directors.
(Several of the most eminent and liberal-minded of the new directors had been proposed by MacArthur on the basis of advice by a
former vice-president of the Ford Foundation, Champion Ward.)

A test of strength between the factions on the expanded board
was not long in coming. It took the form of a showdown between
MacArthur and Simon, which reached its climax in late 1981. During the preceding year Simon had proposed that the foundation
make a number of substantial grants to politically conservative institutions with which he was associated, and a number of such
grants—to MacArthur's great annoyance—were in fact approved.
At board meetings clashes between him and Simon became very
sharp. MacArthur did not hesitate to denounce in public some of
the board's actions as "just plain dumb," and, with obvious reference to Simon, he charged that some of the worst grants were
pushed by directors "who wanted to assist their favorite think tank,
or support a pet cause, or aid those with whom they had personal
connections."

Finally, Simon, who is singularly unfond of being contradicted or criticized, made a move to have MacArthur ousted from the board. But his challenge failed, and Simon in high dudgeon resigned at the end of 1981.

TEMPORARY CEASE-FIRE

Thereafter things quieted down for a while. The two most powerful figures to emerge were MacArthur and Kirby, and the two of them, who formerly were in the habit of denouncing each other to the press in such terms as "liar," "fool," and "crook," in the interest of the foundation's reputation apparently took vows if not of silence at least of greater restraint. As a result it was possible for the foundation to get on for a time with organizing the work of the board, developing a staff, defining its program, and diversifying its assets.

John Corbally became full-time president, and an able executive vice-president, James Furman, formerly head of the Illinois Board of Education, was named. Others, mostly relatively young, were hired to provide largely routine administrative services to the board members.

The board itself was organized into a number of committees and subcommittees to involve the trustees directly in program development and grant making. There was a committee to direct the MacArthur Fellows Program, chaired by Rod. There was a committee for the foundation's second major program, which works in the field of mental health, headed by Kirby. A committee on "special grants" was set up to deal with gifts to cultural and institutions and community organizations in the Chicago area.

Finally, a "general grants" committee would handle everything else, areas declared by the board to be of interest to the foundation but not addressed by other programs. At first most of its grants were given on a one-time basis in response to pressure on the foundation to meet its statutory payout obligations. But gradually more of them took the form of exploratory efforts in new fields. Subcommittees of the committee were created to deal with specific areas such as environment and resources and international affairs, and from these subcommittees have come some major new undertakings.

Although these several committees are made up of designated members of the board, any director can join the discussions of any committee. Rod MacArthur rather regularly did so to express his opposition to particular proposals.

The procedure of the foundation in considering grants is as unusual as is the dominant role of trustees in the grant-making process. Proposals received are each summarized by the staff in a two-page memorandum, which the committees review and judge to be worth either further examination or immediate rejection. If a proposal is deemed worthy of further study, a committee of the board then does whatever it deems appropriate to give it further consideration and eventually decides whether or not a grant should be made. Thus board members are directly involved in receiving, processing, and deciding on all significant grants.

A second distinctive feature of the foundation's approach to grant making is that it has formally structured "initiative taking" and "responsiveness" into its procedures. It accepts outside requests for funding in only two of its four current program areas: "special grants" in the Chicago area and "general grants" in the fields of education, public affairs, justice, and mass communications. The MacArthur Fellows Program does not accept applications but gathers nominees through its own network of "finders." The health program solicits proposals in specific areas of research and invites participation in its research networks through public announcements. But it does not receive uninvited applications.

EARLY GRANTS AND PROGRAM EVOLUTION

The foundation began grant making in 1979, a year after the donor's death. Under the pressure of statutory payout requirements it was obliged to make substantial outlays even though its program was still undefined and its operations not yet organized. In the fashion of a number of other foundations who found themselves in the same situation, MacArthur solved the problem by lump-sum gifts to a variety of recipients. In 1979 it gave $2.5 million to the Better Government Association of Chicago to look into problems of governmental waste and corruption. In 1980 its grant level jumped to more than $40 million, $22 million of which was represented by a grant of land to the state of Florida for the MacArthur Beach State Park. In that same year it made a much-publicized grant of some $5 million to rescue the dying monthly magazine *Harper's*. (Four years and several million dollars later the magazine claimed to have cut its deficit considerably. It had incidentally also acquired as head of the nonprofit organization that is now its owner Rick MacArthur, son of the redoubtable Rod.)

In 1981 the foundation distributed another $40 million, a good part of it in special out-of-program grants: one-time awards of $300,000 each to seventeen colleges and universities for MacArthur Fellowships and awards of $1.2 million each to nine colleges and universities to endow MacArthur Chairs.

Thereafter, such "irregular" grants became less frequent, and the principal ongoing programs plus major new initiatives emanating from the "general grants" committee and its subcommittees began to consume the bulk of the foundation's income.

As of 1983 the program of the foundation, which was still in a process of evolution, had these main features: its most widely known activity was its MacArthur Fellows Program. Of equal scale, perhaps because of some kind of agreement by the board to give MacArthur and Kirby roughly equal funding for the two programs they lead, was the program in mental health research. The general grants program, which is the rubric for experimentation and expansion of the foundation's activities, was being developed vigorously and boldly. A succession of important ventures was launched, and each was backed with substantial funding. In 1982, a commitment of $15 million was made for the creation of a new World Environmental and Resource Institute. Nobelist Gell-Mann was the key person on the subcommittee that recommended the action. In 1983 a $20 million appropriation was made to apply developments in genetic engineering and immunology to the study of parasitic disorders. Dr. Salk played an important part in the development of this venture. Another subcommittee, under the leadership of Dr. Wiesner, initiated a new international affairs program to deal with arms control and national security, to which $25 million was eventually committed.

At that moment it appeared that the foundation's tumultuous early years were coming to an end and that more orderly progress could thereafter be expected. President Corbally worked hard and with some success to mediate the continuing rows at board meetings. He also managed to improve the foundation's image with the press and to convey an optimistic picture of its future. Arrangements were even set in motion to lay longer range plans for its institutional and program development. Dr. Jonas Salk was named head of a special board committee for this purpose.

But such appearances were deceptive, for in fact another major upheaval was in the offing.

ROD MACARTHUR'S VISION AND HIS DISCONTENTS

As they developed, the internal struggles of the MacArthur Foundation involved three factors or factions: the Bankers Life executives, the notables, and Rod MacArthur. MacArthur was the loner and the dissident. He was also the mover and shaker who was responsible for the foundation's trademark program and for the fundamental and most constructive change in its original structure, namely the addition of the prominent national personalities to its board.

He was intensely, even ferociously engaged in the foundation's affairs from the start. He was determined to be the MacArthur of the MacArthur Foundation, and he fought every issue in alley-cat style. At the same time, whatever the underlying psychological forces motivating him, he fought his fights over questions of principle, and he was the boldest and most visionary donor's descendant in any of the large American foundations at the time. It is important to understand his vision and the issues that agitated him to understand the climactic upheaval that occurred in early 1984, and to understand the significance of his death later that year for the future of the foundation itself.

Roderick MacArthur was a self-made millionaire and as eccentric, opinionated, and individualistic as was his father. Father and son never got along. Reportedly the father thought Rod was "to stupid to come in out of the rain," and although he helped him from time to time, he generally operated on the principle that "if he made it easy for his children, they would never amount to a damn."

After World War II Rod worked for a time in Europe as a reporter for United Press International. In the early 1950s his father hired him to run a publication he owned, *Theatre Arts Magazine,* and then fired him over a policy dispute. Rod then tried working in a bank controlled by his father, but quit when the old man refused to raise his ten thousand dollars a year salary. In 1973, with one of his father's companies paying for the initial advertising, Rod started a company that sells commemorative plates to collectors. The venture turned out to be extremely profitable, and in 1975 his father demanded a share of it. Rod refused, and his father seized its inventory. Rod then hired seven semi-trailers and with the help of forty employees "raided" the building where the plates were stored and reclaimed them. A year later the two patched up their differences after Rod paid his father a settlement of $175,000.

He had a very large—some might say romantic—notion of the creative and innovative role that philanthropy should play: "The American foundation is unique in the whole damn world," he once said:

> This is the only institution in our society that does not have constituencies that it has to keep looking to. All the others have to worry about pleasing a lot of people, so they're bound to tend toward conventional wisdom, respectability, and the lowest common denominator.... Foundations should be striving to do the kinds of things that government cannot do. I repeat, *cannot do:* things that are not politically popular, things that are too risky, things that are just too far ahead of what the public will put up with.... A private foundation, where the board of directors is answerable only to itself, is in a completely different situation, and if it doesn't take advantage of that uniqueness, it's just blowing its opportunity, and perhaps even its moral obligation.

In his mind, the role of philanthropy and of government had to be considered in relation to each other, even though the two are clearly different and the differences should not be blurred. He was "appalled," for example, that President Reagan called on the private sector to take on responsibilities that the federal government had dropped and that a good many foundations were going along with the administration's wishes:

> I personally think that both we and other foundations should refuse to pick up where government is pulling back. The government was doing little enough as it was, and the whole idea that this society should move back to the nineteenth century just because the government wants to save money is absurd.... The unfortunate folk in our society have the right to rely on their government for a little help. In effect private foundations should not encourage the government to go backwards. We should be out there in the forefront, ahead of where government thinks it's safe to be.... Only in that way can we use the unique ability that a private foundation has. If we don't

use that unique ability why should we have the privileges we enjoy? We should only have them if we use them to maintain fluidity in our society, the random element, the opportunity to make mistakes while striving to make a better world, as corny as that sounds. . . . If you don't try a few things, if you don't take chances, then you don't change the world. . . . I want to encourage a little more free-wheeling and chance taking, which seems to have been diminishing in philanthropy for quite a long time.

Rod MacArthur had his own small foundation, and its program has clearly reflected the philosophy he wanted to see his father's philanthropy follow. It has worked on unpopular civil liberties cases and controversial environmental questions and has analyzed critically the policy of the Reagan administration in Central America.

Because of his rough manner and his unorthodox views, Rod was an enormous annoyance to all the other board members of the MacArthur Foundation from the beginning. In their view he was constitutionally unable to be a "team player." But from the standpoint of the public interest he was on the right side of most of the issues he raised, and he was the only member of the board who enunciated a concept of the foundation's role commensurate with its huge resources. If his views had been effectively translated into its program, then out of Chicago once again, as in the time of Jane Addams after the turn of the century and of Julius Rosenwald in the 1920s, would have come an authentic and powerful new perspective on philanthropy. The fact that that did not happen was his primary frustration and discontent.

The second disappointment was what he saw as the loose and irresponsible handling of the foundation's money and assets: the taking of exorbitant fees by many of the trustees, the mismanagement of the insurance company, and the mishandling of its sale.

The problem of mandatory disposition of "excess business holdings," which has been a major distraction for a number of the large foundations, troubled the MacArthur Foundation from the beginning. Part of the difficulty arose from the nature and complexity of its assets. It owned all the shares of a major insurance company, which in turn owned a vast amount of real estate and some ninety-five subsidiary companies, in wood processing, car rental, printing, whiskey making, and many other businesses. An equally serious difficulty was that the donor built the senior executives of the insurance company into the board of the foundation, creating a maze of problems of potential conflicts of interest.

Almost as soon as the foundation took ownership of the company, its profits began to fall. An actuarial firm was hired to look into the causes, and they concluded that its management was at fault. The foundation board also appointed two leading investment banking firms to advise it on the sale of the company and a specialized real estate firm to advise on the disposition of its properties. Gaylord Freeman, former head of Chicago's First National Bank and a trustee of the foundation, thereafter devoted himself diligently for many months to the task of negotiation with possible buyers.

The insurance company's cloudy reputation, poor management, and sagging profits made it difficult to sell, particularly in a period when the economy remained sluggish and when the financial services industry was in a period of dramatic change and restructuring. In June 1983, no sale having been made and the statutory deadline for divestiture approaching, the foundation appealed to Congress and the Internal Revenue Service for an extension of time in order to avoid a "fire sale" liquidation of its holdings.

What was not known publicly at the time, but subsequently became clear, was that Rod MacArthur had become convinced that so many acts of dereliction and irresponsibility had been committed by the board that nothing less than its total restructuring was required. The degree of his unhappiness was suggested by the fact that when nineteen of the company's real estate holdings were sold in December 1983, for some $400 million, Rod said publicly that the deal had been made over his opposition and that it was a "giveaway" of the properties. Another hint of what might be coming was a suit he placed a week later against the president of the foundation, accusing him of overpaying himself $114,000 in salary plus other unauthorized reimbursements.

Six weeks later, in February 1984, the entire ugly mess became public, and the foundation was thrown into turmoil by a suit placed by MacArthur before the Cook County Circuit Court containing a catalog of allegations against all but two of the other members of the board and asking that the foundation be put into receivership or dismantled.

One set of charges accused his fellow directors of squandering the foundation's assets and enriching themselves, and he demanded their removal.

He cited President Corbally for taking almost $500,000 from the foundation and from Bankers Life in salary, fees, and perquisites between January 1982 and September 1983 for "less than full-time work." He accused Director Kirby of taking $340,000 in part-time director's fees for the five years up to 1984, plus hundreds of thousands of dollars as legal fees paid by the foundation and Bankers Life to a law firm of which Kirby was "of counsel." He accused Director Ewing of increasing his salary and benefits from Bankers Life to nearly $500,000 per year and of taking, along with his wife, still additional fees from the foundation.

Of those who were not "dual directors" of both the foundation and the insurance company, he cited Nobelist Gell-Mann for taking nearly $270,000 in part-time fees from the foundation between 1979 and 1983 and Dr. Jonas Salk of taking nearly as much.

He further accused Doolen, Kirby, and Ewing of mismanaging Bankers Life, whose profits had sharply dropped, and of arranging lavish "golden parachutes" for themselves, which any buyer of the company would be obliged to pay. He also charged them and other members of the foundation's finance committee of reducing by some $200 million the value of the company as a result of their incompetence.

He therefore asked the court to appoint a receiver to take over the management and sale of the company or alternatively to dissolve the foundation.

The formal response of those accused did not contain any rebuttal of the charges of self-enrichment but concentrated on the technical claim that MacArthur did not have "legal standing" to bring his charges and that he was simply a troublemaker. They asserted that he "was not trusted or relied upon by his father," that from the foundation's inception he had been "a dissident, disruptive loner," and that his lawsuit was only "the latest ploy in plaintiff's efforts to badger and coerce his fellow directors into giving him outright control of the foundation. . . ." Neither did they refrain from quoting various private letters from John MacArthur to his son throwing adverse light on his character. One of these read in part, "I think you should go back to your psychiatrist and get some more treatments . . . this time at your own expense."

A RUBICON CROSSED AND A KEY FACTOR SUBTRACTED

Until Rod placed his suit against nearly all the other trustees in early 1984, the foundation despite its internal discord had managed quietly to improve its program effectiveness considerably. The "geniuses program" continued to be handicapped because the "finders network" for the identification of possible grantees was inadequately developed and still captive of a circle of academic "old boys" concentrated in the Northeast and in California. But in the mental health program, as the sophistication of the trustee committee in charge grew, competent outside advisers were drawn upon, particularly Dr. David Hamburg, now head of the Carnegie Corporation, and in time a small but able staff was built. Likewise the international affairs program increasingly turned to experienced experts like McGeorge Bundy, former head of the Ford Foundation, and as a result the professional quality of the work noticeably improved.

Major program and organizational decisions, however, continued to be made—quite often, it appeared—by resort to threats and counterthreats among the trustees and sometimes simply by cutting the foundation up and allocating the parts to contending subgroups. But even that mode of operation was made impossible by Rod's legal action. The majority in the face of his all-out attack decided to stand firm, and their resolve was strengthened when the first court to which he had turned dismissed his charges.

They pressed ahead with plans to sell the insurance company, and in early May made a deal with a Kentucky corporation to purchase it for $384 million. Rod acquiesced in the sale, pointing out that it was for $116 million more than the transaction the board had previously proposed and that he had blocked.

This having been accomplished, President Corbally expressed the hope that the sale would remove one serious bone of contention and enable the foundation to "get together." But MacArthur reaffirmed his determination to take his suit to higher courts. A number of the trustees thereupon planned to try to remove him as a trustee at their next meeting.

The prospect at that moment was for months, perhaps years, of paralyzing litigation and for the work of the foundation to be carried on by the trustees with the greatest caution and with careful attention to compiling a legally defensible record of all proceedings. Then suddenly and unexpectedly a new element was injected:

Rod MacArthur was diagnosed as having pancreatic cancer and a very brief life expectancy.

Out of consideration for his deteriorating health, the board postponed the election that could have led to his removal as a trustee. But MacArthur defiantly declared his intention to continue his efforts to have drastic changes made in the board and the management or to have the foundation dismantled. "If my time is limited, I will just have to work faster," he asserted. But by November 1984, with his strength running out and in the face of imminent death, he relented and withdrew his suits. Three weeks later, on December 15, he died.

He had been the most powerful and most contentious element in the foundation's affairs. His disappearance from the scene calmed and simplified the foundation's problems somewhat, but it did not by any means eliminate them. Ironically, whether the foundation now proceeds to build on some of the good things it has done and becomes not merely a more peaceable but a more creative, influential, and productive philanthropy will largely depend on those individuals not connected with the company that he had forced the initial group of trustees to elect the board.

Rod MacArthur was an unloved figure, but he left an indelible mark on what he considered to be "his" foundation. It could yet turn out to be a fine one.

Robert Wood Johnson: Bright New Star

In the emergence of new foundations, there can be some bad surprises, as the MacArthur case proves. But there can also be some very happy ones. Of these, the happiest of all in the past fifteen years has been the Robert Wood Johnson Foundation.

When it was activated in the late 1960s, it seemed unlikely to amount to much, and there were several reasons to believe that it might turn out to be a rather poor show.

First, federal government funds were pouring into medical research and training, and the recently enacted Medicare and Medicaid programs were making health care available to the elderly, the poor, and minorities on a scale never known before. These had long been the problems on which foundations such as Rockefeller, Commonwealth, Hartford, Milbank, Markle, and others had concentrated, and they appeared to have been preempted by government. Indeed, many knowledgeable observers felt that the field was awash in money and that it was the last place where more foundation help was needed. But the trustees of Robert Wood Johnson decided that they would commit its huge resources precisely to that area.

Second, leaders in philanthropy had long accepted that a donor's foundation should not work in the same field as that in which his company operated in order to avoid the appearance of indirectly serving commercial interests. For this reason, the Lilly Endowment, for example, deriving from fortunes made from the Eli Lilly Pharmaceutical Company, has carefully stayed away from the health field. But the trustees of Robert Wood Johnson, whose assets were based on money made from the Johnson & Johnson company, a leading manufacturer of health-care products, were not deterred by this unwritten but strong ethical standard.

Third, excessively close ties between the foundation and executives of the donor's company have generally spelled trouble for newborn foundations, as MacArthur and many others have shown. But the new Johnson Foundation was totally in the hands of executives associated with the donor's company, another disquieting sign.

Finally, quite apart from their company links, the initial trustees were all individuals of conservative outlook and with intimate relationships with the medical establishment, which had long been the principal vested interest blocking more equitable availability of health care in the United States. It seemed most unlikely, therefore, that a foundation under their control could be anything more than an adjunct to the old and exploitative fee-for-service medical monopoly.

But all those omens and indications, in the event, turned out to be wrong.

THE GENERAL

The story of all foundations begins with an individual, the donor, and in the case of the Johnson Foundation, an individual whose qualities appear the more impressive the more carefully he is studied.

Robert Wood Johnson was born with a silver tongue depressor in his mouth. His father and uncle had founded a little company in the late 1900s in New Brunswick, New Jersey, to manufacture plasters, an all-purpose remedy of that era, and sterile surgical dressings. The idea for establishing the company was inspired by the work of the famous English surgeon Sir Joseph Lister. The success of the firm, Johnson & Johnson, in mass-producing sterile dressings eventually caught his attention, and he wrote to the brothers in 1891, requesting details about their manufacturing processes. Their reply was as follows:

New Brunswick, New Jersey,
December 28, 1891.
To Sir Joseph Lister, London.
Honored Sir — In response to your request for specific information as to the special methods employed in our laboratories in the preparation of surgical dressings and materials used in wound treatment, we cheerfully give herewith our processes in detail, feeling this is due to you, both in answer to a proper request and in recognition of the fact that the whole system of modern wound treatment and the manufacture of materials for the same have been made possible largely by your labors. . . .

The young Robert Wood Johnson, who was born in 1893, attended good preparatory schools and probably would have gone on to college except for his father's untimely death in 1910. Then seventeen, he entered the family business over his relatives' objections by simply going to the plant and hiring on as a mill hand.

Twenty-two years later he became president of the company. The year was 1932, the pit of the Great Depression, so the position was hardly a sinecure, and he worked hard to overcome its problems. When he took over the company, its sales were $11 million, largely domestic. By 1967, the year before he died, the company operated ninety plants and had sales over $700 million in 120 countries.

In manner and appearance, Johnson was not an overpowering figure. Though slight of build, because of his intensely competitive spirit he became something of an athlete: swimmer, horseman, and tennis player. He flew all the early types of airplanes, including the original single-motor biplane, the monoplane, and the Autogiro, as helicopters were first called. He also liked to race his oceangoing sloop and was evidently good at it, as he won a case full of cups.

He was a fastidious dresser and always looked as if he had just stepped out of a haberdashery. He was also, perhaps because of having grown up in the sterile surgical dressing business, something of a fanatic about cleanliness. He visited all the company's plants at least twice a year, for example, and went so far as to require that all the corners in all of them be painted white so that the dirt, if any, would show.

About his personal life little information is available. But it does not appear to have been particularly happy. His first two marriages ended in divorce, and his only son, whom he reportedly banished from the company, died within a year of his father's death.

While he was a young man, he became interested in civic affairs and was elected councilman and later mayor of his hometown. This experience led him to introduce a Sound Government Program into Johnson & Johnson to encourage employees voluntarily to engage in public service. By 1955 that program included some eighty employees holding elective or appointive office.

He also had a strong, old-fashioned sense of patriotism. When World War II began, he was appointed a colonel in the army and named chief of the New York Ordnance District. Later he was promoted to brigadier general and was appointed by President Roosevelt to be vice-chairman of the War Production Board in Washington. He took great pride in his wartime service and was thereafter always called "General" by his associates.

What was little known and never recognized during his lifetime were his unusually visionary qualities as a businessman.

He was, for example, one of the early environmentalists in the modern sense, in contrast to the Teddy Roosevelt type of conservationist. As early as 1927 in Gainesville, Georgia, he pioneered the "factories can be beautiful" concept by building a community for the workers in one of the company's cotton mills so handsome it gained international attention. In 1949, looking back with pride on that facility, he said, "There was a time when no one objected to ugly factories, to smoke, chemical fumes, polluted streams and run-down industrial slums." But today, he went on, "we realize that business has no right . . . to make its community unfit for civilized life."

He was also surprisingly, even radically, prolabor. He wrote four books on corporate management and social responsibility, and in them he put heavy stress on the need for employers to treat their employees as fellow human beings. "Wage earners are men and women; they have rights, dignity, ambition, pride; and they feel a deep need to stand well in the eyes of their associates," he wrote. "Until employers treat them accordingly, business will not act in accord with sound moral principles."

He advocated giving workers a say in the organization of their work long before anyone had ever heard of Theory Z management or quality circles, and he felt too many of them were underpaid. In testimony before a Senate committee, he urged a higher minimum wage than even the labor unions were seeking at the time. "To ignore the conditions of the many underpaid people in the United States," he told the senators, "is as foolish as it would be to ignore public health, crime, and the need for education."

Perhaps the best summary of his social outlook was the credo he wrote for his company in 1944 that set forth its five basic responsibilities:

> Our *first* responsibility is to the doctors, nurses, hospitals, mothers, and all others who use our products. . . .
> Our *second* responsibility is to those who work with us. . . .
> Our *third* responsibility is to our management. . . .
> Our *fourth* responsibility is to the communities in which we live. . . .
> Our *fifth* and last responsibility is to our stockholders.

Not many business leaders would agree with those sentiments and that ranking even today. Forty years ago when they were written they were enough to cost a man his membership in the Union League Club.

In some inexplicable but indisputable way, the good citizen, patriot, and visionary in this intense little man has been carried into the foundation he created.

THE PHILANTHROPIST

From early on, philanthropy was one of Johnson's interests. In 1936, four years after becoming head of Johnson & Johnson, he set up his foundation, and he used it thereafter to support various projects in which he was interested. One of the most important of these was his collaboration with Dr. Malcolm MacEachern, then president of the American College of Surgeons, to establish the world's first school of hospital administration at Northwestern University, in Evanston, Illinois.

Years later, when he was preparing to transfer the bulk of his estate to the foundation, he evidently was aware of the damaging legal quarrels that have affected a number of large foundations in their first year and took care to avoid them by creating a separate philanthropy, the R. W. Johnson, Jr., Foundation, through which members of his family could fund their favorite charities. But no family members would be involved in the Robert Wood Johnson Foundation itself.

To direct its development, he then did something that was understandable for a man whose lifework had been the building of his company, but that, nonetheless, was on its face imprudent: he gave control of his foundation to a group of his company executives by making them the trustees, an action that has foiled the hopes and good intentions of many other donors. To head the board he designated Gustav O. Lienhard, with whom he had worked for more than thirty years and who, at the time of General Johnson's death, was president of Johnson & Johnson.

This obviously could have resulted in a hopeless entanglement of the foundation with the company and its interests, but it did not. All the trustees soon separated themselves from the company, and not a trace of conflict of interest can be detected in their performance in the years since. After the General's death in 1968, they set seriously to work to try to make the foundation not only a good but an outstanding one.

There is some reason to suppose that the Patman hearings and passage of the 1969 Tax Reform Act contributed to the scrupulousness with which their plans for the activation of the foundation were made. Lienhard and the other board members had a strong desire to avoid public controversy, and the Patman hearings were clear warning that serious criticism could arise if the Johnson Foundation should be guilty of any of the kinds of abuses that had drawn such fire from the Congress and the press and that had led to passage of the new legislation.

But beyond that, it seems evident that some deeper and inbuilt standards of ethics and social responsibility deriving from the character of the donor were at work and that he had chosen from among his executive colleagues men of character and quality to be his trustees.

ACTIVATION OF THE FOUNDATION

When the General died in 1968, the shares of Johnson & Johnson stock he had willed to the foundation were valued at about $300 million. Over the next four years, while the will was in probate, the stock increased in value to almost $1.2 billion. (On December 6, 1971, *The New York Times* ran a front-page article about a previously obscure little foundation located in New Brunswick, New Jersey. The headline read, "$1 Billion Legacy Makes Foundation the Second Biggest." The story made a strong impression on many people, including a follower of the philosophy of the late Willie Sutton. That very night, the three-bedroom Victorian house in which the foundation had its offices was broken into, apparently by someone looking for the money.)

Eleven months before the bequest was actually received by the foundation, Lienhard, who was an executor of the General's estate as well as the designated head of the new foundation, retired from the company and began to study the field of philanthropy. He read widely, visited many of the larger foundations, and consulted with various knowledgeable people.

That the foundation would work in the health field was probably a foregone conclusion. The General had not stipulated that in its charter or in his will, but he had indicated that he would like to see it happen, and all the trustees, who themselves had long been involved with health matters, were strongly disposed to respect his preferences. They were well aware of the impacts of large-scale public funding of medical research and health care and of the prevailing view that philanthropic funding in the field had become quantitatively marginal. But they believed that although the new situation would greatly change the role previously played by private philanthropy, it could well create new problems that would lead to great need for foundation initiatives. Whether or not this may have been mere rationalization for a predetermined course, it turned out to be correct.

To develop the foundation's program, trustee Lienhard set out to find a president who was not only able and respected but who, consistent with the board's intention, could make the Robert Wood Johnson Foundation a leader in its field. After a considerable canvass, the man he proposed was Dr. David Rogers, then head of the first-rate medical school of Johns Hopkins University. Rogers had an outstanding reputation as a physician and teacher. He was also an important figure in the national debate on health policy and had a record as an innovator in organizing new kinds of systems for the delivery of health services.

He was therefore not only a prestigious expert but an activist and a reformer, and the Robert Wood Johnson trustees, all businessmen of generally conservative outlook, had to make a clear choice whether they wanted their foundation to be essentially a respectable and establishmentarian one or a force for change. They chose Rogers.

Once on the job, he got under way quickly. He brought with him from Johns Hopkins a brilliant young man, Robert Blendon, who had wide knowledge of the health-care system. Earlier in the 1960s he had served as assistant to Secretary Elliott Richardson of the Department of Health, Education and Welfare and was therefore also thoroughly familiar with the vast array of government health programs and policies. Blendon would be analyst, planner, and evaluator.

To bring someone on board with successful philanthropic experience in the health field, Rogers in effect bought out the Carnegie Corporation's small but greatly admired program in health policy, which had been ably developed by Margaret Mahoney. She transferred with the program to the Johnson Foundation. (Mahoney has since become president of the Commonwealth Fund, the first woman to head an American foundation in the $100 million-plus category.)

Then, on the theory that in addition to brilliance the staff needed wisdom and even a sense of humor, Rogers in a most unusual step named a sage, an elder, to round out his core group. His choice was Walsh McDermott, one of the most admired, even revered, figures in American medicine. In addition to a long career as teacher and practitioner, McDermott among his other achievements had helped form the National Academy of Medicine to advise the government on health issues. The memorial service following his death in 1981 was a celebration of his special humane qualities. One old friend said, "He was one of the very few larger-than-life humans who drop in on our world and leave an indelible imprint upon it. . . . He was blissfully unaware of his uniqueness, and totally unimpeded by any sense of his own importance." An academic associate said, "Though it may strain credulity, even committee meetings could be fun if Walsh were there." A hard-bitten journalist who knew him quoted a poetic old statement that he said fitted the man perfectly: "If everyone for whom he did some loving service were to place a single blossom on his grave he would sleep tonight beneath a wilderness of flowers."

With the nucleus of his staff formed, Rogers began the process of program definition in close consultation with the board.

THE BIRTH OF A PROGRAM

What then occurred was a sequence of fortunate improbabilities. At the start it was not at all apparent that the board of business-men and the staff of reform-minded foundation officers would be able to agree on what the role and objectives of the foundation should be. The hope of the trustees was to apply business experi-ence and concepts to philanthropy. They were determined that the Johnson Foundation should be "productive": that it have clear goals and priorities, meet its deadlines, show results, and stay out of trouble.

Rogers and his associates, all of academic or philanthropic background, shared a strong sense of concern for the social and eco-nomic aspects of health care, including its inequities. Their hope was that the foundation by strategically placed grants could correct some of the worst faults and deficiencies of the huge and decentra-lized system, knowing full well that from such an effort controversy could well ensue.

Not unimportantly, all of the trustees were older males. Rogers's team included both young and old as well as a woman.

Against the odds, they reached agreement not only on general objectives but also on specific priorities. There was agreement that, given the immensity of federal funding in the field, even a founda-tion as large as Johnson, if it were to make any impact, would have to target its efforts as precisely as possible. (In recognition of the preponderant role of government, one of Rogers's early actions was to establish a Washington Research and Information Office to maintain close and continuous contact with the development of federal and state activities in the health field.)

After several months of consultations with experts from all over the country and of many meetings between board and staff, an ambitious and activist program emerged. The foundation's grants would not be used for such activities as funding cancer research or building wings on hospitals but would go to projects to improve the availability of primary health care. It would not be concerned with training surgeons in open-heart procedures but family doctors in general practice. It would help set up not new biomedical laboratories but group practices to coax doctors back to inner-city and rural areas. It would fund research not on gallbladder removal procedures but into ways to organize health-care delivery more equitably and efficiently.

Within one year the program framework was finished. How that result was achieved, and how the tensions in the situation became useful rather than destructive, must in part at least be surmised. The leadership of both Lienhard and Rogers, and their determination not to let emotional and jurisdictional obstacles block the construction of a first-rank foundation, was probably the basic factor. The willingness of the board to deal responsively with the extraordinarily able and independent-minded staff group Rogers had assembled and the professionalism of the staff in dealing objectively with even the most highly charged issues must both be given credit. Perhaps the wit and wisdom of McDermott also helped.

In any event, the first and crucial phase of the foundation's activation was impressively and rapidly accomplished.

WORK BEGINS

In the first months while it was formulating its program, the foundation because of federal payout requirements had also to distribute its income at a rate of some $44 million a year. In the same period the staff was enlarged to include a balance of skills and backgrounds. The board was also gradually enlarged by the addition of several "outsiders," all men. (Among the anomalies in the structure and procedures of the Johnson Foundation, it should be noted that the Chairman of the Board retains the title of Chief Executive Officer and works full time in an office adjacent to that of the foundation's strong-minded president. This arrangement would seem to be a perfect recipe for endless confusion, irritation, and conflict. Yet Rogers and Lienhard, the in-law constantly in his kitchen, have managed to get along. More than that, this odd couple—improbable as it might seem—has made a highly effective team.)

As the program took actual shape, it had these distinctive characteristics:

1. The main emphasis would be on the organization of large-scale field trials of promising new ideas for rectifying deficiencies in the health-care system.
2. The foundation would invest heavily in objective, third-party evaluations of the results of these actual pilot models.
3. It would wherever possible, in order to gain additional leverage, work in collaboration with other relevant organizations: government agencies, medical schools, hospital associations, other foundations, and so on.
4. It would put the knowledge gained from the grants to work by a program of wide dissemination to all the institutions that could make use of it.
5. It was therefore a program scaled to the large resources of the foundation; it represented a new kind of "scientific activism"; and it was carefully designed to achieve maximum practical impact and replication.

Over the next ten years Johnson developed some thirty of these field-trial programs, all of national scope. Among them were the following:

Health services for high-risk young people. Twenty grants with four-year terms to teaching hospitals throughout the country to sponsor efforts to consolidate health services for young people vulnerable to such serious problems as venereal disease, teen-age pregnancy, alcohol and drug abuse, violence, and mental illness.

Dental training for the care of the handicapped. A program involving eleven dental schools to develop special teaching guidelines for care of the handicapped.

Emergency medical care. A program to develop emergency medical communications systems in thirty-eight states throughout the country.

Municipal health services. Co-sponsored by the American Medical Association and the U.S. Conference of Mayors, a program in five large cities to combine the resources of their health departments and municipal hospitals to offer primary care through twenty-two urban neighborhood clinics.

Rural infant care. Assistance to ten medical schools to collaborate with state health departments in reducing infant mortality and morbidity in isolated rural counties.

School health services. Working through four state agencies, a program to demonstrate the feasibility of using school nurses, backed up by practicing physicians located nearby, to provide student health services. Seventy schools serving thirty-seven thousand children were involved.

Clinical Scholars Program. Operating at eleven academic institutions, it is designed to help young physician-clinicians acquire special skills in certain nonbiological disciplines such as epidemiology, demography, economics, management techniques, and other related fields that can better prepare them for leadership in new and more complicated systems of health and medical care. A related program, Fellowships in Public Policy, developed under the auspices of the National Academy of Sciences' Institute of Medicine and the American Political Science Association, offers midcareer health educators the opportunity to spend a year of intensive work on health policy issues in collaboration with members of the United States Congress and senior executives in the executive branch of the federal government.

Community hospitals. Grants to at least one community hospital in every state in the nation to help it establish a group medical practice to meet the ambulatory general medical needs of people in its area more effectively. This five-year $29 million venture is the foundation's largest national program to date.

In 1974, after its first three years of activity, the foundation had gained enough experience to refine and improve its methods of organizing such major field trials and at the same time to avoid the hazard of building a huge permanent staff that could impede its future flexibility.

It would continue to make grants in each instance to a number of interested institutions, selected competitively, to test the same concept or attack the same problem simultaneously in different regions and in a variety of ways. But these "national programs," as the foundation calls them, would be administered not by the regular staff of the foundation but by *senior program consultants:* leading experts usually on a medical faculty or the staff of a prominent research institution. They would be employed by the foundation to administer and coordinate the program during its limited term of years, and thereafter they would return to their regular posts.

This decentralized method of operation has brought many advantages. It is a protection against the bureaucratization of the foundation. It has made possible the involvement of outstanding individuals and institutions who would have been unavailable as regular employees or contractors in the national programs. It has also made it possible to increase the representativeness of decision making in the programs because minorities and women serve on the various program advisory boards, even though they are not found on the Robert Wood Johnson board itself.

In these programs, as in all it has done, the foundation has proceeded from a recognition of the complexity and the decentralization of the American health-care system, which includes not only government agencies, medical schools, and foundations but also public and private hospitals; child-care centers; facilities for the elderly and the handicapped; pharmaceutical companies; the insurance industry; trade unions; associations of doctors, dentists, nurses, and other health-care workers; the great voluntary health associations such as the American Cancer Society and the American Heart Association; health advocacy groups; and many others. It has also recognized that any changes that may be introduced have to be induced. They cannot be "directed" from some remote "headquarters."

Thus Johnson has worked from the premise that any idea for change or improvement has first to be tested and proved in practice and that the proof must be carefully, objectively, scientifically assembled if it is to be persuasive. Then, all the information and evidence must be communicated to those who decide the policies of the many independent groups and institutions that compose the system.

Following this reasoning, Johnson has gone further than any other foundation in adopting a policy of continuous communication and interaction with all relevant organizations by means of printed reports, films, conferences, seminars, and individual consultations.

To a unique degree it has also made use of various communications techniques in every step of its programming process. To stimulate the widest participation in the competitions for grants, it disseminates prospectuses for its national programs to all eligible institutions and in some instances provides posters for their use. To help make programs it has funded more effective, the foundation has sometimes employed live video teleconferences. In connection with its program of health services for high-risk young people, for example, it organized such a conference in seventeen cities for grantees, cooperating agencies, public officials, and the press. Edited videotape cassettes of the teleconference were then used by the grantees locally to build further support for their projects. To increase the impact of one of its grants on the prevention and treatment of child abuse, a 438-page manual of information and recommendations was distributed, together with a schedule of available training seminars, to the child-protection officer in the local welfare agency of each of the 3,041 counties in the United States.

IN-COURSE CORRECTIONS

After its first seven years of full operation, the foundation reexamined its program priorities in light of what had been happening on the national health scene during the intervening period. Its primary concern from the beginning had been to identify groups and areas that did not have access to medical care or were underserved by the system. By 1978 research findings by a number of independent institutions indicated that significant changes for the better had taken place and that the poor and minorities were on average seeing physicians about as frequently as the rest of the population.

On the basis of such encouraging evidence, the foundation decided to concentrate greater attention on the needs of people in rural areas and the elderly and on the quality of care received in the rapidly increasing number of outpatient visits to hospitals.

Two years later, a second and more complex adjustment in its program focus was made: In light of the fact that 80 percent of health-care resources in the country are currently devoted to the treatment of chronic diseases such as high blood pressure, emphysema, arthritis, asthma, and heart ailments, the foundation decided to address the new kind of health problem being presented: namely, not the "curing" of the patient, as is possible in cases of infectious disease, but rather restoring the afflicted individual to "maximum feasible function" in everyday life.

But the foundation quickly discovered that there existed no reliable measure of the results of most of the nation's multibillion-dollar health expenditures in terms of helping people with chronic diseases to function adequately and independently at work, at school, or at home.

This led to an effort to replace the available gross statistics on mortality with more sensitive and relevant yardsticks. The foundation also decided to give more emphasis to medical procedures that could significantly reduce the likelihood of a person's having to enter a hospital or nursing home. In a related initiative, it launched a $20 million program to encourage ecumenical coalitions of churches and synagogues to develop model "volunteer caregiver" programs to enable elderly and disabled persons at risk of institutionalization to remain in their homes and receive the help they need.

Thus, in fundamental ways the foundation was redefining the nature of the nation's major health problems to correspond with the realities of a shifting U.S. population mix, changing habits, and new resource constraints; it was also charting some of the new approaches to health care that those developments were necessitating.

In 1982, with public and governmental concern over skyrocketing medical costs reaching a crescendo, the foundation made its boldest move—in political terms—to reaffirm its commitment to equity in the availability of health care. With an administration in Washington not distinguished by its concern for the needy, the foundation foresaw the possibility of drastic federal measures to control costs that would in effect destroy the great gains in access to medical care of the previous fifteen years. Such measures could most easily achieve their purpose simply by dropping the poor out of the system, and this in its view began to loom as a serious possibility. The foundation therefore decided to create a system by which to measure the impact of changes in public policy to control health-care costs on the quality and accessibility of health care for all groups in the population. This would be done by monitoring how often people saw doctors and by keeping an eye on where they went for their care, whether to their own physicians or to the emergency rooms of hospitals. An increase in the latter would be a sure sign that access to personal physician services for the needy and vulnerable was again becoming out of reach. The foundation would also watch maternal mortality rates, particularly whether the twofold gap between white and black infant mortality began to widen or to narrow. It proposed in effect to make itself a national ombudsman in the field of public health policies and programs.

Early in 1984, the foundation launched still another groundbreaking program in collaboration with the Pew Memorial Trust, this one to serve the special health-care needs of the increasing number of homeless people in the nation's major cities. Cosponsored by the U.S. Conference of Mayors, the multiyear program offered $20 million of grants to voluntary organizations, churches, public agencies, and medical groups to design and deliver health-care services to the chronically and the temporarily homeless, as well as to the growing number of deinstitutionalized mentally ill who are now wandering the streets.

The Johnson Foundation in its first thirteen years has already spent more than $600 million on its programs, and the pistons of this powerful new social engine are still busily pumping.

AN OVERALL ASSESSMENT

No institution working in a field as important, changing, and value-laden as health care, however technically competent, can entirely escape criticism, for the politics of health and medicine are as fierce and cannibalistic as any.

The Johnson Foundation has staked out its philosophical and political ground on both sides of the liberal-conservative divide. Its goals are liberal, egalitarian, and reformist; its methods are ameliorative, evolutionary, and in this sense conservative.

In the broad middle of the spectrum of medical politics in which it attempts to operate as a stimulative factor and force for gradual change, the Johnson Foundation is highly respected.

There are some, however, outside the center who are very critical. Those on the rapacious Right, who resent any interference with medical profiteering, see the foundation as a meddler and, because of its acknowledged expertise, as a potential threat.

Those on the far Left, who believe that only radical surgery, not homeopathic methods, can cure what is wrong with the American system of health care, also see the foundation as an enemy. In this view, although American medicine is technically and scientifically outstanding, it operates within a system that has been very carefully constructed so as to maximize the personal income and profits of the medical professional, the drug companies, the insurance companies, the hospital-management corporations, and other commercialized groupings. It is also seen as a system built primarily to serve the affluent; only to the extent that philanthropy or government subsidizes the access of the poor to its services will they be admitted, and then only so long as the built-in patterns of profiteering are left undisturbed. According to this view, the Johnson Foundation can nibble around the edges of the system and make minor improvements. But if and when it should ever touch the sensitive money nerve, the backlash of the central and powerful elements of the medical establishment would demolish it.

Both of these perceptions of health care in America are vigorously rejected by Dr. Rogers. In his view, despite its faults and weaknesses, the system is working reasonably well and is increasingly working better and better. Anything other than such a pluralistic system simply could not function in or be accepted by our kind of pluralistic democracy. Therefore, talk of going back to the old days of the AMA or of resorting to radical surgery is nonsense. The only way to proceed is, in his view, by the steady and reasonable method of identifying problems, experimenting with solutions, and mobilizing various elements to introduce proven improvements.

The one serious concern that is expressed by some well-informed figures in the health field is that the foundation, under the businesslike pressure of its board to be a "productive philanthropy," may have gone somewhat too far in its tough purposefulness and initiative taking.

One such person who has worked closely with the Johnson Foundation and is intimately familiar with its operations puts the view in these words:

> There is no question that it has high purposes and superb competence. A danger that may arise, however, when a force this powerful and with substantial resources at its command goes to work on a problem is that it may forget to exercise self-restraint. At the present time, for example, when Johnson identifies some problem as a priority issue and develops a national program to attack it, that almost instantly becomes the conventional wisdom in the field. Those who may have differing views tend to fall silent or to be ignored.
>
> Likewise when the foundation then proceeds to identify the several options or alternatives to be tested to deal with the problem and makes grants strictly within that framework, it tends to eliminate at least for a time consideration of other possibilities. In this respect it creates the danger of blind spots and missed opportunities. There would be a greater degree of public protection in these tremendously important matters if

the foundation were a little less self-confident, a little less absolute, a little more open to unexpected possibilities or different ideas than it sometimes seems to be.

Such comments may have some validity. But the Johnson Foundation, judged by the standards of performance normally applicable to foundations, is virtually in a class by itself.

In the clarity and ambitiousness of its purposes, in the intellectual power that has governed its strategy and grant making, in the social sensitivity and political skill by which its programs have been shaped, in the able and creative way in which its programs have been managed, and in the general qualities of integrity and independence that have characterized all it has done, the Robert Wood Johnson Foundation is the best of the big foundations today.

6

THE LIBERAL ACTIVISTS:

Carnegie,
Edna McConnell Clark,
and William Penn

Carnegie Corporation

The Carnegie Corporation of New York, one of the oldest of the big foundations, had by the late 1960s become the finest in the field in terms of the effectiveness of its board, the caliber of its leadership, and the craftsmanship and creativity of its grants. In the years since, it has gone through considerable evolution in response to the changes and tensions in American society but without diminution of the overall quality of its performance. Under the strong hand of its president, Alan Pifer, in the period from 1965 through 1982 it moved from a general concern about inequities in American life to militancy on behalf of the disadvantaged: children, women, racial minorities, and the handicapped. By the time he turned over the helm to his successor, David Hamburg, in mid-1982 Pifer had become the most ardent voice in philanthropy on behalf of government and private efforts to alleviate the plight of the disadvantaged, and the Carnegie Corporation had become the quintessential liberal, activist, entrepreneurial foundation: more a combat force than a conventional charity. Now Hamburg, with a firm grasp on the tiller, has steered the foundation to a somewhat different but potentially exciting new course.

BRILLIANT BEGINNINGS

The Carnegie Corporation was founded in 1911 by Andrew Carnegie, one of the greatest of the early American philanthropists. (He called it the Carnegie Corporation because he had run out of other names, having already established a Carnegie Foundation, a Carnegie Endowment, a Carnegie Trust, and a Carnegie Institute to carry on programs for the advancement of teaching, international peace, scientific research, and other purposes.)

Carnegie had come to the United States with his impoverished family from Scotland before the Civil War. Starting as an uneducated bobbin boy in a cotton factory, he controlled several large companies by the age of thirty-three. Even at that early point his interests had begun to turn to philanthropy. According to a note he wrote at the time that was found among his papers after his death, he admonished himself in these words: "Beyond this, never earn—make no effort to increase fortune, but spend surplus each year for benevolent purposes."

But good fortune continued to dog his heels, and in the closing quarter of the nineteenth century he had by a series of combinations and mergers made his coal and steel complex so powerful that he was able to challenge the entire banking and industrial empire of J. P. Morgan. In the end Morgan was forced to buy out Carnegie virtually on the latter's terms. Carnegie was paid nearly $500 million for his companies, of which he personally received $225 million. Thereafter this five-foot, two-inch dynamo turned his prodigious energies to philanthropy. His writings on the subject urging his fellow industrialists to avoid the "disgrace of dying rich" and to devote their wealth to social purposes gained him great prominence, and at least a few converts. There were those who pointed out the discrepancy between his public moralizing and the policies of his companies in strikebreaking and the brutal treatment of workers. But this ebullient and complex man did not allow such inconsistencies to deter him from his efforts as a social benefactor. In the 1890s and the early twentieth century his major gifts made a dazzling list:

He gave more than $43 million to build and equip public libraries in the United States and other English-speaking countries. More than 2,500 were built as a result, firmly implanting the idea of community responsibility for free library service.

In 1896 he created the Carnegie Institute of Pittsburgh as a museum and in 1900 founded the Carnegie Institute of Technology (now Carnegie–Mellon University), one of the nation's finest technological institutions.

In 1902 he established the Carnegie Institution of Washington to encourage basic research in several scientific fields, and it continues to be an outstanding center of such work.

In 1905 he established the Carnegie Foundation for the Advancement of Teaching to provide retirement pensions for college professors and to conduct studies on the problems of American education. One outgrowth of the foundation's work was the establishment of the Teacher's Insurance and Annuity Association, which now has assets over $30 billion and has made a great contribution to the financial security of college teachers and employees of nonprofit institutions throughout the country. The research studies of the foundation, beginning with the famous Flexner report on medical education in the United States in 1906, have also had great influence. The Boyer report on the American public high school, published in the fall of 1983, is the most recent example of this continuing output.

In 1910 he founded the Carnegie Endowment for International Peace, which remains to this day one of the most vigorous and respected private centers of foreign policy studies in the country.

In addition he made many other sizable benefactions, including gifts to various universities and Negro colleges and even donations to provide churches with pipe organs. (A nonreligious man, Carnegie thought the only good part of a church service was the music.)

Yet by 1910, after more than a decade of active giving, his personal fortune still totaled more than $150 million, which led him in 1911 to create the Carnegie Corporation. He transferred to it the bulk of his wealth, reserving to himself the right to administer it as long as he lived. The purpose of the trust, according to its articles of incorporation, was broadly "the advancement and diffusion of knowledge and understanding among the people of the United States and the British Dominions and colonies."

In principle Carnegie believed in the delegation of authority to the trustees of his foundation and recognized the danger of donor domination. But in the closing years of his life and in the case of his own greatest philanthropic endowment, he behaved in the dictatorial and somewhat dotty fashion of many elderly philanthropists. Ignoring all advice, he set up a passive and conflicted board that included the heads of the five philanthropic institutions bearing his name, as well as his financial and personal secretaries. For the last eight years of his life Carnegie used the foundation to distribute large gifts to other Carnegie institutions, mainly for public libraries and medical education. Following his death in 1919 the corporation was left with no professional staff, heavy encumbrances on its future income because of commitments he had made, and a board dominated by built-in recipients. In the next two years nearly $28 million was appropriated without benefit of long-range planning or serious consideration of the implications of such a spending spree for the foundation's future. Predictably, most of the money went to institutions represented on the corporation's board.

Soon thereafter another $10 million was spent for a variety of less than imperative purposes. This interval of profligacy ended in December 1922 when a majority of independent trustees was elected and an able man, Frederick P. Keppel, was named president. He remained on the job for the next nineteen years.

For much of that time Keppel had to devote himself mainly to piecing out the corporation's income to pay off its overhang of prior commitments. But he did set a warm and unbureaucratic style for the foundation's operations and he began a tradition of well-written annual presidential essays on matters of philanthropic interest, a tradition that continues to the present time.

With the limited uncommitted funds at his disposal Keppel led the corporation into two new fields, adult education and the fine arts, breaking some new philanthropic ground.

His greatest weakness, however, was the narrowness of his social outlook. Through the years of the worldwide Depression, the New Deal, and the outbreak of World War II in Europe, Keppel's annual reports contain hardly a hint of the great issues and problems of the times. In the isolated environment of the corporation, training for librarians, adult education conferences, and the distribution of art-teaching sets were the preoccupations. Yet his long career with the foundation was to end on a note that anticipated one of the greatest social issues of the United States in the postwar period. In 1938 he had commissioned the Swedish social scientist Gunnar Myrdal to study the condition of blacks in America. Myrdal's now classic report was published in 1942. Keppel in his foreword to the two-volume study almost apologetically sought to justify the involvement of a foundation with contemporary social issues: "Provided the foundation limits itself to its proper function, namely to make the facts available and then let them speak for themselves, and does not undertake to instruct the public as to what to do about them, studies of this kind provide a wholly proper and, experience has shown, sometimes a highly important use of their funds."

Keppel died the following year, and his successor as president, Dr. Walter A. Jessup, was equally embarrassed or frightened by the corporation's association with the controversial document. As a result he hastened to point out in his report for 1944 that the corporation had never had and did not intend to have special programs in behalf of blacks. For the next ten years the study, despite its national acclaim and impact, was, like an illegitimate child, apparently considered unmentionable. In philanthropy, as elsewhere, success often has many fathers, but failure is always an orphan. In this curious instance, a triumph had to wait a decade before its real father would avow paternity.

For the next ten years under a succession of uninspiring and ineffective heads the corporation meandered along. But in 1955 with the election of John W. Gardner as president it entered into its first period of high performance.

His first annual report was a tour de force. In a memorable essay, "A Time for Decision in Higher Education," he brilliantly analyzed the implications of the flood of students then beginning to inundate American colleges and universities.

Clearly his cause as president of the corporation would be "excellence" in American higher education. To help achieve and maintain it he, with the able assistance of James A. Perkins, who later was to become president of Cornell University, laid out a careful and comprehensive strategy. They recognized that although the country's colleges and universities were entering a period of dramatic change, there was no group engaged in long-term study of the fundamental forces, needs, and issues that would shape their future. During the period 1960–1965 Carnegie therefore financed a series of projects to provide a national perspective on higher education and to inform the judgments of educators and public policy makers. Gardner's particular personal concern throughout was to head off "galloping mediocrity" as educational institutions grew in size to cope with the great enlargement of the student population.

In 1964, however, by which time the federal government had enacted major new civil rights legislation, including provisions for school desegregation, Gardner was moved to write in his annual essay that "the most important task facing American education today is to remove the remaining barriers to educational opportunity, whether the barriers are due to race prejudice, urban slum conditions, economically depressed rural life, or just plain bad education."

That sentence, and the fact that the corporation that year devoted roughly one quarter of its grants to educational projects for the poor, was unmistakable evidence of its belated but definitive shift from preoccupation with blue-ribbon colleges and universities and the maintenance of academic "standards" to an awareness of the urgent problems of race and poverty in American life. (Gardner has described his own evolution in these words: "I started out as the most academic of academics—the kind of faculty member who never even bothers to attend faculty meetings. . . . I spent 19 years in foundation work, in the conviction that if you understood a problem well enough and could communicate that understanding, somehow the world would be better. I believed in education in the broadest, deepest sense. Only when I went to HEW and then the Urban Coalition Action Council did I come to understand how much could be accomplished by activist groups." Still later in his career as the founder of Common Cause, Gardner became one of the most outspoken and effective advocates of governmental reform, civil rights, and equality of opportunity in the country.)

In 1965, when Gardner left Carnegie to join President Johnson's cabinet as secretary of the Department of Health, Education and Welfare (HEW), he had become the eloquent liberal voice of the establishment. As his last major contribution to the corporation, he had led it into an awareness of the social changes sweeping the United States and to a series of initial responses to those changes that represented a major advance in sophisticated, strategic grant making by a major foundation.

FROM EXCELLENCE TO ACTIVISM

By the time of Gardner's departure, his successor was clearly in sight. Alan Pifer, who had joined the foundation staff several years earlier, had done an extremely good job running its international program focused in countries of the British Commonwealth, and he had strongly impressed the trustees as a comer.

He was named acting president, partly on the grounds that Gardner might possibly want to return to the foundation after a brief tenure in Washington and partly to give Pifer an opportunity to prove himself.

Then forty-four years of age, Pifer had elegant educational credentials, having been trained at Groton, Harvard, and Cambridge. He had served for a time as a cultural officer in the U.S. Embassy in London before joining the foundation. In the course of his twelve years on the foundation staff he had come to be known as an exceptionally clear-headed analyst of issues, a highly articulate and persuasive advocate of his viewpoint, and, rarest of all in the field of philanthropy, a writer of forceful and graceful style. What was not fully appreciated at the time was that beneath his mild and somewhat academic exterior beat the heart of a passionate reformer.

He took over the helm at a particularly turbulent time: the Vietnam war was producing great domestic strains and damage, urban violence was rampant, and the civil rights, women's, and youth movements were on the rise. Less spectacular but nonetheless profound changes in technology, weaponry, the economy, and mores and moral values were also under way. For Pifer, whose background included not only Groton and Harvard but also a boyhood in Indiana in a family with very strong attachment to democratic values, these multiple shifts and traumas in national life were powerfully affecting his own perceptions and priorities.

He inherited a well-functioning organization with a competent, unified, and responsible board; a small, strong staff; a set of almost uniformly excellent programs; and high prestige and influence in a number of fields: education, public affairs, and international affairs. He brought to his task, in addition to a growing concern about the dangerous condition of the society, a highly developed ability, learned under the tutelage of Gardner and Perkins, to utilize the potentialities of philanthropy skillfully and strategically to bring about institutional and social change.

In a retrospective essay on the occasion of his retirement Pifer well described the concept of a modern foundation that he had in mind at the time and the two major objectives he wanted the Carnegie Corporation to pursue: The mission of the modern foundation "in the simplest terms is to better the world, not by assuming the conventional tasks of charity, as worthy and necessary as they are, but by using private wealth constructively and imaginatively in the search for basic solutions to human problems. . . ." A foundation "if it is to be worth anything at all, cannot be morally neutral. It must be guided by a set of values—must stand for something."

What the Carnegie Corporation would stand for under his leadership and the tasks to which it would devote its energies in the most carefully planned and targeted manner were to be "guided by a single motivating force—a life-long belief in social justice and the equality of all people under law. . . . The key questions for me . . . with respect to any proposed action have always been: will it promote equality of opportunity? And will it to some degree make the world a fairer and more just place?'

This outlook was supplemented by an equally strong interest in human resource development. This problem, which grew in significance in his mind during the early 1960s, led him, by 1965, "to the view that the very future of our society depends absolutely on the broad development of all our people, and especially of our children, irrespective of race, sex, economic status or any other consideration."

These two purposes reinforced each other: "Investment in such things as nutrition, health, decent housing, education—for the poor as well as the more affluent—is therefore, not only a matter of social justice but of practical necessity," he wrote. "Failure to appreciate this fundamental truth, I have come to feel, is more dangerous for this nation than any alleged missile gap or other shortcoming in armaments."

The Carnegie Corporation as of 1965 was therefore perfectly poised for takeoff into its second major period of achievement: It was already an effective and prestigious organization. Its new leader knew the institution and had completed his apprenticeship in the techniques of philanthropy. He also had a clear sense of the activist kind of foundation he intended Carnegie to be and the direction it should take. Over the next two years he got off to a fast start, building on the program momentum he had inherited.

In late 1965, the corporation launched two blue-ribbon citizen panels, the Education Commission of the States and the Commission on Educational Television. In both instances the distinction of the members of the panels, the political skill by which they had been assembled, and the quality of their analyses and recommendations led to important practical results. The former helped spur action and reforms on a number of urgent educational problems by state governments. The latter led directly to a proposal by President Johnson, subsequently approved by the Congress, to create the Corporation for Public Broadcasting. In his handling of these two important initiatives it became apparent that Pifer's foresight and sense of timing were not inferior to those qualities in his great predecessor, John Gardner.

Shortly thereafter, the foundation joined with the Carnegie Foundation for the Advancement of Teaching to create a major project, the Carnegie Commission on Higher Education, headed by Clark Kerr, former president of the University of California at Berkeley, to carry on a continuing and comprehensive study of the future of higher education. Over the next fifteen years the commission published twenty-three reports plus numerous specialized and technical studies. In breadth of coverage, quality, objectivity, and impact on public policy the work of the commission constituted probably the most important body of descriptive and analytical literature about American higher education ever produced. Altogether the commission's reports, testimony before legislative bodies, and advice to federal and state officials directly affected the spending of billions of dollars of federal funds and led to the creation of major new federal programs such as Basic Education Opportunity Grants and the formation of the Fund for the Improvement of Post Secondary Education, a governmental foundation to encourage innovation in higher education.

On a less monumental scale, but nonetheless with great eventual impact, Carnegie in 1966 commissioned a study of the possibility of producing television programs of outstanding quality for children that they would want to watch regularly and that would teach them basic skills. This led in turn to the creation three years later of the program "Sesame Street," which is now watched by more than 9 million preschoolers in the United States and is distributed in fifty different countries abroad.

Only after these major initiatives were under way did Pifer turn to a systematic series of reviews of the major elements of the foundation's program. But in contrast to the sluggish and paper-ridden practice of many foundations in this procedure, the Carnegie reviews, with strong leadership from the top, presented the trustees with crisp and well-reasoned options, which in turn led to timely decisions. In 1967 a staff and board review of the entire grants program in relation to the persistence of poverty in American life was made. The outcome was a decision that the promotion of equal educational opportunity and rights should thereafter cut across all of the foundation's programs, a decision undoubtedly influenced by growing evidence of a diminished interest of the federal government in social programming caused in part by the drain on the Treasury because of the Vietnam War.

By this time Pifer's leadership qualities were fully established, and the board confirmed him as president of the corporation in May 1969.

From the early 1970s onward, as the foundation shifted its concerns more and more to the problems of the disadvantaged, the homogeneous upper-class, WASP quality of its board became more and more of an anomaly. In 1971 this problem was forthrightly addressed. A special committee of the trustees reviewed the structure and functions of the board and recommended major changes, most of which were adopted. As a result the board has since been enlarged and diversified, with more women and minority members and a wider geographic spread and variety of occupational backgrounds. This development, similar to that taking place in some other large foundations in the same period, did not result in the case of Carnegie—as it had in several other instances—in fracturing the board, reducing trustee involvement, and creating board-staff frictions.

In the various changes made in the foundation's program some general patterns were clearly discernible by the early 1970s: Pifer with the full support of his board had one by one deemphasized, reformulated, or stripped away activities that did not center on social justice, equality, and human resource development. In 1972 the foundation's excellent program in medical education and the delivery of health services was discontinued and the activities and personnel taken over by the Robert Wood Johnson Foundation, which by that time had become a major presence in the health field. In 1973 the foundation, which had long been strongly identified with problems of higher education, formally established a program in elementary and secondary education that was to focus on the problems of disadvantaged children and on the improvement of the public schools. In 1975 activities in countries formerly associated with the British Commonwealth were substantially reoriented. From an emphasis on university development in Africa, the Caribbean, and the South Pacific, the focus was shifted to national (that is, indigenous, nonwhite) leadership development and the integration of women into economic development in those areas.

The foundation was steadily becoming leaner, more concentrated, more targeted in its programs. But a second and equally important quality began to be apparent, namely an increasingly sophisticated understanding of the various elements or instruments that had to be fitted into a comprehensive strategy of social change and an increasingly bold, even militant, willingness to employ the most powerful and controversial of these when necessary.

In broad terms the foundation's principal objectives from the mid-1960s until Pifer's retirement in 1982 remained operative. But the strategies for achieving them evolved considerably. In the late 1960s research studies, public policy panels, experimental projects, and leadership training were characteristic. But by the end of the decade some activities with a sharper and more controversial edge could be noted in the grant list. In 1969, for example, the Earl Warren Legal Training Program was started to recruit and give scholarship help to black law students to help them begin civil rights practice in the South.

In the early 1970s, partly as a consequence of a decision by the Nixon administration to cease giving legal help to minority students and their parents who were suing school boards and other government agencies to force them to comply with desegregation orders, the corporation began to support projects to help fill the vacuum that had been created, including fact gathering, mobilizing expert witnesses, and carrying out other activities preparatory to litigation. Beginning in 1972 and continuing over the following decade, the corporation gave more than $4 million to such organizations as the NAACP Legal Defense and Education Fund, the Native American Rights Fund, and the Mexican-American Legal Defense and Education Fund for litigation on educational issues. It also financed the Puerto Rican Legal Defense and Education Fund to monitor the compliance of the New York City Board of Education with a federal court mandate to offer bilingual education programs to more than eighty-five thousand Hispanic school children.

During the same period the corporation committed nearly $15 million to several governmental monitoring and advocacy projects in behalf of minority, female, and handicapped children. One of the groups to which it has given great help has been the Children's Defense Fund in Washington, D.C.

A particular concern of groups supported by the corporation has been Title I of the Elementary and Secondary Education Act of 1965, the largest source of federal funds to local school districts for "compensatory education" programs. Both program audits and independent studies demonstrated that Title I funds were, contrary to law, being used to replace rather than supplement local expenditures for the benefit of disadvantaged children. Such organizations as the Federal Education Project of the Lawyer's Committee for Civil Rights Under Law were thereupon given Carnegie grants to investigate and oversee the use of these monies by various levels of government.

In addition to support for litigation and the monitoring of government, Carnegie in the early 1970s established an independent study group, the Carnegie Council on Children, to gather facts about the status of children and to propose changes in public and private policies to meet their needs. Headed by psychologist Kenneth Keniston, of Yale University, the council produced five studies that caused considerable controversy but without question increased public awareness of the impact of larger social forces on children's lives. The most debated feature of the council's work was that it ranged well beyond educational matters to express a radical critique of American economy and society in general. In its report, *All Our Children: The American Family Under Pressure*, the Council stated that of all the "insults and injuries families face, none is worse than that of financial deprivation caused by the unfair distribution of economic rewards in the society. . . ." It went on to say that better schooling alone could not create equality of opportunity when equality did not exist in the world of jobs, of social relations, or of politics. Among its specific recommendations, it proposed a full-employment strategy, supplemented by a system of income support for families with children.

The storm of criticism that broke over the report did not detectably deter the foundation from its chosen course. It went on to finance a controversial book, *Inequality*, by prominent scholar Christopher Jencks, which suggested that educational reforms were powerless to equalize educational achievement, much less reduce social inequities, when the society itself was inherently unequal, a conclusion that seemed to imply that the various programs being supported by a number of foundations, including the Carnegie Corporation, to find better ways to improve the skills of disadvantaged students and to raise their test scores were pointless unless and until the United States could be transformed into a fully egalitarian society.

Other activities of the corporation through the 1970s and into the 1980s were less controversial but not less reformist. One of the most important of these was support for new structures and opportunities by which individuals could receive higher education. It had long supported the idea of a degree program through independent study comparable to the highly respected external degree program of the University of London, which had operated since the turn of the century. One such project was the college-level examination program (CLEP) administered by the College Entrance Examination Board. However, acceptance of CLEP for college credit by the higher education community was slow, and the participation of unaffiliated students was at first small. A major breakthrough came in 1970 when the State University of New York announced it would award the first true external degree in the United States solely on the basis of tests or of off-campus learning experience. This has grown into a national program now including more than ninety thousand individuals taking the examinations each year, and one thousand colleges recognize the results of the tests for the purpose of course credit. A high proportion of the enrollees are members of the armed forces, and about half are women.

By the time of his retirement as president of the Carnegie Corporation in 1982, Alan Pifer, like his predecessor John Gardner, was eager to move from the confines of philanthropy to a still broader and more direct involvement in public policy issues on behalf of social change. In his departing essay "Final Thoughts," he delivered himself of an ardent statement of personal convictions and conclusions following his nearly thirty years in philanthropy that amounted virtually to a political declaration. With sadness and some bitterness he reflected on what he felt was a new mood of "meanness of spirit" abroad in the land and the dereliction of responsibility by the Reagan administration in behalf of the nation's children and its disadvantaged. He saw in the situation abandonment of a great national mission launched in the 1960s and early 1970s on behalf of justice and human dignity. He hoped that the nation would recognize the situation for the disaster it was and would reverse course, in the interest of its own survival, before it was too late. In his words,

> one can see now that the nation is at a fork in the road. If it goes down one road, the guiding philosophy will be clear: this is the view that a federal social role is wrong in principle and cannot, in any event, be afforded if we are to retain a strong defense capability. It must therefore be reduced, if not totally eliminated. . . . The federal taxing and spending power should be used for no other social purpose than basic social insurance and the provision of assistance to the "deserving poor"—those who qualify by virtue of old age, illness, or physical handicap.
>
> If the nation goes down the other road, the guiding philosophy will be equally clear but totally different. The basic assumption will be that the federal social role is entirely legitimate—indeed mandated in the general welfare clause of the Constitution—and even, perhaps, expanded into new areas of need. The assumption, further, will be that no matter how buoyant the economy becomes there will always be a sizable group in society whose members must receive public assistance if they are to live decently and if their children are to have anything like an equal chance in life. Finally, it will be assumed that, since a vigorous social role by the national government is fundamental to the maintenance of a stable society and to the development of its human resources and hence its security, the country will give the social role the priority necessary for it to be fully funded. . . . It is my firm conviction that sooner or later, and probably sooner, the nation will revert to the second road. I say this because I believe that down the first road there lies nothing but increasing hardship for ever growing numbers, a mounting possibility of severe social unrest, and the consequent development among the upper classes and the business community of sufficient fear of survival of our capitalist economic system to bring about an abrupt change of course. In short, just as we built the general welfare state in the 1930s and expanded it in the 1960s as a safety valve for the easing of social tension, so we will do it again in the 1980s. Any other path is simply too risky.

He concluded, "For my part, although I will no longer be at the helm of the foundation, I will be continuing to exert my fullest efforts in other, and, I hope, no less productive, ways to help build the kind of society in which I believe so staunchly, one that is humane, caring, and provident in developing the talents of all its people."

In obviously defiant mood, this capital example of the social reformer in philanthropy moved into the next phase of his career.

Not all, indeed very few, of his peers in the field shared his passion for social justice or matched his skill and determination in employing a foundation and its resources to realize a personal vision. In his zeal he sometimes displayed an unattractive self-righteousness. But he will be long remembered as a man who tested, developed, and demonstrated the ultimate potentialities of the foundation instrument in American democratic society to assist and encourage processes of institutional and policy change. He also set a very high standard of social principle, courage, and professional competence that will influence younger foundation executives in the future.

Pifer's successor, Dr. David Hamburg, who assumed the presidency in mid-1982 is a man of quite different background, largely in medicine and health affairs. He came to Carnegie from Harvard University's Division of Health Policy Research and Education, which he headed, and before that the presidency of the Institute of Medicine at the National Academy of Sciences.

DECISIVE REDIRECTION

Hamburg is a man of quiet and scholarly manner, beneath which is great intensity of feeling. A catalyzing event in his life occurred in the mid-1970s, when four of his students were abducted from a wildlife research station in Tanzania by guerrillas. Dr. Hamburg immediately went to the scene and devoted more than two months to delicate negotiations that led to their release. He came away from the experience vowing to commit his life to social and public service.

In spirit, therefore, he is an appropriate successor to Pifer. But he has his own, and rather different, ideas about the issues to which the Carnegie Corporation should devote its energies and the style it should adopt in its operations.

Having served three years as a trustee prior to his appointment as president he was entirely familiar with the foundation's programs and did not find it necessary, therefore, to carry out the usual long and laborious "program review" as a basis for preparing his own recommendations for future directions to the board. Instead he engaged the staff directly in that task and within twelve months of his arrival was able to present a comprehensive new program that included a number of elements from the previous period but also some important new ones.

He proposed that the foundation direct its future efforts to four major goals:

- the avoidance of nuclear war and the improvement of U.S.–Soviet relations;
- the education of all Americans, especially youth, for a scientifically and technologically based society;
- the prevention of damage to children and young adolescents as a result of various social and other hazards, ranging from drug and alcohol abuse to teen-age pregnancy; and
- the training and development of human resources in Third World countries, with a special emphasis on Mexico.

To deal with all these sweeping problems, Hamburg placed special confidence in the sciences, both the "hard" sciences and the behavioral ones, as "our most powerful problem-solving tool." In December 1983 the Carnegie board considered Hamburg's recommendations and with only minor alterations approved them.

Quickly thereafter the actual shift in programs began to be apparent: a wider global scope of activities, a general approach of bringing able and influential individuals from various backgrounds and experience to work on urgent issues of public policy, and efforts to affect the course of events somewhat less by advocacy and litigation and somewhat more by "collaborations of competence."

There were those, observing his initial moves, who wondered whether Hamburg's deeply ingrained commitment to the scientific approach as well as his own academic background would lead to programs long on analysis but short on practical impact. But in relatively brief time these doubts have been dispelled. In the foundation's program on nuclear issues, he has managed to leverage its efforts by collaboration with the MacArthur Foundation, which has now committed $25 million to similar objectives. And to connect the program with the movers and shakers in government, he has created an ongoing series of dinners, briefings, seminars, and conferences in Washington, to which congressional leaders as well as high-ranking individuals from the executive branch, including on occasion the president himself, have been prepared to attend.

In similar fashion, he has created the Carnegie Forum on Education and the Economy, which will periodically bring together some one hundred leading Americans from business, labor, government, education, and the scientific community to consider the issues and options linking educational policy with the future economic needs of the nation.

Whether Hamburg, in his enthusiasm and intensity, had bitten off a good bit more program than a foundation with $500 million of assets could chew remained to be seen. But what was impressive was to see such an individual of clear vision, high intelligence, and a strong framework of values assume the leadership of a major philanthropy. He has accomplished the first phase of his new task with both grace and authority, and the visible signs all indicate that Carnegie, though perhaps less militant in style, will continue to be a vanguard foundation in standards and effectiveness. At a time when the other older leader in the field, namely Rockefeller, is stumbling about, this is more than ordinarily encouraging.

Edna McConnell Clark Foundation

When Edna McConnell Clark's father sold books door to door, he gave his customers bottles of perfume as well. It soon became evident that the perfume made a bigger hit than the books, so in 1886 he set up the California Perfume Company. David H. McConnell's creation, renamed Avon Products, Inc., eventually became the world's largest cosmetic manufacturer and door-to-door operation. Today, several hundred thousand "Avon Ladies" are in the streets here and around the world. (Japanese housewives need a signed permission slip from their husband before buying.)

His daughter, Edna, and her husband set up the foundation that now bears her name. She had a Christian upbringing in upstate New York and as a young woman was involved in social work and wanted to become a missionary, until she met and married W. Van Alan Clark, who had joined Avon Products as a young chemist. He led the company during its great period of growth after World War

II. From 1950 until the early 1970s the value of a share of Avon stock increased more than one hundred times.

As their wealth began to pile up, the Clarks asked their lawyer for advice about how to organize their charitable giving. In a brief conversation lasting perhaps twenty minutes he persuaded them that to gain maximum tax benefits and for the sake of convenience they should set up a foundation. That was done in 1950, and for the next fifteen years they made modest but gradually increasing gifts through it.

From the start, Mrs. Clark was the dominant individual in determining the foundation's direction. Mr. Clark, though a very successful businessman, was a less assertive personality. It was she who gave it its strong commitment to the needs of children and the poor and its style of operation: purposeful, nonacademic, and not a little erratic.

In 1961, to get the foundation started on a regular grant-making program, the Clarks asked their sons and their wives to explore possibilities in three fields, child welfare, education, and hospitals, and to report back. Not much happened as a direct result, but the active involvement of the younger family members in the foundation's work, another of its special characteristics, had begun.

By 1966 the family's wealth had reached such a scale that the donors were able to put 1 million Avon shares worth $44 million into the foundation. It was what one family member called "an unentailed puddle of money." But it did require some changes in mode of operation, and Mrs. Clark decided that it was time to employ someone to "assist with the keeping of the files." Thus began what was to be a long and troubled pattern of relationships between the family and staff.

The first employee, a family friend, had the temerity to do a little more than keep the files, and she was promptly removed. Clearly, nobody was going to tell Mrs. Clark how to spend her foundation's money.

In 1969 the Clarks gave an additional 1.5 million Avon shares to the foundation, raising its endowment to $210 million. In that same year the Congress passed the Tax Reform Act that mandated that foundations had to pay out at least 6 percent of the value of their assets annually. For the Clark Foundation the result was a series of very large gifts to familiar charities: Smith College, Mrs. Clark's alma mater, received $3.7 million; Cornell, Mr. Clark's alma mater, $2 million; Lincoln Center in New York City, $5 million; and many others.

The years 1969 and 1970 marked the end of the period when the foundation was used simply as a channel for family giving. The next phase was to be so different that, except for the continuity of the three Clark sons on the board, it was virtually the birth of a new foundation.

By 1970 the pressure for some kind of staff assistance had become irresistible and Charles Menagh, who had been with a corporate foundation, was hired. He saw himself as a foundation president, the board saw his function otherwise, and he soon departed.

The next expedient was to make one of the three Clark sons, all of whom were busy with their various careers, a part-time president. But the work was getting to be too much for anyone to do on that basis, and Dr. Arnold Zurcher, former head of the Alfred P. Sloan Foundation, was consulted. He recommended that the foundation should have a staff of twelve and an administrative budget of $1.5 million. At that point Van Alan Clark, the son who had approached Zurcher, recalled, "I clutched my skirts and ran for the door."

Finally, in October 1970 the board decided to hire an executive head. James F. Henry, a lawyer for the family and for the company, was chosen and given the title of vice-president. By the end of 1971, having evidently allayed some of the family's apprehensions, he became president. Thereafter, one by one the professionals began to arrive: an office manager, the first program officer, and in 1972 two more program officers, both of whom had worked for a management consulting firm, McKinsey & Company. The staff was to be a small, hardworking group of generalists—not out of academia or philanthropy—and it would rely heavily on the use of consultants and advisory boards in specific program areas.

At the outset Henry had been optimistic about relations between staff and board. The answer, he felt, in building rapport and unity was to have "a collection of very good people with manageable egos and lots of communication. This is not a difficult requirement if we work at it." But in practice it turned out to be very difficult.

During 1972, Henry and his colleagues began energetically to scan the grant-making possibilities in a number of fields before making their recommendations to the board as to which few should receive priority. But the board almost immediately began to complain that the staff worked too slowly, did not always listen to its directives, and sometimes wandered too far afield. The staff, on the other hand, felt the board members were often divided among themselves, sometimes showed inconsistency in their directives, and did not always study the background papers provided to them.

Despite the strains, sufficient agreement on program priorities (largely reflecting the individual enthusiasms of the family members on the board) had been reached by 1973 that organized grant making could begin. From then through 1976 Henry led the foundation through its first experimental period of program development. Despite sharp differences among the Clark brothers, which at times nearly immobilized it and at other times threatened to break it into fragments, each controlled by one of the brothers to support his favored projects, some useful results were achieved.

Hays Clark, the eldest brother, had a special interest in problems of the elderly. So in 1973 and 1974 a number of grants were made to open up educational and employment opportunities for them. The program attracted considerable favorable comment, but at that point, for reasons that remain obscure, the foundation began a long search for some other organization to take the program under its wing.

In mid-1973 a second program began. It would address the problems of the poor. Because urban poverty was getting a great deal of attention at the time and the field was crowded, the Clark Foundation directed its early efforts to rural poverty. The principal idea was to create a "national center for rural development," a counterpart of the prestigious Urban Institute. The board made a commitment of up to $10 million over a five-year period "if the right person with the guidance of the right kind of board" could be found. In the end, after much hunting about and endless consultations, no such combination was identified, and in early 1976 the foundation liquidated its interest in the subject. As a result, a good many misunderstandings and hard feelings toward the foundation were generated.

A somewhat more successful initiative was the foundation's third experimental program intended to reform the criminal justice system. Working with the American Civil Liberties Union the foundation heavily supported its National Prison Project. The purpose was to pressure state governments to provide minimum humane living conditions to prisoners, including the avoidance of overcrowding and the provision of a clean bed, an operating toilet, and some fresh air and exercise. As a result of litigation the foundation subsidized, the federal courts ordered the state of Alabama in a landmark case to improve conditions for its prison inmates. A number of other states have now followed suit.

By the end of 1976 the foundation concluded that the program had "contributed to new thinking about the complex question of why Americans lock up so many people who are different" and decided to continue it, despite its mixed results in the first years.

On the other hand the foundation's efforts to work through the American Bar Association to stimulate its members to be agents of reform was eventually abandoned as a failure. And a grant to the Antioch School of Law in Washington, D.C., to train lawyers in public interest practice ended in bitter disagreements and public accusations by the school that the foundation had reneged on its funding commitments.

Two more programs were launched in the early 1970s, one directed to the problems of children and the other to health needs in the developing countries. The program for children initially embraced a wide range of needs experienced by "children in trouble." It included support for research, improvement in the availability of services, and development of leadership in the field.

To head it the foundation in 1973 hired its first specialist, Peter Forsythe, who had been a leading advocate for the rights of children in Michigan and head of the state's program for children. As refined by him, the program became more narrowly focused on one troubled group: children in foster-care institutions, especially older and otherwise handicapped children. No other foundation was helping this group in a substantial way, and institutions for foster care were notably deficient. Within a few years the program began to make its mark. Gradually the foundation helped educate a group of new professional leaders in the field of adoption services; it has improved communications between judges and social workers; and it has promoted greater acceptance of new methods of finding adoptive families. Of all the domestic programs of the foundation, this one by late 1976 had acquired the most creditable reputation.

Clark's program directed to problems of developing countries was undertaken essentially because of the interest of W. Van Alan Clark, Jr., the middle son of the donors. It began with very broad and ill-defined objectives. But after a relatively brief period and a few initial grants directed mainly to economic development, the foundation by late 1973 decided to concentrate on research in tropical and parasitic diseases—a most improbable choice for a foundation without competence or credentials in medical or scientific matters. Schistosomiasis was selected as the specific target of the effort.

In spring 1974 a strategic plan for the research program was produced, after much consultation with scientists and medical schools and the governments of several developing countries.

The following year, 1975, a group of leading scientists was convened (with the cooperation and under the auspices of the Rockefeller Foundation) to update the strategic plan and give guidance on further steps to be taken. That same year the foundation appointed Dr. J. Stauffer Lehman, a recognized authority on the disease, to direct the work.

THE CHANGING OF THE GUARD

By early 1976 James Henry's days as president of the foundation were coming to an end. He had made some valuable contributions to its management and programs, but the board in its impatient and sometimes contradictory way was dissatisfied. His departure was to be effective on December 31 of that year, and in the meanwhile the board spent considerable energy trying to find a successor. Robert F. Goheen, former head of Princeton University and then president of the Council on Foundations, was hired as a consultant. In mid-1976 he submitted a diplomatically phrased but trenchant report on the foundation's needs. Among other things he noted that the strains the foundation was going through were not unusual for a family foundation, and that in the case of Clark these might have been magnified by Henry's highly disciplined management style. Nevertheless the differences among the trustees made the situation for any chief executive officer "catastrophic . . . whatever his ability or style." Goheen also pointed out that the foundation's general reputation seemed to be one of "indecision and indefiniteness—a lack of bite except in its two most specifically delineated programs. . . ."

Although the report was critical, the trustees liked it, so much that they asked Goheen to take on the presidency. He agreed, but with the understanding that if newly elected President Carter offered him the ambassadorship to India, a country in which he had been born and raised, he would accept. The appointment to India was offered, and after only four months as head of the foundation he resigned. The presidency was then offered to John Coleman of Haverford College in Haverford, Pennsylvania. Coleman had been head of that institution for some ten years and was ready for a change. Moreover he was embroiled in a dispute over coeducation at the all-male school that he expected to lose. In any event, he accepted the foundation's offer and became its third president in July 1977.

In inviting an individual like Coleman to take the post the Edna McConnell Clark board was acting at its irrational worst and its ambitious best. It had always found willful executive officers to be intolerable and had fired a series of them. And in Coleman they were taking on a strong-minded, experienced man of established reputation as an economist, foundation executive (he had served with distinction for a period with the Ford Foundation), and college president. There was every reason, therefore, to expect not only clashes but possibly fierce ones. At the same time the board's courage and its aspirations for the foundation had to be admired. For in Coleman they selected a very different breed of man from the usual bland academic administrator that most foundations turn to for "leadership." It has been one of the paradoxes of the Clark Foundation that although family members have dominated it, have endlessly quarreled among themselves, and have had generally miserable relationships with staff, they have at the same time wanted it to address urgent problems and to "make a difference." To achieve that they have been willing to sponsor unorthodox and unpopular causes and to stand fast in their convictions in the face of public controversy. If the yammering of the board could be kept under control and if its high sense of mission could predominate, John Coleman was a good choice for the job.

JOHN COLEMAN: THE PUBLIC PERSONALITY

Son of a working-class family in Canada, Coleman was trained as a labor economist and was a reputable academic for some twenty years. He had taught at MIT and Carnegie–Mellon, among other good schools, and published his share of treatises and textbooks. But he says about that period, "Nobody ever thought of me as a scholar, or even as being particularly bright." His real rise to prominence, and to great personal fulfillment, came in the early 1970s. The triggering event was the attack of a group of construction workers in New York City on a parade of peace demonstrators. At that point he decided he had become out of contact with the American reality and that he needed to take a fresh, personal look at the nation's working class. He took off for the first of what has become a famous series of sabbaticals to break free of his professional cocoon. For two months he cleaned sewers and dug ditches in Atlanta, made sandwiches and salads in Boston, and collected garbage in a suburb of Washington, D.C. His only intervals of professional contact came at two meetings he attended as board chairman of Philadelphia's Federal Reserve Bank.

The response to his chronicle of his adventures, a book titled *Blue Collar Journal*, encouraged him to think his forte might be as an activist reformer, not an administrator. This feeling was an important factor in his ready acceptance of the offer from the Edna McConnell Clark Foundation when it came in 1976.

Since becoming its head he has continued his periodic excursions into the lower economic and social depths. In 1977 he wrote a widely discussed article about one of them, "My Life as a Garbage Man," for *The New York Times Magazine*. He has also, voluntarily, pulled time in several state prisons and a Texas county jail. In the early winter of 1983 he spent ten days wandering the streets of New York as a homeless derelict, and the article he wrote about it for *New York* magazine evoked international attention and acclaim.

It contained such passages as these from his diary of the experience:

> Saturday, January 22—I slept little. The forecast was for more rain tomorrow, so why wish the night away?
>
> Thursday, January 27: A man I squatted next to in a doorway on 29th Street said it all: "The onliest thing is to have a warm place to sleep. That and having somebody care about you. That'd be even onlier." He had what appeared to be rolls of paper toweling wrapped around one leg and tied with red ribbon. But the paper, wet with rain by now, didn't seem to serve any purpose.

And,

> Until now I haven't understood the extent of nicotine addiction. Dependencies on drugs and alcohol have been around me

for a long time, but I thought before that smoking was a bad habit rather easy to overcome.

How many times have I, a non-smoker, been begged for a cigarette in these days? Surely hundreds. Cigarettes are central. A few folks will give them away, a smaller number sell them for up to 8 cents a piece, and almost all give that last pathetic end of a butt to the first man who asks for what little bit is left. I know addiction now as I didn't before.

Newspapers and magazines have delighted in telling the tale of this cloistered executive who wrestles with trash barrels and copes with convicted felons. There are those in philanthropy, however, who dislike, indeed resent, his occasionally publicly voiced criticisms of the performance of American philanthropy. And there is perhaps a touch of envy in the sentiment common among them that he is simply a dilettante and publicity seeker. But Coleman offers at least three reasons for pursuing his form of sabbatical: to counteract what he calls "the isolation in all our lives"; to help him develop information germane to Clark Foundation projects; and to pursue his economic specialty, employment: how and under what conditions people work.

He has as a result become something of a media hero and at times the most widely discussed foundation officer in the United States.

THE OTHER, DESK-BOUND COLEMAN

Immediately upon taking office in July 1977 Coleman talked at length with each of the program heads, following which two of the four promptly resigned. To replace them, in accordance with his own preferences and consistent with the habits of the foundation, he appointed nonacademics.

After a review of the existing programs, that for the elderly was turned over to another organization, with some funding for its temporary continuance. Ending the schistosomiasis program was considered, but after more consultations with scientists, medical authorities, and other foundations, the foundation judged it to be worth continuing. Likewise the programs on behalf of children and in the field of criminal justice were reaffirmed.

In addition he recommended launching a new program to find jobs for the disadvantaged. "The emphasis," he wrote in March

1978, "will be upon finding ways to help those people—young or old, urban or rural, male or female, of minority or majority races, or mentally or physically handicapped—who are least well served by institutions which traditionally link people to jobs."

With time, certain modifications in these programs have been introduced: the work on tropical diseases has now shifted from a concentration on schistosomiasis to the problem of infectious blindness, for example. But the four programs, for children, justice, jobs, and tropical disease, remain the areas of primary interest to the foundation today and consume more than 90 percent of its outlays. It remains committed to the idea of trying to do a few things well and to maximizing the impact of its programs on people, institutions, and public policy.

Coleman's belief is that this is accomplished through increasingly sharp and precise definition of subgoals within the fields of foundation interest. Thus, in the program for jobs for the disadvantaged, the foundation states its objectives in these terms:

To improve the school-to-work transition of urban disadvanged youth by:

- developing model work-education programs among private industry, schools, community organizations and unions to help such youth move into jobs;
- increasing the private sector's role and effectiveness in hiring such youth;
- testing a very few new youth employment models; and
- monitoring government initiatives, particularly as they relate to disadvantaged youth.

The aims and interests of its other programs are just as sharply delineated and confined.

Coleman acknowledges that such concentration entails some risks, but he defends it as necessary to produce results. "In a sprawling area like prison reform, you can't hope to make a big impact *without* specializing." In any case, he adds, the foundation's program priorities are not set in cement. They are expected to change over time, at least in emphasis, partly under the guidance of the foundation's advisory committees. These committees, a Clark innovation, are composed of outside experts who counsel the board as well as the staff on general focus as well as specific program content.

Until early 1984 important uncertainties about the Clark Foundation's longer future existed. To that point its program priorities and policies had largely been governed by the personal preferences of the three sons of the donors. However, the most involved of them, Van Alan Clark, had recently died and whether either of the other two would exert himself to assume a role of leadership was unclear.

Other than family, the board included two nonfamily members, but only one genuinely "outside" trustee. This narrow and fragile governance mechanism after Van Alan Clark's death obviously would have to be revamped, possibly with major consequences for the foundation's program strategy and continuity.

In April 1984 a major step was taken with the election of three able outside trustees. Also, the daughter of W. Van Alan Clark, Jr., was elected to replace him. She continues his active interest in tropical diseases.

The result is that active family involvement is maintained, but a significant new element of independent, outside influence has been added, which should strengthen and stabilize the foundation's position in the period ahead.

A NOTE ON INVESTMENTS

The Clark Foundation has had many problems in its first years, largely due to divisions within the board and to frictions between board and staff. But it has also had to try to develop its programs while on a roller coaster ride in the stock market. It presents a vivid example of the great losses to philanthropy that can result from an undiversified portfolio, even one made up of a very strong security.

The assets of the foundation were acquired in the form of stock in Avon Products, Inc., in the 1950s and 1960s. The stock at the time was growing rapidly in value, and indeed Avon was ranked by *Forbes* magazine in 1970 as the most consistently profitable company in the United States, first in average return on stockholder equity and on total capital over the preceding five years. The value of the foundation's shares by that year had grown to more than $300 million.

In 1972, 1 million of its Avon shares were sold for $113 million, which was reinvested in a diversified portfolio.

When the bottom dropped out of the stock market in 1973–1974 the foundation's assets sank along with the value of Avon stock from more than $300 million to $98 million. The drop would have been even greater except for the stock sale in 1972.

In 1975, to protect itself against such calamities in the future, the foundation created an investment advisory committee to carry out a strategy of diversification, and in the years since the portfolio has outperformed the stock market averages. The foundation's assets, with the gradual recovery of the market, have now regained their earlier level of value.

Because of the extreme variation of the value of its assets the foundation's level of grants from year to year has also had great swings: 1970, $14 million; 1971, $12 million; 1972, $21 million; 1973, $9 million; 1974, $7.5 million; 1975, $5 million; 1976, $7.5 million; 1977, $9 million; 1978, $11 million; 1979, $13.6 million; 1980, $15.6 million.

AN APPRAISAL

The Clark Foundation with its heavy and sometimes distracting family involvement, staffing problems, and incomprehensible program switches has resembled a number of the poorest large foundations of this type. But it has been different in its high aspirations, activism, and willingness to stir public controversy.

And some of its programs have had great impact. Indeed they have administered strong shocks to American society, shocks whose consequences the foundation has then ignored. For example it played a key role in bringing about the court decision in the case of *Wyatt* v. *Stickney* in the early 1970s to deinstitutionalize large numbers of individuals who formerly had been kept in mental institutions. But now that those pathetic people are to be seen sitting on park benches and sleeping in doorways in cities all over the country because community service facilities to care for their needs have not been created, the foundation has taken no action to address that problem. Likewise in its program for prisoner's rights, the foundation has helped stimulate a flood of litigation, some of which has helped redress real grievances but much of which has cluttered the courts with nuisance suits and added further to their backlogs. For this consequence the foundation takes no responsibility. Its defenses for its actions, and inactions, are perfectly plausible. But so are the criticisms that others may feel.

By its strategy, Clark has taken the fullest advantage of the freedom allowed to private foundations in American life to take initiative, exert leverage on social processes and institutions, and contribute to the qualities of pluralism and the competition of ideas in American life. Without question, the willingness of the society to endure the pressures exerted by a foundation like Edna McConnell Clark is maintained in part at least by the fact that so many other foundations are conservative in approach and do not disturb the status quo. From their point of view Clark is exploiting the public acceptance they have generated and is operating in the lee of their political protection.

The Clark Foundation in some ways represents big American philanthropy's ultimate example of the concept of a targeted, reformist foundation and a test of the tolerance of American society for such high-powered activism. At one time in the past the Ford Foundation constituted that test, partly because of its activism and partly because of its monumental size. In the context of the era of McCarthyism, conservative forces struck back very forcibly at the challenge that they felt Ford presented. And that foundation, though it has remained comparatively activist as a social force, did in fact then retreat substantially from the kind of "arrogant radicalism," as some then called it, epitomized by its most prominent officer, the late Robert Maynard Hutchins. Whether the Clark Foundation, large but unthreatening by its sheer size, will generate strong backlash to some of its initiatives remains to be seen.

Since Coleman's arrival, the foundation has essentially followed a policy of focusing on increasingly specific portions of its chosen fields of activity at the same time that its resources have grown considerably. This policy of addressing less and less with more and more raises some problems. In its domestic programs, for example, the foundation has sharpened their focus step-by-step to the point where almost all "responsiveness" to the ideas and felt needs of other institutions has disappeared. They are simply ignored if they do not serve the foundation's own purposes. If this tendency should be combined in the future with the foundation's earlier practice of ignoring the negative effects and fallout of its actions, it could encounter serious reactions.

However, and quite apart from specific questions or criticisms that can be raised about the Edna McConnell Clark Foundation's activities, it is an impressive example of the power of commitment and ideas in the service of social reform. It is a refreshing contrast to the dullness and conformism of many foundations. And it is a precious demonstration of the great freedom that exists, though not without limits, to be sure, for private philanthropy in the American system to pursue a particular vision and attempt to "make a difference."

William Penn Foundation

The Haas family of Philadelphia, whose fortune derives from the Rohm and Haas Company, has been vacillating and uncertain about the name it wished to give its foundation, but in other and more important respects it has been strong and steady in its philanthropic purposes. Its foundation, originally called the Phoebe Waterman Foundation, then the Haas Community Funds, and now the William Penn Foundation, is one of the finest of the big foundations whose program focus is on a particular locality, in this case, the cities of Philadelphia, Pennsylvania, and Camden, New Jersey, and the surrounding counties of the Delaware Valley.

The founder of the family fortune, Otto Haas, was a son of impoverished parents, who from his early years in Germany was driven by an insatiable hunger for wealth. It began, he told an intimate friend, when as a young man he walked in the hills outside Stuttgart and "saw all those roofs and realized that not one belonged to me." He came to the United States in 1909 and over the next fifty years built up his industrial chemicals company into a huge and hugely successful organization. He rarely missed a day at the office, working in a black silk coat in a room furnished only with a simple wooden table and four straight chairs. He kept the reins of management firmly in his own hands until days before his death of cancer in 1960 at the age of eighty-eight.

His two sons, John and F. Otto Haas, until recent years remained deeply absorbed in the family business. As one of the company's executives has remarked, "They were the first to arrive in the morning, the last to go at night, and they knew every employee in the plant. They represent paternalism of the very best kind."

Their father's interest in philanthropy, initially at least, derived from a simple desire to save estate taxes and ensure family control of the company. The foundation was established in 1945 and named in honor of his wife, Phoebe Waterman Haas. Perhaps because of her own background as an army colonel's daughter who grew up on an Indian reservation, she had a strong interest in social welfare activities. For its first ten years the foundation operated with limited resources and no professional staff. Its grants went largely to existing hospitals and research and educational institutions in the locality.

But in 1955 it came to life with the appointment of a consultant, Richard K. Bennett, who had come to the attention of the Haas family as a result of his outstanding work in race relations in Philadelphia, and incidentally as an outspoken critic of their company's employment policies with respect to blacks. Bennett subsequently became the foundation's executive director, a post that he held for the next twenty-five years.

That the family should have chosen a person like Bennett and given him its full support over a long period says a great deal about its values and philanthropic purposes. Bennett is a Quaker who was interned during World War II as a conscientious objector. He later worked with the American Friends Service Committee on interracial affairs and the problems of minority groups. He brought his strong social commitment, outspokenness, and activism with him to the foundation, and its program quickly began to give increasing emphasis to social welfare projects, housing, and scholarship assistance to underprivileged children.

By the time Bennett retired in 1982, the foundation had distributed more than $100 million in grants, a third of it for social welfare programs, nearly 30 percent for education, 16 percent for health care, and 12 percent for cultural activities. Toward the end of his tenure, the proportion going to social welfare projects was further increasing and that for education, the second largest category, decreasing. During the 1970s, his last decade in office, the foundation's program was concentrated on several "clusters" of projects:

1. From 1971 to 1978, for example, a number of grants were made to create a new system of burn-treatment facilities in the Philadelphia area.
2. From 1974 through 1981, the foundation made a series of grants to various neighborhood health services to improve the availability of health care for the poor and underserved.
3. From 1974 onward a series of major grants dealt with the problems of unemployed minority youth.

4. Another "cluster" addressed the problems of housing for the poor; still another the problems of crime, the criminal justice system, and the rights of victims of crime.
5. In the early 1980s a number of grants focused on creating a system of hospices in the Philadelphia area primarily to serve the dying and their families.

A special quality of the foundation under Bennett's leadership was its sensitivity to the changing needs of the community. Writing of the situation in Philadelphia at the end of 1981, he said, "Just as foundations try to influence the nature of life around them, they are—in turn—influenced by their environment," and he added, somewhat bitterly, "The programs and effectiveness of foundations (ours included) cannot fail to be affected by inflation, unemployment, recession (rapidly becoming a cover word for depression), a sharp turn to the right by the Administration accompanied by an especially jingoist type of military posturing and expansion. . . ."

Bennett was succeeded as president of the foundation in early 1982 by Bernard C. Watson, a black, and an educator of national stature. He had come from the University of Chicago to become deputy superintendent of the Philadelphia school system in the late 1960s and later was appointed professor and academic vice-president at Temple University. He came to the attention of John Haas in the course of his work on various civic boards and commissions in which both were involved.

One of his early actions was to institute an ongoing program of consultations between local government and private leaders in fields of social welfare, health, education, and culture to keep the foundation informed of needs and new developments. As one outcome of this process the foundation in early 1982, despite a long-established policy against crisis funding, created a temporary emergency fund to help meet the desperate needs of some Delaware Valley residents. The combination of the state of the local economy and stringent cutbacks in aid by all levels of government led to the action. In announcing the fund, Watson emphasized that foundations should do nothing to relieve government of its responsibilities to the people, but "neither can the philanthropic world blind itself to the individual's need for food, clothing, shelter, warmth, health care and such other things as may be required by many for survival." The grants under this special program have been used for such purposes as helping individuals to buy food, to make emergency heating system repairs, and to obtain otherwise unavailable care such as replacement of broken eyeglasses and aids for various physical handicaps.

By 1984, Watson had put his own mark on the foundation and had taken it several steps further in its development, including a new emphasis on collaboration with other foundations, but always with a characteristic concern for basic human needs. In its grant list for 1983, for example, such actions as the following could be noted:

1. a cooperative program with eight other foundations to provide shelter for the homeless;
2. a program in cooperation with twenty-five other foundations to provide summer jobs and vocational guidance for more than twenty-five hundred inner-city youth;
3. several projects that combined an interest in historic preservation and responsiveness to current social needs, such as a grant to renovate the mother church of the African Methodist Episcopal denomination, a designated national shrine, which is used as a summer day camp and shelter for the homeless as well as for religious services;
4. a program to provide special services to youth returning from imprisonment that has led to an 84 percent reduction in recurrence of delinquency;
5. a three-year grant to strengthen self-help groups among southwest Asian refugees;
6. a multimillion-dollar grant to the Negro Trade Union Leadership Council of Philadelphia for a youth employment program to rehabilitate facilities of nonprofit agencies; and
7. two programs to provide management training for the heads of some two hundred human services and cultural organizations.

GOVERNANCE AND FAMILY ROLE

The strong social and humanitarian concerns of the Haas family have provided the base on which the exceptional record of the William Penn Foundation has been built. They administer three large family charitable trusts with total assets roughly equivalent to those of the foundation, namely $275 million, which are operated separately from it. In the affairs of the foundation itself they also play a very strong role. For nearly forty years the donor's sons, John

C. Haas and F. Otto Haas, have given active personal leadership to its work. John, who is currently chairman of the board, meets weekly with the president to review foundation business in detail. To some extent their approach has been similar to that of most other donor families in making substantial gifts to leading local schools, hospitals, and cultural institutions. But their distinctive quality has been their determination to have the foundation serve the most basic and urgent needs of the people of the area. To keep it in touch with those needs they have been willing to make the foundation a genuinely biracial institution, and they have encouraged the staff members to be entrepreneurial and experimental, not confining themselves to the kind of safe and conventional grants that typify the programs of most locally oriented foundations.

The senior members of the family have also sought to prepare their successors to play a role in the foundation's work in the future. As a result, four of the younger generation or their spouses at any one time serve one- or two-year terms as board members as a kind of "in-service training" in philanthropy.

On the board itself, family members are, by unwritten policy, always in a minority. The composition of its seventeen members represents a good mix by race, sex, and religion. The board meets for five grant-making sessions each year and for three sessions for more general discussion of policy and procedures. Additional meetings are called as required. A spirit of serious dedication to the public interest has been fostered in the proceedings of the board: no fees are paid, and attendance at meetings is virtually 100 percent.

The foundation staff, like the board, is diverse in age, sex, and racial and ethnic background. The foundation publishes full and informative reports on its activities.

FAMILY, COMPANY, AND FOUNDATION LINKAGES

Although the Haas family is strongly represented on the foundation's board, there is no direct communication between the foundation and the company, which carries on its own program of corporate philanthropy. There does remain, however, a questionable linkage on the investment side. The various private trusts established by the donor have their assets almost entirely in shares of the Rohm and Haas Company, and this is true also of the foundation's portfolio. Moreover, the family makes no bones about its intention to maintain concentrated control over the company. For example, a spokesman for the Phoebe Waterman Foundation, Albert E. Arent, told the Senate Finance Committee during its hearings on the Tax Reform Bill of 1969 that the foundation had been created in 1945 "to establish a major philanthropy and to enable the family to satisfy their desire for such philanthropy without jeopardizing their control of the family business. . . . The company is a prime target for raiders and is protected only by the fact that as much as 49 percent of the stock can be considered in friendly hands." The foundation itself still owns 19 percent of the company shares outstanding, and the holdings of the individual members of the family plus the three family trusts presumably constitute an additional 30 percent.

This position is defended as a legitimate exercise of the rights of ownership and also on grounds of benefit to charity because the value of the assets of the foundation and of the Haas trusts has significantly increased over the years.

All in all, and despite the arguable appropriateness of the financial linkages that exist, the William Penn Foundation is probably the best family-type, locally oriented large foundation in the United States today. It operates with the benefit of a strong value framework of social concern established and maintained by the donor family; it maintains open communications with all elements of the community; it is willing to take initiatives and try unconventional projects; and it has employed strong executive heads and professional staff to carry out the foundation's work.

7

THE EVOLUTION OF TWO DYNASTIES:

The Pews and the Mellons

*The Fundamentalist Pews: Pew Memorial Trust
and J. Howard Pew Freedom Trust*

The Pews of Philadelphia have been very rich for nearly one hundred years. In their business activities, mainly oil, they have been both daring and sagacious. In their two principal sidelines, philanthropy and politics, they have been until quite recently reactionary in spirit and inferior in performance.

In the past five years, however, following the deaths of the senior members of the family, some quietly dramatic changes have taken place in their philanthropy, all for the better.

The story of the family's rise begins on a farm owned by John Pew in western Pennsylvania before the Civil War. Like five generations of Pews before him, he was a righteous, fundamentalist Presbyterian. There was only the Word of the Lord—and everlasting damnation for those who disobeyed it. As traders on the pre-Revolutionary western Pennsylvania frontier, earlier Pews had refused to sell whiskey or gunpowder to the Indians and as a result had to abandon trading altogether and become farmers. John Pew and his family were abolitionists because the Bible said slavery was evil, and they made their farm a refuge stop on the underground railway for runaway slaves escaping to Canada.

The first American oil well was struck in 1859 at Titusville, Pennsylvania, just forty miles west of John Pew's farm, and it was the oil and gas boom that subsequently developed in the area that enabled his son, Joseph Newton Pew, to become a millionaire. The young man was among the first to see the possibilities of natural gas for heating and lighting in private homes and in industrial processes. Later, after the great Spindletop strike in 1901, the Sun Oil Company he had founded shipped the Texas oil to Philadelphia, refined it, and then, because the American market at that time was virtually monopolized by John D. Rockefeller's giant Standard Oil Trust, sold the products in Europe.

He died in 1912, leaving his wealth in a trust to be administered jointly by his wife and his five children. Within three weeks of his death the six surviving Pews had met and agreed on the company's new leadership. Arthur, the oldest son, who had developed the company's European markets, was drinking himself to death, so the choice for president was J. Howard, then only thirty years old. He would hold the office for thirty-five years and see the company grow from three hundred employees to more than twenty-seven thousand by the time he died in 1971.

He was a stiff-necked, bushy-browed six-footer who had a bearing so fierce and formal that a U.S. senator once remarked about him, "He not only talks like an affidavit, he looks like one." His idea of a joke was to say that as a boy he had hated school, and so he had graduated when he was fourteen. That degree of gaiety was about the limit to which he allowed himself to go.

Aloof and dogmatic though he was, he had a gift for taking carefully calculated risks in business and a brilliant sense of timing. In 1916, in anticipation of America's entry into World War I, he constructed the Sun Shipbuilding and Dry Dock Company in Chester, Pennsylvania, and within two years was making millions from it. In the 1920s the Pews stayed away from the stock market, and after the collapse in 1929 the company was able to use its huge cash reserves as a basis for major expansion. "In many ways," J. Howard later reflected, "the Depression was the best period we ever had." He then chose precisely the right time to withdraw Sun from its European sales operations. In anticipation of World War II, be began in 1933 to sell off the company's investments on the Continent. By 1939 when war broke out, Sun was free and clear.

In the mid-1930s Sun took another gamble in supporting the research of Eugene Houdry, a French chemical engineer, who then developed a method of cracking crude oil to produce greater quantities of gasoline of higher octane quality than that of previous processes. This strategic investment, which led to what was arguably the most important industrial achievement of the 1930s, again richly profited the company.

J. Howard Pew and his wife, Helen, for all their money were plain people who lived deliberately plain lives. Once when they went to buy a new station wagon, Helen insisted they buy a black one; J. Howard suggested that perhaps they could get red wheels on it, but she objected, saying that that would make people think they had money. They did not like to entertain; their rare parties usually consisted of one other couple for dinner, followed by bridge in the upper living room until 11:00 P.M. with a break at 10:00 P.M. when ginger ale was served. Alcoholic beverages were not permitted in the house, although in 1936 when one of their three adopted children was married, they did order ten bottles of French wine to serve a reception of nine hundred guests.

In his general social outlook, J. Howard remained a rock-hard capitalist of the nineteenth-century kind. He was paternalistic, even sentimental, about his own employees. But in his views about trade unions, government regulation of business, and other economic issues, he was as absolutist and conservative as he was in his Presbyterianism.

Joseph Newton Pew, Jr., Howard's younger brother, known as Joe, was the politician of the family. He was the best suited of the brothers and sisters to deal with politics because he was the most worldly and outgoing of the five, which is to say that he was not really very worldly and outgoing but only seemed so by comparison. He entered politics in the early 1930s, supporting Franklin D. Roosevelt for president. But he turned against FDR in his first term and shifted his allegiance to the Republicans. Almost overnight J. Newton became the nation's leading Roosevelt-hater. He became convinced, as *Time* magazine put it in 1940, that the New Deal was a "gigantic scheme to raze U.S. businesses to a dead level and debase the citizenry into a mass of ballot-casting serfs." He was opposed, he said, to "Communism, Fascism, planned and dictated economies, governmental paternalism and all the other isms," and he called the U.S. government "the wickedest racket the world has ever seen."

Following the Democratic landslide in 1934 he declared, "The Republican Party stands today where the Continental Army stood at Valley Forge, and if Haym Solomon and Robert Morris could empty their purses to keep that Army alive, so can we." And so the Pews did: They gave millions to Republican presidential candidates throughout the 1930s, 1940s, and 1950s and to countless other city, county, state, and federal political campaigns.

In exchange, Joe asked for nothing except obedience and attention. Candidates who came to his office, where he sat beside an American flag and under a portrait of Abraham Lincoln, to receive their weekly or monthly campaign contributions often had to submit to hours-long lectures from him. When he came to feel the need for a wider audience, he purchased the *Farm Journal* and controlling interest in another publishing concern, the Chilton Company, to try to influence public opinion.

In contrast to his older brother's knack for good timing and success in business, Joe in politics had a real gift for poor timing and failure.

Thus in 1940 he was determined at all costs to keep Wendell Willkie from winning the Republican presidential nomination. According to his strategy, Pennsylvania's seventy-two delegates were supposed to switch their votes on the fifth ballot from their favorite son, Governor James, to Pew's conservative favorite, Senator Robert Taft, thereby breaking a convention deadlock and starting a Taft landslide that would bury Willkie. But when the fifth ballot arrived, the delegation refused to switch without direct orders from Joe, who was at his home in the Philadelphia suburbs. Frantically the Taft managers tried to reach him by telephone, but the butler told them the master was at his bath and could not be disturbed. More than half the Pennsylvania delegates thereupon switched to Willkie on the sixth ballot, thus setting in motion a bandwagon for the man Pew had spent $2 million to stop.

Indeed, over time Joe's ineptness acquired a comic quality. For example, at the 1952 Republican convention he stood up to cast his vote for General Douglas MacArthur. Absentmindedly he announced his vote for "that great General of the Army, Ulysses S.

Grant." The fact was that the family politician, if politics is the art of practical compromise, was not a politician at all but rather a polemical Presbyterian, always ready to go down with one's principles rather than to accommodate to reality. He once said, "We don't want the votes of any s.o.b. who *ever* voted for FDR." When a liberal Republican suggested that such a policy would wreck the Party, J. N. replied, "Maybe so, but we'll own the wreckage."

To the Pews their purchase of the allegiance of hundreds of legislators, congressmen, governors, county and state officials, and party workers through campaign contributions was a patriotic gesture designed to save the American people and the free enterprise system. But to a good many Americans there was something outrageous about these sanctimonious Presbyterians who spent their time preaching down to the rest of the world from their mountains of money. In 1945 Congressman Adolph Sabath called the Pews the "outstanding American Fascists."

The two sisters of J. Howard and Joe, Ethel and Mabel, were gentle, fragile, even rather pathetic people. Ethel never married, but in 1919 Mabel married H. Alarik W. Myrin, a minor Swedish nobleman she and Ethel had met during their European travels. Myrin was extraordinarily handsome and a talented bridge player. He was also a man whose Continental values clashed with the Protestant ethic of the Pews. They insisted he work for his living; Myrin insisted that work was improper for a member of the aristocracy. The Pews solved the dilemma by acquiring more than 3 million acres of ranch property in Argentina and sending the Myrins to manage it. They lived there like a feudal lord and lady for ten years. But after he and Mabel returned from Argentina in the early 1930s, Myrin never worked again. In his later years he suffered a brain disease that rendered him virtually dead, incapable even of recognizing his wife for nearly twenty years until his death in 1970.

PHILANTHROPIC MISANTHROPES

The strong religious beliefs that made the Pews so dogmatic in their social and political views also impelled them to give generously to charity and "good works."

Until 1948 their gifts were distributed as personal donations. These went in three directions: to hospitals, schools, and cultural institutions in the Philadelphia area; to Presbyterian Church activities; and to conservative organizations and publications.

In 1948, the four surviving children of Joseph N. Pew, founder of the family fortune, incorporated the Pew Memorial Trust in his memory. In addition the brothers and sisters also set up their own smaller trusts to carry out more limited programs reflecting their individual concerns. These include the Mary Anderson Trust, the Mabel Pew Myrin Trust, the J. N. Pew, Jr. Trust, the Knollbrook Trust, the J. Howard Pew Fund for Presbyterian Uses, and the J. Howard Pew Freedom Trust.

The assets of the seven principal Pew trusts have grown substantially in recent years. Including the Pew Memorial, they totaled $619 million in 1973, $1.24 billion in 1979, and over $2 billion in 1984. Of this amount, the Pew Memorial had a worth in 1984 of $1.2 billion and the J. Howard Pew Freedom Trust, the second largest, $300 million.

The Pew Memorial was given a simple and broad charter: "to help meet human needs through financial support of charitable organizations or institutions in the area of education, social services, religion, health care and medical research." The J. Howard Pew Freedom Trust was given much more specific directives reflecting the donor's strong convictions about the importance of fundamentalist Christian religion and of free enterprise. In the wording of his trust can be sensed not only the intensity of his own convictions but also his near-paranoia toward those forces that he felt were undermining the American Christian tradition.

In article three of the charter he wrote, "Settlor is conscious that enemies of freedom employ sophistry, obfuscation and semantics in order to destroy the true meaning of individual liberty and freedom.... Socialism, welfare-state-ism, Marxism, Fascism and any other like forms of government intervention are but devices by which government seeks the ownership or control of the tools of production...." More specifically, he instructed that his gift be used:

> to acquaint the American people with the evils of bureaucracy and the vital need to maintain and preserve a limited form of government in the United States ... to expose the insidious influences which have infiltrated many of our channels of publicity ... to acquaint the American people with the values of a free market, the dangers of inflation, the need for a stable monetary standard, the paralyzing effects of government controls on the lives and activities of people ... and to promote

recognition of the interdependence of Christianity and freedom. . . .

The stated purposes of the other smaller trusts were on the whole broadly charitable and nonideological.

The motive of the Pews in creating their foundations was clearly practical as well as philanthropic. At the time about 85 percent of the family fortune consisted of Sun Oil stock, which accounted for about 45 percent of the company's outstanding shares and was sufficient for the Pews to maintain control. By donating most of their Sun Oil stock to their own charitable foundations they protected themselves from substantial inheritance taxes and at the same time avoided the need to sell off large blocks of their Sun shares to pay such taxes, which would have greatly diluted the family's power over the company.

A few years later, in 1957, the family then created a private bank, The Glenmede Trust Company, to handle their personal investments and to manage their various foundations. It was felt that such an agency would not only provide more coordinated and professional management of the family's wealth but could also more effectively protect the privacy of their philanthropic activities on grounds of the confidentiality of the bank-client relationship. This strong desire to prevent public knowledge of their giving has been explained by Glenmede on grounds of the Pews' religious belief that charity is a private matter of individual conscience. In those critical of the militant conservatism of the Pews, however, the suspicion has been strong that the real purpose was to hide the use of philanthropic funds for ideological and political purposes.

Through the 1960s and the mid-1970s the head of Glenmede was Allyn Bell, a rigid, vehemently conservative individual who certainly could not be called "more Catholic than the Pope" but did appear to be more Presbyterian than even the Pews. As long as he was in charge Glenmede issued almost no information about the trusts it administered, and Bell steadfastly refused to discuss Glenmede's giving policies. At the time of the hearings on the 1969 tax bill, Bell and Glenmede lobbied vigorously against all the reforms proposed, and after passage of the act, Glenmede complied minimally with its requirements for public disclosure.

From the information that can be pieced together, however, it appears that the general pattern of the family's charitable giving did not change as a result of the creation of their foundations and of the Glenmede bank. Their numerous gifts continued to be lavished largely on the Philadelphia area, and there were few institutions of reputation in the city that were not affected. To take the year 1974 as an example, grants included $1.1 million to Lankenau Hospital, $1 million to Children's Hospital, $250,000 to Hahnemann Hospital, $375,000 to the United Fund, $220,000 to the Franklin Institute, $250,000 to the Philadelphia Lyric Opera, $40,000 to the Philadelphia Orchestra, $2.8 million to the University of Pennsylvania, and $86,000 to the local Red Cross.

In addition to support for hospitals and cultural and educational institutions the Pew trusts continued to give heavily to various religious organizations, mainly Presbyterian, but also others. In 1974 in addition to a number of grants to Presbyterian institutions, these gifts included $36,000 to Catholic Charities of Philadelphia and $35,000 to the local Federation of Jewish Agencies. Fundamentalist churches also received generous help. The Billy Graham Evangelistic Association received $100,000; the National Association of Evangelicals, $100,000; the International Congress on World Evangelization, $100,000; the Moody Bible Institute, $100,-000. Fundamentalist Presbyterian Grove City College, which for many years has been a favored Pew grantee, received $1.1 million in 1974.

The third general field of interest of the Pews and particularly of the J. Howard Pew Freedom Trust has been research and public policy institutions of conservative tendency. In 1974 the Foreign Policy Research Institute in Philadelphia received $50,000; the Christian Freedom Foundation in California, $300,000; the Hoover Institution at Stanford University, $100,000; and the American Enterprise Institute, $320,000.

Many of the institutions favored by the Pews through the 1970s received annual grants of generous amounts. Typically they made their gifts with no publicity or fanfare and indeed seemed uncomfortable and half-embarrassed if any tribute to their generosity were expressed.

The method of their giving, both in personal gifts and in grants by their foundations, was simply to send checks to institutions of their preference in their general areas of interest. There was no planning, no professional processing, no evaluation or follow-up, and no public reporting. It was old-fashioned Lady Bountiful charity on a grand scale.

In the 1960s and 1970s, that older generation of donors one by one passed away: Joe in 1963, J. Howard in 1971, Mabel Pew Myrin in 1972, and Ethel, the last, in 1979. Their charitable impulse remained strong to the very end. Without exception they left virtually all of their wealth to their philanthropies. (As a result the personal wealth of the Pews has greatly declined in the past fifteen or twenty years. *Forbes* magazine in its 1983 listing of the richest families in the United States credited the remaining Pews with only $300 million, a small fraction of the assets of the family's foundations.)

THE FORCES OF CHANGE

In the 1960s and 1970s the United States was going through profound social, economic, and political changes from which not even Philadelphia and the Pews were spared. The family itself, as the grandchildren of the founder of the empire came on the scene, began to travel different roads and adopt different life-styles. One grandson had problems with alcoholism. Another became a midget race car driver and later killed himself. The eldest daughter of J. Howard Pew married four times, her last husband being a black former disc jockey.

In political outlook the old monolithic and fervent conservatism of the family also began to crack. One younger member of the family became a free-lance writer for liberal publications such as *The Progressive* and *The Nation.* Another turned up as the Wyoming director of the 1968 presidential campaign of Senator George McGovern.

Although a good many in the fourth generation have now abandoned the stern code of their forebears, some have maintained the serious interest of the family in charity and good works. Among these are Ethel Benson Wister, granddaughter of J. N. Pew, Jr., who is active in cultural and charitable affairs in Philadelphia, and R. Anderson Pew, who will someday probably be the closest thing the Pews will have to another patriarch. In contrast to J. Howard, he is easy and outgoing in personality, and though a Republican, he occasionally has supported liberal candidates. Both are now on the board of Glenmede Trust, and "Andy" is also a board member of Sun Oil.

In addition to the general evolution of the social and political outlook of the family by the 1970s, a number of more specific events helped bring about the considerable changes in the family's philanthropy that have now taken place. One was the fact that the older generation, particularly J. Howard, had died. Another was passage of the Tax Reform Act of 1969, which forced the Pew trusts to increase the level of their grants sharply over the following years (particularly since the value of their assets also rapidly increased), to begin to divulge some information about their activities to the general public, and to diversify some of their holdings in Sun Oil.

A third was the retirement of Allyn Bell as head of Glenmede Trust in 1977. He was succeeded by Robert Smith, a young vice-president of the oil company. Smith had completed his studies at Yale University, Harvard Law School, and the Graduate School of Business at Columbia before joining the Sun Oil Company in 1957 in the accounting department. What he has accomplished since 1977 in rationalizing the procedures of the nonprofit operations of Glenmede Trust, in clarifying the program priorities of the various trusts, and in generally improving the effectiveness of their operations has to be ranked as the finest example of managerial overhaul in the field of big philanthropy in recent years. It also has to be ranked as an extraordinarily skillful and diplomatic achievement because Smith in carrying out these transformations has had to win the approval of a board on which three generations of Pews have been represented and that also includes several nonfamily individuals with long association with Sun Oil and with J. Howard.

PROGRAM REDIRECTION

Under Smith's leadership a careful step-by-step effort to review, refocus, and upgrade the grant programs of the various trusts has been made. In this process outside consultants of high standing have been drawn upon, and new and more sophisticated techniques of grant making have been employed. The traditional fields of activity of the trusts have been respected, but little by little new priorities have been identified, and marked shifts in the pattern of grants have been made. In the case of the Pew Memorial Trust, for example, beginning in 1977 grants to conservative policy–oriented organizations became fewer and by the 1980s had virtually disappeared from its grant list.

With the changeover, the foundation's concept of its role in grant making was also affected. In the first report of the Pew Memorial in 1979 a shift in attitude was hinted at, but its guard was up against any charge that it might be turning "activist": "We avoid the temptation of seeking proposals that seem to fit preconceived notions of our own design. Our primary policy is to seek out and respond to imaginative and worthwhile requests, not to create them." But two years later in the foundation's report for 1981 this had been modified to accommodate a considerably greater degree of initiative taking: "We must choose wisely those priorities where we will concentrate our grants so as to produce the greatest possible good for the largest number of people. Many philanthropic organizations over the last half century—ours included—often have reacted to applications for help rather than resolved to seek out and identify priorities, and then actively support projects in those areas."

The Pew Memorial does not yet have the self-confidence, or zeal, to take an entrepreneurial approach in attacking some of the most urgent needs and difficult problems of American society, but it seems to be moving in that direction. And in any event it has already moved in a relatively short time far beyond the condition of passivity and parochialism that characterized its grant making in earlier years.

The highest-priority field in the foundation's new program is health. Over the years the Pews had made a large number of substantial grants for capital improvements in hospitals in and near Philadelphia. Through 1979 that pattern continued, but in January 1980 the trust convened its first advisory group meeting of national leaders in health and medicine to discuss needs and specific opportunities for philanthropy. The result was a shift in emphasis from the old brick-and-mortar grants to three areas: training of health-care professionals, especially in fields of health-care policy and management; health policy research, especially on such issues as financing, organization, and cost-benefit assessments; and health services delivery, including preventive medicine on a national basis and community-based health services, particularly for the elderly. Going a step further, it joined with the Robert Wood Johnson Foundation in early 1984 to fund a major new program to serve the special health-care needs of the homeless.

After 1980 the trust stopped any further grants for hospital construction or renovation of facilities, for equipment, or for research in specific diseases. By these shifts the Memorial Trust aligned itself with the priorities of the most advanced foundations in the country in the medical and health field.

In early 1981, a year after it began the overhaul of its health programs, the trust convened another advisory group to help formulate future funding guidelines in higher education. In earlier years the grant making of the trust to colleges and universities was for general operations or capital projects. Many of the recipients were small private Christian schools, sometimes of indifferent quality. Now, on the basis of recommendations of its education advisory group, the trust has begun to identify institutions of outstanding quality in various segments of higher education. One result has been a program of grants to various private black colleges and universities. Another has been a program of grants to strengthen humanities programs at a number of colleges and universities across the country. Most recently it has launched two broad programs to assist leading individual scholars in the natural and physical sciences, the humanities, and the social services, and it has committed $3 million for a program in the Philadelphia public schools to improve the employability of students, especially blacks and Hispanics.

In the human-services field the trust traditionally had funded various conventional charitable agencies in Philadelphia. But in more recent years its grants are spread throughout the country and include such recipients as the Planned Parenthood Federation of America and the Center for Community Change in Washington, D.C., liberal and activist agencies that would never have been found on a Pew grant list even a few years earlier.

As of today, just eight years after Smith's advent to the presidency of Glenmede, new guidelines have been formulated for all of the major programs of the Pew Memorial Trust, generally with the advice of outstanding outside experts, and these are now clearly reflected in recent grants. By the time clock of philanthropy this is a remarkably rapid and sweeping change.

J. HOWARD PEW FREEDOM TRUST

The problem of bringing about similar changes in programs and procedures of the J. Howard Pew Freedom Trust, the second largest under the management of Glenmede, has been far more difficult, basically because the directives of the donor regarding its activities were rather narrow and specific.

In his effort to overhaul the various Pew trusts, to open them up to public view, and to clarify their purposes and priorities, Smith's first step was to shift more and more of their grants relating to religious activity and the encouragement of private enterprise to the Freedom Trust. The first annual report for the Pew Memorial

Trust was issued in 1979; by 1981 enough progress in working over the Freedom Trust had been made to make possible the publication of its first annual report.

In that document, Smith in his introductory president's letter presented a calm and contemporary restatement of the donor's beliefs and intentions that provided an agreeable contrast to the tough and ugly antisocial language of the old man himself. According to Smith's perfumed version, J. Howard Pew's commitments were to the free enterprise system, limited governmental regulation, the rights of American citizens, and the interdependence of Christian principles and freedom. He tactfully did not mention that J. Howard never expressed the slightest criticism of Hitler and the Holocaust or of military dictatorships in all the years that he denounced every effort of the American government to deal with unemployment, problems of civil rights, and so on.

Smith also wrote, in a statement that might surprise, even stun, those familiar with the donor's close association with various fundamentalist religious leaders who were deeply involved in politics and power brokerage in Washington, that J. Howard "vigorously disapproved of activism by churchmen, either social or political," and that he and his close friend, evangelist Billy Graham, who was at his funeral, had had their disagreements.

Smith argued, quoting such authorities as pollster Daniel Yankelovich and Yale theologian Colin Williams, that religious fundamentalism—Christian, Jewish, and Moslem—is now on the rise throughout the world because "the inner decay in our culture has left us with no clear sense of purpose." From this he took a long leap to the conclusion that nonprofit organizations, including foundations, now had to offer "even more imaginative leadership to help society create new approaches to the quality and purpose of life." Among these, Smith said, would be the J. Howard Pew Freedom Trust, administered so as to "intelligently continue its purposes in a changing society." In hooded language this seemed to be saying that the old Freedom Trust, which had long supported many of the most reactionary, militaristic, and backward-looking institutions in the country, would henceforth be looking for more reputable and responsible agencies to work through.

And indeed a review of recent grant recipients of the Freedom Trust suggests that Smith has now begun to do just that. Prominent among these are institutions like the American Enterprise Institute and the Hoover Institution, both conservative in general viewpoint but with high standards of scholarship and wide influence.

Very broadly, such public policy grants now constitute about 30 percent of the Freedom Trust's outlays. Education receives 40 percent, churches about 20 percent, and miscellaneous health-care and human services organizations such as the Boy Scouts, the Red Cross, and the Salvation Army the rest. In early 1985 it gave nearly $1 million for an emergency relief program for victims of the massive famine in Ethiopia.

There are those of course who might feel that the Freedom Trust is still extreme in its conservatism as reflected in its continuing support of the Heritage Foundation in Washington, for example. But a fair judgment would be, given the stated interests of the donor, that it is carrying them out faithfully but in a more moderate, balanced, and constructive way than was characteristic of the trust before 1977.

THE GLENMEDE INNOVATION

The philanthropic resources managed by Glenmede Trust are exceeded in scale only by those of the Ford Foundation. It is therefore a very important institution in this field.

In concept it is unique: a private profit-making bank that serves the Pew family both as its investment arm and as a kind of cooperative philanthropic service agency. The board of the bank, which is a tight in-group of family members and close business associates, not only oversees its investment operations but also serves as the board of trustees for all the eleven charitable trusts under its control, meeting six times a year to decide on grants. Likewise, a single staff of twenty-five serves as the common facility for receiving, processing, and administering all of the grants made by all of the component foundations. Their recommendations to the board on any proposal cover not only the merits of the project itself but also which foundation's funds should be used if the action is approved. The efficiency of these arrangements is very great, and the administrative costs per million dollars of grants compared to those of the great majority of other large foundations are very low.

In making the many useful changes that he has, Smith has sensed and responded to the best in contemporary thinking about foundation management and has opened up the operations of Glenmede, at least partway, to public view and outside ideas. He has kept the staff working on philanthropic activities small and flexible and has supplemented the generalist skills of the full-time employees by drawing on the advice of leading experts in the fields in which the foundations work. The Pew trusts thereby have avoided paralyzing themselves by loading their staff with heavyweight, full-time specialists.

In management style, Smith has also struck a nice balance, making the operations of the foundations more focused but at the same time avoiding overrefinement of procedures. For each of the foundations Glenmede administers, program priorities have been clearly defined, but at the same time excessively fixed and detailed criteria for guiding funding decisions have been avoided. It is recognized that the requirements of organizations differ greatly even among similar ones working on the same problems, and therefore there must be a pragmatic flexibility if the foundations are not to lose their humane qualities. The internal environment at Glenmede Trust is not quite warm and inviting—it still more resembles a bank than a social service agency—but it is not so obsessed with technocratic notions of rationality and efficiency that real productivity in philanthropic terms is sacrificed.

In substantive terms, the improvements in the programs of the Pew Foundations though considerable are somewhat less impressive. The Pew Memorial Trust and the J. Howard Pew Freedom Trust, though greatly improved, are still some distance from being great foundations. The Memorial is now competent and reputable. But in the field of health care, for example, one has only to examine the programs of the Robert Wood Johnson Foundation and the Commonwealth Fund to grasp that Pew is doing creative work but only on a patchy basis; or what Carnegie has done in education to see that Pew is not attempting to tackle the toughest issues in that field; or what the Ford Foundation and the Local Initiatives Support Corporation headed by Mike Sviridoff have been doing in housing and neighborhood development to recognize that Pew is still only a tyro in dealing with the most crucial and complex problems in the field of human services.

Smith has moved the Pew philanthropies out of parochialism and polemics and has made them professional. The question for the future is whether he and the newer generations of the family will have the motivation to go beyond respectability to distinction. One troublesome factor in assessing the future prospect is the general decline that now afflicts the Pews as a family, a decline in its economic power, in its cohesion, and in the determination of its leadership. It may be a force that on the larger national scene is now largely spent. If so, then, as in the case of the Ford Foundation, which has no base of family support or significant tradition behind it, the Pew philanthropies will have to depend essentially on the quality of their hired managers to raise their level if it is ever to be raised further.

The Patrician Mellons: Richard King Mellon and Andrew W. Mellon Foundations

The Mellon family constitutes one of the top three dynasties of the United States in wealth and also in philanthropy. They rank a rather distant second after the Rockefellers but far ahead of the generally second-rate charitable activity of the even more numerous and wealthy du Ponts.

The founder of the Rockefeller line, John D., Sr., had great interest in philanthropy, and his vision and skill in organizing his foundations were as great as his talent for business. The founder of the Mellon dynasty, old Judge Thomas Mellon, son of a destitute farmer from Poverty Point, Pennsylvania, however, was about as uncharitable a man as could be imagined. But now in the third generation of his descendants the two main branches of the family have produced three large foundations. All have become increasingly influential, two of them in traditional philanthropic work and the third in militantly ideological activities.

Of his eight children, his son Andrew most reflected the qualities of the kind of people Thomas Mellon most admired: "Solid, steady, careful men who appear to have no nonsense in their composition." His judgment was correct.

In the late nineteenth and early twentieth centuries, Andrew built on the base the judge had laid a huge financial and industrial empire. He mastered the skills of merger and corporate combination to achieve the vastly greater returns of large-scale production and monopoly. He was quick to sense the possibilities of new technology and created the Aluminum Company of America by taking over a small Pittsburgh enterprise that had the rights to a new electrical process for refining the light metal. He foresaw the possibilities of the emerging petroleum industry and with his brothers, Richard and William, organized the Gulf Oil Company.

Largely as a result of Andrew's financial genius the family today has major holdings in perhaps one hundred large American corporations, including Alcoa, Koppers, Carborundum, General Reinsurance, First Boston, and the Mellon National Bank. They hold these directly and through various holding, insurance, and investment companies, as well as their several foundations.

Andrew's private life, however, was less than brilliantly successful. He did not marry until he was in his forties, when, with unusual impetuosity, he took Nora McMullen, the vivacious daughter of a Dublin distiller, for his bride. Before they separated nine years later they had had two children, Paul and Ailsa. The divorce proceedings provided a glimpse of their bizarre marriage and of the wealth-gathering neurosis of Andrew. Nora in her deposition to the court said of Pittsburgh and her husband: "The whole community spirit was as cold and hard as the steel it made and chilled my heart to the core. . . . Nights that I spent in my baby boy's bedroom nursing these thoughts of his future, my husband, locked in his study, nursed his dollars, millions of dollars . . . always new plans, bigger plans for new dollars, bigger dollars, dollars that robbed him and his family of the time he could have devoted far more profitably to a mere single 'thank God we are living.' " The children, who were to play an important role in the eventual philanthropies of the family, had a difficult childhood, shunted back and forth between hostile parents and suffering the competing demands of the cold banker and the warmhearted Irish woman.

In the 1920s at the peak of his financial success, Andrew turned to a new career in politics. He became President Harding's Secretary of the Treasury and soon came to be regarded as the éminence grise behind Harding's economic policies, winning lavish praise from the conservative press and arousing the deep hostility of the trade unions and the farmers, who called him the spokesman of the trusts and the war profiteers.

After President Harding died and Coolidge took over, Mellon remained in his cabinet post. The new president found the secretary his own kind of man, laconic and severe. It was said they got on so well because they conversed mainly in pauses. In 1926 he engineered the passage of a tax plan that drastically cut taxes for the wealthy and provided postwar rebates to a number of leading corporations, one of which was the United States Steel Corporation, in which the Mellons were important shareholders. Its check totaled $27 million.

Andrew Mellon's political conservatism was a reflection of the primitive laissez-faire philosophy he inherited from his father and practiced in his business dealings. The Mellon companies from the beginning had a reputation for ruthlessness, even by the standards of the time, in the treatment of the laborers in their mines and mills. A critical biographer, Harvey O'Connor, has written, "If native labor was too expensive, the Mellons and their fellows used thousands of Southern and Eastern European workers imported to do the Nation's dirty work. If these in turn rebelled, the Mellons imported hordes of Negroes from the South." In 1915 a savage labor outbreak took place in a mill of the Mellon-controlled Aluminum Company of America in Massena, New York, which was broken by the employment of an army of Pinkerton gunmen and industrial spies. Later, that same company's labor policies were judged by a congressional committee to have been responsible for the bloody race riots that occurred in East St. Louis in 1917.

Through the Depression years, the Mellon companies not only were antiunion but did even less than most others to shield their discharged employees from destitution. They provided no unemployment benefits and refused all responsibility for those who were cast off. To Andrew Mellon the Depression was a passing thing, and he repeatedly said that its victims would come through the storm better disciplined by its rigors and better qualified for survival.

Although he was a nineteenth-century American capitalist of the most rapacious kind, Andrew Mellon was also attracted to the "gospel of wealth" preached by his fellow Pittsburgh millionaire Andrew Carnegie. In 1908 he and a brother founded the Mellon Institute in Pittsburgh in memory of their father. Two years later Andrew helped finance the physical rehabilitation of their father's alma mater, the rundown University of Pittsburgh. But he did little to improve its intellectual or scientific standing. Indeed there is evidence that a condition of his benefactions was compliance by the university in suppressing the teaching of doctrines considered antithetical to Mellon interests.

Then beginning in the early 1920s Mellon began to invest in

works of art, acquiring a collection of paintings of first rank importance, and this in time led to his principal philanthropic enterprise. (He made his purchases through the renowned art dealer Joseph Duveen. The story is told that Duveen made his largest single sale to Mellon by renting the apartment on the floor below him in Washington and filling it with forty-two masterpieces. He gave Mellon the key and encouraged him to look at them at his leisure, and in the evenings the silent Secretary of the Treasury, in dressing gown and carpet slippers, frequently did. After six months, he bought the entire collection with a check for $21 million.) In 1934 after Franklin Roosevelt's election he offered his collection to the government and agreed to pay the costs of a gallery to house it in Washington. Whether this was done as an act of patriotism and philanthropy or as a means of sidetracking a court action then being pressed by the federal government against Mellon for income tax evasion is a matter on which opinions differ.

In the end the Board of Tax Appeals exonerated Mellon of the government's charges. But in making his defense Mellon's lawyers had given such emphasis to his intention of establishing a national gallery that once the tax hearings were concluded Mellon could not very gracefully back out of it.

In 1930 he had set up the A. W. Mellon Educational and Charitable Trust, and from that date until his death in 1937 Mellon gave it more than $100 million in cash and works of art. The main preoccupation of the trust over the next few years, under the leadership of his two children, Paul and Ailsa, was the construction of the promised gallery, a project on which it eventually spent more than $70 million.

After World War II the remaining funds of the trust were given by his children to projects "of significance to the well being of an urban industrial community, that is, Pittsburgh." Its principal single undertaking was the establishment of a graduate school of public health at the University of Pittsburgh, to which it gave more than $13 million. The initiative was actively opposed by the American Medical Association, and at the dedication of the school in 1951 Paul Mellon delicately referred to this controversy by saying, "The medical status quo in Pittsburgh would never be the same."

The third generation of Mellons has been the most philanthropic generation. The four main figures have been the son and daughter of Andrew and the son and daughter of his brother Richard.

RICHARD KING MELLON FOUNDATION

The dominant personality of the third generation of Mellons was Richard King Mellon, son of Richard B. Mellon, who became president of the Mellon National Bank in 1934 and thereby head of the family and of its financial empire. He had been groomed for the position since childhood; ten years after he graduated from Princeton he held directorships in thirty-four major corporations and had convincingly demonstrated his skill in the management of large financial undertakings.

In manner and habits the husky and gregarious six-footer was a far cry from both his austere grandfather and his Uncle Andrew. He was also a far cry from them in his attitude toward the needs of Pittsburgh. By the outbreak of World War II the city's social and environmental problems had reached the point of disaster, and in 1943 he made a personal decision to take the lead in doing something about them. Through his powerful personal position and influence he was able to bring together the corporate elite of the area and the leaders of government in a joint endeavor to clean up and rehabilitate the grimy, rundown city. In 1962, by which time the physical and environmental achievements were clear, as well as the intractability of the remaining social problems, Richard King Mellon made a statement that might well have given apoplectic seizures to his forebears: "We businessmen must participate in the formulation of public policy even though the particular issues may not have an immediate influence on our individual businesses. This necessitates unselfish leadership and personal participation. However important the daily conduct of our business is to all of us, however demanding of our time and energy, it is clear that we cannot isolate ourselves from the universal public service demands and the social problems which surround us. We cannot get away from the fact that the very basis of our industrial society rests upon the environment in which we live."

His deepening interest in Pittsburgh's redevelopment after World War II apparently led him to establish his foundation in November 1947. To run it he set up a small board of four individual trustees and one corporate trustee, the Mellon Bank. The trustees consisted of his wife as chairman and three other close associates, one of them General Joseph D. Hughes, the paid head of its small staff. Its initial assets of $50 million were in the form of shares in Mellon-controlled companies, and its program was centered primarily on the needs of Pittsburgh and western Pennsylvania. Over the following fifteen years the foundation was used largely to plan and launch strategic projects that were subsequently executed through far larger corporate and public funds. About 80 percent of its grants during this period were spent in Pittsburgh, largely in support of its "Renaissance" redevelopment program. The most favored single recipient was the Mellon Institute, which was granted $7.7 million. The Medical School of the University of Pittsburgh received $2.5 million in this period.

By the mid-1960s, as the redevelopment program encountered resistance from the citizens of threatened ghetto neighborhoods, the foundation turned its attention to the social problems of the inner city. In its report for 1966–1968 it announced a number of grants for the specific purpose of aiding blacks and the poor. The programs ranged from remedial tutoring to training of hard-core unemployed; from recreational and cultural programs in the inner city to a mobile library to tour the slum areas with books, records, and films. To carry out these more complex social programs the foundation strengthened its full-time professional staff, and by 1968 it had in addition retained several specialized consultants in the fields of medicine and urban affairs.

Richard King Mellon died in 1970 at the age of seventy, leaving behind a steadily improving record as a philanthropist. He made his foundation a major beneficiary of his estate. In addition he gave many additional millions in anonymous personal gifts to hospitals, local universities, and other charities. He was a thoroughgoing economic and political conservative; he was also a tough pragmatist, never losing his tight control over the board of his foundation, its program priorities, or its investments. But he felt a strong sense of commitment to the improvement of his home city. He vigorously used his philanthropy to fulfill that commitment, and he was willing, when faced with the necessity, to expand his concept of his own social responsibility to include the needs of the disadvantaged.

Since his death the foundation has been ably directed by his survivors. Until her death in 1980 his wife, Constance, headed the board. Today that position is held by Richard P. Mellon, an adopted son. The other adopted son, Seward P. Mellon, is president. The rest of the board is professional, including some officers of the investment company that handles the Mellon family finances. There are now a total of eight staff members.

During its first fifteen years the foundation was concerned primarily with the physical redevelopment of Pittsburgh; during the second fifteen years it focused on "those parts of the community where the force of the Renaissance has not yet fully penetrated . . . [the] disadvantaged members of the community." The third phase, which began in 1977, marked a rather dramatic shift in program priorities: It was announced that concern for the city of Pittsburgh would continue, but as a secondary objective; the major emphasis thereafter, at least for some period of years, would be land conservation and wildlife preservation on a national basis. In the 1977 annual report the trustees stated, "The prime concern of the foundation's efforts in conservation focuses on funding acquisitions of significant natural wilderness areas, both to protect lands from development and to assist in wildlife preservation. . . . It is a consequence and reflection of the genuine concern on the part of the foundation's Trustees for preserving this country's natural heritage."

Until 1977 only about 5 percent of the foundation's grants were given to conservation. But in that year it allocated 42 percent of its total outlays to this purpose, most of it going to the Nature Conservancy in Arlington, Virginia. The percentage of such grants has increased steadily ever since. In 1980 the board approved a $15 million grant to the Nature Conservancy for a ten-year "Rivers of the Deep South" project. In 1982, after a reexamination of the program, it was decided to make education the number two priority after conservation and to increase the emphasis on social service and civic grants.

All of the grants of the foundation except conservation projects are limited to Pittsburgh and western Pennsylvania, and some of these are substantial: the University of Pittsburgh, for example, received five grants in 1981, totaling $1.5 million.

In January 1983 an additional grant of $25 million to the Nature Conservancy was announced. The funds were to be devoted to the National Wetlands Conservation project to "identify critical areas from the Atlantic coastal wetlands to the forests of Hawaii."

Although the primary focus of the foundation's new program is on land acquisition and wildlife preservation, it also includes grants "to enhance the skills of rural communities to protect their historic, natural, agricultural and scenic assets by providing technical advice and guidance." In addition the foundation has funded studies of land policy issues and of environmentally sound industrial siting.

Since 1970 the foundation's assets have increased substantially, from $160 million to $490 million, partly through good investment management and partly through additions to its corpus from the donor's estate. It is communicative with the public and issues excellent annual reports. It has on the whole become an intelligently managed and increasingly effective institution of steadily improving reputation and influence not only among the more traditional environmental organizations but also the more activist.

The Scaife Foundation, created by Richard Mellon's other child, Sarah Mellon Scaife, is not in the size category that is the focus of this study, but it is substantial in size and, as dicussed in Chapter 3, has become very influential as an ideologically conservative foundation.

ANDREW W. MELLON FOUNDATION

The Richard Mellon branch of the family has stayed in Pittsburgh; however, the children of Andrew, Ailsa and Paul, long ago, physically and otherwise, got out. After their father went to Washington during the Harding administration, his interests were never again limited to the affairs of his home city. And his children, with their mother in Europe and their father in the national capital, developed a worldliness and a range of cultivated tastes far removed from the smudge of coal mining and the grime of steelmaking.

Their father died in 1937, leaving a huge inheritance to each of them. Both within a few years had set up foundations, Ailsa her Avalon Foundation in 1940 and Paul his Old Dominion Foundation a year later. Each reflected the particular interests and in a way the complex personality of its founder. While her father was secretary of the Treasury Ailsa had been a social star on the Washington scene. Her marriage in 1926 to a handsome young foreign service officer and son of a Maryland senator, David K. E. Bruce, was the most brilliant the city had seen in years. (Her father reportedly gave the young man a dowry of $10 million "so that he could feel financially independent.") The couple had one daughter before the marriage broke up. David went on to a distinguished career in diplomacy and public life; Ailsa retired from public view and never remarried. The last years of her life were shattered with tragedy when her daughter and son-in-law were killed in an airplane accident.

Her brother Paul, even as a young man, showed no interest in business and preferred scholarly pursuits. He won top prize for excellence in English literature at Yale and went on to become editor of its literary magazine. Later, at Cambridge University in England, he developed a taste for collecting art and first editions. (His initial interest in philanthropy appears to have been the result of psychiatric treatment that he and his first wife underwent at the hands of the great C. G. Jung in Switzerland. "We have all this money," she cried out to Jung at one point, "and don't know what to do with it." His suggestion was that they set up a foundation to publish books like his, and they did: the Bollingen Foundation, named after Jung's Swiss retreat. Since 1969 its publishing activities have been taken over by the Princeton University Press.)

The Avalon Foundation, with a small board that included Ailsa and Paul, gave money to programs in medicine and health, education, the fine arts, conservation, and civic and youth programs. The latter aspect was a reflection in part of the strong interest of Ailsa's daughter and son-in-law in contemporary social issues. Their own small foundation, Taconic, was very influential in promoting civil rights in the 1950s and 1960s.

Paul's Old Dominion Foundation devoted itself to the humanities and higher education, the fine arts, mental health, conservation, and special projects in Virginia, where he has long lived in the lavish style of country gentleman, horseman, and generous patron of the arts. A large proportion of its grants went to prestigious institutions of higher education, mainly his own alma mater, Yale.

In early 1969, Mrs. Bruce fell seriously ill, and her foundation and her brother's were merged into a newly formed Andrew W. Mellon Foundation, named after their father. Two months after its formation she died. Paul Mellon became the controlling figure of the merged institution, whose assets were subsequently greatly increased by a bequest from her estate.

At the time it was not clear what kind of direction and leadership he would be able to give it. The first indications were not exciting. To head the new foundation, Dr. Nathan Pusey, who had just completed a rather undistinguished term as president of Harvard, was chosen. During his brief four-year term, the foundation distributed the bulk of its grants to various Ivy League schools to strengthen them in various ways: to endow chairs in the humanities, to give college presidents some discretionary funds, to subsidize their book-publishing activities, to strengthen their libraries, to improve faculty salaries, and to strengthen theological education, a special interest of Pusey that he had tried unsuccessfully to accomplish at Harvard. The foundation also made grants for buildings and general support to a few medical schools and spent large sums to acquire land for public park purposes. Perhaps the most unusual of its grants in this period were those to twelve major urban universities to strengthen their teaching in the liberal arts for students with strong vocational interests. During these early years it also closed out the various civic, youth, and commmunity programs that had been supported by the Avalon Foundation, activities that were obviously of no interest to Paul Mellon.

The grant pattern under Pusey was with few exceptions an extension of the interests and priorities of Paul Mellon's Old Dominion Foundation: the same kinds of gifts to the same institutions for the same purposes. The program was quiet, uncontroversial, and unexceptional, and it seemed that Paul Mellon with the enlarged resources at his command was going to be the kind of practitioner of middle-of-the road and middling philanthropy that had been an earlier Mellon trademark. But in fact he has turned out to be a much more significant figure.

In the field of art, he has become the nation's premier patron. Through personal gifts of money and paintings he established at Yale the largest and finest collection of British art in the world outside the Tate Gallery in London. With a multimillion-dollar gift, he helped build a new wing on the Virginia Museum of Fine Arts in Richmond and endowed it with a fine collection of paintings by French Impressionists. Most recently he presented ninety-three works of art to the National Gallery that constitute a major addition to its collections. In addition, by personal gifts from himself and his sister, and with nearly $40 million of grants from the A. W. Mellon Foundation, he was the moving force in bringing the magnificent new East Wing of the National Gallery in Washington into being, possibly the most stunning single achievement of American architecture of the decade.

His decision in 1975 to name John Sawyer, then president of Williams College, to succeed Pusey as head of the A. W. Mellon Foundation has proved to be a solid contribution to that institution's effectiveness. Because of the leadership he has given it, Sawyer has now become one of the most admired and influential foundation heads in the country.

Sawyer, once an economic historian at Yale, proved to be a perfect match for Paul Mellon's philanthropic interests and preferred style of operation. He also fully shared the concerns that had preoccupied Pusey about the serious difficulties facing colleges and universities in the United States because of inflation, the prospective decline in student population, and continuing budgetary shortfalls. In its general scope and priorities, the foundation's program, therefore, did not change after his advent. Higher education, especially the preeminent private institutions, has since received the highest percentage of its gifts, more than half of the total, to strengthen scholarly and teaching programs, particularly in the humanities. Major commitments have been made to support research and to strengthen scholarly research libraries and library networks. Some help has also been provided to subsidize the publication of new works in the humanities.

More recently, in addition to its gifts to the most prestigious private "research universities," the foundation has extended its work in higher education to some sixty smaller liberal arts colleges to assist them in faculty development and in securing a greater volume of endowment gifts.

The second major thrust of the foundation's program has been in the arts. In addition to its contribution to the expansion of the National Gallery, the foundation has made a number of sizable grants to leading symphony orchestras, music conservatories, opera companies, and ballet and theatre groups, all carefully designed to stabilize and strengthen their financial position.

A third area of interest has been health, medicine, and population. The present focus is on research and on the development of research scientists. In the field of population problems, research on reproductive biology and the support of promising younger scientists at fourteen major centers of advanced work have been emphasized.

PHILOSOPHY AND STRATEGY

Although the edges are a little fluid in places, the core of the Mellon Foundation's program is clearly defined and stable. In its major emphases it is not unique: a number of other major foundations concentrate on the same kinds of institutions in the same fields. But what are distinctive are the coherence of its program rationale and strategy, its pursuit of long-term goals, and the consistency of its quest for quality in the selection of its grantees.

The foundation's underlying philosophy and its grant-making strategy have been set forth clearly in Sawyer's presidential essays in the foundation's annual reports. His approach rests fundamentally on a belief in Alfred North Whitehead's maxim "In the conditions of modern life the rule is absolute, the race which does not value trained intelligence is doomed." This in turn requires that the very highest priority be given to sustaining the valued elements of our cultural heritage and key institutions of the society. In Sawyer's view, "Knowledge provides the foundation for all human achievement. . . . This capacity rests on an interconnected array of educational institutions that develop human talents, nurture ability to learn, and sharpen critical thought; research institutions that generate new data, ideas and conceptual systems; and arts institutions that add perception, color and depth . . . in the culture."

Having thus defined the critical elements of the "social infrastructure" that must be sustained, the Mellon Foundation has chosen as the segment with which it will primarily work those at the high end of the spectrum of excellence and prestige, and within those institutions, individuals of the greatest talent and promise.

It is Sawyer's conviction that to strengthen important institutions, encourage basic research, and nurture activities of the highest quality in education and the arts, the funding provided by a foundation must be both adequate and predictable: "It is critical that a course be set, made known, and sensibly sustained."

He gives great emphasis to the dimension of time: the response time of foundations in making their decisions, the time horizon toward which funding is directed, and the timing of grants in relation to the fluctuations in funding from other sources. In his view foundations can be particularly helpful when their support is provided "countercyclically," to ease disruptions in the flow of other institutional support, especially the surges from time to time in government funding.

Sawyer feels independent foundations also

have an opportunity—and perhaps a special responsibility—to support programs, institutions or causes that lie beyond the reach of personal or regional philanthropy; or that may be out of favor, or too sensitive, value laden, or esoteric to be a proper field for government; or that require a time perspective stretching beyond the reach of other funding sources. Individual donors and local organizations can respond to needs with immediate appeal. But neither government nor individual donors are a logical or predictable funder of such activities as the sensitive long term research needed in reproductive biology to develop methods diverse cultures will find satisfactory for limiting the population explosion that threatens all economic progress in the Third World. Likewise neither is likely to support for 30 years primary research on the deterioration of organic materials used by artists, the paints, pigments and varnishes, the books and paper that carry so much of our culture. . . .

ACTION AND REACTION

There are those in philanthropy, both admirers and critics, who see Mellon in its program and approach as traditional, uncontroversial, elitist, and purely reactive.

In its three basic fields of activity most of these adjectives would seem to apply: it works mostly with established institutions of high quality and prestige, it avoids controversy, and its style is conservative. But the Mellon model is more complex, and entrepreneurial, than might at first appear. In fact about two thirds of its outlays are spent, after much listening and consultation with others, on program initiatives of its own design.

To clarify this seeming contradiction, a rather typical example can be cited. In early 1980 it launched what it called a "Funds for the 1980's" project. Sawyer then wrote to a number of university presidents as follows:

This letter outlines a program the Foundation has under consideration to help, on a one-time basis, a limited number of leading independent universities and colleges meet particular needs of the 1980's. . . .

We start from the premise that three converging problems confront many institutions with an acute set of pressures in the 1980's: (1) high rates of inflation and new economic uncertainties; (2) the skewed age distribution of most faculties, reflecting the bulge in past faculty hiring and tenure commitments that results in few retirements in the next several years but substantially more after 1987–1988; and (3) the effect of the declining number of 18-year-olds on projected enrollments and thus on academic job opportunities.

This combination of events, as you well know, threatens

the flow-through and advancement of able young talent needed to sustain inquiry in important fields of knowledge and to provide future leadership in academic institutions. . . .

Against this background . . . we propose a program of spendable grants, for use over the next seven to ten years, that would be designed in part to utilize the higher interest rates inflation has caused. Investment of grant funds at 8 to 12 percent, for example, with both principal and interest expended over the period, should make possible annual withdrawals ranging from 15 to 20 percent of the original amount—roughly three or four times the probable yield of straight endowment. . . . Funds of this nature could provide a third revenue stream, supplementing annual giving on the one hand and endowment income on the other, to address critical bridging needs in the 1980's.

We would propose to make our funds available for any of four uses, or for combinations thereof: (1) to appoint or promote junior or intermediate-level faculty members in anticipation of the retirements now expected in the late 1980's; (2) to assist faculty members in early or mid career either to receive further training and to deepen their grasp of substance or methods in their current fields or to shift to fields where prospects are greater; (3) to encourage and facilitate early or partial retirements; and (4) to provide postdoctoral fellowships or, in special circumstances, dissertation support as required to maintain an appropriate flow of the best younger talent through graduate schools and onto a faculty ladder. We would offer the institutions discretion in allocating our funds to these purposes within traditional fields of the humanities (including history) or within interdisciplinary programs drawing heavily on the humanities. . . .

If the program and conditions set forth are acceptable . . . we shall need at least a preliminary statement of plans for the management and use of the proposed grant. . . .

In this formulation there is a blend of considerable directiveness by the foundation and of considerable discretionary authority by the applicants. It is a kind of grant making that is both responsive and entrepreneurial, a picture in shadings and not black and white.

QUALIFIED CONSERVATISM

Likewise, the image of Mellon as a deeply conservative foundation, an image Sawyer deliberately or inadvertently nurtures, is not quite accurate.

In his own writings, Sawyer carefully avoids the liberal buzz-words *compassion, equal opportunity,* and *democratization.* He is, on the other hand, outspokenly contemptuous of "naïve activism," "short term political maneuvering, newly sophisticated manipulation by special interests and diversions offered by the media" as means of dealing with national problems.

When he mentions the major goals on which "most Americans would agree," as he did in his 1981 annual report, he cites "a productive high-employment economy, a healthy environment, and a people educated and motivated to realize their best potentials under conditions of reasonable security, internal and external." But he makes no mention of fairness, equal opportunity, or equal protection of the laws, goals on which a large proportion of Americans have also been agreed for a good many years.

Yet if one listens for other sounds through the tough talk, some can be heard. Since Sawyer's arrival there has been a slow but steady increase in the number of grants addressed to public policy issues in such fields as population control, economic research, and environmental protection. There has also been a growing number of grants to urban universities, colleges in Appalachia, and black colleges, which touch on problems of the disadvantaged in American life.

In his essay in the 1982 annual report, he went so far as to say:

If a nation's attitude toward education is indeed a key to its future, American elementary and secondary education must receive sharply increased attention. The more we move into an information-based, high-technology economy, the more critical become the skills and the educational qualifications—and the need for access to them—that the society requires. To remain "one nation indivisible," we must recognize as major unfinished business the necessity of providing ladders of educational opportunity for sectors of our society that will otherwise be left farther and farther behind. Just as the United States cannot afford monetary and fiscal policies that leave a third of our manufacturing plants idle and unemployment around ten percent, so it cannot enter the next century as a prosperous and progressive leader of the Atlantic democracies if it fails to provide real opportunities for what could become an excluded, growing, and demoralized underclass.

The spirit might have been more one of fear of than sympathy for the disadvantaged, but an evolution of the foundation's concerns in the direction of some of the nation's most pressing social issues was becoming unmistakable.

In his essay for the 1983 report Sawyer went a step further. He announced that the foundation would direct more attention to the secondary school field and to the special needs of "ill-prepared minorities" in the school-age population. In that regard the foundation appropriated $2.1 million to provide partial scholarship help to allow some 250 highly promising Hispanic high school graduates to go on to colleges or universities. He also suggested that the foundation might urge the federal government to provide incentives to state and local governments to encourage able college graduates to become public school teachers and to strengthen high school teaching programs in mathematics and science.

In an almost challenging statement to the Reagan administration he wrote that

> we are in danger of approaching our 200th [anniversary] with a serious underestimation of the crucial role of the Federal government in much that has been accomplished since 1789— and thus of undervaluing the importance of sustaining its positive role in the public-private partnership on which national unity and a prosperous and humane future will depend . . . thus, it is puzzling to hear it now said that there is no proper role for the national government in helping states and localities and the private sector address educational deficiencies. . . .

THE MELLON MODEL

A good many other large foundations in an instinctive and sometimes incoherent fashion seek to support traditional institutions, research, and scholarships—the programs Mellon mainly supports. But none of them has articulated the premises, the strategy, and the purposes of that activity in the reasoned way that Sawyer has. In this sense, he and the Mellon Foundation represent the leading example of intelligent conservative philanthropy in the best traditional and philosophical sense of that term.

Moreover, in the translation of its concepts into a grant-making program, the performance of the Mellon Foundation has been if anything even more impressive. Sawyer's management of the institution has been exemplary. His relationships with his small and prestigious board have been excellent. The foundation distributes some $60 million of grants annually with a professional staff of only six and a total staff of only seventeen, so its administrative costs are remarkably low. Its investment portfolio has been very well managed, and its assets today are just over $1 billion, making it one of the ten largest foundations in the country.

In a rather turbulent time for philanthropy, in which some former leaders have lost their luster and there is much uncertainty and confusion, the example of the Mellon Foundation has increasing appeal for a good number of troubled foundation heads.

In considerable part the prestige that Mellon has now acquired is due to the style and stature of Sawyer. He is a man of "presence" who inspires respect and confidence in those who deal with him: colleagues in the philanthropic world, heads of various kinds of nonprofit institutions, members of the business community and others. However intangible these qualities, taken together they have great weight. The Mellon Foundation with the same program priorities and operating methods but without the hand of Sawyer at the helm would be a far less influential institution in the field of philanthropy and nonprofit activity generally than it has now become.

8

CALIFORNIA COMES ON STRONG:

Kaiser, Hewlett, Irvine, Weingart, Keck, and Hilton

California, now the largest state in the Union in terms of population, is vigorously growing and rapidly changing. It is also widely regarded as the source from which many of the new political, social, and economic trends in the nation derive.

Large individual fortunes have now been acquired in various industries including oil, real estate, hotels, aviation, and more recently, electronics. In a number of cases these have been converted into large foundations. The largest, the J. Paul Getty Trust, is an *operating foundation* (a foundation that spends all its income to operate its own museum or research laboratory, for example, and does not make grants to others) and is not dealt with in this study. But six other California foundations are already in the quarter-billion dollar or greater class. Two of them, Henry J. Kaiser and James Irvine, are in the older group, having been established in the 1930s and

1940s. Four others—William and Flora Hewlett, Ben Weingart, William Keck, and Conrad Hilton—are in the younger group, all having been activated more recently. Three are fully functioning; three are in their formative stage. Their quality is extremely mixed, from very good to very poor.

Henry J. Kaiser Family Foundation

Over the past fifteen years, no large American foundation has improved itself and its program more than the Kaiser Foundation. With recent leadership changes of both the board and staff, it may now take off in somewhat new directions and could become an even more prominent presence on the national health-care scene.

At the beginning of the 1970s Kaiser was a foundation with a highly concentrated portfolio of shares in Kaiser companies, a board made up essentially of family members and company executives, and without professional program staff or defined program. It received almost no income from its assets, gave out extremely little in grants, and issued no public reports. It was in fact a striking example of some of the kinds of abuses that led to passage of the Tax Reform Act of 1969. Since that time it has come a long way to the right direction, but the road has had a few bumps.

THE DONOR

The donor, Henry J. Kaiser, was a man of prodigious energy and ingenuity, one of the great builders and entrepreneurs in modern American history. A high school dropout from upstate New York, he began his business career as an errand boy in a dry goods store. By the time he died at the age of eighty-five, he had built a multi-billion-dollar group of companies that operated 180 plants in thirty-two states and forty-four countries and employed more than 900,000 workers.

In 1906 at the age of twenty-four, having decided to stake his future in the West, Kaiser moved to Spokane, Washington, and entered the construction field. He quickly developed a reputation as a road builder by using new production methods and by doing jobs better and faster than his competitors. In the late 1920s he completed a two-hundred-mile, five-hundred-bridge highway project in Cuba; in the 1930s, the era of the big dams, he headed a consortium of companies that built the Hoover Dam in four years (two years ahead of schedule) and then Bonneville and Grand Coulee.

By World War II his construction company was building roads, bridges, dams, and pipelines all over America and had also set up a large cement-producing subsidiary. When the Allies desperately needed ships, Kaiser applied his innovative methods to shipbuilding, and by 1945 his company had built some 1,490 cargo vessels, roughly 30 percent of American wartime production of merchant shipping, plus 50 small aircraft carriers.

After the war Kaiser entered the aluminum business, developed extensive operations in chemicals and fertilizers, and established the first fully integrated iron and steel complex in the American West. He also established the Kaiser Jeep Corporation, the Kaiser Broadcasting Corporation, and the Kaiser Aerospace and Electronics Corporation, all of them highly successful in his lifetime. When he died in 1967, he was busy building the new community of Hawaii Kai in Honolulu for sixty thousand residents.

Henry J. Kaiser was single-minded in his devotion to business; he had little time for politics or philanthropy. Yet some major projects he undertook for farsighted but practical business reasons had important social side effects. To increase the productivity of his steel plants, for example, he created innovative incentive plans and protected his employees against technological displacement. (The AFL-CIO as a result awarded him a special medal for "treating the worker as a human being.")

His most important social contribution was his "Kaiser Permanente Medical Care Program," a classic demonstration of Adam Smith's contention that the best things businessmen do for human well-being are done out of motives of profit, not charity. Kaiser became aware of the relationship between health care and worker productivity in the 1930s when he was building pipelines and dams in remote locations far away from hospitals and doctors. Later one of the greatest problems faced by his shipyards in meeting their war production goals was absenteeism due to illness. In order to keep his workers healthy and on the job, Kaiser built health clinics at a number of his production sites. The financing for them was provided out of government contracts because their cost was accepted as a bona fide operating expense. After the war the clinics and their equipment were declared surplus war property. The Kaiser Hospital

Foundation was established by Kaiser and his wife, Bess, to buy the facilities at a small pecentage of their original cost and make them available to the general public.

With an initial contribution of $200,000 the Kaiser Medical Plan was born, based on five fundamental principles: voluntary membership open to the public, prepayment for services, group medical practice, emphasis on preventive services, and interrelated hospitals and medical offices. To ensure that the plan would be self-supporting, Kaiser created three separate cooperating entities: the Health Plan itself, which enrolls subscribers and collects their payments; the Hospital Foundation, a tax-exempt entity that finances and operates the hospitals and clinics; and the Medical Group Organization, which now consists of hundreds of doctors organized into their own partnerships. Based on this ingenious combination of industrial management concepts and financial planning in the field of health services, the plan has now become the world's largest private system of prepaid medical care. It operates thirty-one hospitals, with a total of 6,770 beds and more than 110 medical clinics in ten states and the District of Columbia. Over 4.5 million persons are enrolled in the plan, and the numbers are still growing. Currently the program is being expanded into North Carolina and Georgia.

The California Medical Association fought the plan for years because of its group practice aspect, but over time it has established its economic viability and also a reputation for providing high-quality health services. By the 1970s with the upward spiraling of health-care costs, the Kaiser plan became the model for a major government effort to create similar health maintenance organizations (HMOs) throughout the country.

CREATION OF THE FOUNDATION

The foundation received its initial resources from Mrs. Kaiser, who died in 1951. Their younger son, Henry J., Jr., died of multiple sclerosis in 1961 and left it most of his estate. When Henry Kaiser, Sr. died in 1967, he further increased its assets.

In the late 1960s, Edgar Kaiser, the sole surviving son and head of the Kaiser companies, asked George D. Woods on his retirement as head of the World Bank to become chairman and chief executive officer. By 1970 a program had been roughed out: The primary emphasis would be on the extension of the Kaiser Medical Care Program, plus a lesser emphasis on community problems in the San Francisco–Oakland Bay Area. At the time the assets of the foundation had a value of some $200 million, all in Kaiser stock. But within two years the shares fell from a price of $20 to about $4, another example of the potentially catastrophic results that can result from an undiversified portfolio.

At that inauspicious moment, Dr. Robert Glaser was persuaded to become president of the foundation. Its real development begins with the date of his arrival.

Glaser came to the post with an excellent reputation as a scientist and medical educator. He had taught at Harvard and was later dean of the Stanford medical school, the temple of high-tech medicine in the United States. He then served as vice-president of the Commonwealth Fund, a medically oriented foundation in New York City, where he had greater exposure to the serious social and economic problems of the national health-care system.

As a knowledgeable person in the field, Glaser after his arrival at Kaiser promptly staked out the areas in which he felt it should operate. The basis of its program would continue to be to strengthen and extend the system of prepaid medical care pioneered by the Kaiser family, but in addition the foundation would make grants for medical education, health policy research, improving the management of health-care institutions, and controlling health-care costs.

Before the new program could be implemented, however, Glaser had to address a number of prior problems. First, he had to get some help. At the beginning there was only one other professional on the staff, the treasurer, so program personnel had to be recruited. Second, he had no money to spend, because the foundation had no cash income. During the first year, the trustees were able to sell enough of the Kaiser shares in a private placement so that a modest program of grants could be started, and within two years it proved possible to raise the annual level to $2 million.

The board also had its problems, including the need to overhaul its membership. After Glaser's arrival George Woods remained as board chairman, concentrating his attention for the next several years on reorganizing and in some cases selling off the various Kaiser companies in which the foundation was a major shareholder. In 1977 several of these enterprises were disposed of for cash, which the foundation then profitably reinvested. More than half of its assets were still in shares of Kaiser companies, however, and in the early 1980s a decision was taken to dispose of these holdings in an orderly way. As a result of these efforts the income and the grants of the foundation by 1980 had risen to some $14 million annually.

The makeup of the board was also gradually changed, so that it came to consist of a majority of nonfamily, noncompany members, including several individuals of national prominence such as Gerard Piel, publisher of *Scientific American*, Kingman Brewster, former president of Yale University and ambassador to Great Britain, and Joseph Califano, secretary of Health, Education and Welfare under President Carter.

As the foundation's program reached full development, its principal features and accomplishments were its large-scale support for the expansion of the Kaiser Permanente Medical Care Program, the funding of the program of fellowships in general internal medicine at a number of leading universities, major grants to several business schools for programs in health-care administration and management, and support for increasing minority enrollment at medical schools. In addition, some grants were directed to studies of medical ethics, strengthening of the hospice movement for care of the terminally ill, and cost-benefit analyses of new medical technology.

As the end of the 1970s approached, the leadership of the board weakened, Woods and Edgar Kaiser having had a falling-out that led to Woods's resignation as chairman. Then Edgar Kaiser, who had long served as vice-chairman, was stricken with a very painful and debilitating form of cancer, which made it impossible for him to play a strong role in the brief period until his death.

Perhaps because of the vacuum created by their disappearance, strains and division among the other trustees became severe. Some of these related to program priorities, a few trustees feeling that the foundation's work had become too diffuse and that it should concentrate largely if not entirely on the expansion of prepaid medical care systems. But there were others who strongly objected to such a shift and endorsed fully the existing pattern of the foundation's work.

Some separation between Glaser and a few members of the board also developed. This related as much to style as to substance, but it was nonetheless serious. Virtually everyone recognized that Glaser had made a great contribution to the foundation's development and to its reputation for quality and integrity. But he was a man of low-key, conservative style: self-effacing himself and not disposed to seek public visibility for the foundation. Some trustees were therefore quite frustrated that it was not recognized as more of a force nationally.

Edgar Kaiser died in late 1981, and his son, Edgar, Jr., became board chairman that same year. His advent contributed to the rift because young Edgar was among Glaser's critics, and he is not by temperament inclined to leave those under his authority a free hand, as his tumultuous career as an executive in several Kaiser companies repeatedly demonstrated. In any event, Glaser left as he had planned in 1983, having completed ten years as president, to become head of another large foundation then in an early stage of formation.

The Kaiser board chose as the new president Alvin R. Tarlov of the University of Chicago medical school, who had come to prominence in the early 1980s because of his brilliant direction of the Graduate Medical Education National Advisory Committee (GMENAC) in Washngton, Its report to the Secretary of Health and Human Services in 1980, based on a massive two-year study of future needs for physicians and the prospective future supply, had been a bombshell. It demonstrated that unless major changes in medical education were made, the country would have a surplus of physicians by the end of the century, that there would be too many surgeons and therefore too much surgery, and that there would be a serious shortfall of graduates willing to serve as family doctors.

The report made more than one hundred recommendations for action, and Dr. Tarlov in the widespread public and professional debate that followed quickly established himself as a strong personality and a new leadership factor in the health-care field.

To some of the discontented members of the Kaiser board, he seemed the perfect head for the kind of program they wanted the foundation to pursue: an individual highly respected by the medical profession, deeply involved in the large issues of health care and health policy, and an activist and innovator. At the same time, he was no radical, not even antiestablishment. His GMENAC, though it included some members from nursing, law, hospital administration, and insurance, had been made up mostly of physicians. The reforms it proposed and Tarlov advocated envisaged collaboration between the medical profession and government and reliance on voluntary cooperation, not government regulation. On the other hand, those trustees of the foundation who wanted it to be essentially a banker to help extend the Kaiser Health Care Plan had some doubts about the course Tarlov might take.

The trustees gave Tarlov the year following his appointment to look over the entire health field and to identify the critical problems on which he felt the foundation should concentrate.

His recommendations to the board presented in late 1984 included a number of important program shifts. Support for the development and improvement of HMOs, because of their continued rapid growth as a factor in the national health-care system, would continue at a significant level. Several existing programs would be dropped as part of a strategy to develop a more sharply targeted effort. The major new thrust would be a wide-ranging attempt to improve the nation's health by changing injurious individual behavior patterns such as smoking, poor diet, and alcohol abuse. Tarlov is deeply concerned that a very large proportion of health-care costs now go for the treatment of such "self-inflicted" damage and he is convinced that investment of foundation funds in programs to improve health habits and self-care will pay much larger dividends than further investments in the health-care system itself.

Consistent with this general approach, he is greatly interested in measuring the *outcomes* of present medical care: their effectiveness in restoring the mental and physical function of patients and their ability to live an independent life. In this his ideas run parallel to those of the Robert Wood Johnson Foundation; and he indeed brought to his post a $5 million Johnson grant, which the Kaiser Foundation is matching, for a major study that will try to measure the results of medical treatment in these new terms.

The board solidly endorsed Tarlov's proposals in principle, and he and the staff are currently at work trying to design programs that can translate the concepts into effective action.

In its new program, Kaiser will probably shift to a more activist and aggressive, and probably controversial, style. Already the board has become more unified, and board relationships with the staff have reportedly improved. If so, Kaiser under Tarlov's leadership may now become more of a seen and felt factor on the national scene.

Hewlett Foundation

The Hewlett Foundation of California, with assets now of $600 million and rising, is the first major new foundation created on the basis of wealth acquired in the booming business of high technology. At least one more will be coming along shortly: donor Hewlett's partner in the development of the Hewlett-Packard Company, David Packard, has already established his foundation and has begun to assemble its board and staff and block out its program. Within the next few years it may well surpass Hewlett in the scale of its resources. *Fortune* magazine, in August 1983, reported that the surge in stock market prices in the preceding eight months had increased Hewlett's personal fortune by $600 million and that of Packard by $1.2 billion.

The young Hewlett Foundation, which has been in full operation only since 1977, has been in a process of extremely rapid growth—its grant level has risen from $2.5 million in 1977 to $31 million in 1983—but it has nonetheless already acquired a reputation for competence and quality in its work.

The donor, William Hewlett, is the son of a former professor of medicine at Stanford University. He took a degree in liberal arts from Stanford, completed a master's degree in science at the Massachusetts Institute of Technology, and then returned to Stanford for a degree in electrical engineering.

At Stanford he became close friends with an engineering classmate, David Packard, and in 1939 with $538 in capital borrowed from a Palo Alto bank they established their first "plant" in a small local garage. Their product was an audio oscillator based on a design by Hewlett. From the beginning, Hewlett was the detached analytical thinker, the technological innovator, in the partnership; Packard was the businessman.

When Hewlett returned from army duty in 1947, the Hewlett-Packard Company was incorporated. Their venture has since become one of the legendary success stories of American industry. The company today is a major designer and manufacturer of precision electronic equipment for measurement, analysis, and computation. It employs seventy thousand people and has annual sales of more than $4 billion.

The firm's extraordinary growth and profitability have been attributed by many to its distinctive internal culture embodying the styles and values of the two founders. The "HP Way," as company documents describe it, emphasizes high quality, innovative products, "management by wandering around and an open door policy," "belief in our people," and "honesty and integrity in all matters."

Hewlett is an example of the new kind of entrepreneur who

has come to the fore in the era of high technology. In contrast to the rugged individualists of limited education and social outlook who fought their way out of poverty to success in earlier times, he came from a family in comfortable circumstances. He was highly educated, sophisticated in social outlook, and active in civic and social affairs. Keenly interested in education, he served for many years as a trustee of Stanford University and Mills College. He has been deeply involved in health matters, having been board president of the Stanford Medical Center, a director of the Kaiser Health Plan board, and a member of the Drug Abuse Council in Washington, D.C.

Of special relevance to his role as foundation donor is that he was for ten years on the Distribution Committee, the grant-making body, of the San Francisco Foundation. As a result, when the time came for him to set up his foundation, he went at the task in an unusually sensible and knowledgeable way, certainly when compared to that of most donors.

Initially he endowed it with $20 million of Hewlett-Packard stock, and from 1966 to 1972 he distributed its grants from his corporate office with the help of his personal secretary. The money went to the purposes in which he and his wife were interested, namely education, religion, and the environment. The outdoors has been his lifelong hobby, and he is an avid skier, mountain climber, fisherman, photographer, and amateur botanist.

By early 1973, with the flow of paperwork increasing, he took the first steps to convert the desk drawer operation into a more organized form. To judge from the record, he wanted the foundation to be a family one in the sense that he and his wife would direct its work along with their three sons and two daughters, to the extent they were interested. At the same time he recognized that he needed some professional advice as he proceeded, and for this he turned to John May, former director of the San Francisco Foundation, with whom he had worked for a number of years.

An office was set up outside the Hewlett-Packard complex to underscore its separateness, and a part-time staff was hired. With May's help, the foundation's fields of primary interest were defined as education, mainly at the college-university level; population problems; and preservation of the environment. Preference in grant making would be given to the western part of the United States and especially the Bay Area. In 1975 the board, which then consisted of Mr. and Mrs. Hewlett and two of their sons, was expanded, with some prodding from John May, to include two nonfamily members, Robert Brown and Lyle Nelson. Both were close family friends: Brown was Mrs. Hewlett's lawyer, and Nelson was on the faculty at Stanford. At the time, informality characterized the board meetings, which were held at the Hewlett home. Members brought their wives, and everyone joined in on discussions of individual grant proposals. Since then two more nonfamily trustees have been added, Arjay Miller, former president of the Ford Motor Company and later dean of the Stanford Business School, and Robert Erburu, head of the company that publishes the *Los Angeles Times*.

By 1976, as the assets of the foundation continued to grow, it was clear that further steps had to be taken to convert it from a "mom and pop" operation into a more structured and professionalized one. Recognizing that his foundation would in time become one of the largest in the country, Hewlett decided to find a top-flight person of national reputation to become its first full-time president and not to name a mere "faithful footman" in order to maintain his personal control.

The man selected was Roger Heyns, then president of the American Council on Education in Washington, D.C.. Heyns was well known to the Hewletts from his days as chancellor of the University of California at Berkeley. Mrs. Hewlett, an alumna of that school, had followed Heyns's performance during his tumultuous tenure from 1966 to 1971 and had been impressed by the way in which he had been able to win the trust of the students and restore a degree of order to the strife-torn campus.

Heyns brought to his new role as a grant giver a vast experience in the actual administration of nonprofit institutions and an unusual understanding of the point of view of the problems of the grant seeker. He took office in 1977, a few months after Mrs. Hewlett's death. These events, including the expected acquisition of a large bequest from Flora Hewlett's estate, marked the beginning of a new era for the foundation, now renamed the William and Flora Hewlett Foundation. Over the following few years its grants would increase twelvefold, and its program would evolve from a local to a national and even somewhat international one.

Hewlett and Heyns agreed from the outset on the general style and standards the foundation would adopt. Following the A. W. Mellon model, it would have a small, highly competent staff. It would work mostly with established, high-quality organizations and would allow their heads a considerable degree of flexibility and discretionary authority in the use of grant money. In its dealings with applicants it would be courteous and considerate. All requests for funding would be answered promptly, and all letters, whether of acceptance or rejection, would be personalized, reflecting Heyns's view that "fund raising is enough of a pain. We should at least be sensitive and helpful in our communications."

Finally, the style of the foundation would be low-key, and it would not seek publicity, reflecting Bill Hewlett's preference for anonymity in his philanthropy. There would be no grants for Hewlett Buildings, Hewlett Rooms, or Hewlett Professorships.

PROGRAM CONTINUITY

From the beginning, the foundation's fields of primary interest have remained essentially constant: education, population control, environmental protection, the arts, and regional grants in the Bay Area. Under Heyns there have, however, been some refinements.

Educational grants have been concentrated on major research universities and on the strengthening of their research libraries, especially by the development of networks of collaboration among them. In 1977, Hewlett joined the Bush Foundation in a program to augment alumni giving at the nation's black colleges, an effort that has been quite successful. The following year it was joined by the A. W. Mellon Foundation in launching a program to promote faculty and curriculum development in forty-five good-quality but financially imperiled small liberal arts colleges. Most recently the foundation has begun to make some grants to improve elementary and secondary schools.

Next to education, the worldwide problem of population growth is the largest object of Hewlett grants. Within this broad field, the foundation's specific interests are the training of population experts, policy research on population issues, and support of comprehensive family planning services and other fertility-reducing programs. Controversial projects are avoided by a policy of excluding support for "single-issue" groups as well as programs in reproductive biology and the development of contraceptives.

Prior to 1977, the foundation's environmental grants were concentrated almost entirely on the family's interest in the preservation of ecologically endangered areas. Since then, although some land acquisition has continued, the focus has shifted to research on how land use, zoning, and other environmental decisions are made;

the training of natural resource professionals; and the search for ways of averting or resolving environmental disputes by means other than agitation and litigation. In 1983, this interest of the foundation led to the establishment of a new program in the general field of dispute resolution and the encouragement of processes of mediation and other "third-party intervention" techniques.

Hewelett's program in the performing arts is unimpressive to date, consisting mostly of a scattering of small grants to miscellaneous organizations. But its regional grants and its "special projects" are the headings under which it takes advantage of targets of opportunity and addresses a number of current social issues. These include community development and youth employment projects in San Francisco; assistance for the launching of new community foundations in the Monterey peninsula and in the troubled city of San Jose, California; engineering and science scholarships for minority students; and strengthening nonproft organizations and the nonprofit sector generally. The foundation has also now begun in a limited way to work in the field of international affairs, particularly on the problem of U.S. relations with Mexico, and on some national security issues.

THE HEYNS CONTRIBUTION

Although Heyns has accepted and worked within the general framework of program priorities established by the donor and the Hewlett family prior to his arrival, he has made a personal and most important contribution by giving a coherence to the foundation's grants in most of these fields by relating them to a broader set of underlying objectives. These at first were only implied, but he has gradually formulated them into a conceptual structure, an achievement that represents a considerable intellectual contribution to the general development of a theory of foundation role.

In his first annual report in 1977 he stated that one of the foundation's overriding purposes was "to help create an effective democratic society, one whose institutions work." In that latter clause he provided the key to understanding one of the two central beliefs that have governed the Hewlett program since, namely faith in the essentiality of institutions and therefore in the importance of strengthening the best of them. In his report for 1983, six years later, his essay was introduced by a quotation from Benjamin Disraeli that is as good a statement as can be found of this view:

"Individualities may form communities, but it is institutions alone that can create a nation."

Accordingly, the foundation has devoted a good part of its grants in every field in which it works to the strengthening of institutions: general support grants, grants to help them develop their financial base, grants to improve their management and personnel, and, reflecting Heyns's own long experience as an institution head, grants to provide discretionary funds to college presidents, for example, to introduce improvements they feel are needed. Consistently Hewlett has tried with its grants to promote underlying institutional strength and not simply to alleviate short-term specific needs. Needless to say, there are many in the United States who feel that overinstitutionalization and the inherent rigidity and inertia of institutions are among the major problems of the society. Hewlett, on the contrary, does not see them as problems but almost venerates them as essential resources.

A second theme running through the Hewlett program has been to improve the decision-making processes of the country. This has included actions to develop public policy options through research by "institutions with a history of objectivity and a capacity to transmit their results to decision makers." Thus Resources of the Future and the Brookings Institution have been helped to conduct policy studies on environmental issues, the Trilateral Commission on problems of international relations, and the Urban Institute on urban problems.

Related to this purpose has been the foundation's strong interest in conflict resolution by means other than litigation or confrontation. Heyns has repeatedly expressed the view in his essays that environmental and other public issues "are not best resolved by impassioned advocacy." In that statement is obviously reflected his painful experience in dealing with the student rebellion and the Free Speech Movement on the Berkeley campus during his tenure as chancellor.

The Hewlett hope is that social stability can be ensured by reasoned policy debate based on factual evidence, which in turn can lead to the development of public consensus. This logical managerial or administrative approach to the resolution of political questions is seen by some public figures in California as naïve. "If the world were as tidy, prosperous and secure as the suburbs of Palo Alto, it could work," one black Bay Area leader says. "But it has little to do with the reality that I see—the anger and hopelessness in the inner cities, the vast differences in power among various groups, and the need sometimes to break eggs if omelettes are to be made."

Nonetheless, Heyns's concepts have given a common thrust and unity to the grants of the Hewlett Foundation in the several fields in which it has chosen to work. They also constitute the most defensible rationale so far formulated for the instinctive approach of many conservatives in preferring to give their support principally to well-established and well-known institutions and to avoid direct engagement with issues and groups in the arenas of social reform, social equity, and conflicting interests and ideals.

AN EVALUATION

The Hewlett Foundation is one of the group of foundations that might be called "the constructive conservatives," of which Andrew W. Mellon is the prototype and bellwether. They basically buttress and help sustain the leading nonprofit institutions of the country; they avoid involvement in projects of social reform, activism, and public controversy. At the same time they have also avoided the worst sins of a good many of the most conservative foundations: questionable ties with the donor's company, ideological grants to low-grade institutions, conflicts of interest, and poor staffing. Their style is dignified and their standards ethical. Their boards are small, homogeneous, and effective. Their internal relationships are harmonious. Their donors are very influential in setting program priorities, but they are also staffed with strong professionals. Increasingly they are operating with the benefit of a well-reasoned concept of their purposes and role. Because of their low-key approach, they tend often to be underestimated. But they effectively occupy an important middle way in American philanthropy. Because a good many of the larger foundations now find themselves in disarray and groping for new directions, the model that this group of foundations, including Hewlett, represents is of growing influence and appeal.

James Irvine Foundation

In the mid-nineteenth century a Scotch-Irish immigrant named James Irvine, who had made his fortune in groceries and gold mining in California, put together a tract of raw ranch land of some eighty-eight thousand acres located between what are now the cities of Los Angeles on the north and San Diego to the south. After his death in 1886, his son, James Irvine II, gradually transformed the ranch from livestock grazing to field crops and eventually to citrus production. But as late as the mid-1960s some of the land remained as it had been when the first Spanish explorers, members of the Gaspar de Portolá expedition, passed through two hundred years earlier. Spurred and booted cowboys still herded cattle in some places and slept in a bunkhouse that had stood since 1879.

The son established the James Irvine Foundation in 1937 for motives that, in the opinion of the late Congressman Wright Patman who studied the case in great detail, were purely to escape federal and state income and inheritance taxes. In any event, he made running the ranch company his life's work, and his philanthropic interests were nil. According to the minutes of the foundation, he did not attend a single meeting of the board during the ten years between its establishment and his death.

By the terms of his trust setting up the foundation he gave it majority ownership of the company and directed that it should keep its shareholdings intact and should exercise a controlling voice in the company's operations. He gave the foundation's directors broad grant-making authority but stipulated that the money go only to charities in the state of California and that none should go to those "receiving a substantial part of their support from taxation...."

The foundation got off to a very poor start, which lasted almost thirty-five years. The basic problem was the total entanglement of the foundation in the affairs of the ranch company and vice versa. The inherent difficulties of managing and planning for the future development of what was probably the prime piece of undeveloped real estate in the United States were not only distracting; they made giving comprehensive attention to the foundation's needs almost impossible. This was particularly so because of poor family leadership, the relentless litigiousness of a dissatisfied family member, and the highly charged political atmosphere of Orange County, California, the heartland of Nixon-Reagan Republicanism, where the Irvine Ranch is located.

In its first decade, while the donor was still alive, the foundation made a few small gifts to local institutions. But it was essentially lifeless. Myford Irvine, the son of the donor, became head of both the ranch company and the foundation after the death of his father in 1947, and for the next twelve years until his own suicide in 1959, his indifference to philanthropy almost matched the absolute standards set by his father.

Both the donor and his son died under strange circumstances. According to the donor's granddaughter, Mrs. Joan Irvine Smith, he died in 1947 while on a fishing trip in Montana with a company director. Making it clear she viewed the circumstances suspiciously, Mrs. Smith has said, "he was found floating in a stream where he was supposed to be fishing." His son, Myford, who had become involved with a gambling group in Las Vegas, found himself one weekend in early January 1959, in a situation in which he had to raise several hundred thousands of dollars in cash by the following Monday morning. Failing to do so after approaching several family members and friends, he went into the den of his home and fired a shotgun blast into his body and a .22-caliber bullet into his brain.

Throughout the 1960s Mrs. Smith, a large stockholder of the Irvine Company, lodged a succession of lawsuits against the foundation trustees charging them with mismanagement, self-dealing, and self-aggrandizement. Her interest in pursuing these suits had nothing to do with improving the performance of the Irvine Foundation. Rather, she wanted to get more money from her shareholdings in the ranch company. The president of the foundation at the time, M. Loyall McLaren, a San Francisco accountant and businessman, in turn charged Mrs. Smith with the practice, among other things, of "surreptitiously recording ... by concealing recording devices on her own person, private conversations with directors of the company and directors of the foundation." The state and federal courts ultimately rejected Mrs. Smith's charges and vindicated the board. But coping with the siege she maintained in the courts preoccupied the directors of the company and of the foundation for a number of years.

There were also other distractions of a political nature.

When the ranch company gave the University of California one thousand acres of its land for a new campus to be built in the town of Irvine, the action produced a multitude of charges alleging the manipulation of the university for the profit of a private company, as well as various other political and ethical indiscretions. Some of the regents of the university, led by the multimillionaire industrialist Norton Simon, charged the then-chairman of the Board of Regents William French Smith (later U.S. Attorney General under President Reagan) with conflict of interest because he had acted as a lawyer representing the Irvine Company in its negotiations with the university. Ronald Reagan was then governor of California, and his sensitivity to the Irvine fracas was indicated by an item in the *Los Angeles Times* of October 17, 1970:

> SAN FRANCISCO—A U.C. Board of Regents meeting erupted Friday into an angry, shoving, name calling confrontation between Governor Reagan and Regents Frederick Dutton and Norton Simon. Reagan called Dutton a "lying-son-of-a-bitch."
>
> The incident took place just after the meeting adjourned, minutes after Dutton accused the board majority of postponing a controversial Irvine Company land development plan for political reasons. . . .

Such was the lively and unusual atmosphere in which the philanthropic work of the Irvine Foundation through its first thirty-five years was conducted. Until the mid-1960s it had no paid staff and no defined program. In 1964 after more than twenty-five years of operation the foundation issued its first public report, a document light on factual information but heavy with rhetoric about its high purposes. Its second report, in 1969, was again a deceptive document clothing a banal, even trivial record of grant making with pretentious verbiage. Up to that point Irvine stood as perhaps the most glaring example among the big foundations of the negative effects of allowing foundations to concentrate their holdings in and exercise control over business corporations.

After 1969 changes for the better began to occur. The tax reform act of that year, among other provisions, prohibited control by a foundation of a profit-making corporation, and this rquirement was the triggering factor that has led to the gradual transformation of the Irvine Foundation into a good and still improving philanthropy.

The requirement of the new tax law that foundations dispose of their "excess business holdings" posed a particular problem for the Irvine Foundation because the donor's original trust stipulated that the foundation should keep its shares of the Irvine Company intact. To clear away this obstacle the foundation promptly filed suit in California Superior Court to amend the trust to conform with the new federal law. In 1973 the court gave its permission.

But the process of disposing of the shares of the ranch company led to further legal problems. In October 1974, an agreement to sell its land to the Mobil Oil Corporation was reached, but Mrs. Smith challenged the agreement, contending the price was inadequate. In early 1975 the attorney general of California also filed suit to delay the transaction until it could be ascertained that the sale would not be to the disadvantage of the foundation. Finally in April 1977, the court permitted an "auction" of the shares of the company. The top bid from a group of real estate investors enabled the Irvine Foundation to receive $184 million for its shares. In approving the sale the superior court of California at the same time dismissed Mrs. Smith's allegations against the foundation's directors for improper conduct. (That decision did not discourage her from pestiferously protecting her interests as a shareholder in the new company that took control of the Irvine Ranch. Its head has reported receiving more than eleven hundred letters of comment and criticism from her during his first three years in office.)

With that decision the foundation was finally freed of the incubus of its intimate involvement with the company and of the endless quarrels and contests that had produced.

Immediately thereafter the board named Kenneth Cuthbertson, who had been a financial vice-president of Stanford University, to become administrative vice-president and chief operating officer. Since then Irvine has turned into a well-managed and productive philanthropy. Cuthbertson developed an effective plan for managing its investment portfolio; he has built a good staff, which now numbers fifteen; he has introduced a number of moderate and incremental changes in the foundation's program that have greatly improved its quality; he has made the foundation's communications with its clientele as well as with the general public models of clarity and forthrightness; and he has worked well with a board of very strong individuals in accomplishing this major transformation in a relatively few years.

PROGRAM DEVELOPMENT

One cannot dignify the grants of the Irvine Foundation over its first thirty-five years as constituting a program reflecting a strategy or even a decipherable concept of philanthropy. Scattered gifts, mostly small, were made to institutions in the field of higher education, health care, community service, and the arts. The recipients were mostly in the vicinity of the ranch in Orange County or in the area of San Francisco where Mr. McLaren, who served on the board for forty years and was president of the foundation from 1959 to 1976, made his home. A number of organizations received small grants year after year. In addition more substantial capital grants were made to hospitals, educational institutions, and community service agencies, a few at first and a gradually increasing number over time, until by the end of the 1960s most of the foundation's income was being distributed in this form.

In 1978 the board, after the appointment of Cuthbertson, reaffirmed the foundation's commitment to the several fields in which it had been making grants. But within that broad framework clear patterns of change can now be discerned. There are stricter standards in choosing recipients of capital grants, which now tend to be larger in size and fewer in number. To strengthen selected institutions, more grants are being made to help them improve their management, fund-raising capabilities, and other forms of self-development. Also the institutions chosen for capital and development grants are more widely dispersed throughout the state of California.

There is some indication that the foundation is rather cautiously making "seed money grants" to newer and less well established organizations, particularly those seeking to meet new community needs. Thus La Raza Centro Legal received ninety thousand dollars in 1980–1981 to establish a project to disseminate immigration and naturalization information for Hispanic and Asian immigrants and refugees. Similarly a grant was made in 1980 to help establish the Bay Area Hospice Association to assist the rapidly expanding hospice movement in that part of California.

The grants of the foundation are also increasingly sophisticated in leveraging other philanthropic contributions. Thus it took the initiative in 1981–1982 in authorizing $8 million to fund an annual alumni-giving incentive program among nineteen colleges and universities in California. The program is designed to help the recipient institutions overcome something of a historic lag in the state in the habit of alumni giving. The foundation matches the increases in such giving the participating schools achieve over a three-year period. The foundation also gave the University of Southern California nearly $3 million to develop and strengthen its program in

Urban and Regional Planning. A major part of the grant was designed to encourage others to make endowment gifts to build an improved financial base for the activity.

Within the confinement of a program focused on a single state, the foundation has made some effort to support local projects that relate to broad national issues. One of the more important of these was a recent grant of $500,000 to the National Chicano Council on Higher Education to create an advanced fellowship program to encourage Hispanics to pursue careers in education.

Irvine is moving toward more problem-oriented and creative grant making, but slowly and cautiously. How far it may wish to go remains to be seen. But there are at least signs of growth in this direction.

THE FUTURE AND THE BOARD

Once the Irvine Foundation was released from the burdens and distractions of running the Irvine Company, and after the arrival of Cuthbertson, very beneficial changes have been made in a continuous succession of careful, purposeful steps. But his 1986 retirement will require the board to decide what kind of foundation under what kind of leadership it wants for the future. Looking at the composition of the group that will make this decision gives both reason for hope and perhaps some cause for concern. In recent years it has changed considerably and has become very much stronger. Of the eleven directors who were serving in 1970 only four remain. There was one woman on the board in 1970, and three in 1985. It includes a number of the most influential individuals in California: the president of Bank of America, the chairman of Carter Hawley Hale stores, the chairman and president of Fireman's Fund Insurance Companies, the president of the Hewlett Foundation, and others. Indeed the Irvine board is probably as a powerful of group of business, financial, and civic leaders as can be found on any foundation board in the country. They give the foundation, therefore, the benefit of the input of knowledgeable and widely experienced individuals. They also can give it immense influence quite beyond its own financial resources, which now total $300 million, in forming coalitions of foundations or of other institutions, for example, to generate funding for major undertakings or to achieve other broad social objectives.

On the other hand the board is conservative by disposition, and the main base of the foundation's activity is an area far removed from—and seemingly often unsympathetic to—many of the most pressing problems of an urban, industrialized, and rapidly changing nation. Whether such a board operating in the atmosphere of Orange County will be able to make the Irvine Foundation increasingly relevant to American realities cannot be foretold. But as of now the trends have to be judged as hopeful.

Weingart Foundation

California has always attracted down-and-out dreamers aspiring to fame and fortune. Ben Weingart was one of these, and one of the rare few who realized their dream.

He was born of a poor family in Kentucky, and his father died in an accident before Ben was five years old. He was then sent to an orphanage in Georgia. From there he went to live with a foster family on a farm near Atlanta. He dropped out of school in the third grade and did field work until his early teens.

To escape from that, he drifted to St. Louis, Missouri, and found employment delivering laundry in a horse-drawn wagon. "It was good money," he said, "and it was interesting work because it was a whorehouse district—the red light district, you know—and I was fascinated. What adolescent boy wouldn't be?"

Thereafter he joined forces with an itinerant "doctor" who peddled eyeglasses. When the law was about to catch up with them, Weingart hopped a freight train to California. The year was 1906; he was eighteen years old. He then went back to delivering laundry, this time in Los Angeles's skid row. "I met some nice people there," he was to reminisce later, "as nice as you would meet anywhere. An awful lot of them just had bad luck or were simply old and unwanted. I remembered them the rest of my life."

He began his business career by saving enough money to lease one of the boardinghouses on his laundry route. One lease then became several, and he was started on his way to success. When the stock market collapsed in 1929 Weingart suffered losses. But with the onset of the Great Depression he was soon able to recoup his fortunes by buying up or leasing foreclosed properties and making them profitable.

By World War II Weingart owned a variety of businesses in addition to substantial real estate holdings and was considered a very wealthy man. At war's end he moved himself into the ranks of the superrich by having the foresight to buy thirty-five hundred acres of beet and bean fields south of Los Angeles in anticipation of America's move to the suburbs. On the land he eventually built eighteen thousand medium-priced tract homes and a 156-acre shopping center, creating his own totally planned city, Lakewood.

In his personal life, Ben Weingart had a reputation as an eccentric and a Casanova. He wore thirty-year-old suits, high-button shoes (he had several dozen pairs made by a Boston firm), and a black beret. He never touched liquor and lunched daily on peanut butter and jelly sandwiches at one of his hotel restaurants.

Friends recall him as a man of great natural intelligence, self-educated and highly articulate. "He could express himself on his feet or on paper with the fluency of an Oxford don," one of his business associates has said. An inventor, he designed and patented a number of items, from a toilet paper hanger to a vacuum cleaner.

He also loved women and was involved with a number of them. He met and married his wife Stella before World War I, and they lived together until she died in 1955. But in the 1920s he met a divorcée, Helen Hazel Walsh, with whom he maintained a parallel and lifelong relationship. Later he met an aspiring young actress known as Laura Winston (she took her first name from a popular song she liked and her last name from that of a prominent New York diamond dealer because it suggested elegance). In the last period of his life she became his confidante and paramour and eventually moved into his home.

Helen Tarashita, Weingart's housekeeper for over thirty years, explained in a court proceeding that Weingart managed these complicated relationships by dividing his time between the two women, seeing Walsh on Wednesdays, Fridays, and Sundays and Winston on Tuesdays, Thursdays, and Saturdays. (On Mondays, presumably, he rested.)

ESTABLISHMENT OF HIS FOUNDATION

Weingart established his foundation in 1951 after the success of his huge Lakewood project had boosted his fortune to a wholly new level. Just why he created it is not clear. Possibly it was in anticipation of eventual inheritance tax problems, since he and his wife were childless. It was certainly not because of any great interest in charity. He did not take part in cultural or philanthropic activities of the Los Angeles Jewish community, and indeed he considered himself nonreligious. Neither did he have any interest in creating monuments to himself. Once he had become rich he was courted by various members of the city's establishment to endow buildings at one or another of the local universities. He consistently declined, often with the remark "Why in the world would I want to have my name cut in marble at that price?"

But in discussions with close friends he explained his tightness with money in more revealing terms. "I was so poor for so long," he once told a business associate, "I have never been able to get any joy out of giving. Moreover I know that it is my wealth that gives me whatever standing or influence I have. So I am going to hang on to it until the day I die." His friend then asked him, "But what will you do with your money after that?" to which Weingart replied, "Maybe I'll buy an extra big shroud and just take it with me." The only exception to his dislike of charity was the many small gifts he made personally to the derelicts of Skid Row.

Weingart died a rather messy death, and the settlement of his estate was a rather messy process. In 1974 when was eighty-six, the Los Angeles Superior Court declared him mentally incapable of handling his own affairs and placed his estate in the hands of conservators. Three years later he was moved to Good Samaritan Hospital, where his mental and physical condition deteriorated to the point that he no longer spoke or recognized friends. His personal physician Dr. A. F. Pierce was quoted in a 1979 court document as saying, "the more I observe this man, the more I think this is brain deterioration due to neuro-syphilis." Dr. Pierce speculated that Weingart might have contracted the disease some twenty years previously. Three days before Christmas in 1980, Ben Weingart died at the age of ninety-two.

ACTIVATION OF THE FOUNDATION

Well before his death Weingart had selected three longtime friends for his foundation's board of directors, two of them men who had been executives of his company for many years and the third a prominent California retailer. These three were also appointed as conservators when the court declared Weingart incompetent, and they served as his executors upon his death. In carrying out their responsibilities, their lot during the first few years was not a happy one. They had to help the court determine the donor's condition. They had to cope with a number of lawsuits, particularly those laid by Laura Winston attacking various actions of the board and seeking to obtain a larger share of Weingart's estate for herself. (The final twist to the conservators versus Winston story was a last-minute court order received in the middle of Weingart's funeral services that stopped the interment. The order was obtained by Winston on the basis of her claim that Weingart wished to be cremated. Four days later after a hearing the court allowed the body to be buried.) They had to settle a large and complicated estate worth some $50 million and consisting of various properties and shareholdings in a number of listed and unlisted companies. They also had to manage the assets of his foundation, which at the time of his death were valued at almost $200 million, most of them in the form of real estate holdings. At one point the attorney general of California made formal charges of mismanagement and malfeasance against the board, charges that were subsequently dropped but cost the trustees considerable time and effort to rebut. Some of them even began to wonder whether they had taken on not only a thankless responsibility but one potentially damaging to their reputations.

Gradually, however, the lawsuits were disposed of, the estate settled, and the investments of the foundation put into some kind of order. During the same period, the board was strengthened by the addition of two prominent businessmen and a well-known surgeon and the naming of Dr. Lee DuBridge, former president of the California Institute of Technology, as "advisor to the board."

THE FOUNDATION'S OPERATIONS

In creating his foundation Weingart expressed the desire that preference be given to charities located in southern California. But beyond that he gave the trustees full discretion in determining the use of the money.

Despite the difficulties arising from Weingart's final illness and eventual death and from the troubled settlement of his estate, the board activated his foundation rather quickly and well. By 1976 a grants officer had been hired, along with a specialist in real estate investments and some administrative staff. During its first years it granted some $3.4 million to capital projects in the city of Lake-wood for a library and a YMCA.

In 1979 it issued its first annual report, a handsome and informative document, in which the trustees stated that the foundation's interests were being extended to such areas as research on the aging process, problems of senility, and improvement of the quality of life for the elderly and disadvantaged. Among the principal grants that year were one of $1 million to Cal Tech for research on aging; $500,000 for a new residence to house the needy elderly; and $125,-000 for an alcoholic detoxification and rehabilitation program in the skid row area of Los Angeles.

The program emphasis was distinctive; Weingart had become the sole large foundation in the United States with a major program interest in the poorest and most derelict of the poor. Over the following few years, however, this feature of its work was diluted as the level of its grants rose to more than $14 million a year.

By 1983, a pattern had become visible: Grants to higher education consumed 35 percent of the total; grants for health and hospitals, 25 percent; and grants for "community social services," 25 percent. These included some for abused children, the elderly, and the severely disabled, but also at least as many for such organizations as the Red Cross, the Boy Scouts, Girls Clubs, and the YWCA. The focus had clearly shifted away somewhat from skid row and toward more conventional grantees. As it searched for its eventual course, the foundation also made several large general support and bricks-and-mortar grants: $5 million to Dr. DuBridge's former institution, the prestigious California Institute of Technology; $3 million to renovate a stadium at Los Angeles City College to make it usable for the 1984 Olympics; and a matching grant of $3 million to build a new $6 million YMCA. The renovated stadium is in a predominantly Mexican-American community, and the YMCA is in Watts, a black neighborhood.

In early 1984 a distinctive new feature had been added to the Weingart program: nearly 10 percent of its grants were devoted to "governance and public policy" projects, including one of $250,000 to Stanford University for a study of arms-control problems and one of $605,000 to the Urban Institute in Washington for a study of the impacts of Mexican immigration on the Sunbelt states.

In the next phase of its program development, it is likely that the Weingart Foundation will commit a major part of its income to a large new scholarship program for talented and needy students. The design of such a program is now under detailed study.

TRUSTEE ADMINISTRATION

To date, the foundation's program has been carried out largely by the direct involvement of the trustees in the screening, evaluation, and administration of grants. To aid them, Dr. DuBridge serves as the board's permanent adviser, attending meetings and actively participating in decision making. In this regard Weingart is a reflection of an impulse now felt by many individuals who are invited to serve on the boards of foundations, particularly in their formative years, namely the desire to direct not only the financial affairs and overall policy but also actual grant making. The Weingart Foundation has hired some professional staff, but more to "shield the trustees" from grant applicants than to shape decisions on major grants. The trustees themselves serve in effect as the professional staff.

It is clearly recognized by the board that direct involvement in grant making is time-consuming and strenuous. Therefore retired persons not heavily burdened by business or professional responsibilities are felt to be in the best position to make the commitment required. To compensate them for their efforts the foundation pays its trustees an annual fee of twenty-four thousand dollars.

But already some unexpected problems have arisen. The legal and financial difficulties of getting the foundation under way have proved to be more burdensome and aggravating than anticipated. Had they been foreseen, it is doubtful that some of the present members of the board could have been persuaded to serve. One of them, after reading newspaper allegations against him and the others at a moment when they were laboring to unravel some of the complications of settling the donor's estate, looked up at his portrait on the wall and exclaimed, "Ben, you old bastard, you got me into all this!"

Also, a number of the foundation's projects have proved to be much more intricate than the trustees originally expected. Giving away the six-hundred-room El Rey Hotel, one of Weingart's properties in downtown Los Angeles, was a case in point. At first the trustees thought they could just "get rid of it" by giving it to the Volunteers of America as a residence for the homeless. But as the project unfolded, it became clear that to make the project viable additional capital and operating funding would have to be provided and a consortium of other donors organized. The negotiations to accomplish this took many weeks. The Weingart Rehabilitation Center, as it is now called, is the largest institution of its kind, providing detoxification, medical care, and social services for two thousand persons a day.

Despite their frustrations at times, the Weingart trustees seem determined to keep the foundation under their close control in program as well as other matters for at least the coming few years. Whether the concept will work with a "second generation" of trustees who did not know and have great regard for the donor remains to be seen.

A more immediate question is whether the trustees, as the foundation's resources and grant level grow and as the established health, educational, and cultural institutions of Los Angeles develop their various strategies for getting to them with their appeals, will continue to devote a good part of the foundation's resources to the poorest and the powerless. If they do, the foundation will fill an important gap in the spectrum of interests of big American philanthropy and make a major national contribution. Even though Weingart is confined geographically to California, it can create models for dealing with the down-and-out, alcoholics, and the homeless that could influence other public and private agencies throughout the country.

But the poor and powerless are poor and powerless, and one of the clearest reflections of their condition is their lack of access to the kind of individuals who generally compose foundation boards. For them not to be ignored and neglected will require a capacity, indeed a determination, by the Weingart trustees to disappoint the rich and influential institutions that will approach them skillfully and incessantly and to feel a strong commitment to a cause shared by few in their social circle.

W. M. Keck Foundation

Keck is a low-grade foundation controlled by persons with low standards of philanthropic responsibility. It is new, having been activated in 1980, and in the period since it has been continuously embroiled in controversy, litigation, and scandal. It has assets of $490 million.

The donor, William Myron Keck, was a crusty wildcatter who founded the Superior Oil Company in 1929. By the time of his death in 1964 his estate was estimated to exceed $180 million. "The Old Man," as Keck was known to almost everyone, devoted his whole life to building the company, which until its recent acquisition by Mobil was the largest independent oil and gas producer in the country. As long as Keck was alive, Superior was a closely held and unusually secretive corporation.

A civic leader, even a family man, he was not. His political outlook is suggested by the fact that when "Tail Gunner Joe" McCarthy was flying around the United States in the 1950s pushing his brand of anticommunism, the converted World War II bomber in which he traveled was provided by Keck.

He had six children, but as one of them has said, "This is not a family. This is a collection of people with the same name."

One daughter died in infancy. One son was killed in an automobile accident as a young man. Another daughter lived as a recluse in Europe for many years until her death a few years ago. The oldest son, W. M. Keck, Jr., who died in 1982, was president of Superior for a while in the early 1950s but was ousted by his brother Howard in 1952. The two surviving children are Howard Keck and Willametta Keck Day. She and Howard live in a state of open warfare, and their lawsuits and accusations against each other have made the headlines repeatedly.

Trouble between them apparently began early. Willametta says that as a little girl she cried for days after Howard killed her pet ostrich. The bird's neck had become caught in a fence hole, but instead of freeing it, Howard stuck an orange in its mouth, and the bird strangled to death.

As far as is known, the donor created his foundation essentially to save inheritance taxes and perpetuate family control of the oil company. He left individual trusts to his widow and the children and to several California colleges—Occidental, Pomona, Stanford, and the University of Southern California—and also to an Episcopal church. His will was in probate for fourteen years, a proceeding that did not come to an end until 1978. When the foundation was finally activated in 1980, Howard, who was chief executive officer of the oil company at the time, also became its head.

The father's will contained rather elaborate provisions for continued family control over the company and specified that his favorite son, Howard, should be the dominant factor in the affairs of the company, the family, and the foundation. Thus, he placed the 8.6 percent of the shares of Superior destined to benefit the foundation in the W. M. Keck Trust and empowered Howard to exercise exclusive voting control over those shares, a very important block in determining control of the company.

The will also called for all of the donor's descendants to sit on the foundation's board. Thus until recently it was made up of a combination of eleven members of the family and eleven others, all but two of whom had long and intimate business association with Howard and with the company. Because a majority of the directors were large shareholders, directors, or lawyers of the company, the board was riddled with conflicts of interest. Since the family directors included, and still include, members of both the warring clans of Howard and Willametta, it has had, and still has, a built-in potential for great strife.

For a brief period after its activation, affairs at the foundation were peaceful enough. But there were soon strains. Howard and his wife chose most of the grant recipients, and Willametta along with several other members of the family began to protest that they were excluded from any voice in grant making. But the underlying and most divisive factor was one in which the foundation was only incidentally involved: the desire of Willametta and her supporters to sell off their shares in the company or if necessary to sell control of the company itself in order to increase their personal income, and the determination of Howard on the other hand to resist the public sale of any family or foundation holdings and to fight off by every device possible any takeover bids for the company.

The implications of this struggle in dollar terms for the foundation as well as for members of the family were considerable. Superior Oil long held to a policy of paying out dividends at a relatively low rate, namely about 5 percent. Thus in 1979 the foundation received some $13 million of dividend income from its Superior shares owned by the trust and slightly over $20 million in each of the following two years. A more "normal" return on a portfolio of some $500 million in market value at the time would have been nearer 10 percent, and its income would have nearly doubled.

Because of Howard's flat refusal to consider selling Superior Oil shares, Willametta in 1982 began discussions with other large oil companies and with investment bankers about the sale of her personal stock. As soon as Howard learned what was going on, he flew to New York to tell the bankers and various oil companies that

Superior was "not for sale at any price." Not long after that, according to an insider's report, Howard asked Willametta why she had voted against him as a director at Superior's 1982 annual meeting. She replied, "Because you're a dumb son-of-a-bitch and you ought to get off the board and sell the company."

Willametta had no prospect of prevailing over Howard on her own, but in late 1982 power shifted dramatically in her favor. In November of that year W. M. Keck, Jr., died, and control of his 2.4 percent of the shares passed to his son, W. M. Keck II, who decided to support Willametta. Explaining his decision, Bill II said, "What shareholder wouldn't be in favor of at least taking a look at an offer? It doesn't take me long to figure out I can do a lot more with a 10 percent yield than a 6 percent."

In the course of the following year Willametta decisively broke Howard's control. In spring 1983 she won a bitter proxy fight to force Superior's board to consider offers to buy the company. By fall, Howard was forced off the board; shortly thereafter, in a final admission of defeat, he announced that he was ready to sell all the shares he controlled. Early in 1984 Mobil made an offer of $5.7 billion for the company, which was accepted.

THE BATTLE OVER TRUSTEES' FEES

In parallel with the running battle over control of Superior Oil and the public sale of its shares, another bitter fight erupted in mid-1982 over the fees taken out of the foundation's assets by Howard Keck and, until his death, his brother William in their capacity as trustees of the William Keck Trust.

The decree establishing the trust for the benefit of the foundation had become effective in December 1978.

In October 1980 the two, apparently without informing the board of the foundation, submitted a request to the Superior Court of California for fees as trustees of $1 million for the year 1979 plus $150,000 in legal fees to be paid to the firm of Howard's son-in-law.

The court in mid-1981 reduced their claim somewhat, allowing the two brothers $550,000 in fees and $110,000 in attorney's costs. Then in July 1982 they requested their fees as trustees for the year 1980. This time they asked for $1,022,448 for themselves and $204,489 for their lawyers.

While the court was considering the request, two enterprising reporters of the *Los Angeles Times* uncovered the story and inquired of Willametta about her reaction to the fees being requested by her brothers and also about $185,000 in campaign contributions by her brothers to the gubernatorial campaign of Attorney General Deukmejian. She exploded.

The following day the *Los Angeles Times* story appeared, and Deukmejian, whose office was directly involved in negotiations over the fees to be allowed the Keck brothers, immediately and with some embarrassment returned their campaign contributions.

A week later Deukmejian's office and the lawyers for the Keck brothers agreed on a mathematical formula for their trustee fees in the future, a formula that allowed them $825,000 for their "services" in the year 1980 plus $190,000 in legal expenses.

At that point Mrs. Day declared herself "outraged by her brothers' audacity in seeking these outrageous fees" and informed the trustees of the foundation that she intended to submit resolutions at the next board meeting demanding an investigation of the whole situation. She did so, and the board, still dominated by Howard Keck, rejected all of them.

By whatever reasoning the California attorney general's office may have arrived at its decision concerning the "reasonableness" of the fees it approved, the ordinary citizen in appraising the ethics of Howard Keck's claims against the charitable assets of the foundation might want to take into account such factors as the following: Keck is himself an immensely rich man with a fortune in the hundreds of millions of dollars; his duties as trustee did not involve more than a few hours of work per year at most; and although he has sought to justify the fees on grounds of the "risk" to which he was exposed in handling the foundation's finances, his father's trust specifically absolved him from any such liability.

Indeed, it appears that Keck has been in the habit of supping with a large spoon from the resources of any institution he controls. Until 1982, as CEO of the company, he took a salary of more than half a million dollars per year and in addition enjoyed perks that were lavish even by the standards of oil companies. The company maintained a luxurious hunting lodge in south Texas for him and the few guests he invited, which had running expenses of more than $450,000 in 1981. Says an oil man who has been there, "all the waiters wear tuxedos. They have about eight help per hunter and raise their own quail. The cost per bird must be about $1,000."

In addition, the company provided him his own jet aircraft, in which he commuted weekly between his homes in Houston and Los

Angeles. After his retirement as CEO Keck remained a director and consultant until late 1983 at a fee of twelve thousand dollars per month, plus use of his company plane.

In this continuing spectacle of caterwauling and greed, the foundation has had to carry on its philanthropic activities, such as they have been. In 1979, its first year of operation, the foundation distributed some $9 million in grants; by the early 1980s they had reached an annual level of $15 million.

Grants have gone mostly to institutions in California: colleges, hospitals, museums, and miscellaneous welfare organizations. A few have been addressed to such matters as alcoholism and wife abuse, which some observers believe derive from personal problems that certain members of the family have experienced. There is a trace of conservative ideology in a few of the grants. Pepperdine University, for example, was given more than $1 million for its Institute of American Ideals and Institutions, for its Teacher Institute for Economic and Political Education, and for its Free Enterprise Building project. Rumors of illegal self-dealing have circulated about the foundation's grants totaling some $7 million to the Colorado School of Mines, but no basis for such rumors has so far been established.

On the whole the grant list of the foundation has been typical of those foundations with little staff competence and no identifiable sense of serious purpose. (Mrs. Day calls it "an embarrassment" and a disgrace to the memory of her father and mother.)

By 1981, because of the rapid rise in the mandatory level of the foundation's grant making, it was decided that executive staff should be hired. A search firm located a prominent East Coast financial expert who was offered a salary of $325,000 to take the job, and the appointment was publicly announced. But the man after reconsideration declined, and the search began again. This time around, the board hired a prominent Los Angeles businessman, former head of the Security Pacific Bank Carl Hartnack, who brought in Joseph Dempsey, former head of the Southern California Regional Association of Grantmakers, as his chief operating officer.

A few months thereafter both Hartnack and Dempsey were summarily fired by Keck, who then had himself elected chairman, president, and chief executive officer of the foundation at a special meeting of the board on August 12, 1982.

Precisely why they were dismissed is not known. Neither will talk about the situation, perhaps because, in the case of Dempsey, of a three-year terminal "consulting" contract at $50,000 per year that reportedly includes a "confidentiality clause," including penalties for its breach. But it appears that their sin was offering a grant of $500,000 to the public television station in Los Angeles, which was at that moment in acute financial distress, without getting prior approval from Howard Keck.

Keck has been noted for high-handed firings. *Fortune* magazine reported on May 30, 1983, that during a twenty-one-month stretch in 1980–1982, while he was still CEO of Superior, he dismissed Broward Craig, president of Falcolnbridge Nickel, a major subsidiary company, who had been on the job less than six months; Joe Reid, president of Superior; as well as the president of the Keck Foundation and the entire foundation staff. People who know him say that he can be vindictive and that he often acts capriciously. The trouble with Howard, an acquaintance says, is that "he was born on third base and thinks he hit a triple."

After Howard Keck's assumption of all executive responsibilities in the foundation, a number of useful organizing steps were taken, and the board was strengthened. Compensation rates were established for trustees, including the several family members, at a level of twenty-two thousand dollars per year. A statement of grant policy was adopted in the fall of 1982, and an executive committee was created to establish grant-making procedures and to arrange for the preparation of annual reports. During 1983 the first independent trustees of stature were elected: Walter Gerkin, head of Pacific Mutual Life Insurance Company; Simon Ramo, an eminent scientist and entrepreneur; and Thomas R. Wilcox, chairman of the Crocker Bank. Bob Rawls Dorsey, a business executive who first came to fame in connection with the political scandals at Gulf Oil, which he headed at the time, was also made a trustee.

The addition of some nonfamily and nonretainer members to the board was a possibly encouraging sign. But Howard Keck as of mid-1984 still was in control, and the foundation judged by its record up to that point was the worst big foundation in the country. It was operated essentially as a device to control Superior Oil, and the evils that flowed from that connection were many: The foundation's assets were undervalued, and its income abnormally low; most of its grants were random, even trivial; it was milked by the controlling individuals for unconscionable fees; and it was a battleground and victim of unending family quarrels. It was indeed a disgrace.

But then came a turning point. Once the linkage between the

foundation and Superior Oil was broken by Mobil's acquisition of the company in June 1984, a series of important and encouraging changes began to occur. The foundation's shares were increased in value and when they were sold and the proceeds reinvested in a diversified portfolio of securities, its income substantially increased. With the sale of the Superior Oil shares, the trust that the donor had created to hold those shares was dissolved, in turn eliminating the hoggish fees that Howard Keck had been taking as its sole trustee. Also, with the complete separation of the company and the foundation, the company executives on the foundation board departed, to be replaced by additional independent members.

By late summer it had been decided that a full-time professional in philanthropy would be made president, and trustee Ramo had begun to play a significant role in helping define the foundation's program and role and in laying out a long-term grant strategy.

The creation of a number of Keck Chairs at various universities was considered, along with a number of other conventional means of disposing of a large accumulation of grant funds. Finally in early 1985 it was announced that $70 million would be given to the California Institute of Technology and the University of California jointly to construct the world's largest optical telescope. The Keck Observatory, as it will be known, will be built atop an extinct volcano on the island of Hawaii. This huge grant was scientifically useful and at the same time satisfied other criteria important to the Kecks: it was something they could put their name on and it was eminently uncontroversial. Symbolically, like the Keck Foundation itself, it was aimed at problems as far away as possible from the life and concerns of people on earth.

One telescope, even of four-hundred-inch diameter, does not a program make, and the Keck Foundation, though it has now done something consequential, is still a miserably deficient institution.

The family factionalism and quarrels are still unresolved and whether a new outbreak of fighting or another tantrum by Howard Keck will derail the hopeful new developments cannot be predicted. But his seventieth birthday is approaching, the date of his intended retirement, and there is therefore even the prospect that his disturbing and divisive influence may disappear. If these positive possibilities are realized, it may become necessary at some point to take away from Keck Foundation the one prize it has so far earned in philanthropy, the booby prize.

Conrad Hilton Foundation

The Conrad Hilton, the youngest of the large California foundations, after only three years of preliminary operation already shows
some promise.

If the donors of some of the big foundations were grim, colorless grubbers, the man behind this newest one decidedly was not.
Born in the New Mexico Territory in 1887, he died at the age of
ninety-one, having become the undisputed king of the hotel world,
head of a chain of first-class luxury establishments stretching from
the Waldorf-Astoria in New York to London, Madrid, Cairo, Istan-
bul, New Delhi, Jakarta, and dozens of other capitals.

His father, a son of Norwegian immigrants, ran a successful
general store in Apache country and for a brief time in the early
1900s became quite wealthy. Conrad, one of eight children, had a
patchy education in various schools in the area. As a young man he
worked as a store clerk, managed a female musical trio, and was
elected to the state legislature in 1912. In World War I he served in
the army as a junior officer. Then, after his discharge, and determined somehow to get into business, he bought a hotel in 1919 in
the oil town of Cisco, Texas. For the next thirty years he struggled
to build up a string of small, second-rate hotels. But in the Great
Depression he lost much of what he had gained. Thereafter, with
his flair for finance and theatrics and with a willingness to take large
gambles, he not only recouped his losses but went on to achieve fab-
ulous success. At his death, his wealth totaled some $400 million.

Hilton was a tall, broad-shouldered man who dressed in high
style. In his younger days he cultivated the reputation of being a
tycoon by day and a playboy by night. It was not uncommon for
him to dance until three in the morning, appear for coffee and orange juice at eight, and then go on to a full day's schedule. (As a
young man he "thought very well of himself romantically," in his
words, and once had a calling card printed that read "Conrad Ni-
cholson Hilton/Heart Breaker/Beware of Fakes, as I am the Original 'Honey Boy'/Love, Kisses, and Up-to-Date Hugs a Specialty.")

Hilton was married three times, the first two marriages ending
in divorce. He had three sons by his first wife and a daughter by his
second, the actress Zsa Zsa Gabor.

There was a touch of the showman in much that he did. For
the openings of his major international hotels, he took planeloads of
celebrities to the elaborate dedications. These usually included Hil-

ton's doing an old dance called the *varsoviana* at some point in the proceedings with a pretty companion. His home in Los Angeles had some sixty rooms. Among other features it included a three-apartment doghouse, air-conditioned and adorned with oil paintings of dogs. For years the gatherings of movie stars at his parties made headlines, and an important aspect of the public relations program of his hotel company was its smooth integration with his personal publicity.

In later years, as his status and fortune grew, Hilton's personal promotional activity became more formal, with less emphasis on ballroom accomplishments and more on matters such as world peace and his religious beliefs. He hosted the first annual congressional prayer breakfast, and he provided the newspapers with numerous stories on the way he practiced his Catholicism, some of which were later reprinted in inspirational anthologies. (He prepared a prayer for the breakfast somewhat ambiguously titled "America on Its Knees." The prayer was subsequently reprinted in four colors by his company and distributed in more than 2 million copies. In his autobiography, *Be My Guest*, copies of which were placed in every Hilton hotel room, he wrote: "We humbly believe that our Hilton House flag is one small flag of freedom which is being waved defiantly against Communism. . . . With humility we submit this international effort of ours as a contribution to world peace.")

In the case of a man like Conrad Hilton, who literally swam in publicity for decades, it is difficult to separate the persona from the person. He lived the high life, loved the company of celebrities, enjoyed beautiful women, and was a master of all the tricks of image making. However, if one searches carefully through the records, it becomes clear that in philanthropic terms there was more substance to the man than might at first be supposed.

During his lifetime he was generously charitable, giving to various children's organizations, as well to several orders of Catholic nuns for humanitarian work throughout the world. In 1973 he made a personal gift for a research facility at the Mayo Clinic of $10 million. At his death, although his relations with his children had on the whole been warm and friendly, he left them only relatively modest amounts and put the great bulk of his fortune into his foundation.

His directive to his trustees in his will suggests something of his character. It is in his flowery style, but it also reflects great feeling, and it is in sharp contrast to the bloodless lawyer's boiler plate in which the goals of most foundations are expressed:

> There is a natural law, a Divine law, that obliges you and me to relieve the suffering of the distressed and the destitute. Charity is a supreme virtue, and the great channel through which the mercy of God is passed on to mankind. It is the virtue that unites men and inspires their noblest efforts.
>
> Love one another, for that is the whole law; so our fellow men deserve to be loved and encouraged—never to be abandoned to wander alone in poverty and darkness. The practice of charity will bind us—will bind all men in one great brotherhood.
>
> As the funds you will expend have come from many places in the world, so let there be no territorial, religious, or color restrictions on your benefactions, but beware of organized, professional charities with high-salaried executives and a heavy ratio of expense.
>
> Be ever watchful for the opportunity to shelter little children with the umbrella of your charity; be generous to their schools, their hospitals and their places of worship. For, as they must bear the burdens of our mistakes, so are they in their innocence the repositories of our hopes for the upward progress of humanity. Give aid to their protectors and defenders, the Sisters, who devote their love and life's work for the good of mankind, for they appeal especially to me as being deserving of help from the FOUNDATION.

His Catholicism, which he advertised extravagantly, was increasingly important in his life in his later years, and in his will he asked his trustees to take a special interest in Catholic charities:

> I know the Sisters of Loretto very well, as it was this order who first established educational institutions in my home state of New Mexico. I have had an opportunity of observing the fine work they do. The Sisters of the Sacred Heart is another order that I have assisted in Chicago, but there are many deserving support in other fields, particularly hospitals. Deserving charities exist everywhere, but it is manifest that you cannot help all; so, it is my wish without excluding others, to have the larg-

est part of your benefactions dedicated to the Sisters in all parts of the world.

At his death he left $750,000 to his son Barron, $300,000 to his son Eric, and $100,000 to his daughter by Zsa Zsa Gabor, Francesca. The rest, more than $300 million, he gave to his foundation. His daughter contested the will and kept the estate in litigation for more than three years because she felt she had been shortchanged.

She claimed he left her a relatively small amount because he had "insane delusions" about his fathering her. These, she said, were caused by his guilt over marrying her mother without obtaining an annulment of his first marriage or a special dispensation from the Catholic Church. He renounced her in 1971, two years before making out his last will. The change, she said, "from a caring and loving father to a fear-ridden old man . . . was the result of the ravages of old age, illnesses, cerebral accidents and his extreme obsession with his religious beliefs."

However, the judge in the case ruled that Hilton's quandary over parentage was based on a logical suspicion since the young woman was born about two-and-a-half years after Hilton and Gabor separated. An attorney for the Hilton Foundation said, "This case is an attack on the moral values and work ethic of Conrad Hilton. He believed his children and grandchildren should work for a living, and that was a virtue, hardly an insane delusion."

The initial board of nine members was made up of the donor's two sons, five old business associates, and two outsiders. Donald Hubbs, an attorney who had worked with the Hiltons on tax and other legal matters for many years, was chosen to head the foundation. Lacking philanthropic experience himself, he sought the best advice he could find and began to build a small staff of able professionals.

Since 1982 the foundation has had to operate with only the first portion of its funding, the remainder being tied up in unfortunately protracted negotiations over the transfer of certain securities. The grants paid out in 1982 and 1983 were the usual scattering of funds to various favored charities of the donor either to fulfill specific directives or to satisfy what were regarded as moral commitments. In this first year of unsystematic giving $5.6 million was paid out in grants, and an additional $29.5 million of pledges to be paid out over future years was incurred. A large number of health, education, and social service organizations, a good many of them in California, received small grants. The principal gifts were to the Conrad N. Hilton College of Hotel and Restaurant Management at the University of Houston and to the Rand Corporation for a major research study directed at combating chemical dependency.

During that same year with the help of a document called "Managing the Transition to a Major Foundation," prepared by staff member Terry McAdam, formerly with the New York Community Trust, the board began a two-year effort to educate themselves about American philanthropy and to study systematically the different program areas in which the foundation might choose to operate, the different approaches to grant making that it might consider, the management style it might adopt, the kind of staff it should seek to develop, and even the future composition of the board, the criteria for selection of members, and the role the board should play.

To suggest the clarity, brevity, and quality of the document, the following is McAdam's way of presenting to the board, made up largely of businessmen, the fact that grant-making styles can range from passive to active and that they could choose from among three options:

The Bank Teller	*The Loan Officer*	*The Investment Banker*
• Totally reactive	• Fairly reactive	• Initiates and reacts
• Minimal analysis of projects	• Some analysis	• Thorough analysis
		• Seeks philanthropic leverage —Builds partnerships —Syndicates grants —Assumes moderate but prudent risks
• No follow up on grants	• Moderate follow up and analysis	• Thorough grant accountability

Naturally, the choice among these models has implications for us in terms of the time and cost of our managerial efforts as well as the character of the staff we recruit and train.

By mid-1984 a number of tentative decisions had been reached about these basic policy choices. The foundation would be an active, entrepreneurial one and would seek to become a leading force in its chosen fields of activity:

1. Education for the prevention of juvenile drug abuse;
2. The problems of family violence;
3. The improvement of elementary and secondary public education; and
4. The human services programs of Catholic charities.

Some of these programs would be conducted on a national basis and some on an international basis, particularly the work carried out through Catholic charities. This latter activity would probably become the largest program of the foundation.

It had been expected that the foundation would receive all its assets from the donor's estate and become fully activated by 1983. But since then there has intervened another example of conflict between philanthropic interests and the maintenance of family control over a donor's company.

After Conrad Hilton's death his son Barron became president of Hilton Hotels. In a relatively short time he began to steer the company away from hotels and into gambling, from which it now earns some 40 percent of its profits. That in turn has involved the company with various organized crime figures, as a result of which the New Jersey Casino Control Commission in 1984 rejected Hilton's application for a license to operate a casino in Atlantic City, a project on which it had already spent some $320 million—"the largest undertaking in the company's history." This huge misadventure immediately put it under threat of takeover by others in the gambling industry.

The foundation has been seriously affected by these maneuvers because Conrad Hilton in his will gave Barron an option to buy those company shares "in excess of the permitted holdings of a private foundation." Control of these holdings is Barron Hilton's main defense against the takeover of the company. But the interpretation of the terms of the will and the exact number of shares to which he can lay claim have for more than two years been entangled in court proceedings.

The takeover contest has bolstered the value of Hilton company shares and therefore of the assets of the foundation. But those assets will not become effectively available until the ongoing game of corporate high finance comes to an end.

Because of these complications in the final settlement of the donor's estate and of the delay in fully activating the foundation's program, it is still too early to judge it on its grant-making performance. But the way it has prepared itself for the launching of its program remains encouraging.

The family members and company officers on the board clearly want to make the Hilton Foundation, in Hubbs's words, "a substantial force in the philanthropic world." There has been no petty factionalism among them, nor do they seem to have the insularity or small-mindedness of a good many foundation boards. Perhaps most important of all is that the donor, a fabrication of Hollywood hype though he may have seemed, was a genuinely charitable man, who communicated that spirit to his foundation. About him Hubbs has said, "In human terms he was warm and gracious with a genuine feeling of care and responsibility toward the less fortunate of the world. We intend to have this foundation reflect his personality and character. . . ."

9

THE COMMUNITY FOUNDATIONS,
AN IMPORTANT VARIANT:

Cleveland, New York, and San Francisco

All of the large private grant-making foundations discussed in other chapters of this study have had an individual or single family as the source of their funds. But three with assets over $250 million are of a different character: the Cleveland Foundation, the New York Community Trust, and the San Francisco Foundation. They administer a number of charitable trust funds representing the bequests of many families and individuals, and they focus their work on the needs of their particular communities or localities. Called *community foundations*, they are an American social invention conceived by a little-known but very important figure in the history of philanthropy, the Cleveland banker Frederick Goff.

Since the founding of the first in Cleveland in 1914, community foundations have now sprung up in most large U.S. cities. They play a major role in local civic life and are increasing in number, size, and influence. There are now more than two hundred of them with assets in excess of $2 billion and annual grants of more than $200 million. They constitute in fact one of the most vigorous and promising new movements in American philanthropy.

For present purposes community foundations deserve careful study for several reasons: First, their record has been singularly free of the kind of abuses by private foundations that led to passage of the Tax Reform Act of 1969. Second, the spreading popularity of community foundations suggests that by their structure and mode of operation they are remarkably in tune with the times and have been able to build for themselves a kind of public involvement and credibility that relatively few private foundations have been able to achieve. Third, they stand as a reminder that there still exist great possibilities of public benefit from the creation of new and different kinds of philanthropic vehicles fitted to the changes now taking place in the society and economy of the United States. To take just one example, there are some three hundred highly educated, younger scientists and entrepreneurs who have become millionaires and multimillionaires in the Silicon Valley of California in recent years who are different in many ways from typical donors of the past. It may well be that some new version of the traditional foundation model may have to be developed to fit their intellectual and civic interests and trigger their philanthropic impulse.

Cleveland Foundation

ONE MAN'S IDEA

Frederick H. Goff single-handedly invented the concept of the community foundation and then built a working model and promoted the idea indefatigably across the country. A lawyer and civic leader in Cleveland, Ohio, Goff showed a predilection for public service in 1908, when he left a $100,000-a-year partnership in the celebrated Cleveland law firm that was counsel to John D. Rockefeller and took a precipitous drop in income and prestige to become president of the struggling Cleveland Trust Company, known as "the people's bank." During his fifteen years there he instituted a number of reforms to strengthen the bank's public accountability. He also became fascinated by what he saw as the great unrealized potential of banks and foundations to contribute to the welfare of the community and its changing needs through a more flexible management of the charitable bequests of deceased donors. Under traditional legal concepts in the United States as well as Britain, the wishes of the deceased prevented any diversion in the use of charitable bequests, even when their purposes had become irrelevant, except after long delays and heavy legal expense. He was determined to find a way around this restriction.

Goff was well acquainted with such examples as Benjamin Franklin's folly in setting up a huge trust that could be used only for "loans to respectable apprentices" even long after apprentices had disappeared from American life, and the famous Mullanphy Fund in St. Louis to aid western pioneers (finally committed, after four decades of court interpretation, to the work of the Traveler's Aid Society).

He became obsessed with the thought that tens of millions of dollars of social capital was being left to molder because of the "dead hand rule" (known in legal terminology as the *cy pres* doctrine). (A book by the British jurist Sir Arthur Hobhouse titled *The Dead Hand* and published in 1880 in London had deeply influenced his thinking. The margins of the pages of his personal copy were filled with his penciled notes, and he had underlined such phrases of Hobhouse as "the deadly superstition of blind obedience to the demands of the dead" and "no human being, however wise and good, is able to foresee the special needs of society even for one or two generations.") To try to find a solution that would make those funds available for useful purposes he discussed the problem with almost every banker, lawyer, public official, and businessperson he met. (Indeed he discussed it so frequently at the dinner table with family and friends that his daughter many years later said that as a child she hesitated to go up any dimly lighted staircase for fear "the dead hand would reach out and grab her.")

It was out of this search that the community trust idea was born.

The solution he finally devised was as simple as it was sensible. A new type of foundation directed by a partnership between trustee banks and a responsible group of citizen leaders would be formed. It would provide unified management for a number of charitable trusts. When leaving their endowments to the foundation, donors would agree that their charitable directives would be honored so long as they were not obsolete or harmful and that they could be altered by the foundation's directors as changing circumstances might require without resort to the courts.

Goff's blueprint for this new kind of foundation, which came to be known as the *Cleveland Plan*, also contained other unusual features. It divided the administration of the foundation into two parts. Local banks or trust companies, acting as trustees, would be responsible for the investment of funds. The power to make grants from the income from such investments would be lodged in a separate Distribution Committee, composed of prominent local citizens. To ensure the independence and integrity of the committee and to win public confidence in the foundation, the majority of the members would be appointed by designated public officials and local civic leaders, such as a state or federal judge, a university president, and the head of the local bar or medical association. Public disclosure in the form of an annual report and a published annual audit were also important elements of the plan.

CLEVELAND: THE FIRST COMMUNITY FOUNDATION

In 1914, Goff took his plan before the board of the Cleveland Trust Company, which approved it and brought the Cleveland Foundation into being. The trust company had to serve for a time as the sole trustee of the foundation because the city's other bankers were initially skeptical about the "new-fangled, overidealistic and tricky" concept and held back.

News of the new foundation spread promptly over the country with the help of an energetic campaign directed from Mr. Goff's office to put its details before newspaper reporters as well as bankers, lawyers, and other community leaders. Andrew Carnegie from New York gave it his blessing, as did John D. Rockefeller's office. In Cleveland itself the local political firebrand Peter Witt said, "What a pity it was not thought of a long time ago!" and a surprised and thankful chorus also went up from the directors of the city's charities and welfare agencies.

The idea having been initially well received, Goff then moved quickly to meet the two greatest needs of the new foundation: public recognition and money. His strategy was a clever one that was later successfully copied by other community foundations. Using his own money and that of the Cleveland Trust he launched a series of studies of Cleveland's most pressing municipal problems. The year

1914 was a sad and hungry one for most American manufacturing centers, including Cleveland, where many thousands were unemployed and soup kitchens operated in the downtown streets.

Goff set up a prestigious "survey committee" and hired an outstanding social scientist to make a full study of the shortcomings of the city's welfare system and recommend reforms. The report produced was critical and constructive. (One of the problems uncovered was that the public relief director himself had spent much of his time that year trying 3,708 pairs of shoes on indigents.) Almost every word of the survey's report was carried by the newspapers to the citizens and within two years major reforms were instituted. The study became a landmark in the history of American relief and welfare work and helped establish the Cleveland Foundation's place in the city.

In 1916 a second survey was done, studying the public school system, which at the time was the object of much criticism. Some twenty-five factual reports were produced along with recommendations, again resulting in major reforms. And because the issues involved touched virtually every family in the city the reputation of the foundation was further strengthened.

In late 1916 a third survey was begun to study the city's recreational system, the results of which were the creation of a municipal recreation department and a comprehensive summer playground program, the funding of a set of neighborhood centers and bathhouses open during evening hours, and the birth of Cleveland's noted "emerald necklace," a system of interlinked wooded parks that now encircles the city.

By 1917 donors were beginning to entrust the new foundation with funds, and by 1919 it was receiving sufficient income to permit the employment of its first full-time director, Raymond Moley, later to become famous as a member of Franklin Roosevelt's "brains trust." The Distribution Committee was then formed and began to make its first grants. The survey program continued, and in 1921 an inquiry into the local administration of criminal justice produced in Cleveland the greatest reforms of this century. It was directed by two of the Harvard Law School's most eminent teachers, Dean Roscoe Pound and Professor Felix Frankfurter. The reports produced are classics of their kind and have since been used as "case readings" by law teachers all over the world.

By the mid-1920s the foundation decided that the survey program had matured and that thereafter greater emphasis would be given to distributing its income more directly to philanthropic purposes. At that point Mr. Moley resigned and went on to teach at Columbia University and later to Washington.

THE MOVEMENT BEGINS

As soon as the Cleveland Foundation was established, Goff began a one-man campaign to promote the concept throughout the United States. He tirelessly proselytized among his friends in law and banking. He even persuaded the Trust Division of the American Bankers Association to create a standing committee on community trusts. He visited a number of cities to present the case to their leaders personally, finding fertile soil for his idea wherever he went. During 1915 alone, the year after Cleveland Foundation's founding, eight new community foundations came into existence: in Chicago, Detroit, Milwaukee, Minneapolis, St. Louis, Los Angeles, Spokane, Attleboro (Massachusetts), and Boston. By 1923, the year of Goff's death, thirty-one were in operation, all modeled on his Cleveland Plan. By 1931, as the country entered the Great Depression, there were seventy-four. The movement was well under way.

Most of the community foundations established in the years before the Depression were products of the interest of individual bankers who had been directly influenced by Goff, such as Albert W. Harris of the Harris Bank and Trust Company, founder of the Chicago Community Trust; and Frank J. Parsons of the U.S. Mortgage and Trust Company, founder of the New York Community Trust.

Most also followed a pattern of growth similar to that of the Cleveland Foundation: slow development in the first few years, with the primary emphasis placed on establishing the foundation's presence in the community, then a surge in assets, led by large bequests of one or more wealthy individuals or families.

The Chicago Community Trust, for example, founded in 1914, followed Cleveland's lead by promoting itself through a series of community surveys and a publicity campaign among the city leaders. In 1924 it received its first large gift, $1 million from James A. Patten, the "wheat king," and by 1939 its assets had grown to $5 million.

The New York Community Trust, founded in 1923, took a somewhat different route. The strategy of its first director, Ralph Hayes, who had been Goff's personal assistant in Cleveland, was to involve members of some of New York's most wealthy and prominent families in the Distribution Committee. As a result only one year later the Warburg family set up two funds totaling $1 million, and in 1929, a Rockefeller family foundation turned $2.5 million over to the trust.

With the onset of the Depression, as a result of the collapse of the security markets combined with the rapid increase of government social welfare and relief programs, the growth of the community trust movement virtually stopped. The lull continued through World War II. Then, quite suddenly, a general upsurge in philanthropic giving brought new funds to the existing community foundations, and many new ones were formed, the initiative coming in this phase more frequently from community leaders and planners than from bankers.

The San Francisco Foundation exemplifies those begun during this period. The directors of two local foundations, Columbia and Rosenberg, took the lead in its establishment. All nine of the city's trust companies agreed to serve as trustees. Prominent members of the Distribution Committee devoted themselves energetically to spreading the word about the new foundation throughout the Bay Area, and as a result its standing as a worthwhile organization grew rather quickly. The growth of its assets, however, was slow. It took eight years before the first $1 million of gifts and endowments had been acquired. Thereafter a large additional sum was received from a private foundation that had been the target of allegations of impropriety by the state attorney general. The questionable foundation disappeared, and the San Francisco Foundation in effect laundered the funds by making them part of its own corpus. By the early 1960s a rush of money began, and the foundation today includes 105 separate trusts and endowments, including one that has produced a mass of problems, which will be examined later.

During the 1960s the development of community foundations was greatly encouraged by changes in the tax laws. In 1964 federal legislation expanded the tax benefits available to donors of "publicly supported organizations," including community foundations. Such donors were allowed to deduct gifts of up to 30 percent of their adjusted gross income as distinguished from the 20 percent limit applying to other types of foundations. The Tax Reform Act of 1969, which imposed various restrictions on private foundations, left community foundations in the most advantageous tax category.

As a result, in the two years following passage of the 1969 act their overall assets grew by some 30 percent, a portion of this increase representing the transferred assets of private foundations that dissolved.

Thus the community foundation movement has passed through three periods of growth: from 1914 to the Depression, from the end of World War II until the 1960s, and from 1970 to date.

THE BIG THREE AT PRESENT

The community foundations that now have assets in excess of $250 million are Cleveland ($260 million); the New York Community Trust ($370 million); and the San Francisco Foundation, the largest ($400 million). All three are structured according to the basic tenets of Goff's plan. Their grants each year amount to 6 to 8 percent of the value of their total assets, well above the payout requirements stipulated in federal legislation. All give substantial support to health, social services, education, the arts, and neighborhood revitalization. They fund a large range of grantees, from established pillars of the community to small storefront organizations. All are intimately knowledgeable about local problems and resources; all are widely known and influential in their communities; all issue excellent annual reports each year.

At the same time each has its own special history and its distinctive characteristics.

The Cleveland Foundation, after its strong start in the 1920s, has had a consistent record of good performance. It has been deeply involved in dealing with the periodic governance crises of a historically troubled city. In the absence of other adequate leadership factors, it has on several occasions literally saved Cleveland from disaster. As a result, its prestige and influence in its own community are unmatched. In 1974 Homer Wadsworth became its head, and he maintained its position for the following decade as a force in the affairs of Cleveland and as the outstanding community foundation in the country. Wadsworth was especially well fitted for the post, having worked in the city government of Pittsburgh, administered the New School for Social Research in New York City, and directed the Kansas City, Missouri, Association of Trusts and Foundations. A solidly built, silver-haired and silver-tongued man, Wadsworth during his tenure came to be widely respected as the statesman of the field.

When he arrived in Cleveland the city was once again afflicted with an immobilized local government, flagrant fiscal irresponsibility, and corruption. The city council was split along racial lines. The mayor and the council for a number of years had deferred maintenance on the city's streets, bridges, and sewers and had resorted to every fiscal trick to avoid asking for new taxes. But in December 1978 the bills all came due, and Cleveland became the first major American city since the Depression to slide into default. That same year saw the city's police chief fired, teachers go out on a two-month strike, the public schools go into receivership, and the city council president and five council members indicted in a kickback scandal.

In that highly charged situation the Cleveland Foundation, working with local leaders both in and out of government, provided financing and guidance for a number of key actions to rehabilitate the city government and reestablish its solvency. A team of eighty-nine business leaders, the Operations Improvement Task Force, was created. They examined every city department during a three-month period and made hundreds of recommendations to improve efficiency, almost all of which were then implemented. A study of the conditions of Cleveland's capital plant was made, and a plan to fund the vast repairs needed was developed. An analysis of tax policies performed by the foundation became the basis of a successful campaign for voter approval of a necessary tax increase. Then to help ensure against another breakdown the foundation established several management training programs for senior officials to overcome the problem of unauditable books and archaic procedures throughout the city administration.

The resurrection of Cleveland from the shambles of the 1970s was due to the collaboration of many factors: businesses, banks, universities, neighborhood groups, and others. But there is general agreement that the Cleveland Foundation, operating skillfully along the margin of politics but avoiding partisan involvement, played a powerful catalytic role. Its ability to do this depended on its extraordinary reputation for integrity and responsibility among the population of the city, the prestige and representativeness of its governing board, and the skill and stature of Wadsworth.

Still more recently Cleveland has been hard hit by economic recession. Unemployment in the early 1980s was very high and the stories of human suffering shocking. Again the Cleveland Foundation moved to improve the city's delivery of human services, despite increased demands and depleted resources. It helped finance fifteen hunger centers operating out of the city's churches, took the initiative in bringing together other foundations and potential funders to provide emergency help, and gave a substantial grant to Case Western Reserve University to improve the management skills of the executive officers of Cleveland's fourteen hundred human-service agencies.

In January 1984 Wadsworth's successor, Steven A. Minter, took office. He had been head of the Welfare Department of Cuyahoga County (in which Cleveland is located) in the 1960s and commissioner of Public Welfare for Massachusetts from 1970 to 1975. From the mid-1970s until his new appointment he was on the staff of the Cleveland Foundation with the exception of a year in 1980 spent in Washington as undersecretary of education during the Carter administration. Like Wadsworth, he brought a broad background of experience in public administration to his new post as well as great knowledge of the Cleveland community.

After seventy years the Cleveland Foundation remains a vigorous, responsive, and creative influence in a major city under siege by a brutal combination of racial, economic, and political problems.

New York Community Trust

The New York Community Trust from the time of its creation in the 1920s until the late 1960s had a steady if unspectacular increase in its assets and developed a solid reputation as a competent foundation with unusually wide knowledge of the needs of the city and of the activities of the many agencies, private and governmental, attempting to deal with them.

Over the past fifteen years, a period of vigorous development, it has more than tripled its assets, which now total some $370 million. Even so, it cannot play the kind of powerful role in the metropolis that the Cleveland Foundation does in Cleveland, partly because of the sheer mass of the city and partly because of the presence in the situation of a number of other very large foundations.

That circumstance plus the fact that its funds to a greater degree than those of some other community foundations are under restriction, designated by the donors for distribution to particular grantee organizations or fields of activity, has obliged the New York

Community Trust to find different ways in which to play an influential role and to leverage its resources.

This it has done imaginatively and effectively.

Because of its almost unique knowledge of the city it has become a kind of philanthropic service center both for other foundations and for major corporations operating in the area. They have increasingly begun to turn to it both to assess projects they might support and to monitor projects after they have been financed. Nonprofit agencies seeking funds have also increasingly sought the advice and assistance of the foundation, whose endorsement is taken by a good many funding sources as a kind of Good Housekeeping seal of approval.

Because it enjoys the respect of other foundations and nonprofit organizations, the trust has been able to promote cooperation among grant makers in the city both in the exchange of information about prospective grantees and in actual funding. In the words of one of its officers, "We have a sort of unearthly neutrality, which is the key. We don't need jobs; we don't need resources; we don't need contracts; and we are not running for office. Which in New York at least makes you about as neutral as you can get."

The foundation has also distinguished itself by the strong effort it has made to form partnerships of various kinds with government and other foundations and corporations in the joint development, funding, and administration of projects.

Because New York is the financial and business capital of the country, the trust has been the pacesetter among community foundations in providing philanthropic services to corporations. With them it maintains three basic types of relationships: First is a corporate philanthropy consulting service, by which it provides advice on funding strategies, special consultations on specific projects, and evaluations of potential grantees.

Second, the foundation has a Special Projects Fund to which eight national corporations based in New York make a yearly contribution. The trust then distributes the proceeds. The fields of interest in which grants are made are selected in consultation with the participating companies. One of the most attractive features of the idea is the opportunity it offers for corporations to make a greater impact with their dollars both in terms of helping nonprofit organizations and of receiving more recognition for their contribution than if they operated independently.

A third relationship is the "one-company" fund. The Exxon Corporation, for example, in 1978 began to give the trust an annual allocation of some $500,000 from which to make grants to revitalize neighborhoods, help needy families, and provide job training for disadvantaged youth. Exxon maintains its corporate identity through the use of a letterhead and special check for all grants made.

Such "servicing" functions, which could have become purely routine and placed the trust in a subservient role, have, because of its strong institutional character and high quality of staff, led to a number of unusually interesting and creative joint projects: one to overhaul the city's foster care system, another to improve services specifically for Puerto Rican elderly, and another to help establish a program for training in advanced management of nonprofit institutions at Columbia University.

With its own unrestricted funds, the trust has also been able to take some effective initiatives. An enterprise for which it became well known during the energy crisis in the late 1970s was a program, based on an idea learned from the Chicago Community Trust, to provide technical assistance to nonprofit agencies in the city to have a technically competent "energy audit" made of their facilities as a basis for introducing cost-saving measures. In a number of instances, given the prospective savings, the institutions were able to finance necessary improvements in insulation and heating equipment on a self-liquidating basis.

Most recently, the trust has begun to offer new kinds of services to the state and federal governments on a contract basis. One of these relates to the use of *restitution payments*, that is, penalty payments imposed by the courts on business firms for violations of petroleum price regulations or environmental regulations, for example. In these cases, the "injured party" is most often the community in general, and the problem in utilizing the several billions of dollars of these payments that governments nationwide now hold in escrow has been to find purposes and a vehicle that would fulfill the purposes of restitution. In its pursuit of the possibility of rendering a special kind of public service in utilizing such funds, the foundation may be opening a funding possibility for other community foundations across the country as well as for itself.

For a number of years the work of the New York Community Trust has been led by an interesting combination of an older and experienced executive director, Herbert West, backed up by dynamic younger staffers with a strong sense of social commitment. It remains a solid organization working usefully in a massive and very complex environment.

San Francisco Foundation

The San Francisco Foundation, the third and largest of the big three, was established in 1948 in the early phase of the post–World War II resurgence of interest in community foundations throughout the country. In words that were to acquire special and unexpected significance thirty years later, the defined area of interest and responsibility of the foundation included the Bay Area counties of Alameda, Contra Costa, Marin, San Francisco, and San Mateo. In the chartering document it was also specified that *the foundation's Distribution Committee would have the responsibility of modifying the conditions of a trust if compliance with the donor's instructions should become "impossible, impracticable, unnecessary, or undesirable."*

The first years of the foundation, in the common pattern, were devoted to establishing its reputation as an asset to the community. An executive director, John May, was hired; then ensued eight long years until the foundation had acquired its first million dollars in assets. But in the next eight years its assets increased more that eightfold.

Its earliest work was concentrated in the field of social welfare. But as the foundation grew, grants were made in areas of equal opportunity and housing, jobs and legal assistance, the arts, education, environment, and development of neighborhood organizations.

In the mid-1970s Martin Paley, a former management consultant, succeeded May as executive director. He brought to the foundation a more enterprising style and added a more activist quality to its program. Indeed the foundation began to take some pride in its being in the forefront of certain kinds of controversy: sponsoring litigation to prevent oil drilling off California's coast, to fight problems of discrimination in housing and jobs, and to bring about prison reforms.

The foundation's grant list by the late 1970s reflected the special characteristics of a distinctive and youthful subregion of the United States, including its diverse ethnic composition, social problems, cultural interests, and life-styles.

Were this the totality and the end of the story, the San Francisco Foundation would clearly stand as the most lively and unusual of the large community trusts. But since 1980 it has been involved in a snowballing set of problems that derive from an immense bequest that it received in that year. The Buck Trust, as it is called, has been both a bonanza and increasingly a curse. The San Francisco Foundation is now like the boy who wanted a volcano for Christmas, and got it.

THE BUCK TRUST

More than a century ago an itinerant land speculator named Frank H. Buck moved around California picking up land no one else wanted. Among these properties was a parcel fifty miles west of Bakersfield that was so unappealing that, in his words, even the coyotes spurned it. But oil was subsequently discovered there, and when the widow of Buck's son, Leonard, died in 1975 without any direct heirs she left the property in the form of some seventy thousand shares of Belridge Oil Company to the San Francisco Foundation, with the stipulation that the proceeds could be used only in Marin County. At the time, her gift was thought to be worth about $10 million. When the shares were actually sold in October 1979, the oil embargo and other events having occurred in the interim, they brought a price of $264 million, instantly catapulting the assets of the foundation to a total of $348 million and making it the largest community trust in the country.

From that day the bequest has generated a great and growing controversy.

Although several of the counties in the purview of the San Francisco Foundation are confronted with grave problems of poverty and social distress, Marin County is the richest in California and one of the most affluent in the United States. Although there are some small pockets of need, its average income is some 40 percent above the national median, and the average home costs about $170,000.

When the trustees of the foundation were suddenly faced with the fact that the Buck bequest would add thirty times as much to the foundation's assets as had been expected and would nearly triple the total size of the foundation, it might have been supposed that the most urgent and serious debate would have been aroused among them about the prudence, even the feasibility, of such a vast increase in its grants in Marin County; about the repercussions in the other counties within the Bay Area of lavishing such a volume of money on the most affluent part of it; and about the "responsibility" of the trustees to alter the terms of a trust if compliance with the donor's instructions should become "unnecessary or undesirable."

Some discussion evidently did take place, for in December of that year the foundation issued a preliminary plan for the use of the Buck funds, in which it was frankly stated that "an inordinate spending of philanthropic funds can present a danger to the public welfare. . . ." Suggestions were invited from nonprofit organizations in the region to ensure that the foundation "actions contribute to, and do not detract from, the interests of the county, the Bay Area, and society generally."

However, for reasons that remain obscure, the foundation, instead of taking measures to permit it to distribute the income from the trust more broadly and equitably throughout the Bay Area, chose to accept legal advice to abide strictly by the wording of the trust and to pour all of the income into rich Marin.

Ironically, given the origins of the community trust concept, it was the attorney general of the state of California who filed a court petition in December 1980 contending that such a policy might "result in a condition of charitable surplus or saturation." The probate commissioner of the county also agreed that there was a "reasonable basis for concern" that the Buck Trust might "at some time result in a condition in which the charitable needs of Marin County and its residents have been satisfied . . . and in which continued distributions of all income could result in a detriment to the County." He therefore ordered annual hearings to be held and reports to be prepared on the money's effects on Marin.

THE DRAMA DEVELOPS

Friedrich Dürrenmatt, the Swiss dramatist, in his classic play *The Visit* portrayed the pernicious effects of a promised endowment on the life of a European village. The ugliest aspects of human nature—greed and cupidity, envy and resentment, cunning and cheating—were all brought forth by the prospect of something for nothing.

The atmosphere that developed within Marin County, once the magnitude of the Buck funds became known, had a considerable resemblance to Dürrenmatt's theme. Two schools of thought quickly developed. A good many nonprofit agencies took the view that although the county was generally affluent, they could absorb the total bonanza without strain. A number of Marin officials, elected and appointed, agreed that the county could use all of the money and said they knew of a fine cause that needed support, the county government itself. They argued that because of budget gaps left by Proposition 13 and federal cutbacks, the Buck money should be used to prevent drastic reductions in public services.

On the other hand there were individual citizens, nonprofit agencies, and some government officials who felt that the Buck money presented real dangers. One resident, Gordon Sherman, a successful businessman and philanthropist, said, "The sooner the county discovers this thing is lethal and rises to change the will the better. Let us change it to this extent. They don't have to give Marin all the money—give us as much as we need—enough to fill the spirit of the will. But don't cram us like a Strasbourg goose."

Various nonprofit leaders expressed other concerns. Some feared that the Buck money would discourage volunteer work and choke off donations from other sources. Others worried about domination. "The Buck funds have become the only game in town," the head of a children's service agency said. "We are all dancing to their tune because other funding has dried up." Still another fear was that the money might spoil the county by populating it with migrating nonprofit agencies. And indeed a number from elsewhere opportunistically did move in.

There were also some citizen groups that felt that "cheap" Buck money would tend to create a lazy dependency and jeopardize the basic principle that responsible democratic communities must be prepared to pay for the public services they want. A related concern was that the money would buy the foundation more power over county affairs than that wielded by its elected officials. In this regard a deputy attorney general of California said, "It could very well be that Marin residents will become the unwitting victims of the foundation's benevolence."

THE FOUNDATION'S REACTIONS

Holding fast to its legalistic position that the Buck money could be spent only in Marin County, the San Francisco Foundation worked hard to find plausible grantees there and made great adjustments both in its operating procedures and grant policies to accommodate the demands of the county.

To respond to the criticism that it was administering its activities entirely from its San Francisco headquarters and treating Marin County as a "province," the foundation established an office and a special "program executive" for Marin activities. To allay the criticism that it was operating secretively and "behind closed doors," it made a vigorous effort to open up communications with Marin residents.

Its accommodations in programming policy were even greater. At one time the foundation routinely rejected requests for grants to capital projects or building funds. But in Marin that policy was modified not only for private structures but also for public facilities. One of its largest actions was the expenditure of more than $6 million to acquire some thirty-three hundred acres of vacant land, after which it held public hearings to get ideas on what to do with its acquisition. In its 1982 report to the Marin County Probate Court, the foundation admitted that 98 percent of the acreage would be used for cattle grazing or as a greenbelt in a county that already had dedicated almost two-thirds of its land for parks and greenbelts. Similarly the foundation in earlier years did not make disaster relief grants to public or private agencies. But after a particularly severe storm in early 1982 it put up some $20 million for storm damage repairs, $5 million of that available to local government agencies.

Despite such acrobatics, criticism of the foundation seemed to grow, not diminish, and to spread outward in ever-widening circles.

In changing its program policies to fit the Buck Trust's restrictions, the foundation, perhaps because of a lack of imagination or the habit of "localism" in its thinking, did not attempt to create some major scientific, cultural, or scholarly institution (such as a medical center to study the diseases of the elderly, for example, or a center to do research on U.S.–Asian relations) that would have involved large expenditures *in* Marin County but not narrowly for the benefit *of* Marin County residents. Such projects are clearly permitted by the terms of Mrs. Buck's will and might have prevented some of the problems that the San Francisco Foundation has encountered.

THE CONTROVERSY BUILDS

From the beginning one of the most influential and persistent critics of the foundation's handling of the Buck money has been Robert Gnaizda, head of a San Francisco public interest law firm, Public Advocates. On behalf of a number of Marin County residents and a group of nonprofit agencies in the other counties of the Bay Area, Public Advocates brought suit against the foundation, charging that it had violated the spirit of its own charter by focusing its grants on one small area within its jurisdiction, ignoring considerations of need as well as simple fairness. Gnaizda presented evidence that the foundation had given 3 times as much for health grants in Marin as for the rest of the Bay Area, 4 times as much for social service grants, 12 times as much for education, and 13 times as much for environmental problems. (On a per capita basis, and ignoring the far greater affluence of Marin, the differences were even greater: 50 times as much for social service grants in Marin as in the rest of the Bay Area and 150 times as much for environmental projects.)

To document its charge that the foundation's grant-making policies were extravagantly discriminatory, Public Advocates in its 1982 brief to the Marin County court presented data showing that approximately 70 percent of all grant applications from Marin County, whether or not qualified, were routinely approved for funding. By comparison, the San Francisco Foundation has admitted that it rejects at least four out of every five *qualified* grant applications throughout the rest of the Bay Area.

The discriminatory effect of such "automatic" approval was exacerbated by the large sums given by the San Francisco Foundation per grantee. On average this figure was eighty-eight thousand dollars for Marin County versus eighteen thousand dollars in the rest of the Bay Area.

This "double standard" in the foundation's grant making in the view of attorney Gnaizda was not only evidence of preferential treatment but of "stuffing the goose" in order to dispose of a surfeit of money.

In another study Public Advocates contended that in the year 1982–1983, 36 percent of Buck money was used for government purposes and that for the years 1983–1984, 25 percent of its total funds had been obligated for these purposes. Included in the definition of "governmental purposes" were grants directly to government bodies, grants in support of public schools, grants for community planning and development, and grants replacing funds previously provided to various nonprofit organizations by the county government.

At the same time that the foundation was being assailed in court, the press went on the attack.

Most of the most influential newspapers in Marin at one time or another expressed critical views. Then in early 1983 *The Nation* magazine published a slashing criticism based on a study financed by a wealthy resident of Marin County. Calling the Buck Trust a "curse," the study charged that the foundation's grants in Marin County largely ignored the needs of the small minority of poor and chiefly benefited the affluent.

Among the "frivolous" grants it cited were $25,000 to the "Bio-Dynamic French Intensive Gardening School" in the town of Bolinas, an anonymity-seeking oceanside colony that has eliminated all road signs indicating its existence; and $278,000 to the Commonwealth Center in Marin, whose concept emphasizes "getting people away from the stresses of city life by recognizing the value of organically grown food and a preventive approach to health care." A $300,000 grant was given to the Headlands Foundation for a study of possible improvements in three historic forts in the county. The Sleepy Hollow Home Owner's Association got $20,000 to hire a swimming coach for a pool used by association members and their guests. A $169,000 grant was given to equip a television studio for Golden Gate Baptist Theological Seminary, and $21,000 was spent to provide a van for a private school.

In due course the leading newspapers of San Francisco, the *Los Angeles Times*, *The New York Times*, *The Wall Street Journal*, and the Columbia Broadcasting System all raised questions about the foundation's program and policies. *Forbes* magazine, in a particularly acid review, said, "The charitable grants of California's Buck Trust would be laughable if the implications were not so serious."

THE FOUNDATION'S REACTION

In the swirling controversy the San Francisco Foundation for some time did not distinguish itself by the moderation, reasonableness, or even candor of its comments. Rather it dug in its heels, adopted a snappish and defensive tone, and occasionally looked both foolish and evasive.

In its various reports in 1981, 1982, and 1983, it gave heavy emphasis in referring to the Buck Trust to the wording of the donor's will specifying that the funds be used only in Marin County, but it never referred to the fact that the foundation's charter gave its Distribution Committee the power to modify such restrictions when necessary or desirable.

On one occasion Robert Harris, the lawyer who has played a central role in the drama both as a trustee and as legal adviser to the foundation, admitted to *The Wall Street Journal* that the Buck funds might be used to help other Bay Area counties if the following test were met: "If the day ever comes that we fill every rut in the roads in Marin County . . . then I think it is possible."

In a statement not quite so silly but still rather surprising, Martin Paley, head of the foundation, on another occasion responded to the charge of unfairness in its distribution of Buck moneys with this declaration: "The principle of equity just does not apply in private philanthropy the way it does with tax moneys. . . ." The issues in this regard raised by the champions of the have-nots were to Paley "interesting and intriguing and may even be annoying but they really are irrelevant."

In the foundation's annual report for 1981, he attempted to assuage the concerns of the foundation's "stockholders," namely the people of the five counties of the Bay Area, in these words: "While we have developed regional criteria and standards, there will be a difference in the number of dollars available for Marin. The policies for granting those dollars will be consistent with the policies that apply to the other counties, though there will be special circumstances that will apply only to Buck Trust grants and awards."

That small masterpiece of contradictions and ambiguity was surpassed by another in fall 1983: Conceding that the money could be better spent outside Marin, Paley said, "If it were only a matter of doing the most good, it would be a simple decision" to modify the Buck will. But he added, "It's a much tougher question to ask whether it's right to have that much money for Marin and not for other parts of the community." Then, defiantly, "There is no objective definition of public need, and nobody has the right to tell us where to put our money."

Yet, although the foundation snapped at its critics for "superficiality" and "irrelevance," it put forth no serious rationale for its policies and conduct. It made reference to deliberations by its staff on the basic ethical issues involved, and it even claimed to have consulted philosophers on them. But it remained mystifyingly silent about the outcomes. It appeared to be immobilized by some internal policy disputes or possibly by a lack of courage in confronting a very complex and contentious set of local forces.

THE IMPASSE BREAKS

By early 1984 the whole matter had reached a point of crisis. The value of the foundation's assets had grown to more than $400 million, and the battle in the courts, the media, and public opinion generally had also escalated. Pressures of all kinds had been mobilized: within Marin County to fight any effort to "steal the County's money" and in the other parts of the Bay Area to seek to force the foundation to serve the needs of the several component counties on a more equitable basis.

Then on January 27, the impasse broke when the foundation announced that it would petition the superior court in Marin to permit some of the income of the Buck Trust to be spent outside the county.

The uproar in Marin was immediate. Members of the County Board of Supervisors outdid one another in striking postures of outrage. One called the foundation trustees "grave robbers." Another accused them of a breach of faith, saying, "All along they have been plotting to do this." They also voted a special fund to fight the foundation in the courts.

However, once the foundation decided to grasp the nettle and address the problem forthrightly, its performance in dealing with the situation significantly improved. Director Paley in a brave speech to the Marin Chamber of Commerce in February 1984 stated the facts in full as well as the rationale for the action the foundation had taken. In moderate and reasonable language he reminded his critical audience that Mrs. Buck at the time she made her gift could not have known that it would eventually grow thirtyfold to be worth more than $300 million. He also revealed that in her will Mrs. Buck expressly contemplated that it might at some time become inappropriate to spend all of her money in Marin County and directed that in such case a court should distribute it "to such public charities, for charitable, religious or educational purposes as the Court . . . shall determine proper." He went on to emphasize that community foundations like the San Francisco are specifically vested with discretionary power to alter the use of funds where a donor's original wishes have become "undesirable" or "impractical," and he pointed out to his audience that Mrs. Buck and her advisers specifically chose to leave her money to such a community foundation.

Even though his statement may not have been persuasive to all his listeners, given their emotional state, it was a wholesome and clarifying effort, and it for the first time explained the foundation's position in terms that public-spirited people in the Bay Area and across the country could defend. The foundation had finally put itself back onto the high road, and it was to be hoped that the quarrels, ill feeling, and litigation that its earlier position had helped generate would begin to subside. But whether that would happen and how long it might take remained to be seen.

By its mishandling of this affair, great misuse of funds has resulted as well as damage to the foundation itself. Deep resentments in the other Bay Area counties that have undermined its credibility have been created; in Marin, outlandish appetites have been whetted and vested interests in its benefactions created, interests that once mobilized could be expected to fight long and hard not to have "their" money taken from them. Within the foundation itself, the practice of a "double standard" in its grant making over a considerable period of time has been corrosive to the morale and self-respect of all concerned, and that injury may be slow to heal.

The prospect is that it may take many months, even years, for the matter to work its way through the courts to a final decision, with the possibility that the final rulings could open the gates to all kinds of future challenges to the decisions of foundation boards of trustees.

Because of this, many foundation leaders have watched the unfolding of the Buck drama with great anxiety. Yet the reluctance of foundations to break ranks in criticism of one another even in such a situation is very strong. For example, Gnaizda circulated a letter in mid-1982 to the twenty largest foundations in the United States summarizing the issues in the case and asking for their comment. Of the twenty, nineteen did not reply. The one that did was the Rockefeller Foundation through Richard Lyman, its president. In his response he took the view that Public Advocates was doing injury to philanthropy by its suit and should desist, rejecting out of hand the viewpoint that it was the conduct of the San Francisco

Foundation in this complex matter that was the source of any damage that might occur.

About the best that can be said of the situation is that although it would have been far better for the board to have made its appeal to the court several years ago, it is better that it has acted now rather than to have allowed the situation to fester even further.

The fumbling efforts of the San Francisco Foundation in handling the Buck Trust should not obscure, however, the far more important fact of the extraordinary performance of community foundations in general.

On the whole, the model has been effective in attracting endowment from individual donors; the record shows that first-rate individuals have been nominated for and have accepted appointment to their boards; and the boards have generally functioned responsibly and with great dedication. Community foundations with few exceptions have good professional staffs, good programs, and a good record in reporting fully and publicly on their activities. By their basic design, they have good linkages and feedback loops with their communities, and they have therefore been unusually responsive to local needs. They are a social invention that has worked, and they are destined to grow greatly in importance.

10

THE MAJOR MIDWESTERNERS:
Kellogg, Kresge, Lilly, and Mott

W. K. Kellogg Foundation: Earthy Excellence

Will Kellogg, who created the foundation that bears his name, now one of the ten largest, was as a personality one of the strangest, most driven, and most joyless figures among the golden donors. But despite his shy, withdrawn manner, he was one of those rare individuals who had both a vision for the social use of his great wealth and the capacity to organize an instrument to realize that vision. By his accomplishments, he ranks with John D. Rockefeller, Sr., Andrew Carnegie, and Julius Rosenwald as one of the handful of truly great philanthropists in American history.

The "King of Cornflakes," as he came to be called, in the course of his ninety-one years lived three distinctly different lives.

Born in 1860, he was until middle age a frustrated and discouraged bookkeeper in a health sanitorium in Battle Creek dominated by his older brother. From his forties until his seventies, by a combination of fierce energy and unexpected merchandising genius, he built a worldwide and highly profitable breakfast food company. In the last third of his life he created his foundation.

His father was a Seventh-Day Adventist preacher who also ran a small broom factory to support his family. The rules by which the children were raised were strict, especially the requirement of work. By the time Will was fourteen he was an experienced broom salesman with his own territory. He later recalled that "as a boy I never learned to play." He had little formal education; his only academic degree was from the Parsons Business College in Kalamazoo, Michigan.

In the latter part of the nineteenth century the Adventists had established a sanitorium at Battle Creek based on their beliefs in the simple restorative methods of nature, the use of hydrotherapy, and vegetarianism. Will's dynamic older brother, Dr. John Harvey Kellogg, became physician-in-chief of the institution in 1880. As it flourished, Battle Creek became a health mecca for thousands of Americans, including many of the wealthy and celebrated, and Dr. Kellogg became nationally famous. He wrote more than fifty books and established dozens of companies to manufacture health foods, alcoholism cures, and other products. In the first years of the twentieth century he farsightedly went to the expense of having a film made about the harmful effects of tobacco, particularly its relationship to lung cancer.

Will was employed at the sanitorium working long hours for little pay in a back room as clerk, business manager, and jack-of-all-trades, lost from view in the shadow of his renowned brother. Busy every day and most evenings, he neglected his unhappy wife and three children. He was a slender, intense little man, lacking in self-confidence and discouraged about his situation. "I feel kind of blue," he told his diary after nearly twenty-five years in this humble capacity. "I am afraid that I will always be a poor man the way things look now." But then his fortunes began dramatically to change.

His brother conducted constant experiments to devise vegetarian foods that would be more attractive and digestible than those then available, and in these efforts Will was his general helper. Together they invented a number of new foods, including peanut butter (a product whose sale they did not promote because its taste was judged unlikely to gain public acceptance) and, in 1894, the first precooked flaked cereal. They had no idea they were inventing a breakfast food, the expression itself being unknown at the time. But sales of the new product, primarily to former patients at the sanitorium, began to grow encouragingly. Will sensed the possibility of enormous profits if the marketing could be developed on a nationwide basis. But time was of the essence because the secret of their invention had leaked out, and more than forty little flaked cereal companies quickly sprang up in the town.

At this point another of the many conflicts between the two brothers broke out. Dr. Kellogg was firmly opposed to any active promotional effort to sell the new cereal, feeling that it might damage his medical reputation and the prestige of the sanitorium. So Will acquired the dominant interest in the cornflakes company and went into business for himself. Suddenly the backroom bookkeeper displayed an amazing talent for inventing new concepts of mass merchandising, utilizing the then infant medium of advertising. He introduced door-to-door distribution of new food samples and also new point-of-sale techniques. In New York City in 1911, an intensive advertising campaign daringly invited housewives to "wink at their local storekeeper to see what would happen." What happened was that they got a free sample package of Kellogg's cornflakes. As a result, sales of the product leaped within six weeks from 200 cases a week in the city to 200,000. He drove himself and his colleagues with almost uncontrollable energy. By day he handled the problems of organizing, financing, and increasing the production capabilities of his company; by night, a poor sleeper, he scribbled an endless flow of new promotional ideas for his product.

Within a few years the little company, with sales skyrocketing and profits pouring in, made Will Kellogg one of the great American business successes of the twentieth century. With his new wealth and power, new facets of his complex personality manifested themselves.

One was a strong interest in helping others. He wrote in his diary at the time, "It is my hope that the property that Providence has brought me may be helpful to many others, and that I may be found a faithful steward."

From his personal records it is apparent that as soon as he was in a position to do so he made hundreds of small gifts to relatives and friends to help them send their children to school, to pay hospital and funeral expenses, and for other emergency needs.

Another expression of generosity was in the dealings of his company with its employees. By 1927, a nursery, which included a medical and dental clinic and a dietician, was in operation at the plant for children of female workers. During the Depression he rearranged production schedules so that more workers could be hired and gave preference to those who had families to support. He gave Battle Creek an agricultural school, a bird sanctuary, an experimental farm, a civic auditorium, a day nursery, a Boy Scout camp, and many student scholarships.

Then he began a serious search for an organized way to dispense his vast fortune. His charitable interests undoubtedly derived from his religious upbringing but may also have been influenced by the many tragedies in his life: the deaths of various family members by illness and accident, his miserable relationships with his own children and grandchildren, and his deep personal sense of loneliness and alienation.

One of his hopes had been that other members of the family would succeed him in the company. But in the process of trying to groom his son, John L. Kellogg, to take over, he broke his spirit, and the young man fled the organization. Sometime later at a relatively young age he died unexpectedly of a cerebral hemorrhage.

Kellogg then turned his attention to J. L.'s son, John L. Kellogg, Jr. As the boy grew to young manhood, Kellogg put increasing burdens of responsibility upon him, but in trying to push him too hard also drove him out of the company. Later the young man committed suicide over a business failure. In later years Kellogg never completely overcame his sorrow that he had no descendant to run the business.

As he grew richer and older, Kellogg strove to develop new hobbies and interests and to enjoy himself. He spent months traveling about the world. After the death of his first wife he remarried, but the new relationship seemingly added little pleasure to his life. He built several lavish homes, one in California where he started a ranch for breeding Arabian horses. But after living there several months of each year for fifteen years he turned it over to the University of California, saddened by his failure to make any friends in the area.

Finally, Will Kellogg's interests began to turn increasingly toward philanthropy as an outlet for his energies and as a means of personal fulfillment.

DEVELOPMENT OF THE KELLOGG FOUNDATION

In 1925, when he was sixty-five, Kellogg made his major move to put his donations on a systematic basis. In that year he established The Fellowship Corporation to distribute his gifts anonymously. Over the following five years it financed a considerable number of projects, nearly all in the Battle Creek vicinity. But almost as soon as the corporation began to function, Kellogg began to talk with the other members of the board about his desire "to get a child welfare foundation established and set in operation during my lifetime."

This he did in 1930, calling it the W. K. Kellogg Child Welfare Foundation. Two months later he renamed it the W. K. Kellogg Foundation. In setting up the first organization he had said, "I want to establish a foundation that will help handicapped children everywhere to face the future with confidence, with health, and with a strong-rooted security in their trust of this country and its institutions." But on further reflection, in broadening and renaming it, he wrote: "Relief, raiment and shelter are necessary for destitute children, but the greatest good for the greatest number can come only through the education of the child, the parent, the teacher, the family physician, and the community in general. Education offers the greatest opportunity for really improving one generation over another." The foundation was made the beneficiary of the assets of the W. K. Kellogg Foundation Trust, which were valued at approximately $45 million at the time, largely in stock of the Kellogg Company.

The manner in which he launched the foundation showed once again the extraordinary qualities of this unprepossessing but great man. He gave it a general direction and philosophy based on his own convictions and personal experience. His strong personal interest was in the welfare of children and in the needs of plain, ordinary people. That quality has been, and after fifty years remains, the distinguishing characteristic of his foundation. He believed that a foundation's role was not to serve merely as a vehicle to channel funds into ongoing charitable institutions, so he encouraged his trustees to put its resources behind pioneering ventures and new initiatives. He established from the start the principle that the foundation should operate as an independent and professionalized institution. He delegated broad responsibility to his trustees. Although he followed the affairs of the foundation closely through the rest of his life, he spoke little and stayed only briefly at board meetings in order not to create even the appearance of dictating policy.

He encouraged the trustees to make a systematic study of the operation of other foundations as a basis for their own planning, and they did. And Kellogg launched the foundation itself as an experiment. For the first five years, and until the foundation had proved itself, Kellogg made only annual gifts to support its programs. But in 1935, satisfied with the institution's performance, he made substantial resources available to it on a permanent basis. Mr. Kellogg died in 1951 at the age of ninety-one. During the last ten years of his life he was virtually blind. He remained nonetheless actively interested in the work of the foundation and is remembered in that period for his regular and frequent visits to its offices, always accompanied by his Seeing-Eye dog.

Compared to the egocentricity, ulterior purposes, lack of a genuine sense of direction, and general organizational ineptitude of more than a few donors, Will Kellogg was a giant: compassionate, broad-minded, clearheaded, and with great practical wisdom.

Launched in the depths of the Great Depression, the foundation for a time gave a good portion of its funds to direct relief. This program was discontinued in the late 1930s partly because of the expansion of federal welfare efforts and partly because the foundation had been able to move forward with its own "social laboratory" program.

From the mid-1930s until the outbreak of World War II, Kellogg served its apprenticeship in philanthropy by carrying out its initial program essentially as an operating foundation. On the principle that "little ships should stay close to harbor," it chose as its first target area the seven rural counties immediately surrounding Battle Creek, where it carried out what was called the Michigan Community Health Project to provide specialized services in health and education. Through the project county health departments were strengthened; rural hospitals were reorganized; new diagnostic centers were created; the teaching of health and hygiene in public schools was introduced; adult education programs in nutrition and home accident prevention were conducted; and the results of each project were carefully evaluated. A staff of ten professionals made tens of thousands of visits to homes, schools, and public facilities to give advice on everything from water supplies and sewage disposal to curriculum development.

After Pearl Harbor, further support to the health project, which was by then well launched, was discontinued, and the foundation devoted its resources to the war effort in various ways. One of the most important came as the result of a request from the U.S. State Department, which asked the foundation to help strengthen relationships among nations of the Western Hemisphere by developing activities in Latin America. The foundation in response began funding fellowships for physicians, dentists, and other health professionals from the region to complete their graduate studies in the United States. This became a major program that has continued to the present time.

At war's end the foundation reassessed its program and made two important changes. It decided it would thereafter operate entirely as a grant-making foundation and that it would broaden the scope of its work to include agriculture. The focus of this new program was in Western Europe, where farming and food production had been seriously disrupted by the war.

From then until the late 1960s the foundation's program steadily evolved and broadened.

The earlier concentration on child health and welfare was gradually enlarged to include the general field of medicine and health, but with special concentration on those grass-roots problems and institutions that most other foundations working in the field ignored. Kellogg thus gave important assistance to dentistry and dental education. The foundation's hospital program was directed to the needs of rural institutions, improving their administration and reducing their operating costs. Great attention was given to relieving the nursing shortage and upgrading the nursing profession, including the training of medical auxiliaries, practical nurses, dental hygienists, and occupational therapists.

Likewise in the field of education Kellogg concentrated not on the preeminent colleges and universities but on the needs of the public schools, including the improvement of educational administration, reorganization of school districts and school consolidation, improvement of school libraries, and financing of public education.

Beginning in the late 1950s it began to give support for the creation and extension of the national community college movement. Through its grants it played a leading part in the development of these colleges from a rather narrow vocational focus to the comprehensive educational institutions that now number more than twelve hundred and serve nearly 5 million people throughout the country.

The foundation also had an important role in the field of continuing education during the 1950s and 1960s, both for the professions, particularly health and education, and for the general public. One of its major contributions has been the funding of nine residential centers at regional universities for the continuing education of adults, regardless of their formal educational preparation.

In 1967 Emory Morris, who had presided over the affairs of the foundation for more than twenty-five years, retired. Russell Mawby, who had been the foundation's director of agricultural programs, assumed the presidency. He has led the foundation's development since.

A NOTE ON STYLE AND SUBSTANCE

In terms of outlook and program interests, Mawby was well chosen to provide continuity in the foundation's philosophy and program. He is of rural background, and his academic training is in the practical and applied aspects of agriculture. In operating style he is in the down-to-earth, unpretentious tradition of the Kellogg Foundation. And in general social philosophy he shares the conservatism of its origins and ethos. Will Kellogg was at the same time a man of great compassion and of faithful Republicanism in politics. His hero in public life was Herbert Hoover. He was outspokenly critical of the expansion of the role of government under the New Deal and what he saw as its tendency to encroach on the freedom of private enterprise and on individual responsibility. Mawby shares those general concerns about the dangers of excessive government as well as Kellogg's faith in the importance of traditional family and social values.

About Will Kellogg it could be said that what he may have lacked in style he more than made up in substance. The same is true about his foundation and about Mawby. In the more snobbish circles of philanthropy he has sometimes been regarded as a somewhat stuffy country cousin. But his record as an administrator and in program matters is impressive. He may indeed be the most underrated foundation head in the business.

In the management of Kellogg he has kept costs down and productivity up by taking advantage of the newest information technology. He has made highly effective use of outside advisers to gain expertise and protect the foundation's flexibility. He has developed a model program of public reporting and communications, and his own presidential essays are substantive and to the point.

The changes he has introduced in the Kellogg program reflect responsiveness to changing social needs and priorities, but within a fundamentally traditional framework of values, an unusual combination. Among the major ones are these:

1. Attention to the needs of the disadvantaged and the handicapped has been greatly increased. Since 1968 the foundation has provided more than $20 million in grants to black colleges throughout the country. It has also given nearly $4 million to improve the management of member institutions of the United Negro College Fund. It has given more than $7 million in the same period to improve economic and educational opportunities for native Americans. And it has given some $15 million for programs aimed at improving services and opportunities for handicapped citizens.

2. Programming to improve services and employment and retirement opportunities for the elderly has been greatly expanded. The foundation has provided substantial support for Elderhostel, which pioneered the use of more than 240 college and university residential facilities for educational programs for older Americans. It has also helped professionalize the field of geriatric health care, particularly by increasing the number and training of geriatric nurse practitioners. (In recent decades a number of the better major foundations in the East have also begun to concentrate on some of these same disadvantaged groups. But they have done so more out of a spirit of liberal egalitarianism than a conservative commitment to old-fashioned religious ideals, as in the case of Kellogg.)

3. In the field of health it has supported pilot efforts to increase public awareness of the need for individuals to take personal responsibility through their life-styles for health improvement and disease prevention. Kellogg was also one of the first foundations to support projects aimed at demonstrating alternatives to institutionalization of the elderly

and infirm and testing various incentive programs and other arrangements to reduce the costs and improve the quality of health care.

4. Because of its serious concern with what it sees as the deterioration of social values and the weakening of the family in American life, the foundation has developed a number of programs to deal with the special problems that the increasing number of working women experience.

In the 1980s as a result of its most recent periodic program review the foundation has decided to maintain its emphasis on continuing education both for professionals and other adults; on comprehensive and cost-effective health services; on the promotion of better health habits, including nutrition, particularly for adolescents and the elderly; and on applications of new food-production technology to ensure adequate supplies of wholesome food worldwide.

In addition, it has become increasingly concerned with the problem of leadership development. In President Mawby's words, "the overwhelming tendency of our civilization in the last two decades has been to create specialists in virtually every field of endeavor . . . the disappearance of generalists has loomed ever-larger as a distinct possibility. Yet, without a strong cadre of emerging leaders who can function across lines of specialties . . . our nation will have lost one of its most valuable human resources."

As an outgrowth of this concern the foundation in 1980 established its National Fellowship Program to allow selected individuals to carry out largely self-directed programs to broaden their social and intellectual awareness and "equip them to deal in those complex decision-making areas where expertise in a single discipline is insufficient."

Satisfied with the results of the National Fellowships Program over its first four years, the foundation is now contemplating a new international program of the same kind.

In its most marked change of policy the foundation has now become actively engaged in the support of economic development programs in Michigan. As part of its effort to help rebuild the trouble-ridden economy of its home state, Kellogg in 1983 made a commitment of $9 million to the Industrial Technology Institute to encourage the computer-integrated automation of Michigan industry. The program is expected to attract new firms to the state and to help diversify its industrial base. It is also intended to build new partnerships between industry and education.

Kellogg has on the whole not supported programs of social and political activism or of advocacy and litigation. Neither has it helped spawn new organizations to express the special interests or needs of various groups and constituencies. But in its own fashion and within its own value framework it has moved with the times. And when it has decided to make a program commitment, it has frequently done so with large and sustained funding. As a result some of its efforts have had substantial impact on whole fields.

Although many specific alterations in program have been made over the years, the striking aspect of the Kellogg Foundation is the continuity in its general objectives and philosophy and their consistency with the outlook of its founder. Structurally it has also evolved and improved. The heavy interlock between the foundation and the company board that once existed has now been corrected. The foundation board has also been somewhat diversified.

For many years, the one seriously questionable aspect of the foundation's policy was its unwillingness to dispose of its massive, indeed controlling, block of shares in the Kellogg Company. These holdings, which amounted to 47 percent of the total outstanding shares, were held through the W. K. Kellogg Trust, which the foundation in turn controlled. Such concentrated stock ownership has in the past been highly hazardous to the health of a number of foundations, making their assets vulnerable to sharp changes in share prices, distracting them with involvement in the management of a business enterprise, and sometimes making them the instrument, as the Patman hearings documented, of the efforts of donor families to maintain financial control over their inherited company. It was for such reasons that the Congress in 1969 legislated to prohibit such "excess business holdings."

But the Kellogg Foundation, while its grace period for divestiture under the Tax Reform Act of 1969 was still running, vigorously lobbied to induce Congress either to change the legislation or to grant it an exception. Its motivation in this effort was in part to maintain ownership of its Kellogg shares, which in fact were exceptionally profitable. But more basically its intent was to try to keep the company out of the clutches of a corporate conglomerate. If it were to be taken over by such a group, the foundation officers believed, the results for local employment and the Battle Creek economy could be catastrophic. In November 1984, however, as the expiration of the grace period approached and as Congress showed no inclination to change the existing rules, the foundation reluctantly disposed of a substantial part of its controversial holdings. So this shadow on its shining record was at last removed.

A number of the major foundations seem better than they are, and they devote considerable effort to maintaining that appearance. Kellogg is the reverse case: it is substantially better than it is generally seen to be. It must be ranked very high among the genuinely creative and productive major American foundations. This author fifteen years ago called it "an admirable example of a shirtsleeve, midwestern fund working effectively on a range of problems overlooked by most foundations." Now, on the basis of its continuing performance and its fifty-year record, it stands as the finest large American foundation west of the Atlantic seaboard.

Kresge Foundation: The Capital of Capital Grants

The Kresge Foundation of Michigan is one of the older and larger of the big foundations. Founded in 1924, it currently has assets of nearly $800 million. It is an honorable, well-managed foundation still strongly under family influence in the third generation. Its simple, single, and unwavering practice of using nearly all its funds for capital grants differentiates it from almost all the other foundations encompassed in this analysis, a program approach that some find entirely defensible, and others highly debatable. (The only other major foundation with a similar policy of giving almost exclusively for buildings and facilities and doing so on a challenge basis is the Mabee Foundation of Oklahoma.) But the foundation, unswayed by changing fashions in philanthropy or shifting winds of public opinion, proceeds self-confidently and steadily on its course and thereby contributes its particular quality to the mosaic of foundation activity.

THE DONOR

In many ways the philosophy of the foundation reflects the old-fashioned and eminently practical qualities of Sebastian S. Kresge, its founder, who personally guided the foundation's affairs from its establishment until his death at ninety-nine in 1966.

S. S. Kresge was born to a poor farm family in the heart of the Pennsylvania German country just after the Civil War. By a combination of good fortune, business acumen, and endless hard work, he amassed a huge fortune in the chain-store business.

Starting out as a bookkeeper and then traveling salesman for a hardware company he became acquainted with some of the early pioneers in cash-and-carry merchandising, including Frank W. Woolworth and John G. McCrory. He quickly saw the opportunity for profits in that field and in 1897 acquired a part interest in a small variety store. Within fifteen years he owned eighty-five more, and by the 1930s more than seven hundred. The chain prospered throughout his long lifetime and has maintained its adaptability and vigor since under a new name, the K mart Corporation.

Kresge was an obsessive money-maker and money saver. Stories of his parsimony abound. Married three times, Kresge was divorced by his first two wives, each citing his stinginess as a major complaint. He would wear a pair of shoes until they literally fell apart; when the soles became too thin, he would line them with newspaper. He gave up golf because he could not stand to lose the balls.

His hobby was beekeeping for reasons that summarized the guiding principles of his own life: "My bees always remind me that hard work, thrift, sobriety, and an earnest struggle to live an upright Christian life are the first rungs of the ladder of success."

He was generous to the employees of his company, and because of his religious convictions, he made large gifts to programs opposing the use of cigarettes and alcohol and to many other charities. Without fanfare or ceremony he established his foundation in 1924, at a time of relatively low taxes, with an initial gift of $1.3 million.

During the next forty years under Kresge's guidance the foundation operated with a small board consisting of himself and three close friends, and a staff of one. His son, Stanley, joined the board in 1930 and served as trustee for more than fifty years until his death in 1985. Its assets currently total $790 million. The board consists of seven members including the donor's grandson and has a staff of thirteen, including professionals. With this small staff in relation to the volume of the foundation's grants, one professional for each $4 million of outlays annually, the foundation's total administrative expenses, including investment management fees, are only about 3 percent of its income.

Originally the foundation's assets were entirely in the form of stock in the Kresge Company. It began a diversification program in 1965, four years before the passage of the Tax Reform Act of 1969 required disposition of "excess business holdings." At present its holdings in K mart stock represent less than 4 percent of the company's outstanding shares and only 14 percent of the foundation's total portfolio.

The foundation is located in Troy, Michigan, the headquarters of the K mart Corporation; but the foundation is completely independent, and its grants are unrelated to the location of the company's stores and are not exploited in any way to serve the company's interests. It reports regularly and fully on its operations in annual reports that, during the long tenure of William Baldwin as president (1966–1981), were typically introduced by his literate and charming little essays.

The Kresge Foundation, in sum, is a foundation with a large and growing body of assets and with many virtues: freestanding, publicly accountable, and efficiently operated by a board and staff that work together in harmony.

But what about its program?

NONINNOVATIVENESS ENSHRINED

For more than forty years, under the guidance of the donor, Kresge followed an explicitly noninnovative philosophy. In its first public report covering the three-year period 1954–1956 it stated: "While all applications for grants are judged on their own merits, it is one of the present broad policies of the Kresge Foundation to favor grants providing for the maintenance, expansion or perpetuation of deserving existing organizations over grants which look to the establishment or initiating of new organizations or experimental projects. The policy . . . is based in part at least on the fact that other capable and well advised philanthropic organizations have made and will make considerable funds available for exploratory and experimental projects."

At that time about half the foundation's grants were made to institutions in Michigan and much of the remainder to institutions in states in the Northeast where Kresge's fortune had largely been acquired. Colleges and universities received the largest amount of support, hospitals and medical institutions somewhat less. For a time it supported institutions for religious training, but that activity subsequently diminished. In the late 1950s for the first time the foundation began to assist cultural institutions.

There was a moment in the late 1960s, when racial strife and urban violence were rampant, that the Kresge Foundation seemed to be prepared to take such issues into consideration in its grant making. President Baldwin in the annual report for 1967 wrote, "As much as any institution, and more than most, foundations have a duty not to neglect the world even though they may have doubts about the proposals for changing it. . . . [Kresge] will try to relate its gifts of facilities and equipment to the major problems of the time in the hope that creative minds can use the given facilities and equipment as instruments to the advantage of mankind." But after a few grants in the Detroit area for legal aid, job training, and inner-city schooling, the foundation soon returned to its long-established groove. In 1971, aware that the foundation's policies were generally regarded as regressive by others in the field, Baldwin wrote this rejoinder: "From time-to-time, it is possible to hear sniffs and clucks of disapproval and to observe what appears to be a slightly lifted eyebrow or a looking down of the nose at our dealing in such unimaginative grants. Suffice it to say that we get none of this disapprobation from those who apply to us. Since shelter and facilities are required by both imaginative and traditional institutions, we are commonly and fervently assured by both that we should stay where we are."

In 1975 the policy was reasserted, this time on grounds that it was not necessarily conservative at all: "This Foundation makes what are commonly called 'bricks and mortar' grants—an area, incidentally, we have always regarded as a most liberal form of giving, since it permits people to do work of their own choosing in buildings of their own design. And, as someone has remarked, there would have been little zoological research if Noah had lacked the Ark."

For many years Kresge's capital grants were used primarily for the construction of new physical facilities. More recently the renovation of existing older structures has become increasingly their purpose. In general, partly because of its policy of requiring that its grants be matched with other funds, Kresge's help has gone to well-established, financially sound, fully accredited organizations in higher education, health care, social services, science, conservation, and the arts and humanities.

An examination of the list of grantees indicates that prominent institutions all over the United States are included: from Allegheny College in Pennsylvania, the Art Institute of Chicago, the National Gallery of Art in Washington, D.C., and the Oaks Indian Mission in Oklahoma to the YWCA in El Paso, Texas, and the Zoological Society of San Diego, California.

The foundation supplies applicants with a fact sheet to fill out with information about the project and their organization that is used in judging the proposals received. The form calls for rather detailed financial information about the project and about the accreditation and financial situation of the sponsoring agency.

In the mid-1960s, Kresge conducted a survey of its grantees to ascertain their attitudes toward the foundation and its policies and procedures. In the mid-1970s a similar survey covered both its grantees and applicants whose proposals had been rejected. In the first survey an almost unanimous 99 percent of the respondents said that the project they proposed had been sound, that they thought the challenge grant method was effective and useful, and that they had been treated fairly by the foundation. About 80 percent said the foundation should remain exclusively in the bricks-and-mortar field. From the foundation's point of view the results of the survey left it satisfied that Kresge should continue its general program policy without modification.

In the mid-1970 survey, when both grantees and rejected applicants were canvassed, the grantees were again almost uniformly satisfied that the foundation's policies and procedures were sound, including the requirement that Kresge funds had to be matched by additional fund raising.

Rejected applicants who took the trouble to reply to the questionnaire were somewhat less satisfied with the foundation's policies, but most of them retained hope that they might get help if they applied again. Welfare organizations registered the lowest approval (48 percent) of the present type of Kresge grant. Again the foundation concluded that the survey results justified the continuation of its grant policies without alteration.

In 1981, Alfred Taylor succeeded Baldwin as president. He came to the foundation in 1972 as administrative vice-president after long experience in banking, followed by a period in Washington as associate director of the Office of Economic Opportunity. Under his direction the program has remained on its steady course, with one major and interesting departure. In mid-1984, a grant of $5 million dollars was made to help establish a new community foundation for southeastern Michigan. That metropolitan area, which includes Detroit, was the last major population center in the United States without such an institution. Kresge was careful to point out at the time that it took this unusual action because of the uniqueness of the opportunity, not as a basic shift in policy.

ALTERNATIVE APPRAISALS OF THE KRESGE APPROACH

Because Kresge is the biggest and best practitioner of its particular type of grant making, it provides a good hook on which to hang the pros and cons of bricks-and-mortar grants.

The arguments used by those who defend Kresge's policy include the following:

1. A number of the large foundations are prejudiced against bricks-and-mortar grants, and Kresge is therefore attempting to fill something of an unoccupied niche.
2. The costs of facilities and major capital equipment are one of the fundamental expense items that practically all nonprofit institutions must face; to the extent that Kresge relieves some of them of this burden it is in effect freeing other income, which can be used at their discretion for programming and other costs.
3. Bricks-and-mortar grants, unlike short-term foundation grants for experimental new programs, do not leave the institution when the grant has been spent with quite the same obligation of raising continuing funds from other sources to sustain the activity. Except ongoing maintenance and eventual renovation costs, a bricks-and-mortar grant is somewhat equivalent to a contribution to an organization's endowment.
4. Kresge-type grants for facilities are less intrusive and less threatening to an organization's autonomy in determining and controlling its own program than are targeted project grants. They eliminate the sometimes annoying problem for grantees of pressures and requirements from foundation staff that amount to meddling in the substance of their business.
5. On a more philosophical level, the Kresge approach is one of modesty about a foundation's capacity to conceive and direct significant new programs and is fundamentally re-

spectful of and reliant upon the judgment and competence of established nonprofit institutions to maximize the creativity, diversity, and quality of contribution by the nonprofit sector to the national welfare.

6. By confining itself essentially to judgments about the financial feasibility and managerial competence of its grantees, the Kresge Foundation can operate with minimal staff costs and with minimal diversion therefore of philanthropic funds from donor's gift to grantee's use.

7. The policy of making grants essentially to established, accredited, and respected institutions, and of requiring matching funds, may not seem very daring to some, but its logic is fundamental and important. The matching-fund requirement, given the prestige of Kresge grants, enables a recipient organization to leverage the money and obtain additional resources that in most cases it otherwise could not. Neither is there any reason to apologize for giving preference to those tried and tested educational, cultural, and other institutions of our society. Newly established institutions sometimes are made to seem more glamorous and interesting, but it is the great universities, hospitals, museums, symphony orchestras, and charitable agencies that day in and day out, year in and year out, produce the major flow of benefits offered by the so-called Third Sector to our national life.

Those critical of the Kresge approach have used the following arguments:

1. The "gap" in the funding preferences of other foundations that Kresge claims to fill is in fact as fictitious and evanescent as the various "gaps," missile and otherwise, that have been propagandized in American life in recent years. Small and middle-size foundations, which constitute the vast majority, are largely unstaffed and do little more than contribute to capital fund campaigns and bricks-and-mortar projects of various kinds. Indeed even the largest foundations, if one examines the grant lists of most of them, have a strong predilection for such giving.

2. Likewise the supposed tendency of many foundations to

fund experimental projects, suggested in the Kresge Foundation's first public report of thirty years ago as a justification for its noninnovative approach, simply does not exist. The vast majority of foundation grants goes to conventional activities and the support of traditional institutions. So there is no shortage of noninnovativeness that Kresge should trouble itself to overcome.

3. The Kresge policy of giving essentially to well-established and accredited institutions and its general requirement that matching funds be raised as a condition of obtaining a grant is in effect a policy of giving preference to the already privileged. It effectively excludes all of those institutions that represent new growth and innovation and that attempt to serve the needs of the disadvantaged. It is a snobbish, class-oriented bias and should be recognized for what it is.

4. The idea that by providing physical facilities the Kresge Foundation is somehow making a basic contribution to the nonprofit sector is pure sophistry. One might just as well argue that providing fire extinguishers, toilet facilities, or electric light bulbs is an equally crucial benefit. In truth there is a direct correlation between the incompetence and generally low standards of responsibility among foundations and the tendency to give bricks-and-mortar grants. This type of outlay is the first and the last resort of foundations without ideas of their own, without any sense of their own real purposes and priorities, and without the capacity for making discriminating judgments, let alone taking creative initiative.

5. Bricks-and-mortar grants are an especially nonthreatening kind of assistance that government can give to nonprofit institutions, and it should be left to fill that role. For at least the past thirty or forty years, government funding has been made massively available for educational facilities, health facilities, and facilities of many other kinds of nonprofit institutions throughout the country. As a result, particularly in higher education and health, the problem has more often been the overbuilding of facilities than the lack of them. This imbalance in the availability of funds between physical facilities and program activities was never more clear than in the first half of the 1970s, and yet Kresge in that period,

indifferent to considerations of relative need, plunged forward on its simple-minded course, adding excess to surplus by its fixation on bricks-and-mortar.

6. Kresge has sometimes argued in defense of its policies that great minds after all do need a place in which to work. That may be true, but it is equally true that what is important in a nonprofit institution is what goes on within its buildings and not the buildings themselves. It is that truth that Kresge cannot cope with and is incapable of making any contribution to, by its own admission.

7. Kresge's approach is indeed a modest one, and it is a foundation that intellectually has a great deal to be modest about. A crucial reality about nonprofit institutions, like all institutions, is that over time they become set in their ways, bureaucratized, and even ossified. Their funds also become completely committed to the support of ongoing activities and existing staff so that there is nothing left for adapting the institution to new requirements, experimenting with better ways to accomplish its purposes, or improving its quality. It is the essential, inherent, and most important quality of a foundation, not being pinned down by ongoing heavy operating costs, that it has the freedom and flexibility to contribute to the process of innovation and of self-renewal and rejuvenation by other institutions. From this perspective, what Kresge is doing with its money is not wicked, it is just empty-headed. It totally fails to capitalize on the greatest possibilities and potentialities of the foundation concept. Putting the matter in more concrete terms, there is nothing of any great importance that can be done in relation to the nation's most serious educational, health, and welfare problems—or in relation to the greatest and most dangerous international issues—simply by building a building somewhere.

These are the principal arguments, pro and con, about the Kresge approach. Take your pick.

Lilly Endowment, Inc.: The Athletics Supporter

The programs of a good number of the largest American foundations have a strong local focus. It is also true that urban problems in general and central city decay in particular have moved up in the program priorities of most of them.

In the industrial Middle West, because of the effects of demographic shifts, structural changes in the national economy, and the recent recession, concern about the decline of its cities and the need for economic redevelopment have become particularly great. Two of the largest foundations in the area, Lilly in Indianapolis, Indiana, and Mott in Flint, Michigan, have become heavily involved in such redevelopment programs in their home cities, in ways that raise some fundamental issues of philanthropic policy and role.

The Lilly Endowment of Indianapolis, Indiana, is a case of heavyweight assets and lightweight leadership. The market value of its portfolio is over $800 million, which ranks it among the ten largest foundations in the country. (There was a time in the early 1970s when its assets were $1.2 billion, and it was second in size only to the Ford Foundation.) Nevertheless it has never been able to sustain an impressive program. In the early 1970s there were signs of encouraging development, but more recently it has slumped again into a mediocre program, one element of which can be described as comic, or tragic, or something of both. The resources of the foundation derive from the Eli Lilly Pharmaceutical Company, from which the foundation is not dissociated, and this fact may be at the root of some of its problems.

THE DONORS

The foundation was established in 1937 by the Lilly family. The three principal donors were Josiah K. Lilly, Sr., who built the small drug company founded by his father in 1876 into a giant enterprise, and his two sons, J. K. Lilly, Jr., and Eli Lilly.

The foundation began without professional staff or defined program. J. K. Lilly, Jr., was chairman of the board. His brother, Eli, was the executive director and operated the foundation for the next several years, as he said, "out of the left-hand drawer of my desk." Grants during those years were confined to the family's favorite charities.

In 1949 J. K. Lilly III became the first full-time director; during the five years of his capable administration some progress in developing the program and staff was made. But by 1954 father and son had become embroiled in a quarrel so bitter that the younger Lilly resigned, left Indianapolis, and has never since had anything to do with the foundation. Harold Duling succeeded him as head, and over the next fifteen years the foundation began to develop a creditable record. Most of the grants were made to organizations within the state of Indiana, primarily to educational institutions and religious organizations. A few were made to black institutions, mostly through the United Negro College Fund.

By the 1950s the endowment had become the largest single source of U.S. philanthropic assistance in the specific field of religion. It favored middle-of-the-road Protestantism and played an influential role in improving theological education. This was a reflection of the strong religious beliefs of the family, who also made generous personal gifts to the Episcopal Church. Eli Lilly was reportedly its largest individual contributor in the United States during that period.

J. K. Lilly, Jr., was the dominant figure in the endowment until he died in 1966, but Eli and his wife were also actively involved and were largely responsible for the foundation's general improvement in the 1950s. By 1959 in fact it appeared that the endowment might be ready to move beyond general institutional support and scattered grants to community organizations to some kind of commitment to social change. Such at least was the conclusion of experienced decoders of foundation verbiage upon seeing the following labored sentence in its annual report for the year: "Charitable organizations and agencies such as those supported by the Lilly Endowment and other foundations are now prime movers in the constant reexamination and development of man's abilities and responsibilities which lead the way to great advances in social, economic and scientific horizons and accomplishments."

Whatever that statement was intended to mean, however, it did not in fact lead to a more vigorous program. Within a few months thereafter Harold Duling was replaced by a retired lawyer whose local reputation was based largely on his extremist political activities. And within two years he was succeeded by a junior officer of the Lilly Company, John S. Lynn, known primarily for his affiliation with a bizarre fundamentalist religious group and with leaders of the John Birch Society. Very quickly, the foundation strayed far into the ideological swamps.

Just why the endowment took such a sharp political turn at that moment can only be surmised. Despite the moderating influence of Eli Lilly and his wife on the board, it may simply have succumbed to the relentless pressures of the local political environment of Indiana, which at that time was a center of militant anticommunism and superpatriotism. But some close observers lay the change to the impact of two specific developments on the Lilly family: the Kefauver investigation of the drug industry in the late 1950s, which produced acute resentment and fear of federal "intervention"; and the "radicalization" of American Protestantism, symbolized at that time by the National Council of Churches' declaring its support for the recognition of mainland China and its admission to the United Nations.

In any event, the foundation's grant list thereafter began to be peppered with projects "explaining the free market and limited government concepts" and warning of the dangers of communism. Its annual reports likewise began to suggest that the endowment's major purpose had become its crusade in defense of "human freedom." Even its traditional interest in religion was harnessed to the new cause. The 1962 annual report soberly noted that because "Christianity is the great unifying force" in international affairs, it thereafter would receive the endowment's increased support.

By 1965 the ideological fever had begun to drive out some of the better staff members, and even some signs of public protest became visible. (One group of Indiana doctors, for example, threatened to boycott the products of the Lilly Company.) Thereafter the shrill political note in the foundation's reports was muted, and when John Lynn left in late 1972, grants to extremist groups had essentially ended. (Publication of the author's earlier study, *The Big Foundations* [New York: Columbia University Press, 1972], in which the degradation of the Lilly Endowment was recounted, apparently helped trigger Lynn's departure. After its appearance a member of the Lilly family telephoned to say that "the exposé had rendered a useful service. Lynn had become an embarrassment and had bullied the Endowment into a number of very foolish actions. He should have been removed earlier." A few months later another member of the Lilly board at a public occasion encountered the author and assailed him for "washing dirty linen in public." But he went on to say that the result had been to bring a festering situation to a head and to cause "necessary action to be taken.") Lynn was succeeded by a very different and much more substantial individual, Dr. Landrum Bolling. Before accepting the post Bolling wrote a memorandum outlining the program ideas that he intended to pursue. At the time Eli Lilly and Eugene Beesley, chief executive officer of the Lilly Company, controlled both the company and the endowment. They accepted Bolling's proposals, and he took office in October 1972.

Thereafter the foundation's program and organization went through a rapid change both in the scale and in the direction of its giving. In the years before 1969 when Congress mandated a minimum payout level for foundations, the endowment had distributed only 1.5 percent of the market value of its assets on average in grants. Thus in 1968 it gave out $6.7 million. By 1972 it was forced to increase this to $18 million and by 1975, because of a rapid rise in the value of Eli Lilly Pharmaceutical Company shares, to $55 million. (The Lilly family was always secretive about financial matters and alert to take advantage of tax benefits for their charitable giving. When J. K. Lilly's $5.5 million rare coin collection was given to the Smithsonian after his death, his executors persuaded Congress and the president to pass a special law providing an equivalent reduction of his estate taxes. Company stock was not listed on the New York Stock Exchange until 1970 because of the exchange's disclosure requirements. In that year, probably in order to market blocks of the endowment's shares as required by the diversification provisions of the Tax Reform Act of 1969, the family gave in. As *Forbes* magazine commented at the time, "Families like the Lillys may resist change, but they cannot stop it.")

Bolling had a combination of attributes that enabled him to make the most of the limited possibilities of the situation. He was personally known and well regarded by Eli Lilly, who was the last survivor of the founders of the endowment and a rather revered figure in that small environment. Bolling was acceptable also because of his deep religious beliefs and his experience as head of a private liberal arts college in Indiana. He was a man with strong interests in educational and international affairs, and because of his convictions as a Quaker, he was also a believer in consensus and accommodation to the views of others. This combination of qualities made it possible for him to get along with the local establishment and at the same time do more than settle for the least common denominator of its narrow views.

In Bolling's first year at the helm, the level of the foundation's giving nearly tripled as compared to the previous year, reaching

$52 million. The staff was expanded, and Dr. Herman Wells, the distinguished head of the University of Indiana, was added to the board.

The endowment's educational grants were extended to institutions not only in Indiana but throughout the country. Its established program for the training of ministers became more ecumenical, adding an emphasis on the training of black ministers in the South. For the first time a number of significant international grants was made: for disaster relief in Africa, to improve international understanding, and to support research on major foreign policy issues.

Local institutions such as the Indianapolis Museum of Art and the Indianapolis Children's Museum continued to receive large grants, as did the American Enterprise Institute in Washington. But changes nonetheless were definitely under way.

Over the following four years the endowment further developed its national and international programs. And here and there in the grant list could be found items that only a few years earlier might well have been denounced by Bolling's predecessors as "communistic": a grant to the Federation of Southern Cooperatives, a grant to the Native American Rights Fund, and the like.

Under Bolling the Lilly Endowment became a much larger factor on the philanthropic scene both because of its greatly enlarged assets and because of its improved program. It came to be regarded as an institution with an interesting and useful combination of qualities: a strong Midwestern emphasis, a unique role in the field of theological education, a good international program, and a wide-ranging interest in matters as diverse as early childhood learning and the better training of local public officials.

Then rather suddenly a total change in leadership occurred. In 1976 Beesley and Eli Lilly died within a few months of each other. And at the end of 1977 Bolling decided to move on to become the head of the Council on Foundations in Washington.

Beesley before his death had anointed Richard D. Wood to replace him as CEO of the company, passing over the other contender, Thomas H. Lake. As consolation prize, Lake was then named chairman of the board and president of the endowment in early 1978. (In response to a question raised by a member of the endowment's board about the propriety of swapping individuals back and forth between the company and the foundation, Beesley is reported once to have said, "I know it's questionable and can't last but we will keep on doing it as long as it is legal.") Lake, during his years in the company, was known as a tight, buttoned-down executive type whose outside main interest was an enthusiasm for sports.

In 1977, Bolling's last year, the market value of the endowment's assets had plunged to a level less than half of that of the previous year. In 1978, Lake's first year at the helm, he therefore had to operate within a restricted budget. But the grant pattern did not immediately change.

In 1979, however, as the endowment's assets began to rebound, Lake signaled that the redevelopment of downtown Indianapolis had become its priority interest. Among the grants that year was a $5 million allocation for the planning of White River Park, a proposed giant amusement and exhibition area. In 1980 the shift became a landslide. Of the $32 million in grants approved for the year, about 60 percent went into community development projects, most of them in Indianapolis. Among the larger items were a gift of $2 million for buildings for the local Methodist hospital and $1.5 million to each of two other hospitals for construction costs. Under the heading of "higher education" was listed a grant of $8 million to build a championship swimming pool and diving facility to be located at the campus of the combined Indiana University–Purdue University at Indianapolis (UIPUI, known locally as "OOEY-POOEY," this is an institution of some twenty-three thousand students). The swimming pool project eventually cost the endowment $10.5 million.

By 1981 it had become clear that the Lilly Endowment had become a full partner with the Indianapolis city government and with the local business community in an effort to rebuild the downtown area and thereby attempt to reverse the city's declining fortunes. The strategy was to try to gain recognition for Indianapolis by its variety of cultural and educational resources but most of all as a capital of athletics. The facilities funded by the endowment on behalf of this objective now include a sports center with twenty-four tennis courts and seating for ten thousand spectators at center court; a sixty-five-hundred-seat "natatorium"; a track and field complex seating fourteen thousand and expandable to thirty thousand; a bicycle racing track; and a sixty-five-thousand-seat domed stadium, about which more later.

Eli Lilly during his lifetime said on a number of occasions that he wanted to have the endowment "help make Indianpolis known for more than the Five Hundred," the big annual Memorial Day automobile race. Thomas Lake's version of that ambition focuses on sports.

In the endowment's 1981 annual report Lake insisted "that a foundation has a special obligation to the people of its home community. That is why the Lilly Endowment has always emphasized programs that serve Indianapolis and Indiana." But in his view this was not parochialism: "We are sure the programs that directly benefit a specific community can indirectly benefit all communities." The mayor of Gary, Indiana, an industrial city to the north of Indianapolis with a largely black population, which received only one grant of $50,000 that year, might well have wondered what benefit, even indirectly, his desperately distressed community might derive from such endowment grants as one of $500,000 to the American College of Sports Medicine to enable it to relocate from Madison, Wisconsin, to Indianapolis; one of $1 million to renovate the American Legion Mall in downtown Indianapolis; one of $700,-000 to build a new facility for the Girls Clubs of Greater Indianapolis; several millions of dollars for construction costs of various sports facilities; and a stunning item of $25 million, of which there was no mention in Lake's introduction to the endowment's annual report, for a vast football stadium to be added to the city's convention center. City officials expressed the hope that the facility would enable Indianapolis to win a National Football League franchise by 1984 and "push the city into the big time." In early 1984, it was announced that the Baltimore Colts would move to Indianapolis, which caused a faculty member at the university to comment that "this is the only city in the United States that by acquiring a last place NFL football team would feel that its cultural attractiveness had been improved." (Lake's enthusiasm for using philanthropic money for the advancement of sports was topped in early 1985 when it was announced from Rio de Janeiro that a wealthy Brazilian had bequeathed some $150 million to a local soccer team in the industrial suburb of Bangu.)

By 1982 opinion in Indianapolis with regard to the endowment's huge subsidy program had begun to crystallize. Republican Mayor Hudnut was overjoyed about this demonstration of "partnership" of government, business, and philanthropy and about the willingness of the Endowment "to put its money where its mouth is. . . ." But not everyone was equally enthusiastic. Residents of some older city neighborhoods, particularly blacks, felt that their interests were being neglected and that they had been left out of local decision making. "I am not against progress, but I have difficulty supporting a stadium when our schools are woefully under-financed and other city services are inadequate," said State Senator Julia Carson, a black who had represented an Indianapolis district in the legislature for the preceding ten years. She added, "The Mayor and the Lilly Foundation wanted the stadium, so it was built. That's the way things are done here."

As doubts and criticisms began increasingly to surface, Lake attempted to put a more presentable face on the affair. To the charge that the endowment was simply proving once again that despite its big-time money it was locked in a small-town mentality, Lake took his stance on high rhetorical ground: "Indianapolis in the 1980's is a laboratory of the urban sciences, a place where a cohesive attempt is being made to revitalize urban society, to help cities realize their potential for greatness. If this attempt is successful—or even partially successful—it can profoundly influence the future for all of us." To the charge that the program had simply been imposed on the city by the business community and the endowment without the involvement of the citizenry, Lake asserted that the plans that were being financed had been developed after consultation with a "wide range" of community leaders and that citizen involvement had "received priority attention." But at the same time he did concede that "there isn't unanimity of citizen opinion on programs or priorities."

To the charge that the whole idea of turning Indianapolis into "Jock City" was both neglectful of other needs and somehow unworthy, Lake admitted that "there are problems that need to be addressed in the employment, housing, education and other areas." But about the social and even spiritual value of sports he was unequivocal: "It can contribute to the health of Indianapolis residents, maintain the lively atmosphere that is so important to a community and assist in the creation of new job opportunities. The emphasis on ports also can serve as a continuing reminder of the Olympic ideals of sportsmanship, team work, healthy competition and individual fulfillment."

However persuasive Lake's defense of the athletics facilities program may have been to the skeptics and critics, there is no doubt that the emphasis on these matters in his reports for these years obfuscated important and innovative actions the endowment had occasionally taken, such as a pioneering training program for native American lawyers and its program for the reform of the national juvenile justice system. Neither did they do justice to the useful ongoing programs that he inherited from his predecessor Landrum Bolling. These included its help to liberal arts colleges, its international activities, and most notably its extensive work in theological education, a distinctive and outstanding program under the able leadership of Dr. Robert Wood Lynn.

Indeed the strain of defending his sports program caused Lake to argue the case for even the best work of the endowment by very strange reasoning. Thus in 1981 he rather curiously cited "the Ayatollah Khomeini, religious warfare in Northern Ireland, and the rise of the Moral Majority in the United States" as justification for Lilly's efforts to "strengthen religion" as a contribution to the public welfare. And in his 1982 essay he implied that another miracle of the loaves and fishes had occurred that year by arguing that "In focusing on Indianapolis, neither the Lillys nor the Lilly Endowment turned their backs on national or international concerns. They continue to provide financial assistance to a number of programs designed to help solve problems across America and around the world."

On this assertion at least the grant list could provide a basis for evaluating Lake's contentions. Among the more than $30 million of grants that year hardly a handful could be considered international; the endowment, though it may not have turned its back on such concerns, certainly turned off the money.

HOOSIER DOME

That President Lake chose to treat the largest grant in the endowment's history in his 1981 essay for the annual report simply by overlooking it is understandable, because vindicating such an action by a philanthropic institution could well have been too much even for his demonstrated talents for rationalization.

The domed stadium, called Hoosier Dome, was to be the centerpiece of the expansion of the city's Convention and Exhibition Center. Its total cost by preliminary estimates would be $65 million, of which the Lilly grant would provide nearly half. This massive outlay of philanthropic funds was of course a departure from the traditional concentration of such money on educational, scientific, health, cultural, religious, and social services purposes. But one need not hold the view that sports activities are inherently inferior to these more common objectives of foundation assistance to question the endowment's subsidy of Hoosier Dome both on practical and ethical grounds.

The economic viability of such sports facilities is highly debatable, as the experience of many American cities has shown. Original estimates of costs and revenues are usually wildly distorted by political pressures and the effort to persuade taxpayers to pass the necessary bond issue or tax increase. (The ultimate cost of the football stadium turned out to be $77 million.) Heavy cost overruns and even corruption in the process of construction are not uncommon. If the bookkeeping in such projects were objectively done, most of them in the opinion of students of public finance would be found to have been financial disasters. Stadiums are built "for the benefit of a select and small segment at the expense of the larger population," says Robert A. Baade, a Lake Forest (Illinois) College economics professor who has studied sports finance. They are justified by public officials for a "lot of poorly defined benefits," he says, whereas the real rationale is often just a civic ego trip.

Cities of modest size throughout the country, such as Indianapolis, that have become involved in these political-economic projects have found that the revenues actually earned are rarely sufficient to cover the debt service. In Indianapolis specifically, both the existing local professional franchises, for the Indiana Pacers of the National Basketball Association and the Indianapolis Checkers, the hockey team, have been notorious money losers.

Likewise, the proposition that such sports facilities are effective engines of economic development and neighborhood revitalization is far from proved. "In terms of straight economic development, this stuff is baloney," says Professor George Sternlieb, a Rutgers University urbanologist. "The payoff is trivial."

For a long time, it has been to the Middle West what Philadelphia has been to New York: the butt of innumerable jokes about a dull town with residents to match. Even the mayor has acknowledged the common view of the city "as a place you flew over to get someplace else." But although this perception may be unfair, even some business leaders view with great skepticism the whole effort to turn it into a major convention, transportation, and sports center. Jerry Semler, president of American United Life Insurance Company and chairman of the city's 500 Festival, says that the thousands of people who pack the motor speedway for the annual automobile race do not see Indianapolis as a tourist attraction. They go home after the race and immediately relegate the city, he says, to its usual place as "just another cornfield somewhere in the Middle West."

The head of the local Democratic Party organization objects that the costs will fall on the poor and the benefits go to others. "The people," he says, would not object to an increase in the local sales tax "if the money were going for city services. But when the taxpayers have to pay for a domed stadium that's a frill for the rich, that's going a little too far."

One community leader, who led a fight to require that some of the construction work for the stadium go to minority contractors and that notices of job openings for the project be posted first in the adjoining neighborhoods, has commented "that all this Lilly project is proving is that any city—if it has a foundation large enough and dumb enough to put big money into it—can have a white elephant football stadium."

In the history of American philanthropy, there has never been a foundation expenditure of equivalent size given on weaker economic justification, more questionable grounds of social benefit, and more dubious distribution of benefits among local politicians, profit-seeking entrepreneurs, and the needier elements of the population.

A PHILANTHROPIC MOTH NEAR THE POLITICAL FLAME

To understand the origins and basis of the endowment's enthusiasm for these heavy subsidies of physical facilities in Indianapolis, and the implications of what it is doing for public confidence in the purity of philanthropy's devotion to the public welfare, more is to be learned from a review of recent political developments in the city and state than from the endowment's own high-flown and somewhat inconsistent descriptions of its purposes.

In the late 1960s one of the bright spots on the political landscape for Indiana Republicans was the popularity and good record of former Rhodes Scholar Mayor Richard Lugar in Indianapolis (now senator from Indiana). During his tenure exceptionally warm working relationships developed between his administration and the local business community. In 1970, when the Republicans controlled city hall and Marion County (where the city is located) as well as the state legislature, a bill was put through, without referendum, to consolidate city and county government into what is now called Uni-Gov. The move brought certain efficiencies and strengthened the credit rating of the local government. It also brought major benefits without corresponding costs to the Republican Party and to the affluent white citizens of the suburbs. In the words of Professor Vork Willburn of Indiana University, a political scientist, it was the first major example of "a take-over of a city by the suburbs."

By allowing residents of the outlying areas to vote in the city elections, an unbroken string of Republican mayors has been elected since. At the same time the voting strength of the 20 percent of the county who are black has been substantially diluted. On the other hand suburban area residents have not had to give up control over their own local police and fire departments or school systems or to contribute tax revenues to social, health, and welfare services in the inner city.

Because the business leadership of the area has a large stake in maintaining the arrangement, it is heavily involved in Indianapolis politics. Most of its support is channeled through two groups with close ties to each other: the Greater Indianapolis Progress Committee and the Corporate Community Council. The former makes studies and recommends solutions to city problems. The latter, composed of the "chief decision makers" of the largest firms in Indianapolis, including Eli Lilly Pharmaceutical Company, the largest, places corporate resources behind selected projects. The Lilly Company, through its present and past executives in influential positions at the endowment, has also been able to obtain the foundation's massive financial assistance for these undertakings.

The integration of the endowment into the arrangement was consolidated in 1973, shortly before Mayor Lugar went to Washington, when his chief of staff, James Morris, moved to the endowment as vice-president in charge of activities and grants in Indianapolis. Like Lake, he not only was an Indianapolis booster and a sports fan but came with the blessing and support of both the political and business establishments. His star in the endowment was therefore destined to rise, and in mid-1984 he succeeded Lake as president.

Altogether, the Republican-business-philanthropic coalition in Indianapolis is the smoothest, most powerful relationship of its kind in the United States and its strategic objectives go far beyond sports facilities. Ultimately, by use of a large part of the Lilly Endowment's huge resources, it hopes to build, or buy, and bring to Indianapolis from other parts of the country an array of institutions that might leaven its deadly small-town atmosphere. Thus the endowment has subsidized the move of such organizations as the Hudson Institute, a think tank, from New York, and it has made a multimillion-dollar bid to try to bring an important East Coast museum to the city. The effort has also acquired some curious religious overtones. In early 1985 it was announced that "an informal working group" made up of city officials and the Lilly Endowment had been created to try to persuade four major Protestant churches to move their headquarters from Manhattan to Indianapolis. Mayor Hudnut, a Presbyterian minister himself, said it was his "dream" to make his city the nation's center of Protestantism.

There are those who feel excluded, indeed who are angry about what has been taking place, even though a handsome array of new facilities has been built in the downtown area, which has attracted some major sports events and more tourism. They contend that plutocracy has demolished democracy (and perhaps the Democrats) in the city. But businessman Frank McKinney, Jr., chairman of American Fletcher National Bank, the city's largest, contests this: "Some people say an elite runs this town. I don't like that word. I prefer 'leadership.' Over the last dozen years we have developed a process to hatch ideas and bring them to fruition."

Though opinions on the workings of the local power structure differ sharply, there is no question that it is political in the most partisan and basic sense, and there is no question that the endowment is in the middle of it.

In this, as in a number of the practices and activities of the endowment, there is no clear breach of the law. From its intimate interrelationship with the Lilly Company, its close association with the viewpoints and programs of the local business community, and the remarkable coincidence of priorities between it and the local leadership of the Republican Party, a strong impression has developed that the policies and resources of a philanthropic institution are being closely linked not only to the interests of a locality but also to the interests of a privileged and powerful minority within that community. This is a posture that at best could be assailed as paternalism and at worst as the corruption of a foundation with a subtle and sophisticated kind of politicization.

REDNECK PHILANTHROPY AND THE BOARD

The Lilly Endowment, one of the largest of the big foundations, for most of its history has been an inferior institution with a stunted view of its role and responsibilities. That it has never been able for any sustained period to develop a program of real quality or scope has been a matter of regret and concern among many in the field. Just why this has been the case is difficult to understand. The Lilly family, and particularly Eli Lilly and his wife, had genuine educational, religious, and charitable interests. In the case of foundations like Kellogg and Robert Wood Johnson, close company ties have been complicating but not necessarily crippling. But in the case of the endowment, they seem to have been very injurious.

There are those who explain Lilly's spotty record simply as an inevitable product of the local culture. They cite the fact that Marion County and Indianapolis have been the birthplace of the John Birch Society and headquarters of the American Legion, and even many Indianapolans deride the city as a redneck town. But this characterization is neither fair nor persuasive. The University of Indiana under good leadership has emerged in recent years as one of the finest cultural and intellectual centers in American higher education. The University of Notre Dame in the northwestern part of the state, again under good leadership, has become one of the two or three intellectual standard setters for the Catholic university system in the United States. One of the country's finest business leaders in terms of his sophisticated cultural interests and broad philanthropic perspective, J. Irwin Miller, is from Indiana; his Cummins Engine Company, through its corporate foundation, has won nationwide prestige. So the Indiana ethos cannot be blamed for the faults and failures of the Lilly Endowment. A more probable explanation for its deficiencies would seem to be the limitations of mind and spirit of the individuals who have largely controlled its affairs, particularly from the company side, in recent years.

Given the stature of at least two of the outside directors on the endowment's board, Margaret Chase Smith and Herman Wells, there is a reasonable basis for wondering whether they are fully in accord with the narrowness of its present program. Mrs. Smith was a distinguished member of the Senate with a broad view of national issues, and Wells not only was a major force in the development of

Indiana University but also has been a leading figure in higher education on the national scene.

Now that Jim Morris has become president, it appears that the program of heavy capital grants in Indianapolis may be ending, not to be repeated, and that the endowment will begin to place greater emphasis on social and educational issues, such as the problems of the public schools. The existing programs in youth development and leadership education may also be broadened to a national basis. But Morris's predecessor, Tom Lake, remains on the scene as board chairman. The constraints within which any attempt to upgrade the endowment's program remain, therefore, very severe. If improvement comes, it is most likely to come very slowly.

Charles Stewart Mott Foundation: Moving Up

The donor of the Mott Foundation, Charles Stewart Mott, died in 1973 at the age of ninety-seven. He was a tall, pipe-smoking, moustachioed gentleman with craggy features and immense zest and energy. In his long life he did everything in multiples: multiple marriages (four); multiple careers (engineer, industrial entrepreneur, politician, army officer, community leader, and philanthropist); and multiple business interests (General Motors, U.S. Sugar, several banks, a number of municipal water supply systems, and cattle breeding).

When it came to making money Mott not only did that in multiples but in very large ones. By the time of his death his fortune was probably on the order of $1 billion. As a young man he took over a money-losing wheel factory started by his father in the East, moved it to Flint, Michigan, as the automobile boom began, and made it richly profitable. Then, before World War I he traded the company for a substantial block of shares in the dynamic new General Motors Corporation. This timely stroke provided him with the financial base on which he built his later business interests and his philanthropic activities. (It was in this same period that he had a fling at politics, being elected mayor of Flint in 1912 and again in 1913 and 1918. In 1920 he sought nomination as the Republican candidate for governor of Michigan but lost.)

He was a driving entrepreneur and at the same time a very

charitable and civic-minded man with a deep interest in children and an enduring devotion to his adopted city of Flint.

Friends called him the world's most generous pennypincher, a string saver who never bought a paper clip (he used those he received in the mail), wrote on old envelopes for scratch paper, and bought his suits off the rack in downtown Flint. Once asked to estimate his own worth, he told a reporter, "I don't advertise, that's nobody's business. What I am worth is what I am doing for other people." So that it will not be thought that he was simply a benign old pussycat it should be recalled that on matters such as industrial relations and the protection of private property he was as hard as nails. He called himself a conservative Republican and was a regular contributor to organizations of the extreme Right. In an interview with Studs Terkel reprinted in the national best-seller *Hard Times*, Mott denounced the sit-down strikes in General Motors plants in the 1930s and thought that the police and the National Guard should have used their guns on the strikers. In his words: "They should have said, 'Stop that thing. Move on, or we'll shoot.' And if they didn't, they should have been shot."

ESTABLISHMENT OF THE FOUNDATION

Almost as soon as his fortune began to flourish, Mott began to give liberally to charities in Flint. Between the end of World War I and the mid-1920s he began a series of substantial contributions: to build a hospital building, to acquire land for a city park, and to buy farmland for a YMCA camp for boys.

In 1926, he chartered his foundation and endowed it with two thousand shares of General Motors stock, then worth about $300,-000. From then until 1934 it operated as a typical family foundation supporting a wide range of projects and institutions linked to the family's interests: a children's camp, several churches, and a crippled children's program.

In 1935 the Mott Foundation began its second phase. As the story goes, it all started after a 1935 Rotary Club meeting at which Frank Manly, athletic director of the Flint school district, talked to Mr. Mott about how the schools could be kept open after regular hours to provide recreation for children and keep them out of trouble. Mott, who had been considering building a Boys Club in the city, bought the idea of using the public schools instead as year-round recreation centers. The program began with a six thousand dollar grant to try the experiment for a limited period. Over the following thirty-five years the concept kept broadening until the entire school system was involved and adults as well as young people were able to participate not only in recreational but also a wide range of cultural and educational programs. As a result the traditional role of the neighborhood school was expanded, in the words of the foundation, from that of a "formal learning center for the young, operating six hours a day, five days a week, 39 weeks a year, to a total community center for young and old operating virtually around the clock, around the year."

In 1940 as American entry into World War II approached, Flint became a center of military production, and the program was extended to teaching industrial and technical skills to the city's labor force, many of whom were newly arrived East European immigrants and poor southern blacks and whites.

By the 1960s the Flint community education program had some 90,000 participants in a city of only 200,000. The lights of the schools burned every night, and every room was in use. Frank Manly, whose salesmanship and leadership were important factors in the success of the program, called the schools "poor men's country clubs." To the visitors who came from all over the country to see the Flint experiment in "community education," he often described how people, including mothers with their babies, would line up for blocks on registration night to enroll.

As the program's reputation spread it became a kind of educational movement. By 1974 the federal government had also been attracted to the idea, and in that year President Gerald Ford signed a special bill providing for federal financing of such plans. Eventually some fourteen hundred communities across the country adopted programs modeled after that in Flint.

The "community school" concept became the established trademark of the Mott Foundation. The program, however, was not without its problems and the trademark not without its blemishes.

During a thirty-five-year span the foundation poured a sum on the order of $100 million into the Flint schools through a highly unusual set of working relationships. The foundation in effect had no staff. The Flint Board of Education was the foundation's largest grantee, and the Mott program staff were all employees of the board. At one time Frank Manly carried both the titles of executive director of the Mott Foundation and associate superintendent of the Flint Board of Education. The foundation by the sheer volume of its funding exercised great influence over—and in the opinion of a good number of teachers, as well as other citizens of Flint, undemocratic control over—the city's entire educational system. Some officials of the United Automobile Workers criticized Mott for turning Flint into a "highly sophisticated kind of company town." Sentiment on the whole seemed to be a mixture of gratitude and appreciation for the foundation's generosity combined with a feeling of uneasiness that Mott money had created an unhealthy situation of dependency, favoritism, and factionalism in the city's school system.

In 1963 Mr. Mott turned over the bulk of his investments to the foundation and tripled its assets to $345 million. At that time the first statement of philosophy was prepared, possibly to provide a guide for the enlarged program that was then undertaken. It emphasized that the foundation would attempt to develop strong and responsible citizens and to help them work together to build a better community. Flint would be the laboratory and proving ground. Other communities could observe and learn from its experience.

As the 1960s drew to a close a moment of major transition was clearly approaching. Mr. Mott was beginning to fail, and his working partner in the Flint education program Frank Manly was in poor health. The Tax Reform Act of 1969 required a substantial increase in the level of the foundation's grants, but its principal program was running into difficulty, and the foundation's operating methods had become manifestly inadequate.

Mr. Mott had always run his foundation as a one-man show. He had personally made all grant decisions and had even signed all checks. He also made all the investment decisions. Board meetings were perfunctory and were frequently conducted without benefit of even an agenda.

However, as his strength began to decline Mott recognized the need for a reexamination of the foundation's procedures and program. The person chosen to carry out this task was William S. White, the son-in-law of his son Harding Mott. White had had experience as a management consultant, and that plus his status as a family member made it possible for him to bring about a succession of changes over a relatively few years that perhaps no outside individual could have achieved.

His first objective was to create an organization for a foundation that did not have one: an investment office, a communications function, a program office, and an administrative staff. The new tax law helped induce the board to accept White's recommendations, and by 1970 a number of his recommendations had already been put into effect, most importantly the severance of the program staff from the Flint Board of Education and its transfer to the foundation. This has had beneficial effects both in restoring greater control over its own school system to the community and also in giving the foundation much greater freedom of action in program development.

White then turned his attention to overhauling the procedures of the board of trustees and broadening its membership. In 1973 the foundation produced its first annual report, which contained a comprehensive factual account of the evolution of its policies. That same year Mott and Manly both died within a few months of each other. Thereafter Harding Mott became chairman and CEO of the foundation, and in 1975 White was elected president.

In the foundation's report for 1977 the organizational and operational changes during the ten years in which White had been associated with it were summarized. At the beginning of the period the six-member board of the foundation had been made up of three Mott family members and three nonfamily members. By 1977 the board had been increased to nine, a majority of whom were nonfamily. In the same period the professional staff had increased from fourteen to thirty-eight. At the beginning the foundation issued no publications; at the end it was issuing not only annual reports but also newsletters, specialized books and pamphlets on its programs, and regular press releases. Its assets had increased from $380 million to $420 million, and its stock portfolio had been substantially diversified, particularly its holdings of General Motors Corporation shares.

PROGRAM EVOLUTION

Useful and necessary as these institutional changes were, the possibility of clarifying the foundation's program philosophy and rationalizing the content of its program most excited White's interest. Almost as soon as he assumed the title of president, he turned energetically to that task. White thinks very highly of the results of his labors; others could come to a rather different judgment. But what is indisputable is that there is no comparable example in philanthropy of an attempt to apply the methodology of corporate planning to its programming problems.

To begin the exercise he reviewed in detail the foundation's history and experience. Then he and a colleague "sealed themselves into a room over a period of several months" to develop a statement of basic philosophy.

The atmosphere in that sealed room must have become rather murky because the lengthy deliberations culminated in the following declaration of the ultimate objective of the Mott Foundation: Through its grants it would seek "to demonstrate the contribution of private philanthropy to a fundamental principle—the value of a pluralistic approach to freedom of choice, in search for truth and equality in the fulfillment of human needs."

That studied formulation, which might seem to present certain problems of grammar, syntax, and meaning, nonetheless clearly represented a new breakthrough in the evolution of the esoteric language that Dwight Macdonald, in a memorable series of articles in *The New Yorker* on the Ford Foundation a few years ago, called *foundationese*. He pointed out that sentences written in this language are often reversible, like a trench coat, and he cited two examples from one of the foundation's annual reports: "Democracy is essential if a healthy economy is to function effectively" and "The partnership in progress of all free men depends on the advancement of human welfare." Both, as he pointed out, "give just as good wear either way."

The Mott Foundation has taken the development of foundation prose one step further, from reversible sentences to Tinkertoy sentences, in which the phrases can be rearranged in various ways without necessarily increasing the original ambiguity. Thus the fundamental principle being served by the foundation's grants might be alternatively defined as "the value of the search for truth and a pluralistic approach to equality in the fulfillment of human needs and freedom of choice."

Or the principle might be "the value of freedom of choice in a pluralistic approach to the fulfillment of human needs and of the search for truth and equality." Other such possibilities readily come to mind.

In any event, building on that spongy statement White with relentless logic elaborated a program philosophy and structure that he has reduced to chart form.

Proceeding from the "statement of purpose" to "principles" and "missions," the foundation then formulates the purpose of each mission, breaks it into subparts which are called "thrusts," and then

MOTT FOUNDATION PROGRAM PHILOSOPHY AND STRUCTURE

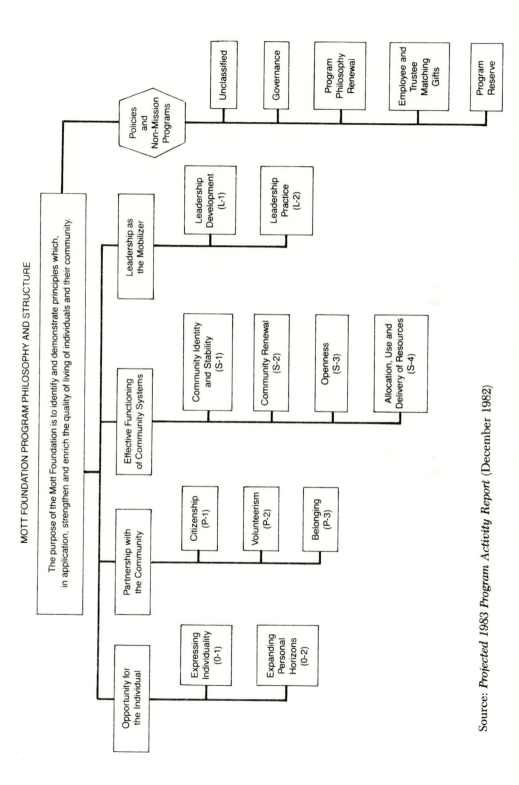

The purpose of the Mott Foundation is to identify and demonstrate principles which, in application, strengthen and enrich the quality of living of individuals and their community.

Opportunity for the Individual
- Expressing Individuality (O-1)
- Expanding Personal Horizons (O-2)

Partnership with the Community
- Citizenship (P-1)
- Volunteerism (P-2)
- Belonging (P-3)

Effective Functioning of Community Systems
- Community Identity and Stability (S-1)
- Community Renewal (S-2)
- Openness (S-3)
- Allocation, Use and Delivery of Resources (S-4)

Leadership as the Mobilizer
- Leadership Development (L-1)
- Leadership Practice (L-2)

Policies and Non-Mission Programs
- Unclassified
- Governance
- Program Philosophy Renewal
- Employee and Trustee Matching Gifts
- Program Reserve

Source: *Projected 1983 Program Activity Report* (December 1982)

subdivides each "thrust" into its component "program areas." Finally, the "program areas" are "prioritized."

Thus, to give just one example, the way the "mission" in the general chart of program philosophy and structure headed "Expanding Personal Horizons" is elaborated in the chart below.

These twisting paths of ratiocination in some cases lead nowhere. The 1983 edition of the elaborately detailed volume outlining "projected program activity," which is produced each year as a basis for budgeting by the board, pointed out about the preceding example that "This mission has been inactive since 1981 and it is likely it will remain inactive for the next two years."

One can develop a splitting headache if the full program plan is studied too carefully. The groupings of activities within missions

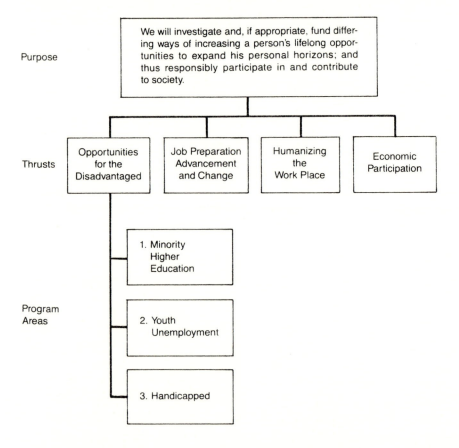

Source: *Projected 1983 Program Activity Report* (December 1982)

in a number of instances have all the coherence of some modern po-
etry. That for "Community Identity and Stability," for example, includes grants for health care, historic preservation, unwed mothers,
crime prevention, surplus food distribution, and teaching high
school students about radio, television, and photography.

In other cases, missions that would seem to be of great scope
and current relevance, such as that dealing with "citizenship,"
prove on inspection to contain no substance. According to the program doctrine this mission "emphasizes the critical partnership between individuals and their communities and encourages the full
and vigorous exercise of citizenship in all of its aspects. It focuses
specifically on ways citizens can overcome obstacles to asserting
their rights and assuming their responsibilities. . . ." The 1980s are
obviously a time when issues related to citizenship are many and
pressing: Floods of immigrants have been entering from Asia, Mexico, Central America, the Caribbean, and elsewhere. The Hispanic
minority in the United States is rapidly increasing and struggling to
gain access to the political process. The problem of political gerry-
mandering as a means of infringing on the voting rights of blacks,
Hispanics, and other minorities is still a widespread national problem. In 1984, a presidential election year, the U.S. electorate once
again demonstrated the lowest participation rate among the leading
democratic nations.

But the Mott program for 1983 indicates that no grants were
made to "explore citizenship roles"; only one grant of $11,000 was
made to "improve citizenship education," and that was to train police school cadets in Flint; and no grants whatever were made
under the heading of "extending the citizenship franchise."

It is possible, of course, to carry such an exegesis too far, just as
the Mott Foundation may have gone to excess in its efforts at codifi-
cation, perhaps because of Mr. White's dedication, as one of his
staff members puts it, to the principle that "whatever is worth
doing is worth overdoing."

He clearly is a firm believer in the idea. On the other hand,
Willard Hertz, his vice-president for program, in a statement that
must have produced some strained expressions at the next staff
meeting, has said, "Oh, forget the mission statements: They're
meaningless when you are trying to determine how to spend
money."

No foundation has so tortured itself as has Mott in trying to
make the definition of its purposes and priorities tidy and logical

and the outcomes of its programs predictable. Nor has any so thoroughly confused potential grant applicants about what the foundation is actually trying to do. And yet, if one forgets the mission statements, as Hertz urges, and looks instead at the reality of the actual grants Mott has made, then a different and quite commendable picture emerges.

It has begun an orderly phaseout of many of the programs supported through the city's board of education and to require the board, through the taxpayers and the city's budgeting procedures, to pay for those it felt were worth continuing. Thus a fundamentally unhealthy, though in some ways productive, relationship of many years' standing has been brought under control.

It has demonstrated an open-mindedness toward a wide range of urgent problems of Americans of every kind: from blue-collar whites to the most disadvantaged minorities, from the needs of police officers to those of advocacy groups, and from problems of the economy to those of the environment.

Among its unusual and in some instances significant actions since 1976 are these:

1. support to the National Council on Employment Policy to study past government initiatives to alleviate the problem of youth employment in order to determine which ones worked and which ones did not:
2. development of a national program dealing with the problems of families, including the elderly and individuals in crisis;
3. a number of grants as part of a national program to prevent or ameliorate the consequences of teen-age pregnancy; and
4. launching of a program on the environment that will focus on the water resources of the Great Lakes area and the problem of toxic substances in industrial processing.

Many of these grants have been of exceptional quality and impact, which seems to have been due to two factors: the able and diverse staff that White has assembled and the creative rather than the scholastical side of this complex man. He is now in full command of the foundation (a board member says, "What White wants he gets") and he has shown that although he sometimes seems almost to make a fetish of the disciplined managerial approach, he also is willing to allow his staff considerable free rein and encourages their initiative. He is at the same time conservative and prepared to take some daring chances. Unlike his beloved program Codex, he makes no pretense of consistency or predictability in his own behavior, a characteristic that may have made possible many of the best things Mott has done.

He is also unusually candid in avowing some of the failures the foundation has had. Its Project SNAP was funded in eleven cities to make small grants to neighborhood groups to work on their own problems. After it had been given a reasonable period to prove itself, White announced, "We're winding it down . . . the evaluation we have received points out that we could have done a lot better and have had more impact if we had directed it differently." In shutting off a program in East Harlem in New York City to help neighborhoods with self-determination, White told the press, "They spent the entire amount of money on lawsuits against each other, with publicity in *The New York Times, New York Post* and all the television stations." Such straightforwardness would alone be sufficient to brand him in the eyes of most of his peers in the foundation world as eccentric.

THE RETURN TO FLINT

Although the foundation's program from 1976 onward in some respects broadened in scope, Flint has remained the center of its work. And since economic recession in the 1980s has hit the industrialized Snowbelt and especially the automobile industry with special force, Flint has become a city in serious trouble.

In the pattern of many other American cities, the signs of its decline appeared not only in the unemployment statistics but very visibly in the decay of its downtown area. Under the circumstances, the fragility of the foundation's commitment to national activities and its vulnerability to local pressures quickly became evident. As a result in the last few years it has poured a large portion of its resources into a major, and some feel quixotic, effort on behalf of "Flint Revitalization."

In a succession of actions it has subsidized the relocation of a University of Michigan campus in Flint to the downtown area with two large grants, one to build a new gynmasium and the other for a new student center. It has subsidized a low-income housing project and has paid the board of education to renovate and expand an old school to serve the new residents. It has provided money to the city to complete the landscaping and entertainment facilities in River-bank Park, located in the Flint River floodplain. It has funded the public amenities in a new 180-acre industrial park. It has subsidized the construction of a new Hyatt Regency Hotel through a gift to a neighborhood improvement association so it could purchase a second mortgage on the property. It has given a tract of land to the Downtown Development Authority for a retail shopping center. It has also given land to the city, on which a new state office building has been built. And it has funded or guaranteed more than half the cost of a $70 million tourist attraction called Autoworld. These projects have already cost the foundation some $60 million, and all the bills are not yet in.

Neither are the results. Some of the projects have done well: the housing development, the hotel, and the shopping center. But the university relocation has not had the economic impact on the downtown area that was hoped. Autoworld, which began operation in fall 1984, failed to attract the hoped-for flow of tourists and was shut down after a few months so that costly alterations could be made. After reopening, attendance continued to lag and that the project might become a financial disaster began to loom as a real possibility.

Reactions in Flint to these heavy "investments" by Mott have been mixed. The city government and the business community have been especially pleased, but the "liberal Left" in the heavily union-ized city feels that the foundation has been wasting money that could have been much better used in other ways than to erect "a giant monument to a fading automobile industry." At the other ex-treme, some working-class whites criticize the program as highly discriminatory in favor of blacks.

The foundation has been drawn deeply, probably more deeply than it intended, into the whole downtown development effort. Quite apart from large loan guarantees that have been made, nearly half of its $22 million of expenditures in 1983, for example, went to Flint. As a result Mott has also come to have mixed feelings and some discomfort about the situation and has now decided to limit its future outlays in the city to not more than $5 million per year on average over the next five years, a substantial cutback.

It defends its heavy commitment to downtown on several grounds: the donor, C. S. Mott, was devoted to the city, and out of respect for the tradition of helpfulness that he established as well as the foundation's own sense of responsibility to its home town, it had to pitch in. Moreover, Flint was not only in difficulty but in real danger at the time. The center of the city was about to turn into a wasteland, and there was also the serious possibility of racial violence. (In addition to its heavy contributions to capital projects, the foundation has put nearly $10 million in recent years into emergency youth services and jobs programs to alleviate the gathering social tensions.) Its outlays have had an underlying economic rationale, namely to give the city's economy a second leg to stand on, tourism, at a time when it could no longer rely solely on automobile manufacturing to sustain it.

On the other hand, the foundation has found that because of the lead role it has taken, it is now expected to fill any shortfall in the financing of individual projects that may develop and that these pressures are difficult to resist. (Some leading individuals in Flint have also once again become uncomfortable with the foundation's role, feeling that although it has been very generous, it has also been inclined to "throw its weight around" in such a way as to undermine the authority and responsibility of both elected officials and private citizen groups.)

The foundation staff is aware that even if the redevelopment effort improves tourism income for Flint, this will be very largely at the expense of other tourist areas in the state and not a boost to the regional economy. There is also clear recognition that Flint remains very vulnerable so long as the economy of the region is in difficulty. But apart from investing a small fraction of its assets in a new venture-capital fund intended to encourage the establishment and expansion of new businesses, Mott has not yet developed a strategy for attacking the deeper causes of the region's decline.

SOME LARGER ISSUES

The heavy involvement of Lilly and Mott in redevelopment efforts in Indianapolis and Flint illuminates a number of fundamental questions of economic justification and of the role, or responsibility, of very large foundations.

First, it raises economic issues: In the American system there are at least three quite different kinds of money: commercial money, government money, and philanthropic money. Each flows in accordance with different forces: those of the financial markets with the prospects for profit, of government with the pressure of political forces, and of foundations with their ideas of public need and social benefit.

The American economy, however, is not one of pure and separated compartments but of mixtures and combinations of every kind. Commercial and government money are of course joined and commingled in many ways, from the construction of housing projects to the production of aircraft. Government and philanthropic money are also frequently combined in the financing of research, education, social services, and the arts. And philanthropic and business funding are not infrequently joined, not only in collaboration between corporate and private foundations but also in the funding of projects on the borderline between viable business ventures and conventional nonprofit activities. The idea of "program-related investments" by foundations is perhaps the most clear example of the application of philanthropic funds in this twilight zone.

The matter of urban redevelopment is one in which the economics are especially complex. Just why certain areas of cities lose their economic viability and decay is not entirely understood; and even less understood is the process by which "redevelopment" or "revitalization" can be made to take place. There are examples across the country in which successful redevelopment has been accomplished essentially by ordinary commercial financing. There are other examples in which predominantly government funding seems to have worked. There are also examples in which neither government nor private funding, nor a combination of the two, has been able to reestablish the viability of a distressed area.

In at least a few cases a limited amount of philanthropic funding combined with government and commercial resources has been successful, as in downtown Pittsburgh, Atlanta, and elsewhere.

Sometimes the problems of the central city are caused by essentially local factors; more often they result from a combination of economic, social, technological, and governmental causes of far-reaching character. Therefore foundation grants for redevelopment raise basic questions: They are necessarily—as the case of the disastrous Renaissance Center project in Detroit, near to Flint and dependent also on the fortunes of the automobile industry, so dramatically and ominously suggests—a highly speculative investment. Is this the kind of "risk taking" that a responsible foundation can properly engage in?

If the effort is one that is highly likely to succeed, then do philanthropic dollars not merely displace commercial or government financing otherwise available? If, on the other hand, the project is very unlikely to succeed, making adequate commercial or governmental financing unavailable, how then can the commitment of philanthropic dollars be justified?

Second, expenditure of philanthropic funds for redevelopment raises issues of the role and responsibility of very large foundations: Why some foundations, including very large ones, are inclined to give disproportionate attention to their home towns is understandable. The combination of civic loyalty, sentimental attachments, and social pressure frequently weakens their will to resist even the most extravagant demands for local preference.

But in the case of foundations with assets in the $250 million range and above, questions of accountability and responsibility at some point do arise. Do the trustees of a foundation based on a fortune derived from the operations of a great national or multinational company have some obligation to distribute the philanthropic benefits over a wide rather than a very narrow area? Does any norm of what might be called "geographical equity" or "demographic equity" have to be considered? Have Mott and Lilly given Flint and Indianapolis an "unfair" advantage over other similarly troubled cities in the region in competing for tourists and new industry? Indeed, does the possibility of overconcentration of philanthropic beneficence and possible deleterious effects on citizen responsibility and authority have to be considered? The cases of Mott and Lilly (and as seen previously, the San Francisco Foundation) make such questions real and not merely hypothetical.

A COMPARATIVE EVALUATION

This group of four major midwestern foundations presents sharp contrasts and great variation in scope and quality of programs.

The Middle West of the United States is a distinctive, important, and at present very troubled region. Historically it has been both the nation's agricultural and industrial heartland. In the earlier decades of the twentieth century it was the great magnet of opportunity that drew millions of immigrants from Europe as well as from other parts of the United States, especially blacks from the South and poor whites from Appalachia, to its booming factories.

The concentration of large foundations now based in the region is just another evidence of the great economic power and the wealth that the region has represented.

But it is now in demographic and economic decline. Its agriculture, though still productive, is in a condition of continuing depression for a combination of economic, structural, and political reasons. Its industry, for equally complex reasons—economic, social, political, structural, technological, and international—is also in distress, a distress only temporarily arrested by various protectionist measures that a combination of automobile manufacturers and automotive trade unions succeeded in persuading the Congress to pass in the early 1980s. Population is moving out, social and racial tensions are serious, and the economic base of the region's former prosperity and growth is now extremely fragile.

Examining the response of the major foundations of the region to this deep crisis is instructive. The Kresge Foundation, which essentially builds buildings for nonprofit organizations, has not been moved to alter its grants policy in any way by the situation.

The Kellogg Foundation, with its long-established interest in agriculture, continues to provide funding for research and training for the development of that sector. It has also since 1980 substantially increased its funding for programs devoted to the problems of youth employment and job creation in the state of Michigan. Its particular strategy is to attempt to harness the large, high-quality educational and scientific resources of the area to the tasks of industrial revitalization. However, this effort is still only a small part of its total program.

Mott and Lilly have made large efforts to revive the central business districts of their home cities, but thus far have done very little to attack the underlying economic problems of the region.

Why the midwestern foundations are making so limited a contribution to solving these regional problems is unclear. It may be that such problems are simply beyond the scope of competence and outside the established modes of operation of even the largest foundations, or it may be a deficiency of leadership, imagination, and courage.

11

THE HORSE LATITUDES:
Surdna, Duke, and Sloan

The majority of the large foundations have, over time, tended to overcome their initial problems and to get better. In an uninterrupted trajectory they have become more independent, more professionally competent, and somewhat more ambitious in the reach of their programs. But of the exceptions to this pattern, three are exceptionally fascinating and instructive: Surdna, Duke, and Sloan. All have existed for half a century or more; all had strong, purposeful donors; all got under way without the quarrels and litigation that troubled others; and all have been useful philanthropies. Indeed, Duke and Sloan have been more than that, each having significant achievements to its credit. But all of them have somehow been cramped or erratic in their development and have failed to reach the highest rank and their full potential.

The reasons are identifiable in the case of Surdna, a donor family that after three generations seems determined to keep it a closed and amateurish family affair, and Duke, which operates within a severely restrictive charter imposed by the donor.

Sloan is more baffling. It has had a zigzag career: a poor start, a gradual recovery, a period of very good performance, followed by a sag. Whether the problem has been the drag of a mediocre board or the misfortune of weak executive leadership is difficult to judge. But it remains an enigma, always on the verge of fulfilling its promise and becoming a leader in the field, but never quite able to take wing.

Surdna Foundation, Inc.

Surdna was established in 1917 by John Andrus (its name is his spelled backward, which has led to its being called the "Serutan" among the brand names of big philanthropy). He was a great bull of a man, who in the course of his ninety-three years built a vast fortune in pharmaceuticals, real estate, gold mining, and lumber. He was also active in politics, having served as mayor of Yonkers, New York, and as congressman for four terms. He proudly claimed that no man had ever shined his shoes or shaved his face, and from his practice of traveling to his office every day by subway, he came to be known as "the millionaire straphanger."

After his wife's death, he created his foundation in 1917 in her honor. Its main activity until the late 1960s was the support of the Julia Dyckman Andrus Memorial, a home for destitute and infirm old people, and of the Andrus Children's Home for orphans. The former is built on the family estate overlooking the Hudson River. As an arcadian amenity, a small farm was maintained on the place for a number of years, including four sheep tended by a shepherdess.

In 1926, nine years before he died, Mr. Andrus announced the allocation of 45 percent of his estate to the foundation. When he died in 1935 he made the foundation in addition a 45 percent income beneficiary of three very large family trusts that he established.

At that point one of his nine children, Mrs. Helen A. Benedict, took direction of the foundation and ran it with a strong hand for the next thirty years. The homes for children and the elderly received about half of its grants over that period, the rest going mainly to local institutions near Yonkers and various colleges and universities located in the Northeast, generally for medical research and buildings.

Since her death in 1969, a number of changes have occurred in the foundation, limited but on the whole positive. The board of nine remains family-controlled. A staff of one professional has been added, subminimal for a foundation of the size of Surdna. The foundation has justified its underprofessionalization on grounds that it has an active working board of directors. But no evidence has been offered to support this assertion, and to judge from the limited information that can be obtained about the foundation, it does not appear that the members are deeply involved.

Surdna's assets have grown considerably since 1970: from $104 million to $260 million in 1984. This seems to be the result of some improvement in the management of the foundation's portfolio plus the receipt of some capital allocations from family trusts as they expire. But given the complexity of the financial structure of the Andrus estate and the paucity of data available for inspection, it is not possible to be more precise.

The noncommunicativeness of the foundation in its first fifty years was breached by the requirements of the Tax Reform Act of 1969, and since then Surdna has issued biennial public reports. They are generally factual and except for those in the early 1970s, are mercifully devoid of foundation-type rhetoric. In 1970–1971 and 1972–1973, however, apparently stung by congressional and other criticism of the failure of foundations to sponsor creative and innovative projects, the trustee president of the foundation, Edward F. McGee, divulged something of Surdna's concept of grant making: "In its experience, the most promising research and productive creative work is being done under the leadership of long-established institutions with records of excellence in their fields. . . ." In his 1972–1973 report he wrote that Surdna attempts "to channel grants to those programs and organizations where important accomplishments can be expected." This articulation has been helpful but less than completely satisfying to those interested in understanding the persistent sluggishness of this obviously well-intentioned institution.

As of the mid-1980s Surdna's program can be summarized as follows:

It continues to commit more than half of its outlays to the Andrus homes for children and the elderly in New York and to another home for the elderly in Minneapolis, where John E. Andrus III, grandson of the donor, lives. In addition it gives another 10 percent of its gifts to other projects for the needy and handicapped.

It continues to make substantial grants to strengthen private higher education and centers of medical research and health care. A major new area of interest is cultural institutions, and grants in recent years have been made to such recipients as the Twin Cities public television station, the Boston Symphony, and the Paul Taylor Dance Company in New York.

On the whole Surdna is a well-intentioned, compassionate foundation with rather broad interests, and its support goes to institutions of quality. Still, given the extraordinary generosity, vision, and boldness of the donor—and the scale of its assets—it remains an underachiever. It awaits the force of strong, imaginative leadership to lift it from being a moderately good foundation to the status of an excellent one. If this happens someday, it will finally correct the impression that not the only thing backward about Surdna is the spelling of its name.

The Duke Endowment

James Buchanan (Buck) Duke gave his endowment the benefit of large resources and a serious commitment to education, health care, and the poor in the region of his birth, the Carolinas. At the same time he gave it the handicap of the most detailed and restrictive charter of any of the large foundations and of tight and permanent ties to the Duke Power Company. With these mixed blessings the endowment has succeeded, against the odds, in becoming a competent, productive foundation. Like the Woodruff Foundation in Georgia, it has been a significant factor in the emergence of the Southeast from the backwardness that characterized it until World War II.

Buck Duke was a natural and precocious genius in business, a horse for work, and a man with definite ideas about everything connected with both making money and giving it away. He was the son of a North Carolina tobacco farmer and as a boy learned to flail out leaf in his father's log barn. By fourteen he was already a foreman in the family's little tobacco business. At eighteen, by threatening to set up his own company, he became a full partner in the enterprise. At twenty-seven he opened their New York factory and within six years made it the largest cigarette and smoking tobacco producer in the world.

By his unusual talent for merchandising and monopoly building, he did in tobacco what John D. Rockefeller at the time was doing in oil: namely establishing a dominant position in what had previously been a savagely competitive business. By 1890 Duke had absorbed the five major companies of the time into his American Tobacco Company by outselling, outbidding, and outworking them all. After the turn of the century he extended his reach abroad, eventually dividing the world's tobacco trade between his own firm and the British-American Tobacco Company.

In the era of trustbusting the federal government broke his stranglehold on the market and dissolved his monopoly. Thereafter several smaller companies were formed from the parts, all managed by men he had trained.

But Duke in the meanwhile had turned his attention to another and even larger field of economic opportunity: hydroelectric power. In 1905 he organized the Southern Power Company to serve the developing textile industry in the Carolinas, and from that base he extended his holdings in hydroelectric development throughout the United States and Canada.

His first love was business. "I resolved from the time I was a mere boy to do a big business," he once commented. "I love business better than anything else. I worked from early morning until late at night. I was sorry to have to leave off at night and glad when morning came so I could get at it again."

But he was also a religious man and generously charitable. As his wealth grew, so did his giving, and in 1924 he took the major step of creating his endowment. He knew of Andrew Carnegie's view about the need to give foundation trustees latitude to fit a foundation's policies to changing times, but he would have none of it. With his usual self-confidence he specified that the Duke Endowment, in perpetuity, keep its funds in the securities of the Southern Power System "except in response to the most urgent and extraordinary necessity" and that the endowment's income be given out precisely as follows:

	Percentage
To Duke University	32
To Davidson College, Davidson, North Carolina	5
To Furman University, Greenville, South Carolina	5
To Johnson C. Smith University, Charlotte, North Carolina	4
For hospitals in North and South Carolina	32
To orphanages in North and South Carolina	10
For superannuated preachers and widows and orphans of preachers who have served in the Conference of the Methodist Church in North Carolina	2
For building rural Methodist churches in North Carolina	6
For maintaining and operating rural Methodist churches in North Carolina	4
Total	100%

The assets of the foundation as of 1984 were $500 million. In accordance with the requirements of the will, the endowment gives the four beneficiary educational institutions annual grants of money without restrictions, plus special project grants. Over the years it has given Duke University a total of more than $270 million and converted it from the small, struggling local college that it had been originally into a major national university. (The creation of Duke University was provided for in the will by the stipulation that if Trinity College at Durham, North Carolina, would change its name to Duke University it would receive a gift of $6 million for its expansion. The offer was accepted.) Most of its physical development, as well as a portion of its annual operating costs, has been funded by the endowment. Because of the scale of its financial assistance the endowment gradually came to play an influential and sometimes decisive role in the management of the university.

In the 1950s the university undertook a basic reevaluation of its future course. Out of this process clear differences of opinion developed among faculty, administration, and trustees, some feeling that the university should continue to be a regional institution emphasizing undergraduate training, others believing that it should seek to become an institution of national standing, a reorientation that would require, among other things, strong emphasis on graduate study and research. Through the 1960s the university was preoccupied by this conflict. The passions that were aroused led to allegations that the endowment, which favored the regional emphasis, had made the university its "captive" and was arbitrarily determining its future. But a number of those who were directly involved in the struggles, including key members of the faculty, were of the view that the endowment used its influence constructively and with restraint.

In more recent years the relationship has greatly improved. Cross-membership on the university's governing board and that of the endowment has been reduced, and the endowment now emphasizes that it intends to maintain open communication in the "partnership" and to be responsive to the suggestions and requests it receives.

A second major focus of the endowment's work is hospitals and health care. In its first published report, covering the period 1924–1928, the stipulations of the donor's indenture with regard to aid to hospitals were restated: First, those operated for private gain were excluded because of his belief that medical care is a community problem and should therefore be handled by community hospitals; second, financial assistance would be apportioned on the basis of the amount of charity work done by each recipient hospital; and third, assistance would be limited to one dollar per day per charity patient. The report then contained an analysis of the inadequacy and maldistribution of hospital services in the Carolinas, one of the first such surveys to be made in the United States.

Over the following decades the endowment steadily developed its professional staff to provide research and consulting assistance to health-care institutions in the region. Because the indenture empowers the trustees of the endowment to cut off funds to inefficiently operated hospitals, the staff interpreted this to mean that its mission includes providing statistical comparisons by which hospitals could gauge the efficiency of their operations and plan their own improvement.

In the period since World War II various developments, including the region's rapid industrialization and the advent of massive federal hospital assistance under the Hill-Burton Act, have changed the nature of the endowment's work in health care. It continues to provide grants to more than fifty hospitals in the Carolinas each year, mostly for construction projects and equipment. It has made major allocations to develop the Duke University Medical Center into one of the finest regional facilities in the country. In addition it has funded programs for improved hospital administration, establishment of rural clinics, home-care programs for the elderly, an alcoholism rehabilitation program, and development of a hospital-based hospice program.

In 1969 it participated in the founding and subsequent support of the Carolinas Hospital and Health Services Corporation to provide cooperative services designed especially for health-care institutions. These now include management consulting and engineering programs, a biomedical equipment maintenance program, a group purchasing program, and a bureau for the collection of patient accounts. Some thirty hospitals now participate in the program. Subscriber fees now pay 96 percent of the total cost, and the endowment's gifts are used primarily for the early research and development of additional services.

In 1973 the Kellogg Foundation joined with the Duke Endowment in helping establish a program for contract management services to Carolina hospitals. This collaboration has led more recently to the establishment of a three-year national project to develop and demonstrate an integrated planning, budgeting, and control system for use by hospital managers. The Duke Endowment provides the funding for the five Carolina hospitals that serve as demonstration sites for the experiment. In this way it manages to play a part in dealing with national issues while serving the Carolinas and abiding by the indenture.

In the mid-1970s the endowment in cooperation with several other Carolina foundations addressed the most pressing health-care problem in the area, namely the inaccessibility of health services for all citizens in rural areas and for the urban poor. On the basis of a comprehensive preliminary study of needs a number of projects have subsequently been funded to help hospitals staff their emergency rooms with full-time physicians, to create satellite clinics in rural communities, and to establish a number of hospital-based primary-care group practice centers in remote areas.

In 1979 the endowment made a long-term commitment of $250,000 annually to support the Center for Health Policy Research and Education at Duke University Medical Center. This is an aspect of its slowly growing concern with problems of containment of health-care costs, as well as of widening access to care. And in 1980 a new six-hundred-bed wing of the Duke University Hospital was completed with substantial help from the endowment.

In its health and hospitals programs the foundation has made its most valiant and creative effort both to abide by the spirit of the donor's instructions and yet to escape from their confinement.

In its work in behalf of orphans as well as with rural churches and clergy, the endowment has followed the approach of assessing needs, providing expert assistance, and inviting ideas for better ways to provide services.

Most recently, the foundation has made some interesting moves to go beyond its established programs of assistance to address policy issues that arise in all of them, including some of the most tangled questions of medical, social, and educational ethics. This is done through a new publication, *Issues*, which is a forum for debate on these matters.

In addition, the endowment in mid-1984 funded a program to develop public discussion among doctors, members of the clergy, educators, insurance executives, lawyers, judges, editors, and citizen leaders in some ten Carolina communities on current issues of medical ethics. The intent is to bring together various points of view, to stimulate wider public interest and understanding, and possibly to arrive at some consensus on a process for dealing with actual cases.

TWO DISCORDANT NOTES

The Duke Endowment has been a significant and constructive influence in health care and higher education in the Carolinas over the years and has some considerable achievements to its credit.

But there are two shadows on its record: One is the level of fees that the trustees take for their part-time services. The board is made up of two members of the Duke family, as well as a number of other prominent bankers, industrialists, and philanthropists. By the terms of the donor's indenture a specific fraction of its income was assigned to be paid to each trustee each year. Currently this fee is $79,000 per member, the highest of any major foundation in the country and quite out of line with the norm. Yet, so far as is known trustees have never suggested that the courts be asked to reduce the amount of the payment, and in the endowment's tax returns it appears that the only trustee who declines the fee is Doris Duke, who rarely attends meetings. This is at the same time a small matter and one that seems to suggest a most unseemly attitude of self-aggrandizement of individuals presumably giving voluntary service to a pro bono institution, individuals moreover who in a number of obvious cases hardly need the income.

The second shadow is the appearance the endowment gives of

being at the same time an agency of assistance and advancement to blacks and a bastion of what has been called the "genteel racism of exclusion and disrespect." This is epitomized by the fact that the board of this institution, which devotes all of its resources and energies to two states whose populations are more than 40 percent black, does not have and has never had a black member.

Leaders of the local black communities are very careful not to express their feelings about this publicly. But one of them, a man of high standing who has dealt directly with the endowment for a number of years, has said the following: "Old Mr. Duke was ahead of his time. When he set up his Endowment, the South was still being terrorized by lynch mobs and the Klan. But he held out the hand of help to us. He was a leading force in the changes which have since come in this area, but his trustees are still a trailing force, a force of drag. They think they honor him by reading his will aloud every year—which they do. But in fact they dishonor him by holding to their lily-white rule. They are decent and good people but they are not living up to the spirit of the man even if they treat the words of his will like Holy Writ."

Something of the same note of lack of leadership is struck in the comments of some others who have observed the endowment at close hand, including individuals associated with other Carolina foundations, university professors, health-care administrators, and editors. "The Endowment is a good institution," one has said in a characteristic comment, "just as good as the ideas that are brought to it. But it doesn't lift things, or generate things or blaze any trails."

That seems to be a reasonable assessment of its performance in the past. But there are indications that it is becoming somewhat less true now. If so, this could be of great significance to its particular region of the country.

Alfred P. Sloan Foundation

The Alfred P. Sloan Foundation of New York with assets of $360 million is unique among the largest foundations because of its commitment to science and technology, to improvement of the management of both private and public institutions, and to support for research and training in economics. Except for the Sloan Foundation these important fields of activity are neglected by most of the other big foundations, so its potential contribution to the national interest and to the overall balance of philanthropic effort could be very important. However, although a good foundation, Sloan over its fifty-year existence has had a very uneven record and after a period of good performance in the 1970s seems now to be backing and filling once again.

THE DONOR

Alfred P. Sloan, the major architect of the success of the General Motors Corporation, was a man of surpassing ability, even genius, as a manager of major industrial organizations. But as a philanthropist he was only second-rate: autocratic, unclear and limited in his social vision, and sometimes ruled by his resentments.

He headed General Motors for nearly thirty-five years. A slender six-footer with hawklike, angular features, he was a functional man, austere and intense. He did not smoke, rarely drank, read little for pleasure, and had no time for hobbies, sports, or other amusements. He dressed like a dapper boulevardier, but he took little part in the social scene. General Motors was his occupation, his avocation, and his recreation. For many years he spent half of each month in New York and the other half in his office in Detroit, which he seldom left even to go to his hotel. In New York he generally dined alone with his wife in their Fifth Avenue apartment (the couple was childless), and after dinner he would study the papers he had brought home. At the office he worked his way through his daily schedule of conferences with metronomic precision. Although he drove himself and others relentlessly, his method of executive leadership was quietly persuasive, not bombastic. He had many close friends in the top echelon of American business and finance, and in the late 1920s and through the 1930s this capable and highly successful man enjoyed a unique prestige among them.

In terms of his public reputation, 1937 was not one of the better times in his life. In that year, when the workers of General Motors struck and conducted sit-ins, Sloan haughtily refused to deal with them "so long as they continue to hold our plants unlawfully," drawing a public rebuke from President Roosevelt. Subsequently, as public opinion turned against him and the company, Sloan had to retreat from his position. In that same year he suffered a more personal embarrassment when Treasury experts reported to a congressional committee that he and his wife had avoided payment of $1.9 million in federal income taxes over a three-year period by the device of personal holding companies. The story made headlines throughout the country. Although there was no charge of illegal conduct, the implications of the allegation were so unpleasant that Sloan went to great lengths to refute them.

Perhaps by coincidence or, as some skeptics have suggested, because of the injury to his pride, Sloan at the end of that difficult year made a gift of $10 million to activate the foundation that he and his wife had created three years before.

Over the next twenty-eight years, until his death at the age of ninety, he personally dominated and directed the foundation, with very mixed results.

Sloan was a man with definite ideas about almost everything, including philanthropy. In announcing his $10 million gift, he said, "Having been connected with industry during my entire life, it seems eminently proper that I should turn back, in part, the proceeds of that activity with the hope of promoting a broader as well as a better understanding of the economic principles and national policies which have characterized American enterprise down through the years." He then went on to say, "This particular foundation proposes to concentrate to an important degree on a single objective, i.e., the promotion of a wider knowledge of basic economic truths." Decoded, this meant that he intended to use it primarily to oppose the economic philosophy of the New Deal.

Thereupon the foundation embarked on a long and shoddy ideological crusade, funding a motley group of organizations to produce publications and films "to carry the doctrines of free enterprise into every American home and high school." The ghost of that effort was to haunt the foundation for more than twenty years. In September 1964 the Anti-Defamation League (ADL) of B'nai B'rith in New York completed a study of the major financial supporters of right-wing propaganda in the United States and named the Sloan Foundation as one of these. The ADL alleged specifically that the foundation had aided extremist assaults on American democratic processes by a succession of major grants to the National Education Program, headed by Dr. George Benson, president of Harding College in Searcy, Arkansas, which the ADL called "the largest producer of radical Right propaganda in the country." The foundation, in a half-embarrassed reply, said that the films and other materials produced through its grants were purely "economic" in content. But the league pointed out that the Sloan-supported materials had been based largely on the writings of Robert Welch, founder of the John Birch Society. The grants to Harding College had been made in the late 1940s, when Sloan's enthusiasm for instructing Americans in the "basic principles of the American enterprise system" was still a significant part of its program. By the mid-1940s even Sloan recognized that the effort was an ignominious failure, and he began to move the foundation in a different direction.

In 1945, using his personal funds, he joined his close friend and long-time associate at General Motors, Charles F. Kettering, in creating the Sloan-Kettering Center for Cancer Research. For the next thirty-five years, with the income from a special fund that General Motors dealers had created to honor Mr. Sloan, the foundation continued to support the center. It has now become the largest private institution in the world for the treatment of cancer and for cancer-related research and training. His action in providing the venture capital for the first stages of the attack on cancer and for the development of this major institution was Sloan's finest single achievement in philanthropy.

In the mid-1950s he supported another major step in the foundation's development, namely the launching of its program of Basic Science Fellowships to identify and support creative young scientists in the United States at the very early stage of their careers. This program has been supported by the foundation ever since, and some sixteen hundred Sloan Research Fellows in total have been selected. Among them are a number of individuals who subsequently became Nobel laureates, as well as several who have received other high recognition for their achievements.

By the late 1950s and early 1960s the foundation had essentially abandoned its earlier interest in economics and was concentrating its grants steadily on scientific training and research and on training in business management. Even though a number of these activities were productive, Mr. Sloan himself appeared to become rather restless with their conventionality. He may also because of his own advancing years have felt the need to begin to prepare the foundation for new leadership. In any event in 1962 he appointed Dr. Everett Case, an educator, to head the foundation. More important, he also brought in Dr. Warren Weaver to help develop some new program ideas. Weaver, a scientist and mathematician who had had a brilliant career at the Rockefeller Foundation until his retirement, then became the principal force for improvement at the Sloan Foundation.

The donor was both a help and a hindrance in these efforts. Although he understood the need to strengthen and broaden the foundation's program, he at the same time found it impossible to break his deeply ingrained habit of absolute rule and remained an autocrat to the end. Weaver has described Mr. Sloan's management methods in these words:

> There were at that time no staff meetings and no general staff discussions; each officer worked directly with Sloan. At trustee meetings Sloan, as the presiding officer, gave extraordinarily clear and complete reports of all financial aspects of the foundation's business, and he himself described, with no notes—in a meticulously accurate way and often with a touch here and there of penetrating humor—the proposals on which the board was to act. The meetings were never long. Sloan always commenced by thanking the trustees for their interest and their presence; and when the business had been briskly concluded—extended discussion was of course handicapped by his deafness—the meetings were promptly terminated.

By the time of Sloan's death in February 1966, signs of some change were evident, but encrusted old habits had not totally been dissolved. Moreover, because of his autocratic methods, Sloan left the foundation with a board of cronies and lackeys and with no real executive leadership. Case left shortly thereafter. In 1969 Nils Y. Wessel, who had been head of Tufts University, succeeded him and became the first president of the foundation unencumbered by the overpowering presence of the donor.

Wessel inherited both a program and staff that had great weaknesses but also contained some strong elements. As a result of the work of some able younger program officers he was able within a year to present to the board a comprehensive set of new program recommendations. It was proposed that the foundation commit itself to three broad and interrelated areas: science and technology, education, and "the range of problems posed by the pressing needs of our current society." Two were of course established fields of interest, but some new wine was poured into the old bottles. In science and technology there would be a new emphasis on the biological sciences and neurosciences; in education the training of blacks and other minority students for the professions, including medicine and engineering, would receive greater attention. The foundation had long given support to schools of business management; now it proposed to support management training for urban leadership and government service.

In its recognition of "pressing social needs," the foundation proposed to concentrate principally on those areas that related to its established interests in science, technology, and education rather than make a complete break with its own past. Still, a distinctly new tack was being taken.

The board in its passive way approved all of the recommendations. In the following year a set of new urban affairs grants was also approved, moving the foundation closer to the turbulent issues of the times than it had ever been before. In 1970, in a further break with its old habits, the foundation created a commission on cable television to develop public policy recommendations in that new and rapidly evolving area of communications technology. (Two of the senior program officers of the Sloan Foundation had served on the Commission on Public Television of the Carnegie Corporation a few years before. Their experience in that highly successful enterprise led to the establishment of the Sloan Foundation's sequel.) The commission's report issued in 1971 was widely and favorably reviewed, and two years later the Federal Communications Commission drew heavily upon its recommendations in drafting regulations for the fledgling cable industry.

In its initial venture in the treacherous task of issuing advice on public policy, Sloan had had a definite success, and it appeared that after years of talking about "risk taking" in its annual reports the foundation had developed enough competence and self-confidence actually to begin taking some.

An interesting innovation in the program recommendations Wessel brought to the board in 1969 was an explicit differentiation between *general programs,* those of broad and ongoing interest to the foundation, and *particular programs* that would be sharply focused on some specific problem and were intended to last for five to seven years and then be replaced by others. Initially it was envisaged that at least two of these particular programs would be operating at any one time and would receive about 40 percent of the total grants budget of the foundation. Although some problems have developed in the application of the concept it has provided a

framework within which the foundation has maintained some ma-
neuverability in its program.

In the fifteen years since the particular programs were begun
some have proved very successful; others have had problems. Those
to train an increased number of members of minorities in engineering, management, and medicine have been among the more
successful. Another intended to introduce new technology in education was a failure. The program in the neurosciences, which
ended in the mid-1970s, won high praise, and a successor program
in the *cognitive sciences* (the sciences seeking to improve understanding of human mental processes) is also well regarded in that
field.

In 1973, the foundation's interest in the field of economics was
revived, but not with the old ideological emphasis. It began with a
problem-ridden five-year program of economics education for journalists at Princeton University, which proved at least that first-class
people in that field were not interested in participating. Two years
later grants were given to support work at ten universities in the
field of applied microeconomics, with somewhat better results.

Then in 1977, remembering the success of its earlier commission on cable television, the foundation decided to create another,
this one on the general subject of "government and higher education," headed by Carl Kaysen, former head of the Institute for Advanced Study at Princeton. But whereas everything seemed to go
right in the earlier effort, in the second venture everything seemed
to go wrong. The commission's report was issued in 1979 after the
expenditure of more than $2 million and made hardly a ripple. In-
deed within the foundation the whole project was regarded as such
a disaster that although the foundation continues to have an interest
in addressing public policy issues, it has apparently abandoned for
good the device of the public commission as being too difficult to
manage and too accident-prone.

Wessel's last year at the foundation was 1978. In his decade at
the helm, the board of the Sloan Foundation was broadened and
strengthened, and the institution developed from an eccentric and
donor-dominated one into a capable, fully professionalized one.
This change was due only in rather small part, however, to Wessel's
input. His unusual management style was to remain largely aloof
from the work of the foundation and to rely almost totally on the
energy and ideas of his three principal assistants, Robert Kreidler,

Arthur Singer, and Stephen White, who were all highly respected among their peers.

In 1979 a new president, Albert E. Rees, a fifty-seven-year-old economist who had been provost at Princeton University, took over. Beginning with his first annual report Rees made it evident that the foundation was now in the hands of a person with a very different conception of what the Sloan Foundation should be and how it should operate. In his first annual report essay Rees stated the classic case for conservative "scientific" philanthropy: "Charity makes no enduring change in the state of affairs that calls for the need for charity." A foundation "should be able to do better than that. We should try to use it in ways that will permanently improve the human condition. . . ."

Therefore, the Sloan Foundation would put its faith "in the steady growth of scientific and technical knowledge and of skills in managing the economy and the public and private institutions of our society. . . ." Neither would it be in a hurry for quick results: "we rarely support anything as clear cut as the attack on polio. Most of the time we are simply helping to add steadily and almost imperceptibly to the slow growth of knowledge and to the training of people who will foster that growth."

The clientele of the foundation, given this approach, would on the whole be colleges and universities, particularly the major research universities. And in making grants to these institutions, quality would be the criterion: "We believe that the proper guide is to try to support promise and excellence. For this reason we are sometimes called elitist, a characterization we gladly accept."

In his second annual report Rees indicated in somewhat more concrete fashion the directions that the foundation's program in the future would take. As an economist he understandably took a particular interest in the foundation's activity in that discipline and hinted strongly that in the future it would probably move beyond the field of applied microeconomics and begin to give substantial support to work in the field of macroeconomics. "When it does," he said,

> I believe it must keep at least one principle foremost. The officers and trustees . . . should not attempt to determine *a priori* which of the warring sects is the true faith and to help furnish its arsenal. It should support scholars of proven ability or dem-

onstrated promise, especially those with innovative proposals, regardless of their view on policy or their adherence to a particular school. It should risk support of scholars whose work challenges accepted wisdom. The truth sometimes lurks in unsuspected places, and it is not given to us, especially in fields surrounded by controversy, to know in advance where these may be.

With that statement the Sloan Foundation after forty-five years had come home again to the field of interest from which it had originally set forth. But this time it was headed in precisely the opposite direction: away from propaganda and preaching and toward objectivity and neutrality.

Before the foundation could switch completely to the new scholarly track advocated by Rees, some of its earlier interests (public policy, education, and the neurosciences) that still had board support and momentum had to be accommodated.

In 1980, despite the discouragement left by the failure of its commission on government and higher education, the foundation launched another effort to make an impact on a major problem of immediate national concern, in this case, the process by which American presidents are elected, which Rees characterized as "interminably long, excessively costly, disruptive of the governmental process and unlikely in the end to offer the voter a choice." Alexander Heard, then chancellor of Vanderbilt University and chairman of the board of the Ford Foundation, would head the multiyear, multimillion-dollar effort. It would be carried out by Heard, a political scientist, but, it was emphasized, he would cooperate and consult widely not only with scholars but also with politicians, prominent figures in the media, and others with practical experience in political affairs. He would, however, operate without the benefit, or handicap, of a formal commission.

Announcement of the program was greeted with much favorable comment because the issue to be addressed had become one of growing public concern. After two years, however, it became clear that Heard was incapable of carrying out the project as originally intended. The foundation thereupon cut back but did not cut off funding for the recast and now purely academic exercise.

By 1982 Rees had been on the job two years; some new directions could be seen, but some new problems also. The foundation had brought to a close a number of its older programs, including its support for the Sloan-Kettering Cancer Center, and had begun to make more grants in the field of economics. But some of its most able program officers had left the foundation, one because he was fired and others because they did not choose to work under Rees.

Also the foundation's program seemed to have developed a wobble. Its declared interest in research in economics had taken the form by late 1982 of a number of actions to replace sharp cutbacks in federal expenditures for research in economics and related social sciences. These rescue efforts, which prevented the interruption of some long-term data-gathering programs that the foundation felt were well worth continuing, were nonetheless troubling. In Rees's words, "What we did seemed to us to be the proper response to a temporary period of adversity. In the long run, however, such policy could have disastrous consequences." Nor did the foundation's other actions in the economic field appear to move in the direction outlined by Rees earlier in his tenure, namely studies to address the great economic issues of unemployment, inflation, national productivity, and competitiveness. Instead it became involved in processing demographic data from the 1980 census and similar useful but seemingly peripheral research. Finally, in late 1984, in a move to get the foundation back on the macroeconomic track, Sloan joined with the Starr Foundation in funding a substantial new research program on the challenges posed to the American economy by changes in the international marketplace, the penetration of the U.S. market by foreign goods, technological developments, and the rise of Third World countries.

Whether the Sloan Foundation, after its various detours, will be able to mount a significant program addressed to major economic issues remains to be seen. As an institution Sloan, even after the death of the donor, has never been distinguished by strong presidential leadership and has often shown a halfheartedness and an ineptness in attacking big and tough issues. If it can overcome these disabilities, it will help fill one of the largest and most crucial gaps in the spectrum of activity of the large foundations.

12

THE SOUTHWEST—
RICH LAND, POOR LAND:

Houston, Brown, Moody, Mabee, and Noble

Despite the association in American mythology of the Southwest with rich cattle barons and wheelerdealer oil tycoons, the history of the area is rooted in poverty and the harshness of rural life. Its economic development, based on the huge hydrocarbon resources discovered below its arid soil, began in Texas just after the turn of the century when the great Spindletop gusher in Beaumont blew in. In Oklahoma the oil boom that has powered its economic transformation started a few years later.

Those who managed to make large fortunes out of the process were with few exceptions men of meager education from farms or small towns and poor families. They were tough, individualistic, and practical, and when they set up foundations to give some of their money away, as a number of them have, they gave it for purposes that reflected their own values and aspirations as well as the special ethos of the region. They preferred to build schools, parks, hospitals, and cultural centers. These great monuments to their generosity have helped fill the need for "social infrastructure" in which the area was so notably lacking. But their foundations have, on the other hand, done little to address some of the serious racial and other social problems that have been endemic to the area, other than to give opportunities for some striving young people to get an education.

Philanthropy in the Southwest, therefore, has acquired a profile as distinctive as the culture of the region itself.

Philanthropy Texas-Style: Houston Endowment

The scene is an office in an older building in downtown Houston, elegant in the style of fifty years ago. The paneling is mahogany; ceiling fans turn slowly overhead, stirring the unconditioned air, and the dominant piece of furniture is a handsome old rolltop desk. At it sits a white-haired and courtly gentleman, Howard Creekmore, the dean of foundation heads in Texas and the man who for the three decades since the death of the donor has personally directed every aspect of the affairs of the Houston Endowment, the biggest and for most of that time the best of the largest Texas foundations. The whole setting suggests the integrity, influence, and responsibility of the institution, and also that time may be passing it by.

The donor, Jesse H. Jones, was a formidable figure in his time and place. A man of imposing physical stature, he went to Houston from a farm in Tennessee early in the century and there began his career in construction and real estate. Within ten years, having started with nothing, he already owned more than a dozen hotels and office buildings and was busy buying others. By the time of his death in 1956 at the age of eighty-two he had extensive interests in oil, life insurance, banking, and ranching. As his wealth and power grew, he became the indisputable "Mr. Houston." More than any other individual in its history he led the city's growth and shaped its early development.

A succession of presidents recognized his extraordinary abilities and called him to Washington for national service. During the Woodrow Wilson administration he served as director general of Military Relief. In the 1920s Herbert Hoover appointed him director of the Reconstruction Finance Corporation. Under Franklin D. Roosevelt, Jones became Secretary of Commerce and served for thirteen years as the leading conservative member of the New Deal cabinet.

It was during his years with the New Deal that he and his wife, who were childless, laid plans for their foundation. With the help of a young lawyer in his organization, Howard Creekmore, whom Jones had come to regard almost as an adopted son, he incorporated it in 1937 and gave it a broad charter. During his lifetime Jones supported the endowment's activities with annual gifts.

In a series of conversations well before his death Jones indicated to Creekmore the general priorities he hoped the endowment would follow. He wanted first that it contribute to the development of Houston as an educational, medical, and cultural center. Second, he felt that "nothing was more important than to educate children, keep them healthy, and make good citizens of them." Those were to be the guiding stars of the endowment's work, "the game plan from which it should not vary."

Creekmore has followed them faithfully, in his fashion. But he has also left his own deep and distinctive mark on the foundation, reflecting his own background and social outlook.

He grew up on a Creek Indian reservation in Oklahoma, the son of an itinerant cowboy and a mother who died while he was still in grade school. He thereafter was raised by relatives in various Texas towns, always working to earn his keep. In high school in Abilene he showed promise both as a student and athlete and won a scholarship to Rice Institute in Houston. After graduation from there in 1923, he went to work directly for the Jones organization as a bookkeeper. It was Mr. Jones himself who, after watching the young man's work for a few months, encouraged him to "improve himself" by studying law at night school. He also offered to pay Creekmore's tuition if he would do so. A few years later when the young man had finished his degree Jones marked the occasion by giving him bus fare to travel to Austin to take the bar examinations.

Except for a stint in the U.S. Navy during World War II, Creekmore has since spent his entire working life in the service of Jesse Jones and his interests.

In his will Jones left the bulk of his fortune, then estimated at more than $200 million, to the endowment. But he also set up trusts for all twenty-two of his relatives and left instructions that after his death checks should be sent individually to each of his forty-four hundred employees. A number of family members were discontented with their shares, however, and Creekmore had to mediate the many quarrels among them and dispose of their legal challenges.

Then for a number of years much effort had to be devoted to the direct management of the assets that the endowment had acquired. These included controlling shares in some twenty-six corporations plus a large portfolio of urban real estate, farm and ranch land, and mineral rights. Several millions of dollars had to be spent, for example, to modernize the Rice Hotel in Houston, which the foundation had inherited, before it could be sold. The National Bank of Commerce, controlled by the endowment, was merged with another major Houston bank to become one of the two leading financial institutions of the city. The *Houston Chronicle*, also owned by the endowment, bought out its ailing afternoon rival, *The Houston Press*, and became the leading publication in the city.

Over the years Creekmore has traded and sold the various properties of the endowment with a good sense of timing and with great negotiating skill. Its assets have steadily risen in value, and as of 1984 they were worth $300 million. In the course of these many dealings he has incidentally become well acquainted with the many possibilities for skulduggery by trustees in disposing of the kinds of assets that Texas foundations tend to inherit. (His own standards of selflessness are indicated by the fact that after many years of handling multimillion-dollar deals he and his wife still live in the small house they bought when they were first married, which still lacks central heating.)

As he gradually converted its property into a diversified portfolio of securities, Creekmore was also able to develop the endowment's program of grants. In the earlier years these went primarily to reputable institutions in the Houston area for the construction of facilities. The grantees included a number of black colleges, reflecting an interest of the donor, who had taken an active part in the development of higher education for blacks for many years. The endowment also gave many millions for construction of a performing arts center, hospital facilities in the Texas Medical Center, a museum of fine arts, and establishment of the Jesse H. Jones Graduate School of Administration at Rice University.

In accordance with the donor's wishes the endowment has given heavy emphasis to education from the beginning. In 1958 it started an experimental scholarship program for graduating seniors from high schools in the Houston area. This program, which continues to the present time, provides four scholarships for each high school graduating class in the Houston Independent School District. Overall more than three thousand students have received such scholarships and have attended more than 240 different colleges and universities.

Except for one puzzling major aberration, the program of the endowment has shown more continuity than change. Mr. Creekmore was a long-time friend and admirer of Wright Patman, the maverick Texas congressman who in the late 1960s had come to be regarded as a scourge by the little world of American philanthropy and whose investigations of foundations led to the reforms of the 1969 tax act. Patman had long counseled him to "get the Endowment out of running businesses, get it out of debt, and get rid of family members on the board." Creekmore, except for the admonition to get the endowment out of debt, has not been particularly responsive to that advice. But he was seemingly very responsive to an interest of Patman's when in 1970, in a drastic departure from all its stated policies and established programs, it allocated $3.2 million to create the Fund for Public Policy Research in Washington, D.C. Immediately thereafter Harold Olscher, Patman's longtime congressional assistant, became its head.

Creekmore feels that the bricks-and-mortar phase of its program is now largely completed as Houston has matured, or exploded, into a prosperous and handsome metropolitan center. In the future he anticipates it will give more emphasis to social and quality-of-life problems. An examination of the grant lists of the foundation through the 1970s and early 1980s, however, reflects only very slow movement in these new directions.

CREEKMORE ON PHILANTHROPY

Howard Creekmore has not only operated a major foundation for many years but has also been a close observer of American philanthropy from a Texas viewpoint. He is a man of strong and salty opinions about what he has seen.

On public reporting. "Foundations should report to the public, and their reports should be brief and straightforward—not the glossy, extravagant things a good many now issue." The reports of the endowment, which have been issued biennially since the late 1950s, reflect his ideas.

On the dangers of malfeasance. "It is not hard to play games with foundation assets if they are in the form of mineral rights, real estate, and such things. Here in Texas the important thing is to be sure we get honest Attorney Generals and encourage them to maintain the honor of Texas foundations. They will have to keep a close eye on at least two or three of our larger foundations in the next few years to make sure some costly accidents don't happen."

On philanthropic foolishness. "McGeorge Bundy of the Ford Foundation did a great disservice to foundations and to the private colleges by his foolish encouragement to them to take greater risks in their portfolio management in the early 70's. A clear case of a man's self confidence exceeding his competence."

On the lowering of the payout requirement. "The pressure in the early 80's generated mainly by the Eastern foundations to persuade the Congress to lower the payout requirement was ill-timed and hurtful both to grantee organizations and to the public standing of philanthropy itself. It came at a bad moment because of the policies of the Reagan Administration and the generally bad economic conditions of the country."

On the new superrich. "The present generation of the very rich in Texas is not of the caliber of the big men of the past—Jones, Hugh Roy Cullen, M. D. Anderson, John Hermann, and others. They were great citizens. The new generation does not have their spirit of civic service and philanthropy. If they create any large foundations it will be largely the result of ego and tax benefits."

On foundation boards. "Very small foundation boards are best for getting the work done. Three is about the right number. They can act promptly and the board is small enough that each member can keep a close eye on the others."

Creekmore has said that Texas foundations are very independent and that each is eccentric in its own way. The same might well be said about him.

THE CASE OF THE *HOUSTON CHRONICLE*

One special and important problem that the endowment must face in the near future relates to its ownership of the *Houston Chronicle*, the largest and most profitable newspaper in the Southwest. The practical problem is when and how, and perhaps whether, the foundation will divest itself of ownership to conform with federal tax law. The deeper question of principle is whether it is in the interest of philanthropy for a foundation to control a major organ of opinion and a major political force like this particular newspaper.

In earlier years it was strongly conservative in its orientation. During the early 1960s, reportedly because of the influence of trustee John T. Jones, Jr., a nephew of the donor and a supporter of John F. Kennedy, a new editor was named, who shifted the paper to a moderate, even mildly liberal, line. In August 1965 Jones for some reason resigned from the board, and William T. Steven, the editor he had brought in, was removed by an act, in Steven's words, "of political assassination. . . . The conservatives won but I am proud of the reason I was fired. As General Custer said, 'I have been scalped right through the neck.' "

Under the terms of the Tax Reform Act of 1969 the endowment has to dispose of its controlling interest in the *Chronicle* by 1989. On at least one occasion it seemed to be prepared to sell. In mid-1966 John W. Mecom, a Texas oilman, agreed to buy a number of the endowment's properties, including the *Chronicle,* for $84 million. Because Mecom was known as a moderate Democrat, a strong financial supporter of President Johnson, and a progressive on questions of civil rights, much speculation in Houston at the time concerned the editorial direction the newspaper would take under his ownership. In the end the deal collapsed, leaving many observers wondering whether it was because Mecom in a tightening money market had been unable to raise the necessary funds to complete his purchase, or whether political factors had persuaded Creekmore to suspend negotiations.

Since then, according to Creekmore, cash offers for the newspaper have been made by interests from Saudi Arabia, West Germany, and Israel, as well as from the Australian publisher Rupert Murdoch. None of these buyers, in Creekmore's view, would have been a "constructive influence in the Texas situation," so no negotiations have been undertaken. On the contrary, the endowment, utilizing its own political muscle and that of the newspaper, was able in 1983 to induce twenty-five members of the Texas delegation to the U.S. House of Representatives to sponsor a special bill that would exempt the endowment from the "excess business holdings" provision of the 1969 tax act so that it could retain its present ownership. The proposal was opposed by the governor of Texas and by the national Council on Foundations, among others.

The Congress in early 1984 rejected its effort along with several others of the same kind, primarily as a result of strong opposition in the House. But the endowment was determined to continue the fight to hold on to its prize property. "We won't start negotiating to sell it so long as we have a chance to save it," a spokesman said.

By 1989, the final date for divestiture mandated in the 1969 tax act, the endowment will either have to persuade the Congress to change the law, a most unlikely development in the judgment of political observers, or complete the sale of the newspaper, however reluctantly.

THE ENDOWMENT IN THE FUTURE

Mr. Creekmore has kept a steady hand on the tiller in steering the endowment along the course laid out by the donor. Its program has been largely localized in the Houston area and in the Southeastern quadrant of Texas. It is basically old-fashioned and rooted in old-fashioned values, namely civic patriotism and a belief in the importance of good health-care facilities and educational opportunity for able and ambitious students of all classes and backgrounds. Over the years the work of the endowment has been honorable and useful and until quite recently it was the best of the big Texas foundations.

In looking at its grant list at present, however, one is struck by the great contrast between the rather staid character of what the foundation is mostly doing and the enormous problems and possibilities of Houston itself. The city in the 1970s after the oil embargo became a booming metropolis, with all the excitement and innovation, and all the problems, of rapid growth. Its gleaming new infrastructure of office buildings, apartment homes, shopping centers, hospitals, cultural facilities, and hotels is architecturally dazzling, but its traffic problems have become monumental. It has drawn a flood of ambitious newcomers from other parts of Texas, from the rest of the United States, and from Mexico, some of whom have suffered serious problems of adjustment and acceptance. But in the endowment grants there is relatively little reflection of the city's transportation problems or the need for better regional-planning guidelines. The city is a center for petrochemical production. But in the endowment's grants there is no hint of concern about the serious toxicological and environmental consequences of such massive activity.

Looking to the future, researchers and forecasters have expressed concern that not only is the oil boom over but that Texas and the Southwest are beginning to run out of oil and gas, a situation that could have the most profound implications for the local economy. But here again, the endowment's grant list does not reflect an awareness of the great changes in the region's way of life that may be impending.

The endowment now has the appearance of a tight, small, ingrown institution rather out of touch with many of the problems that present both great opportunities and dangers for the future development of the area. It almost certainly would receive stimulus for its program from opening some windows and doors to new ideas and social forces. But trends within the institution seem to be moving in a contrary direction. The small staff is not being expanded. The board, which is made up of Creekmore, four relatives of the donor, and the editor of the *Chronicle,* will probably not be broadened or strengthened but will be shrunk further in size, a very discouraging prospect.

Big philanthropy in the Southwest gravely needs leadership in improving the relevance, vitality, and effectiveness of programs. That leadership, to be influential, has to be rooted in and authentic to this distinctive region of the United States. The Houston Endowment has helped set a better standard in its asset management and to some degree in its program for others to follow. But a major change is in the offing when Mr. Creekmore retires. The last direct personal link between the donor and the foundation will then have been severed. That need not be disruptive if it causes the endowment and its board to begin to look more open-mindedly toward the future and toward the dramatically changing needs of the sector of the Sunbelt that surrounds it.

Brown Foundation, Inc.

Herman Brown entered the construction business because his first employer went bankrupt and left him eighteen tired and mortgaged mules and some well-worn equipment in lieu of a year's back wages. With those as his capital and credentials, he went directly to the local county commissioner's office and talked his way into a small road-building contract. From that desperate start, he, his brother-in-law Dan Root, and later his brother George went on to build one of the world's largest engineering and construction firms, Houston-based Brown and Root.

In the years after World War I, when the Tin Lizzie was creating its own revolution in country life, the little company built back roads and bridges throughout the Southwest. During the New Deal period it got its first big contract, one to build the Marshall Ford Dam on the Colorado River. During World War II it won contracts to construct huge military installations all across the country, including airfields and a shipyard. After the war it designed and built dams, petrochemical plants, pipelines, and hydroelectric installations throughout the world. More recently, it was chosen by the federal government to dig the "Mohole" through the earth's crust and to construct the NASA Spacecraft Center.

Herman Brown, born in a little hill town in central Texas, had one year of college before going to work as a road builder. For a good many years he lived the roughest kind of life, constantly traveling from work camp to work camp. He would spend most of a day on one job, then try to get a night's sleep on the bouncing back seat of a car while his driver took him to the next.

He was a salty, plain-spoken man. He and his brother George built their huge enterprise by hard work, hard bargaining, and masterful skill in obtaining contracts in that twilight zone where engineering meets politics. The two of them for more than thirty years were among the most astute behind-the-scenes political operators Texas has ever known. And Texas has known quite a few. Their influence ranged from the selection of school board members to the nomination of senators and governors. Lyndon Johnson was one of their protégés and he never forgot his debt to them. (He suffered his first heart attack, in 1956, while visiting in Herman Brown's home.) They actively backed conservative causes throughout the South and were militantly antiunion. They spearheaded the drives for so-called right-to-work laws in a number of states and, nationally, passage of the Taft-Hartley Act was attributed in good part to their powerful backing.

Herman Brown was essentially a hard-driving businessman, not a do-gooder. But in his later years, perhaps at his wife's instigation, he served on various nonprofit boards. In 1951 he and his brother set up their foundation and through it made substantial unpublicized gifts. Herman died in 1962, leaving it the bulk of his estate. His wife, who had become a prominent patron of the arts and music in Houston, died two months after her husband and also left her estate to the foundation. By the end of their lives, this childless couple had come a very long way in wealth, position, and interests from the dusty road builder's camp where their marriage began.

Ever since, the foundation has had a small board predominantly of family members, no professional staff, and issued no public reports. It carried on a grants program that is the quintessence of the passive, check-writing type: miscellaneous lump-sum grants for buildings or general support to educational institutions (50 percent), museums and arts organizations (20 percent), and hospitals and churches (10 percent). Social welfare programs received only 2 percent of the funds. The grants were given mostly to recipients in Texas, often in the Houston area.

The largest single group of grants made by the foundation was in 1976, when it offered a total of $40 million to Rice University, the Museum of Fine Arts in Houston, and Southwestern University in Georgetown, Texas. The grants were to be spread over a ten-year period and had to be matched by the recipient institutions. As a result, about $2 million a year has gone to Rice, $1 million a year to the museum, and $1 million to Southwestern.

Occasionally in the grant list were organizations like the National Right to Work Legal Defense Foundation. But such politically tinged grants now appear only infrequently.

Although George Brown was particularly "tight-mouthed" and opposed any publicity about the foundation's grants, he reversed himself in the 1970s in connection with a fund for the Lyndon Baines Johnson State Park, for which he was raising money. A number of the donors said they wanted to give but only anonymously, to which Brown said that if they did not want their names revealed, "they should take their money out of it," his one known statement in favor of making information available publicly about charitable contributions.

The last of the donors died in 1984, and the foundation is now in the hands of the children of Herman and George Brown. Currently, Fayez Sarofim, the husband of Herman Brown's daughter Louisa, a board member, is financial adviser to the foundation. For his services he has been paid $1.3 million in the past five years. The foundation promises to remain, therefore, an example of minimal philanthropic performance.

Moody Foundation

The donor of the Moody Foundation, W. L. Moody, Jr., was one of the most mean-spirited, compulsively acquisitive, and generally unattractive tycoons in the history of American capitalism. Slender of build, neat in appearance, and taciturn in manner, he appeared to be an elderly bookkeeper. With a Confederate flag hung on the wall behind him, he labored at his desk throughout his long life seven days a week, often sixteen hours a day.

He began his career in a prosperous cotton brokerage business started by his father in Galveston, Texas. In 1905, when he was forty, having established a successful bank with his father's help, he went on to found the American National Insurance Company, which in time became one of the largest in the United States and the prime asset in his immense fortune. Over the next five decades, with American National providing the wherewithal, he acquired both Galveston newspapers, the *News* and *Tribune;* a large chain of hotels; vast holdings of ranch land; and extensive oil and mineral properties.

Quick to take advantage of the distress of others, he put together much of his real estate empire by foreclosing mortgages. In the early 1920s he made numerous loans to goat ranchers in New Mexico, and when the ranchers failed to meet their payments, he ended up owning most of four counties. The Great Depression and the disaster of the Dust Bowl provided him with still larger opportunities to utilize these skills. Then beginning in the late 1930s, he reaped enormous profit on this land by leasing it to oil drillers.

To his employees he was a thankless and tyrannical taskmaster. He paid extremely low wages, would tolerate no questioning of his absolute authority, and often treated his most senior executives as office boys. Even with others present in his office, Moody would sometimes take off his shoes and order the president of his insurance company to "go get them shined."

Moody's avariciousness warped his relationships with his family, and he was to demonstrate many times that he considered water thicker than blood. As a young man he forced his father to drive his younger brother, Frank, out of the cotton business. His own son, W. L. Moody III, worked with him for a while, but they separated in anger in 1950, and in his will the father left the young man just one dollar. (In response to a note from his father that year suggesting he resign from the company, William wrote: "I have hoped that I came into this world happily for you, but whether or not, my heart beats with your blood. . . . I had hoped with all my heart, as we both grew older and you much more successful, that small but honest differences would appear as trivial as they are, and that the years and better understanding would . . . strengthen the ties of affection and loyalty which should exist between father and son and between son and father." The father responded by firing him.)

The one satisfactory relationship Moody had with his children was with his eldest daughter, Mary. In her lifelong devotion to her father, the childless "Aunt Mary" resembles a character out of a Brontë novel. For a period after her mother's death, she spent every night in her father's thirty-room house, staying awake in his chair on the ground floor until he arose at daybreak, when she would return to her own home to sleep.

Even in his attempts at being witty, the sickness of the old man's spirit was apparent. One of his Christmas cards showed him posing with rows of dead ducks draped over an old truck. The greeting read, "The ducks and I wish you a Merry Christmas." Another of his cards had him posing beneath a tree, with the message: "Seven men and a boy were hanged from this tree. Merry Christmas."

Out of the degraded staff and low ethical standards of his insurance company, along with a tradition of bitter warfare among members of the family, was to come thirty years of scandal, investigations, and litigation for his foundation.

"A SAD JOKE" AND THE SAD CONSEQUENCES

The last will and testament of W. L. Moody, Jr., has been described by one family member as "a sad joke." He wrote his trust indenture and created his foundation in August 1942, twelve years before his death. The terms of the document make it obvious that his primary concerns were for the preservation of his enterprises and the avoidance of taxes; his interest in philanthropy was merely as an instrument to achieve his real purpose, namely to perpetuate as far as possible his control over his acquisitions from the grave. The wording of the lengthy document suggests that the old man and his lawyer pored long hours over the text in an effort to anticipate and block every eventuality that might upset the old man's scheme.

The rather complicated one he decided on, especially in view of the family's quarrelsomeness, made an eventual series of legal contests almost inevitable. He left about half of his estate to the Moody Foundation. The corpus of the trust was to be kept intact, and the income was to be applied to religious, charitable, scientific, and educational purposes within the state of Texas.

The other half was put into a trust for his wife, Libby Shearn Moody. Various members of the family were given a life interest in the income from the trust, but three quarters of its assets were earmarked to revert eventually to the foundation. The remainder was designated for a Methodist church in Galveston of which Libby was a devout member.

When Mr. Moody died in 1954 at the age of eighty-nine, the market value of the assets of the foundation was thought to be about $400 million and those of the Libby Shearn Moody Trust about $200 million. The income of the latter was $1.25 million a year, to be distributed to her, three surviving children, and seven grandchildren. As of 1984, the assets of the foundation had a market value of $270 million. (The fact that its assets today are worth less than they were thirty years ago, although a good portion have been in oil properties that generally have greatly increased in value, raises some intriguing questions of asset management, and possibly of asset stripping, that may warrant future research.)

Moody had firm notions about the way he wanted his businesses conducted after his death. He stipulated in his will that Mrs. Northen, his daughter Mary, should succeed him as president of all the many companies that made up the Moody interests. Already in her fifties, with no previous executive experience, indeed without even one day of formal schooling in her life, she seemed an unlikely choice. But he groomed her during the decade before he died to take over his role, and she did so. "We looked alike, thought alike, and felt alike," she says, and for the thirty years since her father's death she has devoted herself with unfailing determination to carrying out even his most idiosyncratic wishes. She has recently said, for example, "I have never flown in an airplane. I promised my father I wouldn't."

A great many unanticipated problems, however, have interfered. The first to erupt was a series of legal challenges to the old man's will, challenges that outraged Mary Northen, split the four family members who were trustees of the Moody Foundation into two warring camps, and immobilized its activities for five years.

This ruckus was finally settled out of court in the late 1950s essentially by enabling two of the donor's children and four of his grandchildren to swap their life shares in the income of the Libby Shearn Moody Trust for large sums of cash. But the animosity between Mrs. Northen and one of the grandchildren, W. L. Moody IV, who with her had opposed the lawsuits, and the two other grandchildren, Shearn Moody, Jr., and his brother Robert L. Moody, who had received cash settlements, was so great that in their capacity as trustees of the foundation they could not agree on anything, not even a date for a board meeting, for several years.

As a result, the attorney general of Texas filed suit to remove the family members from the board, charging that the foundation was prevented by their disagreements from carrying out its functions. This case was settled out of court in 1960 when the Moody family finally agreed to increase the number of trustees to seven in order to break the two-to-two stalemate. Three prominent businessmen were then appointed as "public" trustees. Thereafter the public trustees and W. L. Moody IV generally voted together, controlling the Moody Foundation and through it the Moody National Bank, the Libby Shearn Moody Trust, and the American National Insurance Company.

Over the following years this group began the process of liquidating the Moody empire. The newspapers were sold in 1963, and then most of the Moody hotels and motels, as well as the family bank and five of the twelve Moody ranches.

In 1968, there was another outbreak of internecine warfare. Shearn Moody, Jr., and Robert L. Moody, the two dissident family members who had split the all-family board in the 1950s with their efforts to break the donor's will by litigation, this time made an attempt to raid the foundation's assets via the legislative route. They arranged to have a bill introduced into the Texas legislature to effect a technical change in state law that would result in the transfer of as much as $50 million of the assets of the trust to the two grandsons. The nonfamily trustees of the foundation fought the so-called Moody Bill because of its damage to the interests of the foundation, and it was defeated.

At this point, the two grandsons, led by Shearn, launched an all-out war on the public trustees through the courts and the media. As it proceeded, everyone was besmirched, and the foundation was again the principal victim.

The action of the state attorney general in expanding the foundation board and adding outside trustees ten years earlier had never been accepted by Shearn Moody. He resented the fact that a non-family group had in effect taken control over the family empire, and he believed that the action of the attorney general was illegal. He also came to feel that the public trustees in collusion with executives of the insurance company were enriching themselves by self-dealing, and he hired a private investigator who compiled a large body of documentation to substantiate his allegations.

His case was aided when in late 1969 a major scandal involving the chairman and the president of the insurance company became public. For at least the previous ten years the pair apparently had used American National's prestige, and in particular its capacity to make large mortgage loans on real estate, to feather their own nests.

Through their transactions millions went to build gaudy Nevada hotels and casinos. Millions more went to friends in the Mafia, the Teamsters Union, and big-time gamblers. Political figures now and then were able to finance a deal or two. And the top company officials avoided taxes by channeling their profits through various dummy corporations and clandestine investments.

In late 1969 the executive committee of the board of the American National Insurance Company, of which the three public trustees of the foundation were members, sacked the offending executives. But they did not bother to inform the seven company directors who were not members of the executive committee, among them the three Moodys, Shearn, Robert, and Mrs. Northen.

When a special committee of the Texas legislature looked into the matter a little later, one of the star witnesses was Roy Cohn, who first came to fame as an investigator for the late Senator Joe McCarthy. He told the committee he had been investigating the Moody Foundation and American National on behalf of a client whose bid for one of the Moody properties had been rejected in favor of a lower bid by one of the foundation's public trustees.

In response to the allegations the Texas attorney general in early 1971 authorized a special investigation of the foundation. In late October his report was made public. It said that no evidence of conflict of interest or mismanagement of the foundation, the American National Insurance Company, or any of the other business interests of the foundation had been found. It went on to commend the three public trustees for "sacrificial service" in the face of "unbelievably adverse criticism, malicious public charges, and unwarranted litigation." At the same time the attorney general called for the removal of Shearn Moody as a trustee of the foundation,

saying that "the law imposes a strict requirement of undivided loyalty upon a trustee, uninfluenced by his personal interest," and that
he had violated his responsibilities as a trustee repeatedly.

Roy Cohn denounced the report as a political "hatchet job"
and urged an investigation of the attorney general's investigation.
"I'm chafing at the bit to get into court [against] those stuffed-shirt
hypocrites," Cohn said. He challenged reporters to check the accu-
racy of his claim that he was offered $100,000 to drop the litigation:

> This shows the extremes to which the majority of the trustees
> were willing to go to try to preserve their billion dollar play-
> ground. When I refused to accept this bribe to get me out of
> the picture, the trustees went to the opposite end of the pen-
> dulum by rigging a report rubber stamped by the Attorney
> General in an attempt to silence their critics. Mr. [Shearn]
> Moody, Jr., was asked to resign because he committed such
> crimes as speaking out against such good deeds by the majority
> trustees as using money originally intended for charitable pur-
> poses to furnish roulette wheels and crap tables for Las Vegas
> casinos.

Shearn Moody promptly lodged a countersuit to keep the
other members of the foundation board from removing him as a
trustee. The judge's unexpected ruling, handed down in 1972, was
that the whole structure of the Moody Foundation board that had
been enlarged twelve years earlier was "invalid" and that the only
two legitimate trustees were Mary Moody Northen and Robert
Moody. These two subsequently elected Shearn as the third trustee,
and they currently make up the board. All the public trustees
therefore were eliminated.

The outcome of this episode of hardball Texas politics and litigation returned the foundation to family control, where it had been
more than ten years before, specifically by the elderly surviving
daughter of the donor and two grandsons who had a long record of
attempts to damage and bleed it.

THE EVOLUTION OF PROGRAM

Despite this continuing struggle for power over the foundation and
its assets, some kind of philanthropic activity had to be developed.
In its first decade, the 1940s, the foundation's only significant grant

was one of $246,000 to a school for cerebral-palsied children. From the early 1950s until 1960, when it was continuously enmeshed in family quarrels and litigation, it received little income from its controlled companies and dispensed almost nothing in grants. From 1960, when nonfamily members were added to the board, until 1965, the foundation went through its first period of real grant making. In those five years it dispensed some $25 million, largely in the form of lump-sum contributions to colleges, hospitals, and welfare organizations in Galveston and the surrounding area. By that time it had also acquired its first full-time professional staff member and issued its first public report. Little by little the beneficial influence of the nonfamily members on the board was beginning to be felt, and by 1969 the foundation had developed a program that included not only the usual building grants but also scholarship programs for talented high school students and assistance to a growing variety of social welfare agencies and arts organizations.

Then in 1969, possibly stimulated by the investigation of foundations by Representative Wright Patman in Washington, the foundation's program began to blossom. In that year the Moody Foundation issued a report called *Coming of Age* in which it committed itself to helping find "solutions to human problems" and to innovation and experimentation.

The rhetoric had changed and the actual direction of the program changed even more. Funds were given to help provide housing for low-income families in Galveston and to strengthen black colleges. By 1970 the foundation reported that "We have found ourselves alive with the excitement of seeing human needs and responding in innovative ways." The professional staff was expanded, and a number of interesting new programs were launched: a special scholarship program to help disadvantaged young people acquire job skills, a loan program for students from low-income families to attend community colleges, and a grant of $1.25 million to the Lyndon Baines Johnson School of Public Affairs at the University of Texas to strengthen its work in policy analysis.

By 1971 the foundation was giving still more emphasis to what it called its "people-oriented programs," including its work on behalf of ethnic minorities, and was focusing some of its grants on the development of greater public-private collaboration in dealing with social problems. It was also assisting arts organizations to extend their outreach. By 1973 it had developed a more comprehensive interest in the solution of community problems and had launched a most unusual program to address the problems of the rural poor and of small rural communities. It was also beginning to give attention to problems of health-care delivery to underserved elements of the population.

At that point the Moody Foundation's program was more responsive to the special needs of Texas and was generally more vigorous and innovative than that of any other major foundation in the Southwest.

The report for 1974, however, cryptically announced that the board of trustees had been "reconstituted." What it did not bother to explain was that Shearn Moody, having won his court battle against the state attorney general, had succeeded in having the nonfamily trustees thrown off the board and the foundation returned to tight family control.

Since then a good part of the earlier program development has been maintained, including work with both the inner-city and the rural poor, as well as assistance to educational institutions to facilitate their adaptation to changing needs.

The changes in emphasis that have appeared, however, have been several: a renewed preference for bricks-and-mortar grants and a much greater emphasis on help to arts organizations and cultural events (including the National Cowgirl Hall of Fame, the Galveston Island Shrimp Festival, and the Reenactment of the Battle of Galveston). More recently, a rapidly growing portion of the foundation's funds has been given to the restoration and preservation of historic monuments—old school buildings, a county courthouse, an opera house, sailing ships, a fire station, and the like.

Some of the increased interest in art and culture may be attributed to the reelection of Shearn Moody to the foundation board in 1977. He has described himself as "a world traveler, art patron, and well-rounded individual of many interests." One of his cultural pursuits is collecting bearskin rugs. The foundation's emphasis on historic preservation is clearly a reflection of Mary Northen's interest in that work.

A program of in-house projects, which includes a projected transportation and commerce museum in Galveston, an office building for nonprofit organizations, a zoo and arboretum, and the Shearn Moody Center for Health and Physical Fitness, has also been developed.

As of the early 1980s, therefore, the program of the Moody Foundation is a somewhat curious mixture of social concern, civic loyalty, nostalgia, cultural pretension, and the monumentalizing of Moody family members.

PUBLIC REPORTS

Since the public members of the board have been removed, the foundation's biennial reports have become a kind of family memorial. Pictures of the donor and his wife and their ornate old home grace the front of the publication. The most recent reports have been formally dedicated to Mary Northen. In that for 1979–1980, rather elaborate quotations from the family board members began to be sprinkled throughout the text. The idea was repeated in the 1981–1982 report, with the further twist of coupling the quotations of the family members with those of such figures as John F. Kennedy, Ralph Waldo Emerson, Benjamin Franklin, and John Dewey.

In these quotations Robert Moody and Shearn Moody, Jr., express themselves on large subjects such as science, the arts, and education. On the last subject, for example, Robert Moody goes on record with the reassuring thought that "the real problems in the world are happening in uneducated societies."

Mary Northen, however, is more down-to-earth. Photographed beside one of the foundation's projects of historic restoration, she is quoted as saying, "I enjoy going to Ashton Villa to celebrate the Fourth of July and ringing the freedom bell. I knew the Browns very well. Alice Sweeney and I played there as children. We were very patriotic. I was very fond of them. I knew all of them well."

About the Mary Moody Northen Amphitheater that the foundation has constructed, she says, "I'm told it's one of the largest outdoor stages in the world. There are real horses on the stage. Grandmother had a horse named Topsy. One of us would drive the buggy. The other would whip."

CONCLUSION

The Moody Foundation has had a very long and rough takeoff. Family quarrels and litigation have not been uncommon in the formative years of a number of the largest foundations, but they have been almost everlasting in the case of Moody. Nevertheless, and despite the fact that great social cost has been involved, the foundation has evolved, and although its program does not have the buoyancy and promise of a few years ago it is very much better than it was in its first twenty years. On balance and overall it remains the most diverse, interesting, and relevant program of any of the very large foundations of the American Southwest.

Moody is still far from a first-class foundation, but it is also a far cry from the deplorable mess it was just a few years ago. It vividly reflects the problems that can result from a low-grade donor, an antagonistic and avaricious family, and the direct implication of a foundation in the operation and reorganization of a set of large economic enterprises. The Moody Foundation may also exemplify the special political and ethical problems that seem to arise more frequently and flamboyantly out of the ethos of its part of the country than in other regions. But if one looks at the matter in deliberately hopeful terms, it provides an example of the willingness of some private citizens to devote themselves seriously to trying to unravel a difficult foundation tangle, and it also perhaps demonstrates that in the career of almost any foundation there is always hope of redemption.

The Oklahoma Variation

Oklahoma philanthropy is young like the state itself, which was admitted to the Union only in 1907. The patterns of activity of the two largest Oklahoma foundations that have now developed have been shaped by the poverty of the area through its first decades of statehood and reflect the outlook of the tough-minded, hardworking entrepreneurs who became principal figures in the oil boom, which for the past fifty years has provided the economy its main stimulus.

In the nineteenth century Oklahoma was known as Indian Territory and became the dumping ground for Indian tribes driven from other parts of the country, mainly the East and the Southeast. With these Indians, especially the so-called Five Civilized Tribes from the area of the old South, also came an influx of blacks, who had been their slaves.

Toward the end of the century and despite federal regulations against it, a flood of impoverished, land-hungry whites entered from the surrounding areas. They were followed in the early years of the twentieth centry, as immigration from Central and southern Europe into the United States swelled, by others from a wide variety of ethnic groups.

The economy of the state from the beginning was based on agriculture. But its soil was brutally mined and in the drought of the 1930s Oklahoma became the heart of the Dust Bowl. The stream of "Okies" driven south and west by the catastrophe became a tragic symbol of the Great Depression.

The huge petroleum resources of the state, which began to be discovered in the 1920s, have been its salvation and have powered a remarkable social, educational, economic, and cultural development that has steadily gained momentum since that time. The two Oklahoma foundations included in this study are both based on fortunes made in oil: the Noble Foundation with assets of $340 million and the Mabee Foundation with assets of $375 million.

J. E. and L. E. Mabee Foundation

The Mabee Foundation was incorporated in 1948 to distribute the charitable gifts of John E. Mabee, a multimillionaire oil operator, drilling contractor, and rancher of Tulsa, Oklahoma, and his wife, Lottie. Its assets of $375 million as of 1984 placed it among the twenty largest foundations in the United States.

Mabee and his wife, before their oil wealth began rolling in, experienced appallingly difficult early years. He was born in Missouri in 1879 of a poor farming family. He claimed he never owned a pair of shoes until he was ten years of age, and by that time he had finished all the formal education he was to receive.

As a young man he did farm work in the Ozarks and later tried his luck as a ranch hand in the West and as a packing-house worker. In 1900 he returned to Missouri to marry Lottie Boren, and for the next several years they scraped a meager existence out of a hill farm there. In 1907, practically penniless, the two of them homesteaded a farm in the southwestern part of Oklahoma. Thereafter he worked for several years in the vicinity of the town of Randlett acquiring leases for the Carter Oil Company.

In 1919 at the age of forty Mabee entered the drilling business on his own. Quickly thereafter the circumstances of his life radically changed. He hit gushers on his first two wells, drilled near Burkburnett, Texas, and over the next few years his lucky strikes continued. By the mid-1920s he was already a very successful and wealthy oilman. He then moved to Tulsa, and with driving energy branched out into ranching, real estate, and various other businesses.

In the 1940s, having amassed one of the largest fortunes in Oklahoma, he began to be more active in civic and philanthropic activities. During World War II he acquired a certain reputation for patriotism by buying more war bonds than anyone else in the state. And in 1945 he began philanthropic contributions on a large scale, announcing in December of that year that he would build two dormitories on the University of Tulsa campus. He was elected to its board that same year and remained active in its affairs until his death in 1961. (The University of Tulsa is an institution with a special relationship to the oil industry. Originally the Presbyterian School for Indian Girls located in Indian Territory, it relocated to Tulsa in 1921 and changed its name. There, in addition to its basic teaching program, it provided special courses to help fill voids in the scanty educational background of many of the early oilmen in Oklahoma. As they became rich and powerful, they rewarded the institution with very generous contributions.)

Three years later, in 1948, the Mabees organized their foundation, and he served as its active head until his death thirteen years later. His motivation in creating it and the purposes he intended it to serve have to be deduced from a very few fragments of evidence for he was not an articulate person or one given to putting his thoughts on paper. He and his wife were childless. He saw himself as a self-made man, and his personal formula for success was "Work 18 hours a day, and don't forget that luck and pluck are partners." According to one of his close business associates he was a man possessing "great compassion for the unfortunate but no sympathy for those who would not help themselves." His foundation concentrates its work in Oklahoma, Texas, Kansas, Arkansas, Missouri, and New Mexico because he felt a strong sense of obligation to return some of his good fortune to the states from which his millions came. He also apparently wanted his foundation to perpetuate his name, which may explain the strong preference it has always had for bricks-and-mortar grants.

In personality he was not particularly outgoing, and his wife, whom he called Lottie J, was a quiet and retiring woman, remaining always in the background. But as time went on he developed a taste for greater visibility. At the Tulsa Charity Show in May 1958, for example, he personally announced a gift of $160,000 to the city's

Children's Medical Center. He then charmed the audience by singing two songs, "Sugar Time" and "Don't Fence Me In."

Mr. Mabee died in 1961 at the age of eight-one, and the foundation was named principal beneficiary of his estate. He left a substantial sum to his personal nurse of the preceding twelve years and sizable gifts to various employees in his Tulsa office. But he left only ten dollars each to thirty-three relatives, including a brother and sister. When Mrs. Mabee died four years later, she also left her estate to the foundation.

The foundation is now controlled by a five-member board, all of whom are also officers and directors of the Mabee Petroleum Corporation. The corporation has been a wholly owned subsidiary of the foundation, but this situation will have to be altered within the coming few years by the diversification requirements of the Tax Reform Act of 1969.

The foundation is run by a part-time administrative officer, Donald P. Moyers, member of a prominent Tulsa law firm and estate attorney for John Mabee, the donor. Its style is low-key: it does not publish an annual report and makes no attempt to distribute public announcements of grants.

It gives its grants largely for the construction of physical facilities to established institutions: colleges and universities, hospitals, social service organizations, cultural institutions, and, in a few instances, churches. Reflecting the ethos of the area there is a manifest skepticism of government in the selection of grantees: with only rare exceptions the foundation abides by a rule of making no grants to tax-supported institutions. In the words of Mr. Moyers, the foundation provides "conservative financial help to good old American institutions."

The program of the foundation is an archetype of the many foundations in the Southwest created by men who, like John Mabee, came up from poverty, had little formal education, and made their fortunes primarily as a result of striking oil. If there are distinctive features about the Mabee Foundation's program they are perhaps just two: a strong preference for *challenge grants*, that is, requiring grantees to match the foundation's funds with additional money from other sources; and giving somewhat greater emphasis to social welfare and cultural organizations (nearly 30 percent of total outlays) than is common among most of the larger foundations in the Southwest.

A few examples of the kinds of grants the foundation has made in recent years are a mirror of its governing social outlook and priorities and those of its directors:

1. to build the Lottie Jane Mabee Dormitory, the John Mabee Dormitory, the Mabee Gymnasium, and the Mabee Speech and Hearing Clinic at the University of Tulsa;
2. to build the Mabee Educational Building on the Stilwell, Oklahoma, campus of Flaming Rainbow University (a school serving a predominantly native American enrollment of three hundred students);
3. to St. John's Hospital, Tulsa, for its building program;
4. to Harding College, Searcy, Arkansas, for an auditorium-gymnasium;
5. to Lubbock Christian College in Texas for its Center for Business and Economic Education;
6. to The Salvation Army, Midland, Texas, for a community center;
7. to Oral Roberts University, Tulsa, for an athletic scholarship fund;
8. to the Pioneer Railroad Museum, Temple, Texas, for air-conditioning equipment; and
9. to the Oklahoma Methodist Home for the Aged, Tulsa, for its building program.

The foundation's offices are combined with the office complex of the Mabee Petroleum Corporation in Tulsa. One wall of the entrance area is covered with colored photographs of the library, hospital, college, and other buildings that its funds have helped to build or renovate, the legacy of childless John and Lottie Jane Mabee to their part of the United States.

Samuel Roberts Noble Foundation

Lloyd Noble established the Samuel Roberts Noble Foundation in 1945, five years before his death. He named it in honor of his father, "the most unselfish person he had ever known."

The elder Noble had found his way to the Indian Territory of Oklahoma in the 1880s. He subsequently ran a hardware store in the town of Ardmore, where his son Lloyd was born and grew up.

Lloyd Noble attended Southeastern College at Durant, Oklahoma, in 1914, dropping out in 1916 to join the U.S. Navy for the latter part of World War I. He then enrolled at the University of Oklahoma in 1919 but dropped out again in the following year to set up a partnership to search for oil. The business struggled at first, but by the late 1930s Noble had become an established success. His drilling rigs were operating throughout the continental United States, as well as in Alaska, where he was one of the first to explore for oil. During World War II he expanded his business internationally and developed production in both Canada and the British Isles. By then he was a multimillionaire and the owner not only of many producing oil and gas properties but also of oil field service companies and extensive ranch and farm land.

With his business activities flourishing he began to be active in public affairs and politics. He made generous gifts to the University of Oklahoma and became a member and later chairman of its Board of Regents. He ran for public office and became the first Republican in Oklahoma to be elected to the state legislature from traditionally Democratic southern Carter County. By the time of his death in 1950 he was the Republican leader of the state.

Physically, Lloyd Noble was slight in stature with tousled blond hair that he never concealed under a hat. In the old brown army shirt open at the throat that he often wore, he looked more like an ordinary roustabout than the prosperous oil lord he was. He was a personable man and is remembered well for his comradeship with the men who worked for him.

He was married twice, both marriages ending in divorce. By his first wife he had three children and by his second, one. Despite his prominence in the affairs of the state he generally shunned publicity, particularly about his personal life.

After his second divorce and with his businesses solidly established, he began increasingly to give thought to what he might do with his wealth that, in his words, "would be in the best interest of the people of Oklahoma."

From childhood apparently he had developed a great feeling for the poor, hard-working farmers of southern Oklahoma and strong convictions about the importance of a prosperous agriculture as an essential factor in the strength of the country. His concern for farmers may have been reinforced by his own observations of the state of farming in the area. In the late 1900s it was one of the largest cotton-growing regions in the United States. However, the land had been depleted by overintensive cultivation and drought, and Noble, who was an early user of private aircraft for business purposes, was repeatedly struck by its drastic deterioration during his frequent trips into and out of his home town of Ardmore.

When he set up his foundation in 1945, his clear intention was to concentrate most if not all of its activity on the human and economic problems of Dust Bowl agriculture, and he himself began to spend a large amount of his time directly involved in its work. Within three years he retired as head of his drilling company and thereafter devoted almost all of his attention to it.

The programs established and directed by his own hand were bold and innovative. They embodied a large and generous vision of public service, and they were obviously inspired by a real concern for the needs of impoverished, uneducated small farmers and by a recognition of the need to provide them with counseling and technical assistance if they were ever to work themselves out of their predicament.

Immediately after the foundation was begun, a technical staff of agricultural specialists was employed to provide local farmers with information about controlling soil erosion, improving the fertility of their soil, and improving their cropping techniques. Farmers who received such technical assistance from the foundation had to agree to demonstrate the new farming methods they had learned to their neighbors in order to expand the impact of the foundation's work. One device used to stimulate the interest of farmers was an incentive plan by which prizes were given for restoring worn-out soil and diversifying crops.

To develop its own understanding of local conditions and to demonstrate what better technology and farm management could accomplish, the foundation created several experimental farms of various soil types throughout the area.

In 1947 U.S. Representative Carl Albert of Oklahoma told his colleagues in Congress of the work the Noble Foundation was doing. In his remarks he quoted Noble on the occasion of the first foundation awards ceremony: "If by our efforts with this foundation, we can bring the knowledge and opportunity to even a few men and women by which the depleted fertility of our soil can be redeemed, if we can do a little part in spreading the information that is needed to destroy forever fear from the hearts of a few, our efforts will not have been in vain."

Over the course of the years the foundation's interest in agricultural improvement has continued. Currently its agricultural division employs some forty specialists in horticulture, agronomy, livestock husbandry, soils, irrigation, and agricultural economics. The foundation now operates three research and demonstration farms, which comprise approximately four thousand acres. And it provides a free farm planning and consultation service to farmers within a 100-mile radius of Ardmore. An additional wildlife refuge and demonstration farm, where ecological studies are to be carried out, was acquired in 1981. On the whole it is this aspect of the program of the Noble Foundation that most authentically reflects the spirit and original intention of the donor and that represents its most distinctive contribution.

Unfortunately, Noble died at a relatively early age in 1950, five years after setting up his foundation. At that point control of its policies and programs transferred to a board made up of his children and various former business associates. Substantial new assets from his estate passed to the foundation, and the trustees decided quickly to add a second major operating program. They chose a field that they felt would be consistent with the donor's general intention to "benefit mankind," namely cancer research, even though Noble had shown no interest in that subject during his lifetime.

This second operating program of the foundation developed its own laboratory, library, and professional staff. At the beginning, in a curious mixture of political attitudes and scientific considerations, the foundation emphasized that the laboratory was unique because it accepted no federal grants or contracts, performed no clinical work, and had no working relationships with universities or hospitals.

For the next twenty years the modest resources of the foundation were largely consumed by its two operating programs. The work of the agricultural division was increasingly accepted by the farmers of the area and gained a national reputation for its quality. The biomedical program got under way more slowly and unevenly. It was regarded by many in that field as a peripheral and second-rate operation, out of the mainstream of the rapidly growing volume of research being conducted nationally and internationally on cancer. In time, however, the work somewhat improved. By the late 1970s the foundation's biomedical division, with the advice and assistance of a visiting committee of outside experts, had broken out of its earlier self-imposed isolation and had widened its collaboration with other research organizations.

The reports of the Noble Foundation during this long developmental period were informative and straightforward and gave a picture of a serious and hardworking institution, not brilliant but little by little getting better.

Then two things happened that have greatly changed the scale of the foundation's activities but not necessarily their quality. The first was passage of the Tax Reform Act of 1969; the second was the international oil crisis of the early 1970s. The combined effect of these developments was to increase the value of the foundation's assets dramatically from some $200 million to $340 million and, because of the payout requirements of the tax act, to increase rapidly the level of its grant making. Its agricultural and biomedical programs were both enlarged, but its grants program had come to constitute the bulk of its outlays. A key indicator of the foundation's approach to grant making was that out of a total full-time staff of nearly ninety only two individuals were assigned to handle grant requests.

In 1979, for example, total expenditures of the foundation were nearly $11 million. Of that amount 26 percent, or $3 million, went to support the agricultural and biomedical programs. The remainder was distributed mostly to colleges, universities, schools, and hospitals, largely for buildings, equipment, and endowment. Many of the grants were concentrated in the state of Oklahoma, but some were sent to other parts of the country. Dartmouth College of Medicine in New Hampshire, for example, received $1 million; Vanderbilt University School of Medicine in Tennessee, $250,000; and the Salk Institute in California, $350,000.

At present, the two most noteworthy features of the grants program are a remarkably small level of funding for social welfare organizations, given the donor's original commitment to the welfare of the rural poor, and the steadily increasing proportion of its gifts, well masked by the confusing categorization of its grants in the foundation's public reports, to organizations fostering economic conservatism and national military preparedness. In 1979, for example, Harding College in Searcy, Arkansas, received $150,000; the Heritage Foundation in Washington, D.C., $750,000; and St. John's Military Academy in Wisconsin, $800,000.

Through 1980 and 1981 the flow of funding to such organizations continued. The Hoover Institution at Stanford University, the Committee on the Present Danger, the National Strategy Information Center, and the Heritage Foundation received repeated grants along with the Religious Roundtable in Arlington, Virginia, the Southeastern Legal Foundation in Georgia, and the American Legislative Exchange Council in Washington, D.C.

A man who has played a prominent part in Oklahoma politics on the liberal side says about these developments at the Noble Foundation, "There is something preposterous about those trustees sitting in their paneled boardroom outside Ardmore playing war games. I imagine them in their battle helmets, down in their bunker, with their war maps on the wall—showing the whereabouts of the combat forces of the Soviets abroad and the liberals here at home—and some Dr. Strangelove flapping his arm and directing their bombardment of grants to protect and defend the Republic."

By 1981 *The New York Times* in a study of foundations assisting conservative causes included the Noble Foundation in the top dozen and estimated its expenditures for such purposes at about $2 million a year. No acknowledgment of this trend has appeared in any of the foundation's literature. (There have been a number of cases in which foundations, most notably the Ford Foundation, have moved in a liberal direction and away from the conservative philosophy of the donor. The Noble Foundation seems to be a switch on that more familiar pattern.)

The annual reports of the foundation are of little assistance in trying to understand either the pattern or the rationale of its grant making. Indeed in parallel with the politicization of its programs in the late 1970s and early 1980s has come an odd, almost comical change in the quality of its reporting. In contrast to the well-organized, factual, and useful publications of earlier years, the foundation's report for 1981 was an assemblage of irrelevancies. It began with a detailed listing of the foundation's administrative employees, including the cook, the bookkeeper, the maintenance staff, and the personnel of the print shop, cafeteria, and laundry. In the section on the agricultural program, substantive matters were dealt with briefly, followed by a four-page detailed listing of the various meetings that staff members attended during the year. The review of the activities of the biomedical division might have been prepared by some of the administrative personnel featured at the beginning of the document because a very brief summary of the scientific work was preceded and followed by an account of operational changes made in the laboratory: "All animal care, which must be maintained on a seven-day schedule, has been combined under one supervisor. Instrument and laboratory maintenance has been centralized in an effort to reduce maintenance contracts while giving us in-house service. Purchasing of supplies has been centralized in the administrative division." Then at the end of the section, it was conscientiously recounted that the safety committee during the year had "in addition to updating first aid cabinets, installed kits designed to facilitate in the clean up of chemical spills."

What the report conspicuously lacked was any listing, description, or explanation of the grants of the foundation for that year, which hit a record high of $10.5 million and made up three quarters of its total outlays.

The report of the following year was much the same but contained a special feature on the summer students program operated by the biomedical division. The work and reactions of the two young people "learning by doing" in the foundation's laboratory were detailed. One, a junior at the University of Oklahoma, was, as it happened, not studying science at all but majoring in finance. His work, according to the foundation report, "has centered on the different parts of the immune system and how those reactions affect the cell's abilities to interact with other cells." The young man anticipated that his work in the following summer would expand on what he had done in the three previous years.

"The immune system really interests me," he was quoted as saying.

The other student, a biochemistry major at Oklahoma State University, was a young man with an obviously fantastic vocabulary: In the foundation's report he is quoted as follows: "Everybody says it's a fantastic program and it really is."

Speaking of his staff supervisor, Joe Clouse, he was enthusiastic. "He was really fantastic and helpful to me, especially in letting me know about a lot of what was going on and letting me do the work myself. He's a fantastic person to work with."

Recognizing that its report on the year's activities might have been deficient in providing information about its grants, the foundation explained that it was doing so many good things in so many areas that it would not be possible to cover all of them. Instead it proposed to report simply on categories of grants. Some of these a reader might not find too helpful. For example, under the category headed "Education–Other-Program/Endowment," in which the foundation in each of the immediately preceding years would appear to have given $6 or $7 million, the total for 1982 had dropped, without explanation, to $6,450.

Perhaps the confusion in its public reporting for these particular years was an incidental effect of a transition of leadership. John March, who had been president for some seventeen years, retired and was succeeded by John Snodgrass in early 1982. On the question of whether the foundation is in the process of a program shift away from the earlier intentions of the donor, Snodgrass insists that no change has taken place, that Lloyd Noble was a deeply conservative man and that his intention in providing help to impoverished Dust Bowl farmers was not to relieve their plight but "to further agricultural free enterprise." He argues also that the grants being given to "ultraconservative causes" are a small portion of the foundation's total outlays.

In basic respects the evolution of the Noble Foundation over the past thirty years has been generally downhill. The first program it started remains its best; its second major undertaking (in the field of biomedical research) has mostly been mediocre; the third, large-scale grant making, has been essentially reactive and almost amateurish. Moreover in its general spirit and direction the foundation's program has moved a very great distance from the donor's original vision of helping the poor farmers of southern Oklahoma restore their land and improve their incomes to an emphasis on miscellaneous bricks-and-mortar grants interspersed with considerable support to ideological conservatism. Despite the protestations of the present leadership of the foundation that they are remaining scrupulously faithful to the donor's wishes, it would appear that the present thrust of the foundation's giving is as far removed from the donor's original interests as his impoverished boyhood was from the oil-rich life-style of his descendants and the wealthy business executives who control his foundation today.

There is not much indication at present that the foundation is likely to recapture the creativity and vigor that it displayed at its beginning. Still it should not be written off, if only because some members of the Noble family are reportedly deeply interested in seeing the foundation achieve first-rank status. As of today, however, it remains largely an entity of contradictions, an enigma with intriguing but largely unrealized potentialities.

13

THE NONIDENTICAL
MINNESOTA TWINS:

McKnight and Bush

The two largest foundations in Minnesota derive from the extraordinary success of the same company, the Minnesota Mining and
Manufacturing Company, known as 3M, the makers, among other
products, of Scotch Tape.

Minnesota is a state with a history of an active citizenry, a
strong tradition of populism and liberalism in its politics, and a pro-
liferation of vigorous nonprofit groups. There are a good number of
private foundations in the state, some of them of outstanding quality such as the Amherst Wilder Foundation, active in the care of the
elderly. Some of the nation's most interesting and effective corporate foundations are centered in the Twin Cities, including the
General Mills Foundation and the Dayton Hudson Foundation. The
Twin Cities are also the area where the idea of corporate "5%
Clubs" first took root and subsequently the "2% Clubs," both of
which after having proved their effectiveness in stimulating in-

creased charitable contributions by local corporations then spread to a number of other cities throughout the country.

The McKnight and Bush foundations, therefore, exist in a context of high standards and strong interest in civic and philanthropic activity. But their donors were not among the most progressive and social minded of the local business leaders, and the two large foundations they created have followed quite different paths and have taken some time in finding their way.

McKnight Foundation

William L. McKnight was the principal architect of the 3M company's development. The foundation he established, with assets of some $450 million, is far and away the biggest in the strip of states from Minnesota westward to the Pacific Northwest.

He was born on a farm near White, South Dakota, but decided early he did not like farm work. In 1906 he went to Duluth, where he could get free room and board by staying with relatives, and enrolled in the local business college. In the next year he was hired as an assistant bookkeeper at a struggling little sandpaper company. In a short time he was promoted to cost accountant, then manager of the Chicago office, and in 1911 sales manager. Within a few years he had revolutionized the company's selling and manufacturing methods. By 1929 he became president, and from then until his retirement in 1966 he directed its extraordinary growth and diversification into a concern with annual sales of billions of dollars. According to an associate, McKnight gave his entire life to the company and never lived or worked for anything else.

His confidence in the Minnesota Mining and Manufacturing Company was such that even in its early years when it was debt-ridden and paid no dividends he began to accumulate all the stock he could with all the money he could afford.

Perhaps his main contribution to its growth was his support of research as a basis for developing high-quality and diversified products that would command premium prices. His slogan was "uninhibited research directed toward uninhabited markets."

In style and tastes he was plain and unpretentious. His favorite foods were hamburger, corn on the cob, and ice cream. His preference in watching television was prizefights and baseball. The office from which he ruled 3M for many years was an unimposing one at the end of a long corridor. The furnishings were ordinary and the carpet even a little threadbare.

As a young man he met and married Maude Gage, a clerk in a local music store. They had one child, a daughter. Their life-style was quiet and private. On an average evening they would read the day's newpapers, he would go through some company reports, and they would be in bed by 10:00 P.M. Neither took an active part in civic or social activities or in public life in any way.

A person close to the family summed up the personality and outlook of the donor of the bigger of the two biggest foundations in Minnesota in these words: "You can't glamorize McKnight. His first name was 'work.' He was perfectly satisifed to work and do virtually nothing else."

However ordinary the lives of the McKnights may have seemed, the fortune that they amassed was anything but ordinary. When Maude McKnight died in 1973, her estate was valued at $267 million, the largest in the history of Minnesota. Most of this was bequeathed to the foundation they had established some years earlier. When Mr. McKnight died in 1978 at the age of ninety his will increased the assets of the foundation to nearly $400 million. (A year after the death of the first Mrs. McKnight, he married the woman who had been his nurse. After his death the second Mrs. McKnight filed suit in a Florida court to break his will and obtain 30 percent of his huge estate. An out-of-court settlement was reached, however, before the case came to trial.)

Orderliness and predictability in its grant making are not the highest possible virtues of a major foundation. But the lack of such qualities in McKnight at least for the first several years after its full activation was quite unusual, even startling.

The development of the foundation, which has been in existence since 1953, falls broadly into three periods: the years from 1953 to 1973, when its assets were small and its few grants were scattered among various nonprofit agencies, mostly in the Minneapolis–St. Paul area; the years 1974 to 1979, when its assets were greatly increased by the settlement of the estates of Mr. and Mrs. McKnight and when it added a small professional staff and began to try to define a program; and 1980 to date, when it has finally begun to emerge from the switchbacks, reversals, and contradictions of its initial efforts to identify its fields of interest, priorities, and grant-making style.

The special character of McKnight at present derives in considerable part from the close working relationship between an Episcopal priest and the daughter of the donor. The foundation was relatively inactive until 1974, when William McKnight turned it over to his daughter, Virginia Binger. At that point Russell Ewald, once the family's minister, was hired as executive vice-president.

Ewald has been close to the McKnight family for a long time. He performed the weddings of two of Binger's children and helped her with her personal charity in the 1960s, much of it given anonymously. Later, when he headed the Minnesota Foundation, she served on his board. Together they developed a strong interest in the problems of minorities and the poor, and the pair still regularly make personal visits to the distressed neighborhoods of the Twin Cities. Clearly Ewald has been a strong influence not only on Mrs. Binger's philanthropic interests but on her personality. "I'm shy," she says. "Work on foundation matters brought me out," even to the extent of occasionally making short speeches. She still avoids publicity, partly because she feels "it's embarrassing to have much said about me."

The board now has six members: Mrs. Binger, her husband (a former head of the Honeywell Corporation), their three children, who live in other parts of the country, and Ewald. The other members of the board defer to Mrs. Binger and to Ewald, who together and in a highly personalized way run the foundation.

She and Ewald seek to keep the organization of the foundation small and maneuverable to permit quick response to emergency situations. It therefore depends heavily on outside consultants and frequently uses other groups to administer its programs. Even today, when the annual grants of the foundation exceed $28 million, McKnight operates with only two full-time professionals, including Ewald, and three administrative staff. The various members of the family reportedly like the informality of the arrangement and also the opportunity it provides for their personal involvement and the expression of their personal interests.

The first effort to formulate guidelines for grant making was in 1974. At that time it was indicated that the foundation would make grants primarily in the St. Paul–Minneapolis area and secondarily in outlying counties of Minnesota. Its primary program interests would be in the fields of human and social services, and it would have a particular concern for the handicapped and disadvantaged. It would also concentrate its energies on fewer and larger projects so that the foundation's objectives could be "pursued with maximum care and impact."

A year later it revised those guidelines to add the field of brain research plus two miscellaneous categories, "special grants" and "discretionary grants" to its areas of interest. (The biggest single grant that year, made with no discernible relation to the published guidelines, was one of $25 million to build a William L. McKnight Science Center at the Science Museum of Minneapolis. Another major grant, also outside the program guidelines, was for $1 million to the University of Minnesota for the training of health professionals.)

In 1977 the guidelines were again revised, and the foundation announced it was ready to consider funding requests in the broad fields of education, the arts, conservation, recreation, and international affairs. (Speaking of the guidelines, Ewald has said, "They're nothing more than guidelines. If we like something, we'll do anything we want to do.") By 1978 the foundation was still making scattershot grants of many kinds, some of them quite large. It gave the appearance of an institution more committed to being responsive to the individual preferences, even whims, of family members on the board than to the idea that its grants should generally fit within some framework of stated program priorities.

Despite, or because of, this, McKnight did fund some creative and effective projects. An outstanding example was its action in early 1978—based on a conversation between Mrs. Binger and Reverend Ewald with Mayor George Lattimer of St. Paul—to contribute several millions of dollars (eventually $10 million in program-related investments and $5 million in grants) to a consortium with organized labor and the cities of Minneapolis and St. Paul to build thirty-two hundred affordable housing units for moderate-income families. With a fine disdain for its own program plans (housing had never been mentioned in any of the foundation's statements as an area of interest) the leadership of the foundation was able to recognize an important opportunity and make a major commitment virtually on the spot. The result was to bring about an important new kind of public-private partnership, one that has been highly successful.

Little by little, however, the foundation was beginning to be more aware of some of the complexities of large-scale grant making. In its public report for 1979 it announced rather plaintively that foundations need to search harder for their areas of "comparative advantage" as the amount of public or governmental support increases for programs previously supported almost exclusively by the private sector. . . . The problem is particularly acute in Minnesota, where the public sector has accepted an unusually high level of responsibility for the welfare of its citizens. In most areas in which the McKnight Foundation is active, support from Federal, State, County, and Local tax revenues far exceeds the McKnight foundation's capacity to give. This is particularly true of the foundation's area of major interest, human services.

The best it could do, however, in trying to relate its private grants to public funding was to take over the support of several projects to train and employ the handicapped and to assist abused women and their children that had been created and initially funded by government. In that same year the foundation discovered program-related investments and revolving loan funds as additional techniques for assisting its grantees.

The year 1980 was a significant one in the foundation's development. In its annual report for that year Chairwoman Binger repeated what had been said periodically in the past, namely that McKnight's primary concern was with the need for services to the disadvantaged and the handicapped. She also made specific reference to the "perilous time for our society" because of the impacts of massive federal budget cutbacks and inflation on the nonprofit community and on highly vulnerable elements of the population.

But this time, for the first time, the tenor of the introductory essay and the actual grant list were in harmony. During the year the foundation made a number of grants directed at alleviating the emotional and physical needs of troubled youth, women, the elderly, the handicapped, Hispanics, and other population groups with special needs for housing, training, and employment. The largest of these was one of $1.5 million to the city of St. Paul to provide job training for some fourteen hundred young people, including working mothers, high school dropouts, and Indochinese refugees.

Apart from the other merits of these individual grants, the foundation has injected into a number of them a requirement that the recipients think about needed improvements in public policy and work to bring about greater collaboration among sometimes competing nonprofit agencies. About this aspect of its work, a former state welfare commissioner, Ed Dirkswager, says McKnight "is making certain that broader policy thinking is taking place in a variety of different locations and under the auspices of different organizations."

As a means of moving money more effectively into the nonprofit sector the foundation in 1980 turned increasingly to the use of grants to umbrella-type agencies. One was a commitment of $200,000 to the Metro Community Health Consortium, to provide support for nine community health clinics. A second was a grant of $100,000 to the Minneapolis Foundation to create a Cash Flow Loan Fund for nonprofit organizations. The United Way of Minneapolis received more than $300,000 for several new programs directed at needy groups.

There were, however, a few aberrations and a new item added to the lengthening and frequently changing list of the foundation's program priorities: $500,000 to The Juilliard School in New York for its endowment fund; $1 million to the University of Miami School of Medicine (Florida), to establish an Immuno-Biology program; $5 million to the Walker Art Center in Minneapolis for its endowment fund; and $1 million to the Nature Conservancy of Portland, Oregon, to create a wildlife preserve in the Rocky Mountains. The new program area announced was in the field of "agriculture, food and rural development."

In 1981 the note of concern in Mrs. Binger's essay about the state of the nation was even more urgent. Events during the year, she wrote, "have even more forcefully demanded that we reexamine our grant making policies and priorities. No longer are our national and local communities concerned only with inflation, unemployment, fiscal crunches and social discord, but now the concern is deeper. Now it is the question of . . . survival." In view of the situation, the foundation had decided to increase its funds for grant making and to reorder its priorities, giving even greater emphasis to the needs of the poor, the disadvantaged, and minorities.

Despite the reduction in payout requirements for foundations enacted by the U.S. Congress that year to 5 percent of their assets, the McKnight Foundation in a most unusual action decided that it would maintain its grant-making level at an amount equal to 6.5 percent of its average yearly assets for the years 1982–1984. Among the major new programs announced were the McKnight Neighborhood Self Help Initiatives Program, which would be administered through the Minneapolis Foundation with the help of a $5 million grant. A second was a $3.5 million four-year program to improve the Minnesota service system to help mentally retarded and disabled individuals. The grant included some support for legal advocacy in their behalf. A third major program was a public-private venture in collaboration with Hennepin County (Minneapolis) to improve mental health services.

In the cultural field, the foundation made a multiyear commitment to the McKnight Arts Funding Plan, which provides $1.6 million annually to build up the endowment income of key arts organizations in the Twin Cities. It also funded a number of "McKnight awards" to assist the work of individual artists, composers, filmmakers, writers, and choreographers.

In connection with its new program in "agriculture, food and rural development" the foundation announced it would undertake a major grant program to support basic research in these areas and perhaps undertake "grant making that has an international dimension." It has subsequently committed $18.5 million for a ten-year research program in plant genetics.

In the foundation's report for 1982 Mrs. Binger's concern for the urgency of doing more to meet the nation's social needs had become exclamatory:

> In the 1980s the challenge to philanthropy is clear!
>
> A demand that we look at and address the basic issues and values of our society!
>
> A demand that we look anew at our areas of activity and convince ourselves we are effectively engaging the critical problems of our age in ways that will aid in solving them! . . .
>
> A demand that we no longer view philanthropy as an amiable custom but rather a belief in the view that the health of the entire private nonprofit sector is crucial to our future!

In preceding years the foundation's distress at the state of things had led it to increasing resort to "special" grants and "special" planning projects. Now it adopted a new category of "emergency services" in its grant listing. Among these was an additional $2 million grant to a Work Opportunities Project that would provide employment to more than six hundred unemployed people in Minneapolis who had exhausted all other sources of benefits. An additional $3.3 million was provided to the Minneapolis–St. Paul Family Housing Fund along with $3.35 million for a comprehensive program to meet the needs of an estimated six hundred thousand Minnesotans suffering from mental illness.

In the grant list for the year were still a few oddities and aberrations: a $350,000 grant to the Gow School in South Wales, New York, for new dormitories and other purposes; $1 million to the city of St. Paul to install a 911 emergency telephone dispatch system; and a $5 million grant to establish an international diabetes center in Minnesota that would do research and training and provide patient care. A few dabbling grants in international affairs could also be noted.

In late 1983 the foundation sprang another major surprise in its program. Mr. McKnight had spent a good part of the later years of his life in Florida, where his most active interest became the training and racing of thoroughbred horses. Because of his interest in the state the directors of the foundation decided to launch a substantial new educational project there. After months of meetings with the governor, state legislators, and higher education officials, the foundation announced in September 1983 a $16 million commitment to improve the quality of higher education in Florida. The program is addressed to three major problems: the lack of access to high-quality education for minorities, especially blacks; the need for more blacks to complete their college and university training; and the disproportionate number of black adults who are functionally illiterate. As the program moves forward it is anticipated that a public-private partnership will be established among the state of Florida and various higher-education institutions, foundations, and corporations to carry forward this effort to broaden educational opportunity and improve race relations.

AN APPRAISAL

There are a number of mysteries about the McKnight Foundation. For example, why it decided to enter the field of brain research has never been explained or how it expected, without technically qualified staff or experience, to plan and carry on discriminating grant making in a specialized field such as this. (The McKnight Foundation could of course clear up such questions as this if it were more communicative. In sharp contrast to the openness of the Bush Foundation, McKnight, although it publishes annual reports that are informative, is otherwise quite inaccessible. It declines interviews and in the case of the present study refused even to provide the author's research assistant with copies of earlier foundation annual reports.) Yet, despite the curiosities and the inchoate quality of much of what the foundation has done, there are a few important consistencies and some significant accomplishments. In accordance with its first tentative policy statement in 1974, the work of the foundation has rather consistently, and increasingly over time, been concerned primarily with urgent human needs and with finding better ways of serving them. It has also rather consistently (with some notable exceptions) concentrated its efforts on assisting particularly vulnerable and disadvantaged elements of the population.

It has been prepared on occasion to make large and bold commitments. It has been willing to try new approaches to work with coalitions of nonprofits, organized labor, city and state government, and private business firms to deal with problems of large scale and complexity. And it has been a foundation responsive to the changing mood and circumstances of the nation and one willing to address urgent short-term as well as longer-term needs.

Although there is some difference of view about the effectiveness of the work of the McKnight Foundation, a number of important citizens of the area speak very highly of it. The editor of a leading newspaper, for example, says that the foundation has been "a catalyst for many of the most important recent developments in the Twin Cities. McKnight is a huge asset for Minnesota in a period of Federal and State budget restraint." Because of the situations in which the foundation has been able to intervene quickly, the police chief of St. Paul has said, "I don't know of any foundation that has done more simple social good than McKnight."

Ewald has most clearly stated the underlying social values that guide the foundation and the rationale of its informal and unprofessionalized approach to grant making. In a keynote speech to the Minnesota Council of Foundations in 1982 he strongly expressed the view that philanthropy had to "assist in the reversal of the existing pattern of maldistribution of wealth and income and return to the original purpose of philanthropy—that of assisting those in need—so that our funds will strengthen the community's capacity for development and self help initiative. . . ."

As to methods of foundation operation, he said, "The professionalization of foundation management . . . has brought many advantages [but] it has also brought disadvantages. It has added an extra layer which further separates foundation board members from actively participating in the identification of needs, and even more basically, separates them from the contacts with individuals and community organizations which are so necessary when decisions are to be made on funding. . . ."

He made reference to recent conversations with some corporate board members centered on questions such as "Who are the poor? Where are they? I don't know any!" and added

> One can only assume that some foundation board members are too distant from the controversies which pervade our society. . . . Staff members in responding to emergency needs . . . are often hampered by regulations, rules, and quarterly settings of meetings, and as a result, their heart-felt concerns are of no avail when they are unable to respond. . . .
>
> There is a need to de-politicize our grant-making process. Those organizations working with the poor, the disadvantaged and with minorities find themselves receiving less attention . . . because the philanthropic sector makes its decisions by where we are placed in the societal structure, by the ethos and values of our peer group, by seeing people as "our kind" of people, by responding to the charisma of a staff person or the overpowering presence of corporate executives serving as board members . . .

Ewald concluded with the appeal that the philanthropic community in the 1980s should "bear witness to . . . an understanding that the gamut of philanthropy extends from whimsy to arbitrariness— the willingness to bet on individuals and ideas as well as betting on sophisticated delivery systems. . . ."

No better statement of the case for direct and personalized philanthropy, and of the dangers of depersonalized and overly professionalized foundation operations, has been expressed in recent years. To a considerable extent the record of the McKnight Foundation under his administration rather clearly reflects both the strengths and, some would contend, the weaknesses of his case.

How long the McKnight Foundation can continue to operate on its present basis remains to be seen. Ewald and Binger are both approaching retirement age. There have been discussions of creating a more public rather than a purely family board, but this is not likely to occur soon, and Binger's hope is that one of her daughters will take over in her place someday.

Bush Foundation

The contrasts between the still brief careers of the Bush and McKnight foundations are striking. If the McKnight Foundation enjoyed a remarkably peaceable takeoff, Bush had a slow start impeded by years of internal conflict. If McKnight has benefited from the active involvement of members of the donor's family and has been entirely free of unhelpful linkages with the company he created, Bush was badly encumbered for years by the influence of the donor's family and the executives of his company. And if the virtues of McKnight have been boldness, inspiration, and opportunism, those of Bush have become professionalism and systematic management.

If McKnight is an example of amateurism in the extreme, from innocent impulsiveness at times to daring free flight on occasion and even brilliance, then Bush is an example of professionalism in the extreme and perhaps of bureaucratization to some degree.

A. G. BUSH

Archibald G. (Archie) Bush, McKnight's partner in the development of the 3M Company, was an equally colorless personality and an equally talented businessman. Their backgrounds were similar, and their careers followed a common trajectory.

Bush was born and grew up on a farm in Granite Falls, Minnesota. The arduousness of farming life was made even worse for him because he suffered from hay fever. So after graduation from high school he headed for pollenfree Duluth to find some other kind of work. Once there he enrolled in the same local business college from which William McKnight had graduated a couple of years earlier. He completed the six-month course in four months and with high marks. At that moment young McKnight had been promoted to cost accountant in the frail little 3M Company, and Bush was hired to replace him as bookkeeper. The two of them became a close working team.

Over the next fifty years, under McKnight's general leadership, Bush managed the company's sales force with driving energy and great creativity. In the late 1940s, by which time the company was producing hundreds of products and its sales figures worldwide were exploding, he was elected executive vice-president. From

1949 until his death in 1966 at the age of seventy-eight he chaired its executive committee.

At the time of World War I he met and married Edyth Bassler, a young Chicago actress and dancer. They had no children.

Bush's business interests centered in but extended well beyond the 3M Company. He was at one time or another chairman of the board of several banks, a mortgage company, a trading company, and other enterprises. He was one of the century's master salesmen, and he was also an able and ambitious entrepreneur. He often remarked that he had only one interest in his life, "making money," which he did rather well. At his death his estate was valued at more than $200 million.

Unlike McKnight, however, and despite his declared devotion to moneymaking, Bush did carry on some civic and philanthropic activities during his lifetime. He gave money for teacher training and improvement of the school system in his home town, Granite Falls; he built the Edyth Bush Little Theater in St. Paul, which during the 1950s and 1960s acquired a good reputation for its many amateur productions; he served on the Distribution Committee of the St. Paul Foundation; he was a trustee of a hospital in Winter Park, Florida, where he spent much of his time in his later years; and he was on the board of Hamline University, a liberal arts college in St. Paul affiliated with the Methodist Church. The latter was his principal pro bono interest, and he gave the school several generous grants during his lifetime. Even so, however, business activities were overwhelmingly his primary interest, and he never could be called, nor would he have called himself, a civic and philanthropic leader.

Both Bush and McKnight were politically very conservative, and personally and through the solicitation of gifts from other 3M executives they consistently gave help to conservative political candidates. In the aftermath of the Watergate investigation it was revealed that the company had illegally charged several hundred thousands of dollars of contributions to Richard Nixon's 1972 presidential campaign to the corporation. This revelation in January 1975 was of considerable embarrassment to McKnight, who during the years he was the controlling figure in the company had never permitted corporate money to be used for political purposes. After his retirement in 1962, however, when Mr. Burt Cross became president, according to the government investigator's report, a scheme to use foreign insurance premiums for nonexistent policies as a means of generating funds for political purposes was then adopted. Harry Heltzer, who succeeded Cross as chairman and chief executive officer, was forced to resign because of the slush funds scandal.

The shady political ethics of the company for a period in the 1960s and early 1970s, and the generally close-knit, all-in-the-family quality of the management group are pertinent to some of the difficulties that the Bush Foundation was subsequently to experience.

Both McKnight and Bush established their foundations in the same year, 1953, at a time when 3M stock had increased very rapidly in market value. Apparently the possibility of great tax benefits that could be gained by gifts of appreciated company stock to a foundation was a factor in their actions.

Until Bush died in 1966 the assets of his foundation were about $22 million. They are now about $265 million. During its early years the foundation made scattered donations to various local charities but not on the basis of an organized giving program. Once the donor died and its resources increased, however, the Bush Foundation began some very troubled years.

THE FOUNDATION

The day after A. G. Bush's funeral in St. Paul in January 1966 a power struggle to gain control of his foundation began between Edyth Bush, the widow, on the one hand and a group of trustees from the 3M Company on the other. A long series of legal battles ensued that continued until 1975, nine years later; involved legal costs of millions of dollars; and finally required the intervention of the Minnesota state attorney general before the bitter impasse could be resolved.

Precisely what the motivation and objectives of the contesting groups were is impossible to comprehend. On the basis of information from the voluminous court records and press accounts, one theory is that Edyth Bush for her own purposes simply wanted to control the foundation and its huge resources and that she was strengthened in this determination by her fear that a group of company officials was engaged in a conspiracy to divert the assets of the foundation to an organization from which she would be excluded. Another interpretation is that the trustees associated with the company were determined that the large block of 3M stock controlled by the foundation had to be kept in "safe hands," and in their view the hands of a frustrated and unstable widow could not be considered safe. A third possible explanation, not to be dismissed, is that the whole episode was powered by simple ego laced with greed and some insanity. But whatever the driving forces, they were sufficient to fuel nearly a decade of legal warfare and to put the foundation at the mercy of its crossfire.

The first attempts of Edyth Bush immediately after the death of her husband to convene a board meeting in order to have herself named as president of the foundation were ignored by the company trustees. The flare-up became so serious that she then threatened to contest her husband's will and reclaim her share of the estate, which she had earlier renounced, whereupon a deal (that the other directors later said was accepted "under duress and coercion") putting a number of dubious arrangements into effect resulted: Mrs. Bush was paid more than $2 million for maintenance of her Florida home and for lawyer's fees; Cecil March, an officer of the company and a board member of the foundation, was given exclusive authority to vote the 1.6 million shares of 3M stock that the foundation owned; and the board was broken into a bicameral body of four "Class A" directors, all executives of 3M Company, and three "Class B" directors, consisting of Mrs. Bush, her nephew, and her lawyer, each group having a veto over any action of the other. That mindless agreement both immobilized the foundation and aggravated the bitterness between the two factions.

In March 1968 a Minnesota court broke one impasse by ruling the foundation eligible to receive Archibald Bush's estate, and a major portion of the assets was thereupon transferred to it. The state attorney general then filed suit in December asking a state court for a complete reorganization of the foundation's board. In a trial in late 1969 the judge forced the two groups of directors into a new agreement. By its terms, the board was expanded from seven to sixteen, the nine new members to be named with the approval of the state attorney general. Cecil March was removed as president, and his personal authority to vote the foundation's 3M shares was cancelled. Mrs. Bush and her two supporters were renamed to the enlarged board, but their veto power over the foundation's actions was eliminated, as was the division of the board into separate classes. Thus, through intervention of public authority, it appeared that the protracted squabble had finally been brought to an end.

During the first three years of the dispute the foundation had disposed of some $4 million of income in various lump-sum grants:

to the greater St. Paul United Fund, to Rollins College in Florida, to the Minnesota Orchestral Association, and to the University of Minnesota for an arboretum.

The board as reorganized included a number of prominent public figures from Minnesota: former Governor Elmer L. Andersen, Chief Judge Edward Devitt of the U.S. district court, and several leading local businessmen, as well as a Chicago investment banker and the head of Tulane University in Louisiana.

In 1971 the board, under the leadership of former governor Andersen, commissioned an executive search firm to find a director for the foundation. Their recommended candidate was Humphrey Doermann, then an assistant dean for financial affairs at Harvard University. Doermann was originally from Minnesota and had once served as a reporter and as an assistant business manager of the Minneapolis *Star*. As soon as he was elected he hired three additional staff members and began the process of defining a program for the foundation.

Squabbling on the board, however, erupted again early in 1972 when two of Edyth Bush's supporters accused ten of the other directors of stock manipulation and of conflicts of interest, an action that the majority of the board regarded as deliberately disruptive and motivated by the desire of the two plaintiffs to gain lucrative legal fees. For the next three years another series of suits and countersuits wracked the foundation. The most important of these were petitions in both the state and federal courts by Mrs. Bush to renounce the will of her husband, a petition that if sustained would have deprived the foundation of a significant part of its prospective assets.

Finally in 1975 these various legal actions were terminated. The courts denied Bush's effort to break her husband's will and dismissed the suit accusing the majority of the foundation's directors of mishandling its finances. In his ruling the judge was sharply critical of the directors who started the action, denouncing them for "attempting to fatten their pocketbooks at the direct expense of the foundation."

The courts at the same time settled the claims of various attorneys for legal fees: the attorneys for the Bush family, the executors of the estate, the board members associated with the 3M Company, and the state attorney general. These costs amounted to more than $3 million.

The effects of these various brawls for power and self-enrichment are probably best summarized in the tribute paid by the board to Governor Andersen on the occasion of his retirement in 1981 at the conclusion of his chairmanship:

> Elmer L. Andersen has been a director of the Bush Foundation since June of 1968. . . . When he assumed leadership of the Board of the Foundation, at a time of uneasy truce, it was not clear whether the Foundation could become a cohesive philanthropic force rather than a battleground. Although sued three times in his role as director and subjected to personal insults, he pursued a statesmanlike course in dealing with critics and adversity. His quiet patience was a decisive element in turning discord into harmony.

Once the legal watershed of 1975 had been crossed matters rapidly improved. In 1976 the terms of almost half the board members expired, which made it possible to replace all three of the Bush "family members," who had become the worst of the troublemakers. In that same year the foundation's assets were also significantly increased by the final settlement of the Bush estate.

It had taken nearly ten years to free the foundation from the family and donor company linkages that had been so distracting and damaging. That the public trustees who had been placed on the board by state authorities had been willing to endure the incessant quarreling and at the same time to devote the time and energy required to help the foundation through its formative period is greatly to their credit. And that Humphrey Doermann was able as executive director to make the progress he did during those troubled years in developing the foundation's program and procedures is equally a tribute to his professionalism and perseverance.

The Evolution of the Program

In the first couple of years after Doermann's appointment and while a staff was being assembled, the foundation made a scattered grants to a variety of recipients in the Minneapolis–St. Paul area and in Chicago and Florida, where Mr. Bush had had certain charitable interests.

In 1971, the board adopted interim guidelines for grant making that were reviewed and revised in 1973. By 1974 the general profile of the foundation's interests had emerged: education, especially private higher education; the arts; human services, especially the welfare of children; health; and fellowship programs for "leadership development."

These broad fields remain the focus of the foundation's program today, but over the years priorities have steadily been refined. In this process the trustees as well as staff have been actively involved, as have outside advisers and evaluators, both individually and in groups.

As a result, by the early 1980s the program of the Bush Foundation had come to this more precise configuration: Geographically 80 percent of its grants go to Minnesota and the surrounding region, including western Wisconsin and the Dakotas. Chicago and Florida have been dropped as localities of special interest. A few projects of national scope are supported.

Education as a field receives more than half the total, and most of this goes to private liberal arts colleges in the region. Major matching gifts have been made to help them increase the flow of alumni contributions and to support capital-funding drives. Large grants have also been made to contribute to faculty development for both public and private colleges in the region.

The two most substantial national programs have also been in the field of education, one a collaborative arrangement with the Hewlett Foundation of California to provide matching capital grants for black colleges to stimulate alumni giving. The other has been to develop a national network of four university centers at Yale, UCLA, Michigan, and North Carolina to provide postgraduate training for specialists in child development.

In the field of the arts, which receives about one quarter of the foundation's grants, the emphasis has been on projects to enable cultural institutions to improve their management and to broaden and increase their sources of income.

In the human-services field the foundation supports programs for handicapped and disadvantaged youth and, more recently, to deal with problems of family violence.

The field of health is one in which the foundation has been determined to find a role for itself but so far without great success. It began by financing some biomedical research projects, but on the advice of experts has since dropped that in favor of giving support for specialized training of medical personnel in ambulatory care, for example, and in provision of medical services in rural areas.

The fifth field of interest to the foundation has been in leadership training, an original interest of the donor. It now supports an ongoing Bush Leadership Fellows program, most of whose recipients study administration and management, as well as similar programs for public school executives, artists, and more recently for rural physicians.

The Bush Foundation's programming and grant making are analytical, dispassionate, and professional. It has systematically explored various possible fields of interest and has developed careful plans before proceeding. It has also devoted an unusual amount of effort to the evaluation of the results of its efforts. An interesting feature of its approach is the practice of setting a termination date for any new program before grants are begun. This "sunset" provision applies after six or eight years. Because a number of the present Bush programs will expire in the coming few years, some changes can be expected.

Perhaps most distinctively, it has gone to considerable lengths to make itself accessible to the public and to open itself to the ideas and criticisms of outside experts. It was one of the first of the major foundations to hold open meetings to explain the rationale for its programs and expose itself to public questioning. It has also maintained an open dialogue with the heads of colleges, arts organizations, and social welfare organizations in its region as a basis for the ongoing development of its programs.

Its grants have a typically managerial touch: They are commonly concerned with the long-term financial and management needs of institutions; they are wherever possible designed to leverage other funds on a matching or challenge basis; and they carefully delimit the term and scope of the foundation's financial commitment.

The Bush Foundation therefore exemplifies the state of the art of philanthropic professionalism today. It not only makes use of the full range of techniques available to experienced grant administrators but does so with sophistication. Its outside advisers, for example, are outstanding experts in the fields of the foundation's interest.

But if professionalism is the hallmark of the Bush Foundation, it may also be its limitation. It makes very few of the impulsive and amateurish mistakes of a good many other foundations. But it is also a foundation that some feel is lacking in both imagination and compassion. Some of its own trustees find it commendable but rather boring. One, after his departure from the board, commented, "It's impeccably decent and useful, but there hasn't been any excitement in the place since all the litigation ended." And some heads of needy nonprofit organizations have found the foundation although interested in their financial problems primarily interested in its own. They carefully noted, for example, that in 1982, as soon as the U.S. Congress had been persuaded to reduce the payout requirement, the Bush Foundation, in the face of widespread social distress and cutbacks in government services, announced that it planned for reasons of financial prudence to reduce the level of its grant making to that of the 1970s.

Given the sharply contrasting, and somewhat complementary, qualities of the McKnight and Bush foundations, it would seem that each has something to learn from the other.

14

A PAIR FROM THE PRESS:

Hearst and Gannett

Private foundations are characteristically linked in some degree and in various ways to the particular corporation from which the donor's wealth derived. These linkages can include some concentration of holdings in stock of the company, concentration of program activities in geographical areas in which that corporation operates, and cross-membership of corporation officers on the foundation's board or occasionally of foundation officers on the corporation's board. There have also been a few examples of publicizing foundation grants in such a way as to advertise the name of the donor's company.

Of the present list of very large foundations about two thirds have or have had such corporate linkages. At present, those with the closest ties would include Hewlett, Keck, Hilton, Edna McConnell Clark, Pew, MacArthur, Lilly, Mabee, Noble, Hearst, and Gannett.

Until 1969 these linkages could be, and in some cases were, abusive and seriously detrimental to the work of the foundations involved. Since then they have become on the whole more limited and benign.

The two cases that represent the most intimate relationship between a corporation and a private foundation both happen to be based on wealth acquired from newspapers and other mass media, namely Hearst and Gannett. Hearst is the more troubling, a rather poor private foundation that in its programs and procedures very closely resembles a rather poor corporate foundation. Gannett, which is also linked to a major media enterprise, has however begun to develop a program of such quality that it more than compensates for what otherwise might be a questionable situation. (A third media-based foundation will begin operations by the end of 1985, the Knight Foundation, established by one of the founders of Knight-Ridder Newspapers. Its assets are expected to be about $360 million.)

William Randolph Hearst Foundation

The William Randolph Hearst Foundation was created by one of the most colorful and controversial figures in American history. He was the first of the great newspaper magnates and a man of unlimited ego and appetite for power. He was also a man with no discernible interest in philanthropy as such, and he conceived his foundation purely as a means of preventing the dismantling of his publishing empire after his death.

As it operated in its original form, it was a clear example of the exploitation of the foundation device to gain various tax and other advantages for the donor without corresponding benefits to charity and society. Such misuse, of which there were a number of examples at the time, helped lead to passage of the Tax Reform Act of 1969. Thereafter the Hearst Foundation had to be restructured to operate as a bona fide philanthropic institution. In its "reformed" status its assets and flow of grants have become much greater. But it remains a foundation indentured to the executives and interests of a profit-making corporation. Its program, conventional and conservative, is that of a functioning and law-abiding but lackluster institution.

THE DONOR

Hearst was the handsome and spoiled only child of a very wealthy father and an indulgent mother. He grew up to be a combination of megalomaniac, publishing genius, and reckless gambler with the considerable financial resources that one way or another he received or acquired.

He started on his newspaper career in a sense while at Harvard, where as student business manager of the *Lampoon* he turned it from a deficit operation into a profitable one. But shortly thereafter he was expelled from the university for a ribald prank and went to New York to work as a reporter on the New York *World*. There he learned the techniques of sensational journalism, of which the publisher, Joseph Pulitzer, was then master. About that time Hearst's father, who made millions in mining and later became a U.S. senator from California, acquired a rundown little San Francisco paper, the *Examiner*, in settlement of a loan. In 1887 he gave the paper to his twenty-four-year-old son.

Within four months after William Randolph took over the *Examiner*, it was losing more money than ever, but it was building its circulation and making a stir. Young Hearst raided other papers for their best writers and paid them premium wages. He featured banner headlines using big type, played sports news on the front page, and spent heavily on various promotional schemes.

When the senator died shortly thereafter it was found that he had willed his entire estate of $18 million in mines and real estate to his wife, evidently fearing that his publisher son would quickly dissipate any money that might be left directly to him. But Mrs. Phoebe Hearst promptly sold enough of her shares in the Anaconda Copper Mining Company to raise $7 million, which she turned over to her son to use to satisfy his budding ambition to make a splash in the New York newspaper scene.

With the money he bought the sickly morning *Journal* and immediately plunged it into a circulation struggle with Pulitzer. He kept the price of the paper at a penny; raided the *World* and other papers to capture their best reporters, cartoonists, and editors; and proceeded to outsensationalize Pulitzer himself.

By the time his *Journal* overtook the *World*, Hearst had gone through the millions his mother had given him plus other funds he had borrowed.

Eventually the paper made money, and Hearst, once he had

learned how to leverage his financing, went on a rampage of acquisitions. By the 1930s his chain consisted of more than thirty newspapers, all of them sensational in style and jingoistic in general viewpoint. In addition he acquired and developed more than a dozen magazines. He also purchased interests in radio stations, built a worldwide news service, INS, and created the King Features Syndicate, which dominated its field.

His compulsion for acquisitions was without limit, and in his day he was probably the nation's biggest spender. Beyond investments in the media he bought vast ranching properties, gold and silver mines in Mexico, a castle in Wales, and a monastery in Spain. His purchases of art and antiques were on an equally grandiose scale. During one period he imported literally boatloads of statuary, furniture, tapestries, and entire historic buildings from Europe.

His pleasure palace at San Simeon in California had more than one hundred rooms. The baths were in black marble and had gold-plated fixtures. It was built and furnished at a reported cost of $40 million.

Hearst married early and had five sons by his wife, Constance. But in middle age he developed a close and enduring relationship with a young Hollywood starlet, Marion Davies, and on her he lavished gifts of royal proportion, including valuable tracts of New York real estate. He even bought a Hollywood studio in order to advance her career and used the palace at San Simeon as the site for an unending series of huge weekend parties where she could mingle with executives and celebrities from the film colony.

As his prominence and influence as a successful newspaper publisher grew, his ambitions for political power vaulted also. He used his papers to bludgeon administrations in Washington and to punish politicians with whom he disagreed. He also used them as a vehicle for his own political ambitions, which were largely frustrated. He was elected to Congress twice, but he sought unsuccessfully the offices of mayor of New York City, governor of New York, and president of the United States. Perhaps his most notable, and dubious, political achievement was that he was the only private citizen in American history to get the country involved in a war. Several of his biographers agree that the faked stories and campaign of political extortion of the Hearst newspapers drove an unwilling but weak President McKinley into the war with Spain in 1898. Indeed the Hearst papers after the sinking of the battleship *Maine* blatantly "declared war" on Spain several months before the government officially did so.

Once his hopes for high elective office had been shattered, Hearst was able to wield political influence essentially through the editorials of his newspapers, which he closely controlled almost until the time of his death.

Hearst had a great knack for making money, for spending it, and also for losing it. He was consitutionally unable, having once acquired a newspaper or other property, to relinquish it, however much of a white elephant it became. As long as times were good and his winnings exceeded his losses, his empire continued to pyramid. But in the 1930s the financial storm that beset the country hit the Hearst holdings full force. By 1937 Hearst, then seventy-four, faced debts amounting to $126 million, and some of his creditors were clamoring for him to declare bankruptcy.

In June of that year under pressure from his bankers he relinquished control of his publishing enterprises to an appointee of the Chase National Bank. In the following few years a number of the money-losing papers were shut down, others were merged, a few were sold off, and bankruptcy was avoided.

By the end of World War II, with improved business conditions in the country, the Hearst Corporation was back on solid financial ground, and it began a new period of growth and profitability, which continues to the present time. It now consists of fourteen daily and thirty weekly newspapers, a string of profitable magazines (including *Cosmopolitan, Good Houskeeping,* and *Harper's Bazaar*), radio and television stations, a cable television programming company, and miscellaneous ventures in real estate, cattle, and timber. Its style now, in contrast to the flamboyance of the years when Hearst was alive, is cautious, conservative, and strictly profit-oriented.

ESTABLISHMENT OF THE WILLIAM RANDOLPH HEARST FOUNDATION

The Hearst Foundation was set up in 1949 three years before the donor's death. (Throughout this analysis, the William Randolph Hearst Foundation established in 1949 in California and the Hearst Foundation, Inc., established in New York in 1945, are treated as one foundation. The two submit separate tax returns each year, but in other respects they operate as parts of a single entity. The same individuals make up the two boards, the stated purposes are identical, they share offices in New York and San Francisco, and since 1975 the assets of the two have been maintained in a commingled account. The William Randolph Hearst Foundation receives 69 percent of the total income of the account each year; the Hearst Foundation, Inc., 31 percent. The total value of the assets of the two in late 1983 reached $250 million. That the donor created two foundations rather than one appears to be simply a historical fact with no other significance. The basic features of the William Randolph Hearst Foundation described in this chapter, and the appraisal made, apply equally to its smaller Siamese twin, the Hearst Foundation, Inc.)

It was established, not coincidentally, the same year attorneys began writing Hearst's will, a will that took three years to finish and was 125 pages long. The creation of the foundation was not the outgrowth of any discernible philanthropic interest of Hearst but rather was set up as the keystone in a complex scheme to accomplish four nonphilanthropic purposes: (1) to maintain control of the Hearst Corporation in familiar and trusted hands; (2) to avoid heavy estate taxes, the payment of which could have required sale of the corporation; (3) to provide some income, but not controlling influence, to his sons and "issue"; and (4) to ensure that company executives with whom he had long worked and in whom he had confidence would control the entire system.

The plan as eventually formulated consisted of these interconnected elements: the stock of the corporation was divided into two classes, voting shares that would receive only a low fixed dividend and therefore had relatively little value for estate tax purposes, and nonvoting shares with variable dividends. All the voting shares were placed in the Hearst Family Trust; all the nonvoting shares were given to the Hearst Foundation and were therefore tax-free. It was further provided that shares of the corporation could not be transferred or sold without the corporation's approval. Finally it was provided that the boards of all these entities—corporation, foundation, and family trust—had to consist of a majority of executives of the company plus a minority of family members. In effect, Mr. Hearst's will was a declaration of no confidence, or at best of limited confidence, in the competence and judgment of members of his own family. This could hardly have been pleasing to them, and it seems that the matter has rankled ever since. Interviews with several members of the family by *The New York Times* in the early 1960s and with various persons inside and outside the corporation indicated that the Hearst sons had long chafed under their inferior position and that the relationship between them and senior company executives was "somewhere between a do-or-die power struggle and one big happy family."

This product of legal skill, while meeting all the requirements of tax and corporate law of the time, also fulfilled Mr. Hearst's primary objectives: The family trust had to pay little tax on the limited value of its voting shares, and there was no need therefore to make public offering of any of the company shares to pay taxes; the foundation had to pay no tax on its nonvoting shares; the family would get some income from the trust; and Hearst's lieutenants in the company retained full control over the whole intricate structure.

It worked beautifully just as Hearst planned for the next eighteen years: The company executives were happy and could run its affairs as a privately held corporation without the intrusion and pressures of outside shareholders; the family was satisfied if not happy and in any event was in no position to make serious trouble; and the foundation took whatever meager dividends the company chose to pay out and did a little grant making.

But then came passage of the Tax Reform Act of 1969, which posed not only inconveniences but threats to the scheme. The most serious of these was an excess business holdings provision that limited a foundation's share holdings to 5 percent of any company's stock. As a result, the Hearst Foundation if nothing were done would gradually have had to dispose of almost all of its shares in the Hearst Corporation by 1984, thereby demolishing the whole watertight system the donor had so carefully contrived.

So a team of lawyers set to work in the early 1970s to figure out how the terms of the new tax act could be met while fulfilling the purposes of Hearst's original plan. The solution developed was elegantly simple. It consisted of a few precise moves worthy of a chess grand master.

First, the foundation sold back to the Hearst Corporation all of its nonvoting stock. Because the stock was nonvoting and had not been publicly traded, courts in California and New York had to approve its valuation, which was eventually fixed at $136 million. The company drew from its accumulated reserves plus some borrowing to pay this amount in cash to the foundation, which in turn invested in a diversified portfolio. The stock that was repurchased was then retired, or extinguished, by the corporation. That left the Hearst Family Trust with all the outstanding shares of the corporation, which then assumed all the rights of common stock. The significance of this arrangement was to eliminate the restriction on dividends on the original voting stock, thereby greatly increasing the value of the shares of the family trust and the income from those shares.

So the family became richer, the foundation became richer, and control of all the entities remained in the hands of company executives.

The benefit to philanthropy was that the foundation increased its giving. Prior to passage of the Tax Reform Act of 1969, it distributed less than $1 million a year in grants; after passage of the act the level of giving immediately more than doubled. Most recently, with the increase in the worth of the foundation's assets, the level of grants has grown accordingly. But the quality of that giving has not improved correspondingly.

BOARD, STAFF, AND PROGRAM

The composition of the board of the William Randolph Hearst Foundation has been and remains consistent with the terms of the donor's will: a majority of company executives, a minority of family members. In the view of those who have been in a position to observe the inner workings of the foundation, the dominant executive in the company tends also to be the dominant individual on the foundation board. Because the donor did not have any particular philanthropic purposes in mind in setting up the foundation, its program has taken its shape and tone from the narrow outlook of the company executives and the Hearst family, the habits of secrecy that still prevail in the privately held corporation, and its commercial interests and profit objectives.

The staff consists of nine full-time employees who serve both the William Randolph Hearst Foundation and the Hearst Foundation, Inc. The head of the West Coast office is a former publisher of the Hearst newspaper in San Francisco; the head of the New York office is the son-in-law of a former head of the Hearst Corporation.

The foundation does not publish an annual report.

THE PROGRAM

An examination of the foundation's tax returns and of other publicly available materials provides the basis for the following profile of its program:

It makes grants in a number of broad areas. Currently health care and medical research receive about one third of total outlays; education, about one third; arts and culture, one eighth; social welfare, about one sixteenth. A few grants are made to churches. The foundation also operates a youth scholarship program and a journalism awards program.

From the beginning the board has followed a generally clear and consistent policy in the foundation's grant making: Their primary objective seems to be to achieve noncontroversial visibility for the Hearst name and to distribute grants, some large and most of medium and smaller size, throughout the country where the corporation has interests, although there is some concentration in the states of California and New York.

In the period before 1970 the foundation established its two principal operating programs, the Journalism Awards Program launched in 1961 and the U.S. Senate Youth Program launched in 1962.

The Journalism Awards Program provides partial scholarships to journalism students enrolled in seventy-eight schools that are members of the American Association of Schools and Departments of Journalism. Awards are made on the basis of writing and photojournalism contests sponsored by the foundation. Participating institutions receive grants equal in value to the scholarship. The Senate Youth Program enables two high school seniors or juniors each year from each of the fifty states and the District of Columbia to spend a week in Washington visiting government offices and gaining an exposure to the operations of the federal government, in particular the U.S. Senate. Each student also receives a fifteen-hundred-dollar scholarship. In both programs, administrative and promotional expenses are heavy.

In 1980, for example, the foundation spent $195,000 for expenses of the Senate Youth Program and $140,000 for scholarships. In the same year it spent $65,000 for expenses of the Journalism Awards Program and $82,000 in scholarship grants. Both of these programs are accompanied by considerable fanfare, especially in Hearst publications.

Although the great majority of the foundation's other grants are of $20,000 or less, it occasionally makes some much larger ones. It pledged $1.8 million to the University of California, Berkeley, for example, to renovate the Hearst gymnasium and has given $1.3

million to the Salk Institute in California to establish a Hearst Research Center. The New York Hospital has received a $2 million grant, the foundation's largest to date.

On the whole the foundation's program is benign and reactive; it gives general institutional support in limited amounts to a rather wide variety of recipients. There are two interesting exceptions, however, to this pattern.

First, during the four years from 1971 to 1975 the foundation gave $800,000 to pay for half the costs of four regional centers that specialize in bilingual and bicultural education for young Spanish-speaking children. The Department of Housing, Education and Welfare and the National Urban Coalition shared in the administration and costs of this program. Both in its relevance to an urgent social problem and in the sophistication of the partnership arrangements with both government and private agencies, the project was in striking contrast to the banality of most of the foundation's grants.

The second exception, one of the most bizarre grants in the history of American philanthropy, was an expenditure of $1.5 million made in 1974 in response to a demand of the kidnappers of Patty Hearst, daughter of Randolph Hearst, a son of the foundation's donor. The case of Patty Hearst and her capture by the "Symbionese Liberation Army," a violent and extremist revolutionary group in California, was one of the major headline stories in the nation's media in the period.

The kidnappers, as a condition for her release, called for her family to give $230 million to establish a free food-distribution program for the poor. On the same day the family received a tape on which their daughter pleaded with them to take some action on the demand within a week, with the implication that if they did not she would be killed.

Her father rejected the initial demand but offered $2 million, $500,000 of which he was able to raise from personal funds. He then appealed to the Hearst Foundation to provide the remainder. His fellow trustees were agreeable, but there was a rather obvious legal obstacle to be overcome, namely securing a ruling from the Internal Revenue Service (IRS) that such a grant would not be considered as "self-dealing" and thus be prohibited.

Over the following frantic few days lawyers for the Hearst Foundation argued with IRS officials that because the grantee would be a bona fide nonprofit institution and the funds would be used for a charitable purpose, namely feeding the poor, it should be approved.

Just before the deadline, they received the ruling they wanted. It declared in effect that in the special circumstances of the case payment of $1.5 million for the ransom of the kidnapped child of one of the foundation's trustees was legally acceptable.

Perhaps the most surprising feature of the grant pattern of the Hearst Foundation is what it does not contain, namely a strong, ideological twist. The Hearst family and the executives of the corporation have traditionally been very conservative, even right-wing in their politics. In the years when Senator Joe McCarthy was on the warpath, for example, two of the most widely circulated Hearst columnists, George Sokolsky and Walter Winchell, were among the leading voices in the country cheering his efforts. Nevertheless Hearst Foundation grants are generally nonpolitical. One does find scattered support to such groups as the Four Freedoms Foundation and the Hoover Institution. But such grants are not numerous, and the amounts involved are normally quite small. Thus in many respects the Hearst Foundation more resembles a corporate than a private foundation. It is intimately linked to and controlled by the executives of a profit-making company. Its program and policies seem governed by the same considerations as those of many corporate foundations: a strong preference for safe, noncontroversial grants in order to avoid damage to the company's image. The executives of the Hearst Corporation on the foundation board, like their counterparts on many corporate foundation boards, tend to regard their power to direct the flow of grants as one of their perquisites of office: At least a few of the foundation's grants each year can be traced to the religious affiliation, school ties, or cultural interests of members or their wives. Finally, in the staffing of the foundation a common corporate practice of using the foundation as a place to put relatives and old company retainers seems also to be evident.

More than a hundred years after the birth of William Randolph Hearst and more than thirty years after his death, the tiger has finally been tamed. His company, once so flamboyant in style and almost indifferent to risks to its profits, is now cautious and careful, its eye fixed steadfastly on the bottom line. Hearst's mania for political power and propagandizing has now been muted in his publications. And even his foundation displays a bland and beneficent visage that the donor would probably have found tiresome and irrelevant.

Gannett Foundation

Both William Randolph Hearst and Frank Ernest Gannett built great newspaper empires. But their backgrounds, temperaments, personal philosophies, and paths to success were as different as east and west. Hearst, the Californian, was from a millionaire's family and acquired his first newspaper as a gift. Gannett, the New Yorker, was the son of an upstate tenant farmer; he began his newspaper career delivering papers. His first acquisition, *The Elmira Gazette*, was a floundering small-town daily that he purchased with his own savings and such money as he could borrow. Hearst was a big, flamboyant, dictatorial man and a roué with the good looks of a movie star. Gannett was an unprepossessing fellow with a tight upper lip, cherubic cheeks, and terrible eyesight that caused him to wear thick rimless glasses most of his life. He was quiet in manner, considerate of his colleagues, and the epitome of traditional Christian virtues. (He was raised a Methodist but later joined the Unitarian Church and stayed in it for the rest of his life.) But their separate paths and styles led them both to the top.

Young Gannett, one of six children, was precocious both in business and in school. By the time he was twelve he had become an employer, paying his friends pennies and candy to collect the bones of farm animals that he in turn sold at a profit to a fertilizer company.

He excelled in school, especially in civics and geography courses, and by the age of thirteen he had developed a knack for political oratory. After the election of Benjamin Harrison in 1888, Gannett condemned in piping voice the protective tariffs engineered by the Republican administration, saying they raised the price of tin, which everyone used, and lowered the price of steel, bought mainly by the railroads. In a speech to his classmates expressing early sympathy for the laboring class, he said: "In this stage of civilization which needs the most protection: the capitalist or the laborer? Why the laborer of course! Then why are we living under a protective tariff? To protect the industries owned by monopolies! That is the only reason we have it."

By the time he finished high school he was writing occasional articles for the *Buffalo News* and had decided to make his career in journalism because it offered an outlet for his interest in public affairs. His good grades won him a full-tuition scholarship to Cornell University, and he covered his other expenses by waiting tables and other part-time jobs.

Because of his outspoken political views, Gannett soon became the working-class hero of the university and beat out a field of Greek-letter fraternity house candidates for the editor's post on the *Cornell Sun*. In this position he was able to share in the paper's profits and to quit his mealtime job at the Cascadilla Dining Hall.

After college he was a reporter on the *Syracuse Herald* and then spent two years in the Philippines working for a commission sent by President McKinley to determine what the United States should do with those recently acquired islands. When he returned to the United States, Gannett became editor of the *Ithaca Daily News* at fifteen dollars a week.

Five years later he resigned after a disagreement with the publisher and then gambled all his savings to buy into *The Elmira Gazette*. As a publisher he had the opportunity for the first time to apply a concept that he had come to feel strongly about, namely keeping objective news clearly separate from editorials and opinion. The formula caught on with readers, and the formerly failing *Gazette* soon overtook its rival, the *Elmira Evening Star*, which had had the biggest circulation in the area, at which point the *Star*'s frightened owner initiated talks to merge the two papers. When the merger was consummated shortly thereafter, Gannett was enriched and his reputation as a successful publisher established. He lost no time in taking advantage of his new position. In 1918 with two partners he bought two newspapers in Rochester, New York; merged them; and again applied his philosophy of objective community journalism, which again proved successful. He then wanted to make other purchases, but his partners refused to go along. So he bought them out and over the next ten years acquired papers throughout the United States. His belief that local publishers and editors should set their own news and editorial policies without interference from the home office was at the time revolutionary for a newspaper chain. The only restriction Gannett put on the papers was that they could not accept liquor advertising. This was a Gannett company policy throughout his life.

In 1922 the two great bulls in the pasture of newspaper publishing butted heads. In that year Gannett found his flagship Rochester paper challenged by William Randolph Hearst, who had decided to run for governor of New York. Hearst had established newspapers in Albany, Syracuse, and Buffalo, as well as in Gannett's home base to shape public opinion in favor of his candidacy. (Hearst lost the race to Al Smith in the primary.)

Hearst's papers used raffles, puzzles, and flashy headlines—as well as boiler-plate editorials written in New York and San Francisco—to attract readers. The local people found the Hearst brand of yellow journalism interesting for a time, but gradually Gannett won the contest for both circulation and advertising, and Hearst folded his papers and left.

During the Depression Gannett became actively political. Although he had once been an ardent partisan of the working class, he strongly supported Herbert Hoover and the conservative cause. Caroline Gannett hated her husband's involvement in politics. "That Frank is emotionally and temperamentally unsuited for practical politics is a credit to him, from my point of view. That he does not know he is unsuited has been a heartache." His greatest humiliation and one of his silliest endeavors was his attempt to become president in 1936 and again in 1940.

As a measure of his political skills, Gannett in 1936 hired as his press agent Edward A. Rumley, a former newspaperman who had been convicted of aiding German propaganda in World War I and imprisoned for a year. He failed in the primaries. He then spent fifty thousand dollars to found the National Committee to Uphold Constitutional Government to oppose Roosevelt's court-packing bill.

The mail campaign the committee carried out helped defeat the bill, and that only whetted Gannett's appetite to run for president again in 1940 as "the man who stopped Roosevelt." When a critic in Rochester said he was out of his mind even to try, Gannett answered: "We constantly hear complaints about the quality of men in public office. For my part without boasting I think the public would be lucky to get a man of my experience and of my character to take the job."

For his second try he hired C. Nelson Sparks, a former mayor of Akron who had been denounced as a reactionary enemy of organized labor, as his campaign manager. At the Philadelphia convention Sparks showed considerable imagination in promoting Gannett's cause. He rented three elephants from a local religious cult leader known as "Dom the Omnipotent" to parade in front of convention headquarters with Gannett placards on their sides. He also paid one dollar a day to flophouse derelicts to stand in front of the center carrying signs that read "Your Best Bet Is Frank Gannett."

Gannett's futile effort was defeated on the first ballot, but one delegate persisted in voting for Gannett long after everyone else had stopped. When told it wasn't necessary to be so loyal, the delegate replied, "I'm going to stay with him until I get paid."

Although his ventures into politics were clownish, Gannett was a man of deep commitment to journalism, a visionary and innovator, and a bundle of contradictions. When he wasn't trying to buy papers he was tinkering with gadgets. He advanced money to develop the Teletypesetter, a time-saving typesetting device. He experimented also in offset printing, which is now used to print most magazines and many newspapers. He worried about petty expenses and hoarded paper clips but forgave an employee who embezzled $250,000 and even gave the man $40,000 to start a new life. He preached local autonomy for his newspapers but occasionally weakened and dictated policy to benefit Republican political causes, including his own. He detested censorship and fought for freedom of the press but tried to kill a book that lambasted him and his associates.

The company he built has kept its dynamism since his death and has now become a leading force in the media. The Gannett chain currently consists of eighty-nine newspapers, thirty-two semi-weekly or monthly papers, thirteen radio stations, seven television stations, a polling service, a billboard company, and a satellite network. The assets of his foundation, which owns 11 percent of the company, are valued at some $330 million.

ESTABLISHMENT OF THE FOUNDATION

As early as the 1930s, Gannett realized that the press empire he had built would probably fall apart after his death because his daughter and adoped son showed no interest in the business. He also worried that various properties would have to be liquidated to meet inheritance taxes. After discussions with his attorney, Gannett decided that setting up a foundation would be the best means of solving these problems. It would keep his enterprises intact by avoiding the necessity of raising cash to pay taxes, and it would protect the jobs of his employees. Most important, it would make possible operating the newspapers as public trusts. In his will he wrote, "Under the Foundation, our newspapers will not be mere business enterprises, seeking only profits; they will not be bound by selfish interests; they will not be subservient to any outside influence or control. Rather they will occupy a position of genuine independence and be able to render the greatest possible measure of service to the public."

He then went on to indicate the principles on which the newspapers should be operated:

We have always tried to produce newspapers fit to be read in any home—clean, helpful, patriotic and inspiring. . . . Especially, I expect that our newspapers will defend the Constitution and do their best to protect and preserve our form of government and the free enterprise system. . . .

Our newspapers should always be sympathetic to the poor . . . should always fight injustice . . . should always fight for progress and reform.

While maintaining strong and vigorous editorial policies, I hope the editors will always be tolerant. One who disagrees with the newspaper may be right, and the newspaper may be wrong.

I have said that I wish our newspapers to be fearless and independent. . . . This means they must be operated at a profit, but profits should be made secondary to basic ideals. Our newspapers must be free from the influence of any interests that may have selfish motives. No advertising should be accepted which may infringe upon our freedom of editorial expression.

The directors of the Foundation should do their utmost at all times to maintain the freedom of the press, freedom of speech and freedom of religious worship—the most precious heritage we enjoy. . . . They should beware of insidious assaults upon freedom of the press by commercial interests which for selfish reasons may seek to force editors to distort or suppress information which is vital to the public.

Oddly enough, in the instructions he wrote accompanying the establishment of his foundation, as in his will, he held forth at length on how the newspapers should be operated but said almost nothing about the principles on which the foundation should be run. And although he was strong in insisting that the newspapers be very careful not to allow "selfish" commercial interests to interfere with their independence, he said nothing about the possibility that a profit-making enterprise, the Gannett newspapers, for example, might interfere with the independence of the foundation.

Gannett provided a small trust fund to take care of the needs of his family but otherwise left them out of his plans for his newspapers and the foundation. He specified that seven of the eleven trustees of the foundation should always be journalists. In 1957 after the death of Gannett the foundation received all the voting stock of the company from his estate.

During its first twenty years the foundation was operated from the office of the company's secretary-treasurer, and the grant pattern was largely random. Until passage of the Tax Reform Act of 1969 its level of grants remained well below $1 million a year. After passage of the act, however, the level quickly doubled, and with the vigorous development of the company since, the total steadily rose to some $13 million by the early 1980s.

From the beginning the foundation has funded the Frank Gannett Newspaper Carriers Scholarship Program. This program now provides each winner with four thousand dollars for a four-year college course. Winners are recommended by local committees in each city where a Gannett enterprise is located. Final selections are made by the board of the program. Hundreds of boys have now received these awards, and the total is increasing at a rate of nearly one hundred a year.

A second interest of the foundation from the start has been journalism education. Until 1973 various small and scattered grants were made, but in that year, triggered by the increase in funds that had become available, the foundation made a broad study of needs in the field. On the basis of its findings it decided to concentrate on five priorities: improved university training and instruction, continuing education for professionals, application of new electronic printing technology, assistance to minorities to enter the profession, and scholarship aid. A year later two $1 million gifts were made to schools of journalism at Northwestern University and the University of Florida. Later, Howard University and Stanford received large grants. A mobile van equipped with computerized typesetting equipment visited colleges in forty-nine states to give journalism students and teachers "hands-on" experience with the new equipment. Over the next ten years grants in this field totaled some $20 million. More recently the foundation has shifted the emphasis of these grants toward programs on newspaper management, defense of press freedom, opportunities for women in media management, journalistic ethics, and research relevant to journalism.

Frank Gannett felt that a good part of his money should go back to the communities in which he made it, and this belief has been the basis of the third sustained element of the foundation's program, the distribution of miscellaneous small grants to localities where a Gannett newspaper or broadcasting station operates. This activity over the years has accounted for more than half the total outlays of the foundation. Until 1970 these mainly went to a few towns in the Northeast. Thereafter the program was enlarged to include every community served by a Gannett enterprise, and a new method of operation, which not only linked the program to, but virtually absorbed it into, the company, was elaborated.

The local chief executive was given full control over the individual grants. The budget of the foundation was divided according to a formula by which each area received an amount proportionate to the contribution of its Gannett newspaper or broadcasting station to the total revenues of the Gannett Company. The local executive, with almost no guidance or oversight from the foundation, was then allowed to decide on the specific grants to be made and also arranged for local publicity when the grant checks were delivered. It became characteristic of the Gannett organization to create as much awareness of its good works as possible in each locality in order to maximize the goodwill benefits to the company. That there might be some conflict of interest in the arrangement did occur to some observers at the time.

In the late 1970s these local grants averaged about seven thousand dollars in size. But in the three years from 1979 to 1982 the average dropped to less than four thousand dollars. The shrinkage was deliberate. In 1978 a policy of "making a little go a long way" was adopted because there had been a great increase in the number of areas served by Gannett subsidiaries without a corresponding increase in foundation income. This increased scattering of the foundation's funds may have served the public relations interests of the company, but it accomplished little else.

In 1981 a new president of the foundation, Eugene Dorsey, was named. His arrival marked the beginning of an important new phase in the evolution of the foundation toward greater independence of the company and greater impact of its grants.

As soon as he came on board, he began tactfully but vigorously to introduce changes, beginning with the "regular grants" program to local communities of which fourteen hundred a year were then being made. In its 1982 report the foundation described the changeover as follows: "In early 1981 foundation staff and trustees began to ask themselves in effect: For all the good these local grants are doing, are they really significant in solving major problems of the communities where they are received?"

In its contributions to advance journalism education and professionalism the Gannett Foundation had defined its goals, concentrated its funds in support of them, and as a result become a national force in the field. But, in the words of the 1982 report, "It became difficult to pinpoint substantial community improvements resulting from the foundation's local grants that, for the most part, funded only relatively small parts of the programs and needs of a wide variety of grant recipients."

Therefore, to attack basic community problems more effectively, the foundation began a Community Priorities Program (CPP). Like the regular grants program, it also makes considerable use of local Gannett executives, but in a significantly different way.

All of them in the spring of each year, in addition to their proposals for regular small grants, are invited to submit CPP applications. If they choose to do so, they must first ascertain their community's priority problems. This is usually done by local Gannett teams, often joined by a variety of community leaders, through systematic surveys. The problems identified have included rising unemployment, increased poverty and hunger, lack of adequate housing and emergency shelter, rising crime and youth delinquency, transportation troubles, and racial tensions.

Once major problems, which vary widely from city to city, are identified the CPP teams then try to develop innovative solutions to those considered to be of the highest local priority. Their recommendations are forwarded to the foundation, where they have to compete with those submitted by other Gannett subsidiaries. In the first year, twenty of forty applications were approved for awards totaling $1 million. In 1982, twenty-seven awards were made, totaling $1.25 million; in 1983, $2 million was budgeted, with the hope of maintaining that amount if possible in 1984 and subsequent years. With this program, the foundation's thrust had become "making a difference" in solving community problems, not merely spreading its grants thinly over a vast miscellany of grantees.

The quality of the program can be judged from the grants that have resulted, including the following:

> In Danville, Illinois, $40,000 to fund a new program to help the elderly and the poor maintain and repair deteriorated homes by employing jobless construction workers and trades people at minimum wages;
>
> In Lansing, Michigan, $62,000 to fund the first year of a program to help eight hundred hungry families to grow their own food on donated land, under competent supervision;
>
> In Ft. Wayne, Indiana, $50,000 to fund the formation of a consortium of local educational institutions and private businesses to develop a "high technology" center to diversify manufacturing and create new jobs; and
>
> In Los Angeles, $75,000 to expand an existing program of volunteer adult guardians to assist abused children through the juvenile court process.

More recently Dorsey has further strengthened the planning and policy role of the foundation by the development of "national programs," major grants initiated by the foundation. These are decided upon by its board, which has now changed from an inside group of Gannett executives to one made up largely of independent trustees of diverse ethnic backgrounds and from the various regions of the country. These national program grants have included emergency help to communities suffering natural and environmental disasters and grants to encourage volunteering and to strengthen nonprofit organizations throughout the United States.

In mid-1984, Gannett announced another action that confirmed its evolution toward entrepreneurial grants. With an initial $15 million, five-year commitment, it brought into being the country's first center for advanced studies in journalism and communications. The new Gannett Center will be located at Columbia University but will be operated directly by the foundation. In addition to continuing education seminars for professionals, it will accommodate advanced research fellows in residence and will maintain a laboratory to demonstrate new technologies in the media. With this commitment the Gannett Foundation carried its established interest in journalism education a long step further and helped fill an area neglected by most other major foundations, namely journalism and issues related to the media.

AN APPRAISAL

The Gannett Foundation has legally been in existence fifty years and has been active in grant making for thirty. In the early decades its program resembled that of an ordinary corporate foundation: mainly miscellaneous local grants to various nonprofit institutions handed out and extensively publicized by local company officers. The large vision of service and independence the donor held for his newspapers was not reflected in the passive and mediocre program of his foundation.

But in the last fifteen years, and especially in the recent few, beneficial changes have taken place.

First, in its work in the field of journalism education and through its Community Priorities Program and now its national programs, it has become a much more effective philanthropy. A large portion of its money is still spent on miscellaneous small community grants, and Gannett offices and the Gannett name are given maximum visibility in the distribution of such grants. But to an increasing degree and with increasing initiative the foundation has now begun to define its program objectives more professionally, to exercise selectivity in making grants to advance those objectives, and generally to strengthen the role of the central foundation staff and the board in the process of program design and in grant decisions.

Because the Gannett company is a particularly vigorous and prospering one, it is quite possible that its already large resources will further increase in the years to come and that the Gannett Foundation, if the very encouraging process of change and improvement that has now been instituted continues, may well become an outstanding one.

The whole case raises interesting questions about the extent to which it is appropriate and ethical for a private foundation to work through and publicize a profit-making company with which it is associated. There are no absolute rules, of course. If such a foundation exerts itself to publicize a poor and pointless program, that is one thing; if the same efforts of publicity are made in behalf of a program of genuine quality and effectiveness, one's judgment would differ.

In the case of Hearst there is not a great deal to commend in the foundation's program in terms of creativity, relevance, or impact on major problems of the country. At the same time the inertness of the foundation extends to its publicity activities, which are relatively minor. On the other hand, the Gannett Foundation offers the sharp contrast of a better and rapidly improving program accompanied by a vigorous program to maximize the visibility of the parent company.

PART
III

Patterns and Prospects

Patterns

In terms of their assets, the few largest foundations dominate philanthropy today just as they did fifteen years ago. In 1969, the topmost thirty-three, with assets of $100 million or more, held nearly half the wealth of all twenty-two thousand American foundations. At present, almost exactly the same proportion of total foundation assets is held by almost the same number of the largest ones, whose assets are now all in excess of $250 million. (Adjusting for inflation, the real value of $100 million in 1969 is just about equivalent to $250 million today.)

On the other hand, the list of foundations in the top group has changed considerably. Of the thirty-three largest in 1969, some twelve have now dropped off: Danforth, Land, Hartford, Commonwealth, Richardson, Scaife, and Longwood, primarily because their assets have not kept pace with inflation; Alfred I. du Pont–de Nemours and Kettering because they have changed their status to that of operating foundations; and Astor, Fleischmann, and Woodruff because they have deliberately spent down their resources. These have been replaced by twelve other private foundations and three community foundations.

Among the twenty foundations that were and still are in the top group, there has been considerable shifting of rank in size. Andrew W. Mellon, Pew Memorial Trust, Kellogg, Kresge, and Lilly are among those that have moved up most vigorously. The Ford Foundation remains the largest by a wide margin, with more than twice the assets of the second largest, but relatively, the value of its portfolio has greatly declined and it is now less preponderant than it was.

Location and Regional Differences

The creation of foundations has generally followed, by thirty or forty years, the migration of economic development across the United States.

The first of the major foundations were established in the East. The region still has more foundations than any other. Some of the largest are among the very finest in the country, including Robert Wood Johnson and Andrew W. Mellon; some are undistinguished, including Surdna and Hearst. It is in the East, distinctively, where the most liberal, international, and activist of the big foundations are located, including Ford, Rockefeller, and Carnegie.

The Midwest is the second area of greatest concentration. The quality of its foundations, with a couple of aberrations, is on the whole very good, including Kellogg, Kresge, Mott, Bush, and McKnight. The Lilly Foundation has had some ups and downs, mostly downs, and the MacArthur Foundation has been until very recently more of a permanent lawsuit than a foundation. If there is any common characteristic of the Midwestern foundations it is that most of them are primarily concerned with the needs and problems of the cities where they are located and the immediate surrounding areas. Kellogg has a significant international program, and the MacArthur Foundation in time may develop one. But they are exceptions.

The Southwest has several large foundations, most of them with programs confined to their particular localities, often with a heavy emphasis on bricks and mortar. The Noble and Mabee foundations in Oklahoma are the newest of this group. All tend to be dominated by members of donor families or donor company executives. They are generally reactive and conventional in their grant making, operating with very limited staff. In philanthropic terms the Southwest is a backward area.

The Far West, more specifically the state of California, is the rapidly rising factor. It now has six very large foundations, all of them relatively young. Three already are effective institutions (Kaiser, Hewlett, and Irvine), and two (Weingart and Hilton) show promise. Keck is still a squalid affair. Although they are based in a state that is increasingly regarded as the point of origin of many new and creative trends in the United States, the California foundations are still rather conventional in interests and style.

The Rocky Mountain region and the Pacific Northwest are not yet represented in the group of largest foundations; the Southeast, which once had two, namely Duke and Woodruff, now has only the former. Robert Woodruff, the great philanthropist from Atlanta, drained the resources of his foundation to complete his major philanthropic enterprises, especially the development of Emory University, before his death in early 1985.

Except for the general inferiority of those in the Southwest, the differences among foundations within regions are as great as those between regions.

Governance

In legal theory, the legitimacy of the institution of private philanthropy rests on the principle of trusteeship. But if in reality the performance of philanthropy depended on the effectiveness of the boards of trustees, it would truly be in trouble. Their mechanism of governance is considered by most observers within foundations and outside to be the weakest element in the structure.

This is not a problem unique to foundations, of course. The boards of other kinds of institutions, including universities, churches, and business corporations, have also developed serious disabilities. Indeed, the governance capability of the U.S. government itself in the view of a good many critics and concerned citizens is the most disabled of all.

Still, the governance problems of foundations are somewhat special for several identifiable reasons. First is that the real function of trustees can change drastically with the evolution of a foundation. In many cases there is an initial period while the donor is still alive and active when the role of the other trustees is simply to rubber-stamp decisions. Then can follow a period when the immediate family takes over his role, in which case the nonfamily trustees are still left in a relatively powerless position, with the difference that they begin rather frequently to spend a good part of their time at board meetings refereeing family quarrels. In another not uncommon situation, if the predominant group on the board consists of executives of the donor's company, the trustee role often becomes that of guarding against "controversial" activities by the foundation that could possibly damage the company's public relations. In a still later phase, once the donor has died, the family has lost interest in the foundation or died off, and separation from the company has been achieved, the trustees are in a more independent and less conflicted situation. But then problems of a far more complex kind confront them: What is, or should be, their role with respect to the foundation's management and programs? To select (and when necessary replace) the chief executive, and to concern themselves with management and investment questions, but otherwise leave substantive program matters to the executive head and the professional staff? Or take an active, even predominant, role in determining program priorities and in making major grant decisions, as well as in directing management and investment policies? There are no clear guideposts, in theory, tradition, or experience, for answering such questions.

The composition of foundation boards has been a frequent target of criticism in recent years. In the past in many cases, once the board was no longer made up of the donor family and executives of the company, it became an "old-boys club": WASP and wealthy. In a few cases the members of these clubs were elderly individuals of great public prominence, the Rockefeller Foundation being a conspicuous example. (Its board at one time was a favorite recruiting ground for U.S. cabinet officers. The Ford Foundation in earlier years also preferred overburdened eminences. One of them, in the 1960s, in addition to being a Ford trustee, was a director of some fifty-nine other organizations and corporations.)

Since the 1960s, pressures and arguments against homogeneous boards of the traditional kind have succeeded in bringing about considerable diversification of membership in a few instances—Ford, Rockefeller, Carnegie, and Gannett—and a degree of it in a number of others.

The performance of all these differently composed kinds of boards is extremely uneven. Some of the in-group boards are working well: Hilton, Hewlett, the Pews, and McKnight, for example; some are not: Hearst, Mabee, and Keck. A number of the homogenous "old boy" boards are effective: Robert Wood Johnson, Duke, Weingart, and Irvine; and on the other hand, some of the more diversified boards are functioning poorly: Ford and Rockefeller in particular.

In the face of such contradictory experience, it is impossible to draw any clear lessons, at least yet. In the matter of foundation governance, as with genital herpes, it is clear that a serious problem exists, but how to treat it, even how to define it, is not yet known.

At a less fundamental level, but also troubling, is the growing tendency for trustees to pay themselves exorbitant fees for their part-time services. The Duke trustees, with only one exception, passively allow themselves to receive nearly $80,000 per year because of an antique formula included in the donor's testament; the trustees of Ford and Rockefeller, with more justification, receive in addition to modest fees generous foreign travel allowances when attending foundation meetings.

Howard Keck of the Keck Foundation may be the biggest individual taker, having claimed fees of some $500,000 a year for his services as trustee and financial adviser. Some of the trustees of the MacArthur Foundation, according to the charges of board member Rod MacArthur, the donor's son, have been receiving $60,000 or more a year. One has allegedly received some $70,000 a year plus huge legal fees from the foundation and the insurance company owned until recently by the foundation. (An operating foundation in Hawaii, Bishop's Estate, perhaps takes the grand prize for generosity toward its board members. For managing the properties of the estate and for overseeing the two schools for children of Hawaiian ancestry that the foundation operates, each of the five trustees receives an annual fee of $250,000.)

This type of self-aggrandizement is not, happily, the general pattern, and there are many examples of dedicated, selfless performance by individual trustees, Elmer Andersen of Bush, John Haas of William Penn, Gustav Lienhard of Robert Wood Johnson, and Harry Volk of Weingart, to cite just four outstanding examples.

But wherever it occurs it represents a deplorable perversion of the idea of voluntary service, and the practice now seems to be spreading.

Public Reporting

Historically, foundations have had a strong preference to operate in privacy, and they resisted determinedly for many years the idea of exposing their activities to public view. After more than fifty years of unsuccessful efforts to persuade them to abandon their secretiveness voluntarily, the Congress in 1969 passed a law requiring them to issue annual reports.

This has resulted in some improvement, but the excessive focus on annual reports as the answer to the communications problem has been unfortunate. Such reports are assumed to have the capacity of informing the public, providing necessary guidelines to grant seekers, building public support for philanthropy, providing outside stimulus to foundation thinking, allaying public and congressional criticism, and serving the needs of students and critics of philanthropy. But on the whole their value in their conventional form has been greatly exaggerated. In fact they are ill-designed and inefficient vehicles to accomplish most of the purposes intended. They do not convey to grant seekers much of the more specific information they need; they do not provide knowledgeable people in special fields (education, health, or whatever) the data and depth of detail they want; they do not provide newswriters the timeliness they require; they do not provide editorialists the basis for evaluation they require; they do not provide students of philanthropy the candid and substantive examination of issues they seek.

Even those of the very largest foundations, which on the whole have had a better reporting record than the vast majority of foundations, tend mostly to be sugary public relations documents. A particularly unfortunate ritual many have adopted is the "presidential essay," in which the foundation head, however vapid his message, seizes the opportunity to lecture the world from this private pulpit. Frederick Keppel, whose stylish essays in the early reports of the Carnegie Corporation started the practice, would cringe with embarrassment at most of the current efforts of his imitators.

A precious few in recent years have been genuinely philosophical and provocative, most notably those of Alan Pifer of Carnegie. Several others are well written, analytical, and reflective, such as those of Roger Heyns of Hewlett, John Sawyer of A. W. Mellon, John Coleman of Clark, David Rogers of Robert Wood Johnson, Mary Semans of Duke, Russell Mawby of Kellogg, and Frank Thomas of Ford. But a good many are windy and uninformative, such as those of Rockefeller and Moody. A few, most notably Lilly, are both pretentious and deceptive.

Fortunately, in recent years the old problem of trying to force or persuade foundations to issue annual reports has largely been bypassed by the invention of a whole new range of communications methods and devices.

Several of the large foundations have been particularly innovative in broadening the range of their publications to serve various special purposes: Carnegie's excellent quarterly reports to provide up-to-date information on its programs, Ford's and Kellogg's series of special reports to provide full background on their major programs, and Robert Wood Johnson's reports containing evaluations of its major programs by independent evaluators. Several of these innovations have now been adopted by other foundations.

Not all these communications experiments, of course, have been equally successful: the Rockefeller multicolored broadsheet has now been quietly abandoned, and the Bush Foundation's practice of holding public meetings to explain its programs has not aroused much enthusiasm elsewhere.

Even more valuable and innovative than the actions of individual foundations has been the development of the products of the Foundation Center, whose guides, handbooks, and other publications, as well as the research files and computerized grant listings in its libraries, have made information about foundations available on a scale and with a convenience never known before.

Indeed, the past fifteen years have been a period of extraordinary development in foundation communications, proving once more the remarkable fecundity and creativity of a diverse, multicentered system in finding effective and sometimes quite unexpected solutions to felt needs.

Program Scope

The geographical scope of the programs of most of these very large foundations is surprisingly limited.

Understandably, the great majority of medium- and smaller-size foundations concentrate their efforts geographically on a particular locality. But the same is true of many of the very large foundations. Though their wealth is enormous, their programs are often circumscribed, even provincial.

Of the thirty-six reviewed here, the three community foundations by definition are committed to work in a single urban area. In addition, eight others, including Mott, Lilly, Houston Endowment, Brown, Moody, Irvine, Weingart, and William Penn, concentrate their activities heavily, in some cases almost exclusively, in a particular city or state. Six more, including Kaiser, Bush, Richard King Mellon, McKnight, Duke, and Surdna, are strongly interested in a particular region. Only eleven can be considered essentially national in their program outlook.

Only four have substantial ongoing international programs: Ford, Rockefeller, Carnegie, and Kellogg. Edna McConnell Clark does some work internationally, and the MacArthur and Hilton foundations may launch sizable international programs in the period ahead. But in no case is international activity the central interest.

Two of the four with heavy international commitment are among the oldest of the foundations, and the other two became engaged during or just after World War II. The younger ones tend mostly to be nearsighted.

Areas of Program Interest and Disinterest

The field of primary interest to the large foundations is education, followed by health and medicine. The emphasis on education is so heavy in many cases that big philanthropy can to a considerable extent be described as a financial adjunct to higher education, particularly the private portion of it. Scientific research is of interest to about a third of the group and the arts and humanities to about a quarter of them. Problems of conservation and the environment in recent years have become a priority for some ten foundations.

Only four have a significant interest in religion: Duke, Lilly, Pew, and Hilton. Building buildings is a favored activity of several, including Kresge, Mabee, Lilly, Mott, Houston Endowment, and Hearst.

Social welfare activities of various kinds are a priority of about a third of the group. On the whole the most conventional and the most unconventional are not included: Almost none give relief grants to the blind or to crippled children, for example, or to the victims of war or famine and other natural catastrophes.

Neither do they spend their funds to ease the plight of AIDS victims, for international programs on behalf of human rights, or, with a few exceptions, even to support the women's movement.

Their priorities in social welfare noticeably shift from time to time and mirror changing national concerns. Some time ago the problems of blacks were a strong focus. More recently Hispanics have begun to receive increased attention. The problems of working mothers, drug abuse, and teen-age unemployment have increased in priority. There has also been a resurgence of concern about problems of mental illness. And most recently the problems of family violence, abused women, and the elderly have come to the fore.

In all these foundation efforts, the scientific or professional approach—planned programs of research, education, and treatment—rather than old-fashioned charity is dominant. (The Foundation Center in its elaborate categorization of foundation grants—which includes rubrics for matters ranging from communications, education, and health to the humanities and the social sciences—does not find it necessary to maintain a category for grants for the poor or the homeless.) It is other kinds of charitable organizations that are the main providers of such direct relief to human distress.

Grant-Making Approach

The crucial matter of grant-making style is the most difficult aspect of foundation behavior to describe, partly because the necessary words are not available. To characterize their varying approaches or philosophies of grand making, and to differentiate between "superior" and "inferior" practice, a vocabulary of terms that are helpful and have some merit has evolved over the years, but they are still coarse and imprecise. "Scientific" philanthropy was one of the earliest, suggesting the idea of using grants not simply to ameliorate symptoms but to get at the "root causes" of problems. Subsequently, active (or sometimes pro-active) and reactive philanthropy gained currency, along with strategic or targeted grantmaking versus "scatteration."

The terms *conservative* and *liberal* have also come into general use not only to distinguish between foundations of differing ideological position but also between those disposed to support established educational, health, and cultural institutions and those inclined to support newer social movements, to become involved in more controversial issues, and to concentrate their grants on distressed groups and urgent social issues. *Excellence* is the watchword of the former, *equity* that of the latter.

All such general terms present two problems: they are necessarily portmanteaux and value-laden, and the actual grant making of the great majority of the large foundations is never conceptually "pure" but is rather a mix, a recipe of differing approaches in varying proportions. Typically, the body and bulk of a foundation's grants can be described by one term, but important other features of its program may be of quite different character. To give proper recognition to the mixture presented by any actual case, and to the variations of mixtures among foundations, is therefore a considerable descriptive and analytical difficulty.

Nonetheless, there are significant and revealing differences in the substructures of concepts and values that shape what problems different foundations choose to address and how they go about it. At the present time, the most actively debated distinction is that between "liberal" and "conservative" foundations. To illuminate this matter, it may be useful to draw some of the contrasts between the two most prominent and prototypical of these among the largest foundations, Andrew W. Mellon the "conservative" and Ford the "liberal."

Mellon has chosen as its areas of primary interest the prestigious private colleges and universities, especially their teaching and research in the humanities and cultural institutions, again with an emphasis on "excellence." Recently it has become interested in conservation, environment, and population control, and still more recently in problems of educational opportunity for minority students.

Ford is a foundation that because of its scale has worked in a great number of fields. But in recent decades it has strongly focused its domestic activities on the problems of the disadvantaged and the urban and rural poor. It has also been actively interested in public policy matters and in influencing government programs relevant to those problems.

Along with such priorities, Ford has given substantial assistance to leading colleges and universities and to the arts and humanities, and it has had active programs in environmental affairs and population. Thus between these two dissimilar institutions there is considerable overlap in their fields of interest, but there are also distinctive differences.

Through examining more closely how they define their broader purposes, the types of grants they make, and how they develop and administer them, still more instructive contrasts can be seen.

Mellon conceives of itself as an instrument of cultural continuity; of sustenance for our finest private educational, scientific, and cultural institutions; and of provision of opportunities for the full development of highly talented scholars and scientists, whatever their race or origin. Its preferred and characteristic grants are therefore for selective institutional support, research, and scholarships and fellowships, given on a competitive basis.

Ford, on the other hand, conceives of itself as primarily an instrument for social change in behalf of justice and equity and for development of new initiatives to help solve impacted and potentially dangerous social problems. Its characteristic grants are therefore less focused on support of well-established institutions and more on the strengthening of inexperienced organizations or the creation of new ones when necessary. It has also frequently supported advocacy and litigation projects, voter registration drives, and minority leadership development.

Even in fields of common interest, Mellon and Ford have taken differing approaches in their general grant making. In environmental matters, Mellon gives greater emphasis to conservation and historic preservation and to basic research; Ford, until it recently reduced its interest in this field, gave more stress to litigation for "environmental defense" and for public policy studies.

The sharpest contrasts between the two can be seen, however, in regard to the disadvantaged, in how they perceive the nature of the problem and the best means to deal with it.

To Mellon, the problem, or the portion of it they choose to address, is the need for educational opportunity. Its principal response is therefore to provide scholarships and fellowships to those strong, talented, upwardly mobile individuals out of the urban and rural ghettoes who can compete for them. Such programs are relatively simple to conceive and carry out, and the depth of involvement required of the foundation with the general situation of the poor and minorities is very limited.

Ford on the other hand sees the problem in more comprehensive contextual terms, involving questions of employment, education, social services, motivation, social and political participation, and public policy. Its programs therefore embrace economic development projects, specialized education, and strengthening of neighborhood self-help organizations and leadership training. Moreover, Ford now directs its grants increasingly to those of the "underclass" who are likely to be condemned by their circumstances to permanent poverty—teen-age unwed mothers, school dropouts and street gang members, and the dependent elderly—who require a variety of kinds of special services and assistance and for whom a competitive scholarship program, for example, would be irrelevant.

Such definition of the problem and of the programs needed to deal with it necessarily involves Ford deeply with racial groups and the poor and requires much staff initiative and "nurturing" of projects, accompanied quite often by controversy, criticism, and relatively high failure rates.

Correlated with these differing program approaches are a number of organizational and stylistic differences. Mellon operates with a small staff and homogenous board, all white—and at low administrative cost. Ford, with its more initiative-taking and hands-on approach, employs more specialized staff (which like the Ford board is highly diversified by race, sex, and occupation), provides more continuing assistance to and oversight of grantees, and operates at considerably higher administrative cost per million dollars of grants.

These contrasting sketches or profiles of a "conservative" and a "liberal" foundation, somewhat complicated though they may seem, are in fact highly simplified and schematic. But they demonstrate the heavy baggage of connotation that such shorthand terms of differentiation among foundation approaches in grant making necessarily carry.

Using the terms *liberal* and *conservative* in the sense indicated, the trend of foundation practice at the moment is toward the Mellon model and away from the Ford brand of liberalism. Among the big foundations that look with increasing interest and approval at the Mellon approach are Rockefeller, Sloan, Hewlett, Bush, the Pews, and Irvine.

In political terms, the programs of the major foundations overall are neither ideological nor activist. They run neither radically to the right nor to the left but down the middle of the road. Their subject-matter interests are on the whole traditional and noncontroversial; their preferred grantees are established educational, health, scientific, cultural, and social welfare institutions. A small minority concentrate on urgent social problems and are committed to "reform." But the great majority are not on the whole disposed to champion the demands of disadvantaged groups or to serve as catalysts of institutional or social change. Several are committed to the advancement of free enterprise; not one advocates or even endorses trade unionism.

It can of course be argued that excessive venturesomeness and controversiality are not appropriate to very large foundations and that such behavior on their part would not be publicly acceptable. But descriptively, not judgmentally, the profile of their activity is clearly conventional, not reformist. They are overwhelmingly institutions of social continuity, not change.

16

A Prescription

As the twentieth century rushes to a close and history's rendezvous with the twenty-first century approaches, the world is an extremely troubled place, with famine, pestilence, and war, including annihilating nuclear war, among the eventualities that must be contemplated. Even within the United States, arguably the most fortunate nation on the planet, an accumulating mass of social, economic, and political problems exists with implications of the greatest gravity. As recent opinion polls indicate, a great many Americans now experience more unease about the dangers and more doubts about the capacity of our institutions to deal with them than ever before in their lifetime.

It is against this sobering background that the ultimate potentiality of the major modern philanthropic foundation can most clearly be understood and the actual performance of the largest existing American foundations can most rigorously be appraised. For these strange and wonderful social inventions have a unique freedom from the dependency of other institutions on markets or constituencies that cripple their capacity to take the long view and to bring a competent and disinterested approach to the search for solutions to complex problems. They are not magical answer-giving machines, but they are instruments by which the best available intelligence, experience, and specialized knowledge can be brought to bear in the least distorting and inhibiting circumstances on such problems. And it is in the United States where they have been given their greatest encouragement and freedom of action, and where they now flourish in greater number and with greater resources at their disposal, than anywhere else in the world.

That the United States is so well endowed with such an array of institutions to analyze its difficulties, devise and test new solutions, and help adapt the social, political, and economic apparatus to the requirements of changing circumstances should be deeply reassuring.

But the gap between the potentiality and the actuality is regrettably very great. All of the large foundations that have been the focus of this study are working on projects of some social utility. But too many of them concentrate essentially on local needs, ignoring national and international problems. And even within that narrow horizon, too many tend to take the easier course of simply providing institutional support rather than developing programs to deal with the substance of tough issues. Moreover, many have such limited staff competence that they could not make a significant contribution to larger and more complex undertakings even if they should try.

With the exception of a splendid minority, our largest foundations are not even attempting to grapple directly with the major and most threatening problems confronting the nation and the world at the present time.

To take three glaring examples from the experience of the past fifteen years, they have ignored or at most have merely nibbled at the edges of the following momentous developments:

First are the problems of war and peace and national security. Some smaller foundations, several of them funded by members of the Rockefeller family, have initiated projects in this field, and recently a few of the larger foundations have become involved. But with the exception of Ford and Rockefeller, the others over recent decades—during which nuclear weapons technology has achieved more and more horrifying capabilities, the arms race has raced on, and the major powers have failed and failed again to achieve control agreements—have been idle and indifferent bystanders.

Second is the degeneration of the productivity and competitiveness of the American economy, the engine of the nation's development and the basis of its power and constructive influence in the world. The marked decline of various industries and of various regions of the country has been evident for some years, and active, even furious public and political debate over the causes and possible remedies has raged for more than a decade. But again, with only a handful of exceptions, the big foundations have chosen not to be involved.

Third is the emerging crisis of the overburdened and underperforming American welfare state. Like all the developed, industrialized democratic countries, the United States in recent decades has been confronted with rapidly increasing demands for social services by more and more groups of the population, rapidly increasing costs, increasing government deficits and taxes, and increasing public dissatisfaction with both the services and the burdens. For both conservatives and liberals, the issues presented are of crucial importance. But most of the large foundations have not only not been moved to become engaged but in many ways have aggravated the problems by urging that more and more demands for services be placed on government.

Historically, the contrasts between the finest few and the mediocre majority of the large foundations have long been very sharp. The few have dramatically and repeatedly demonstrated the immense possibilities of human benefit from the foundation concept—in education, medicine, the sciences, social welfare, cultural affairs, and international relations. But the majority have confined their work to lesser, even parochial matters. In professional terms they tend to be minimally qualified to do anything beyond reacting to ideas that are brought to them. Their vision of their role seems to be that of beneficient crack fillers, doing some useful things that others are not doing, which is not unworthy if foundations are seen as no more than plasterers. But if they are viewed as architects or builders, it is not enough.

Granted, one of the essential virtues of private philanthropy is the autonomy and pluralism of foundations. But recognition of these qualities does not then require a free fall into such absurdities as the conclusion that all the varied actions foundations perform must be considered equal, or that as long as they are diverse in their purposes and methods, they are rendering their highest service to society. As the best of the foundations have so marvelously demonstrated, some programs are indubitably better than others, and some foundations are far better than others. All differences do not lie simply in the beholder's eye.

That there is such striking contrast between those that have developed and tested the limits of this unique social invention and those whose performance conveys an impression of primarily unrealized potentialities is, however, useful. For in the tension of the contrast lies the possibility of defining some criteria to distinguish superior from inferior performance, and in turn of generating pressures for raising the social usefulness of the laggards.

The Elements of a Definition of Maximum Feasible Function

Foundations have their special possibilities; they also have their limitations. President Reagan has vaunted their capabilities and then promptly attempted to offload on them responsibilities that only government has the capacity to carry. And some liberals seem to believe that if only they would, foundations could right most of the wrongs and cure most of the ills and injustices that the American political system and American society itself have been incapable of correcting.

So a little sense of proportion and realism about the limits of the possible has to be the starting point of any effort to create a yardstick to measure foundation performance. They cannot be expected to fulfill impossible dreams. But it can be expected that they make full and effective use of their special institutional position and capabilities.

A reasonable definition of excellence in their performance might therefore be *maximum feasible function*. Those words in turn can best be defined not by a theoretical concept but rather by examining the actual achievements of those foundations that are generally acknowledged as outstanding in their accomplishments.

Any foundation to be considered creditable must obviously meet the requirements of the law: it must devote itself exclusively to bona fide charitable purposes; not have excessively close links to a particular business firm; meet the minimum payout requirements; and be fully accountable to government and communicative with the public.

But beyond this baseline there are four criteria that depict excellence for large foundations by the standard of maximum feasible function:

First, they should concentrate their efforts on matters of a scope and significance proportionate to their resources and their special capabilities as foundations. They should avoid doing those things that other foundations and sources of funding can do, not only to avoid duplication but, of greater importance, to avoid leaving a most dangerous gap in the spectrum of national issues that receive the benefit of diverse, disinterested ideas and criticism. Only the large foundations command sufficient maneuverable social capital in the nonprofit sector to be able to finance a competent private contribution to the discussion of such problems as the adequacy of government regulation of the safety of the airlines or of nuclear power reactors, or the improvement of public secondary education, or the control of health-care costs. If the big foundations do not make possible a pluralistic monitoring, stimulative, or evaluative function at the higher levels of national problems, then those matters will be abandoned to special-interest groups, government, and "solution" by the horse trading of politics.

Second, large foundations should maintain staffs of a competence comparable to the best institutions in other fields and should possess the intellectual vigor to take initiatives in their grant making rather than being purely reactive. This is neither arrogance nor presumption but rather simply the utilization of their situational advantage. A foundation is a crossroads, a marketplace of information and ideas. Heads of individual schools or hospitals from their vantage point can see the needs of their institutions with particular clarity; foundation officers from their vantage point and with a wider scan can sometimes see with special clarity opportunities that can benefit whole groups of institutions or fields of educational, scientific, or other activity. They are also in a position to assemble advisers, commission research, and attract the cooperation of other relevant institutions in an enterprise in a way that persons differently situated cannot. Responsiveness to the felt needs of others is a virtue in philanthropy; but creative action that may relate to needs not yet perceived by others can be an even greater virtue, and some of the most important contributions of major foundations in the past have derived from just such actions.

Third, a large foundation should be open, interactive, and collaborative with all kinds of other private institutions relevant to its purposes. These include not only other foundations but all nonprofit agencies, not only its own grantees. These hundreds of thousands of institutions are not only the clientele of foundations but are the instruments of action through which grant-making foundations must work. Collaboration with business corporations is not only a relatively new departure for foundations, but also a most promising one. The large private foundations can play a valuable role in helping improve the work of corporate foundations, a rapidly growing element in philanthropy, and in encouraging major business firms to expand their programs of social investment in housing, education, and job creation, for example. The kind of isolation and encapsulation that characterized the behavior of many foundations in the past is a serious impediment to the achievement of optimum effectiveness.

Fourth, and of crucial importance, a major foundation must keep itself well informed about governmental policies and programs in its fields of interest, must make its grant decisions in full awareness of their relationship to the activities of government, and must have a conscious and carefully formulated posture toward the role and policies of government in the area of its work. Government, at the federal, state, and local levels, has for the past half-century been a factor of rapidly increasing importance in every field except religion in which foundations operate. It is now overwhelmingly the predominant source of funding in nearly all those fields. Its presence must therefore be carefully taken into account. In some cases a foundation may simply want to avoid duplication of effort; sometimes it may choose to form a joint venture with government; and sometimes it may devote itself to trying to persuade government to alter what it is doing.

There remains a still larger role and responsibility of major foundations vis-à-vis government. This relates to the problem of the growing incompetence, or breakdown, of the means by which the citizenry have traditionally been aided in exercising their critical and evaluative function over government policies and programs. Under the impact not only of the growing scale but also of the growing complexity of many new areas of government action, legislative bodies are less and less capable of overseeing and controlling government economic, social, scientific, and military programs. The newspapers and mass media keep a critical eye on government, but they have been more effective in connection with relatively simple problems such as scandals and graft than in appraising such questions as the effectiveness of government regulation of mass commu-: nications or the defects of federal programs for the training and employment of minority youth. Similarly, for even the most intelligent and informed citizens, many areas of government activity, such as the work of the National Institutes of Health or the Department of Energy, are simply beyond their technical competence and experience.

The large foundations offer one of the few possibilities for subjecting such matters to competent private assessment and for the formulation of meaningful recommendations. A number of foundation-supported public commissions and policy research projects have in fact been extremely useful in this way. Such initiatives are a particularly crucial contribution by the big foundations to the effective functioning of the American democratic system under modern conditions.

What Can Be Done?

Assuming these criteria add up to a reasonable definition of excellence of performance for a major foundation, what can be done to encourage more of them to meet them?

Philanthropy is not a managed or manageable field of activity. The foundations that compose it, and perhaps the largest foundations most of all, are separate, independent, and individualistic private institutions.

What government regulation can do to correct their faults and abuses has now on the whole been done. Conscientious administration of the requirements of the tax laws by the Internal Revenue Service, active oversight of their work by state attorneys general, and periodic congressional hearings on the state of philanthropic affairs will continue to be useful and necessary.

But beyond that, improvement of the effectiveness of foundations depends, and should depend, basically on the interplay of private influence and ideas upon them, both from outside philanthropy and from within it.

In this regard, the media are now beginning to be a more helpful factor. In the past their coverage of philanthropic news was meager, uninformed, and uncritical. But more recently there has been an improvement. *The New York Times* for many years was the only newspaper to assign a staff reporter to the subject, but now *The Washington Post, The Los Angeles Times,* and *The Wall Street Journal* are among the leading papers that give it regular attention. In the universities, student interest in the field seems to be rising, and some centers for the study of nonprofit organizations, most notably that at Yale under Professor John Simon, have been established, and are having a stimulative effect.

But it is from within philanthropy itself that the greatest impulse for improved performance is likely to come. Only a few years ago, this would have seemed a most improbable, indeed almost preposterous, prediction. But various developments, including the shock of the Patman hearings in the late 1960s and the sharp attacks of the neoconservative intellectuals in the 1970s, have destroyed the smugness and complacency of the little world of philanthropy, and intellectually it is now coming to life. Some nonobsequious writing has begun to appear, at gatherings of foundation people actual clashes of ideas now occur, and new light is being thrown on the whole landscape of private and governmental activity relevant to the work of foundations. As a result, horizons are widening as awareness of broader social needs and of the whole context within which philanthropy operates grows. In turn, questions about foundation priorities and foundation roles are being raised in a more knowledgeable and searching way than ever before.

As this process proceeds, ignorant, amateurish, and petty philanthropy, which still characterizes a good part of the activity of even the very large foundations, should become an early casualty. Random small institutional support grants, passivity in grant making, and confinement of the work of a large foundation to purely local matters will more and more clearly be seen as lost opportunities, as a failure of awareness and vision. The surest antidotes to inconsequential grant making are better information and open debate. The influence of such exposure may work somewhat slowly and unevenly, but it is already beginning to be felt.

The Power of Role Models

At least as important as such interaction and argumentation will be the impact on the thinking of other large foundations of the recognizedly superior performance of the few best ones. Role models in philanthropy as in any other field can be a powerful influence.

Robert Wood Johnson Foundation exemplifies this potentiality. It concentrates its efforts on one of the largest, most rapidly growing, most complex, and most dangerously troubled aspects of the American welfare state: health care. Despite the intimidating problems that that field presents, Johnson has been able to identify significant aspects that are amenable to improvement. It has devised its major field tests of alternative solutions in a knowledgeable and creative way. It has won the collaboration of many of the major institutions in the complex American health-care system in carrying them out. It has done the most careful scientific research to measure the results of its experiments and has communicated its findings to all the agencies, governmental and private, that could make use of them as well as to the general public.

Johnson is therefore a living example of the possibility of a large foundation, if it has the intellectual energy, professional competence, and strength of motivation, tackling even the most baffling issues confronting American society—where government and various elements of the private sector are all involved, where the issues embrace subissues of money, science, social values, vested interests, and politics—and of making a real difference.

Johnson has demonstrated that such a foundation, though operating with private resources of relatively limited scale, can not only coexist with the immensely larger factor of government but be a valuable stimulant and guidance factor to government efforts. It can provide a precious safeguard for the public interest by monitoring, evaluating, and on occasion criticizing government policies and actions within its field of expertise. It thus gives proof that pluralistic democracy can operate even at the highest level of national concerns.

Its example gives strong encouragement to other foundations to think that what it has done in the tangled field of health care, they might do in connection with such problems as social welfare policy, or the administration of justice, or housing, or youth unemployment, or care of the elderly, or even lessening the likelihood of war.

THE LOCOMOTIVE EFFECT

The influence of a role model like Robert Wood Johnson increases as knowledge of what it is doing and how it is doing it circulates among others in philanthropy, both staff professionals and trustees, and as the inevitable comparisons are made with their own policies and programs. But the experience and ideas of the ablest and most energetic foundations are transmitted also through programs that they organize jointly with other foundations: the collaboration of Johnson with Pew Memorial in a program to serve the health-care needs of the homeless, of Kellogg and Duke in improving hospital services, and of Andrew W. Mellon with Hewlett and others in strengthening private institutions of higher education. Nothing can be more persuasive to a foundation board and staff of the feasibility and rewards of attacking a large and difficult problem than the experience of having successfully done it as a member of such a consortium. The power of example is considerable; the power of participation is even greater. This type of joint action among the larger foundations is now growing, another encouraging development.

The Fifth, and Metaphysical, Criterion

In the achievements of the few greatest of our large foundations, knowledgeability, professional skills, and rationality have played a very important part. But there has also been present another essential element that cannot be described in the language of scientific or management principles: They have all been animated by a sense of mission, an active commitment to a cause. And for other foundations that aspire to the highest order or performance, this can be stated as a requirement. That vision or cause need not be so transcendental as truth, justice, or world peace, but it surely should be larger than bringing professional football to Indianapolis or buying bulletproof vests for the Chicago police department.

It is a waste of important potential if foundations do not make use of the special freedoms they have been given: to take the long view; to back a promising but unproven idea, individual, or institution; to take an unpopular or unorthodox stand; to facilitate change rather than automatically endorsing the status quo (a reflex that could be called knee-jerk conservatism); to act and not merely react; to initiate, even to gamble and dare.

This point bears emphasis at this stage in the evolution of the major foundations, a good many of which are in midpassage from amateurish philanthropy to a type more organized and productive. One result has been to cause them to bring in experienced executives from business or educational institutions to head their staffs. This has without question resulted in better management. But it has also created the danger of an infestation of bureaucrats and technocrats. For in the end, philanthropy is not an exercise in administrative science by agencies performing ordinary operational tasks. Foundations are not a branch of banking in the business of merely distributing money. Rather, by their special character they are moral and symbolic entities dealing in matters of the mind and spirit. It is not enough therefore for them to be only law-abiding, well-managed, prudent, and dispassionate.

In their sphere they have an obligation of standard setting, of lifting hearts and hopes. As in the case of great concert artists, it is not sufficient that they arrive at the performance on time, play on key, and remember to thank their accompanist. More is and should be expected of them: high aspiration, dedication, and inspiration to others. They must believe in something, stand for something, and with conviction.

The Prospect

The processes for improvement that have now been set into motion pose a deadly threat to inertia and mediocrity in American philanthropy. Though they are diverse and undirected by any central source, they tend inevitably to enable better ideas to overcome poorer ones and to move the large foundations at the middle and low end of the spectrum of effectiveness gradually upward. That those processes are now increasingly under way is the fundamental reason that the prospects for improved philanthropy are now brighter than ever before.

However, the broader political context in which foundations will have to function is not brightening, but darkening, a development that will be discussed in the following and concluding chapter.

17

EPILOGUE:

Double Crisis,
Double Challenge

A heavy cloud hangs over the private nonprofit sector today. From the anxious and angry talk that is heard, it would seem that the crisis is essentially financial, and the cause of it all is Ronald Reagan. In fact, however, it is far more than financial, and it began to take shape long before the president came into office. He has contributed to the problems, but far more fundamental factors are at work in the situation than the force of a single political personality, even a very popular one.

At the time he was elected in 1980, the nonprofit sector had just been through a very damaging decade. Rampant inflation in the 1970s had had extremely severe effects on the costs of all labor-intensive institutions, including the nonprofits, and the erratic performance of the securities markets had badly eroded their reserves and endowments. Financially they were under stress and in seriously weakened condition.

But they were also threatened by other developments, seemingly beneficial, that had begun still earlier. Starting in the 1950s and 1960s, as government social programs of all kinds were enlarged and extended, and as private nonprofit agencies were increasingly employed to deliver the services funded, their income from government grants and contracts also swelled. In the 1970s, for example, their income from the federal government rose dramatically from $15 billion a year at the start to more than $40 billion at the end. Over the same period the proportion of their income from private gifts dropped steadily.

The good part of all this was that the staffs and services of the nonprofits expanded and the historic partnership between government and nonprofit agencies in providing educational, medical, and social services to the population was reaffirmed and strengthened. The bad part was that the whole nonprofit sector other than the churches was becoming more and more dependent on government for its sustenance, more subject to government regulation and oversight; and, fattened with government money, more vulnerable than ever before to any sharp shift in government social policy.

The election of Reagan in 1980 signaled just such a shift. He came into office on the basis of a clearly stated pledge to increase the nation's military strength, reduce taxes, and cut social programs. With strong public support, he promptly proceeded to carry out that program. For nonprofits the cuts in social programs during his first term reduced the federal funds flowing to them by some $4 to $5 billion a year compared to what they would have received under previous legislation. In addition, changes in the tax laws proposed by the president and accepted by the Congress reduced the incentives for charitable giving and thereby cut the level of gifts to nonprofit agencies by some $4 billion a year. Overall, nonprofits other than churches lost about 5 percent of their total income each year during Reagan's first term as a result of the policy changes he introduced.

This aggregate figure masks the more drastic effect of the changes on particular categories of institutions. Thus federal support for hospitals and health-care agencies, because of Medicare and Medicaid entitlements and the general rise in medical costs, increased by some 24 percent for the period. But the real value of federal support to all other kinds of nonprofits except churches declined by some 27 percent.

In November 1984, the president was resoundingly reelected,

and very soon thereafter the White House put forward a new program of major cuts in social programs and a plan for the general overhauling of the tax system. The haste in preparing these proposals was prompted by a wave of concern that swept the business and financial communities immediately after the election because of the huge deficits that had been accumulated during Reagan's first term and the prospect of even larger deficits during his second. Analyses of the proposals by competent experts indicated that the impact on nonprofits would be to reduce further their income from government contracts and grants and from private gifts by an amount substantially greater than their losses during Reagan's first term.

They had been hurt badly by the administration's actions in 1980. Now they were being threatened again, and their outcry was immediate and indignant. But defenders of the president argued that the actions taken in 1980 and the further program cuts and changes in the tax laws proposed in 1985 were simply the fulfillment of his pledges to the electorate, and that just as the nonprofits had benefited from the profligacy and extravagance of earlier Democratic administrations in social spending, so they now had to help bear the pain of the austerity of a new national direction. They also enumerated the benefits they felt had come to the nonprofit sector during President Reagan's first term: the boost he had given to corporate and private giving by his endorsement of voluntarism; the drop in energy costs, as well as the sharp drop in the rate of inflation; the removal of some burdensome government regulations; and the achievement of the first phase of an economic recovery.

Run Silent, Run Deep

But such assertions were not very persuasive to the nonprofit community, partly because it was more convenient for them to feel that their problem was a misguided president than an adverse electorate.

Moreover, they were suffering not only from disappointment but shock—shock because of the brutal demonstration they had witnessed of the extent to which the voluntary sector had become an adjunct and a dependent of government and shock because of the suddenness with which a long-established direction of national social policy could be drastically altered.

Anxiety about the future was also a factor, felt particularly by social welfare agencies serving the needs of the poor and disadvantaged. They consider themselves to be in the very dangerous situation of "double jeopardy." Their income from private sources has been drifting down and their income from government dropping precipitously. At the same time various demographic and other irreversible developments are increasing their caseloads and the demands on them by the elderly; by the growing number of working mothers for day-care services for their children; by the swelling population of ill-educated immigrants now in the country, and others. They feel caught, therefore, in the jaws of a cruel vise and feel they are facing impending calamity.

These fears and frustrations are mixed with a variety of other concerns and emotions. Not just those associated with social welfare agencies but a large proportion of all nonprofit leaders sense not only an indifference but an active hostility toward them on the part of the Reagan administration. In the present adversarial atmosphere they feel that the whole, long-established, carefully developed relationship of mutual trust and cooperation between the federal government and the private nonprofit sector is eroding, even breaking down.

Nor is their situation and state of mind made easier by the kinds of self-doubts and confusions now afflicting many institutions of the nonprofit sector. Across the whole field of human services there has been a strong shift toward professionalization and a parallel downgrading and shrinkage of volunteer involvement. Organizational units, especially hospitals and educational institutions, have greatly increased in scale and in bureaucratization. The pressures of inflation, cuts in government income, and other financial uncertainties have produced a strong push toward the development of profit-making activities and a fee-for-services mentality, which clashes with the qualities of compassion and generosity that have been basic to the voluntarist tradition. The result is a deep and spreading disorientation, an identity crisis, about what the nonprofit sector is, what its role and responsibilities should be, what its relationship to government and to the private profit-making sector should be, and what its special capabilities and limitations are.

The Challenge to Foundations

Grant-making foundations, not being dependent for their income on government contracts, grants, and reimbursement, are not faced with problems of financial survival as a result of the federal cutbacks. But in every other way they are directly affected. Operating nonprofits are the instruments through which they carry out their programs and from which they receive their feedback and much of their stimulus. When the nonprofit sector is strong and healthy, foundations are strengthened and effective; when it is crippled, foundations are equally and immediately handicapped.

The emerging situation urgently calls for a strong and creative response by grant-making foundations. They cannot of course seek to replace the losses in government funding, the disproportion between their resources and their requirements being too extreme. Rather their great challenge and opportunity is to help the nonprofit sector to think through and resolve some of its even more basic nonfinancial dilemmas. Their funding is needed:

1. to gather more adequate and timely data about the general condition of the sector and the precise location of the most urgent and dangerous problems;
2. to help develop greater public understanding of the perils arising and about the grave implications of a possible breakdown of this important element in American society;
3. to help mobilize support to prevent discriminatory tax legislation and other government actions damaging to the nonprofits;
4. for policy studies to develop serious recommendations for a new national policy to strengthen the whole government–private sector partnership. The present chaotic, indifferent, and periodically destructive approach of government to relationships with the Third Sector needs to be replaced by a system of better communication and coordination, including a focus of responsibility within the executive branch for taking effective action when need arises; and
5. to enable leaders of the sector to deliberate with one another and with leaders of other sectors about how nonprofits can cope with their present problems and adjust to their radically new circumstances without losing the essential

characteristics of voluntarism, diversity, compassion, fairness, creativity, and freedom that are the basic values they embody and that constitute their special contribution to the American democratic system.

If resources to support such efforts are not made available, the role and usefulness of the nonprofit sector can only shrivel, and the traditional government–nonprofit sector partnership will steadily, disastrously deteriorate, a process visibly under way at the moment. Yet as of today, American foundations have almost totally failed to grasp the significance of what is taking place before their eyes. A tiny few, such as Gannett, Atlantic Richfield, and Equitable Life, have made some significant grants to two capable existing organizations, Independent Sector and the Council on Foundations, to address some of these problems. But not a single one of the major foundations has yet made this matter so critical for themselves and their clientele a major program interest.

The second evolving crisis confronting foundations and offering major challenge to their competence and creativity is directly related to the first and touches even deeper, broader shifts in American life, including the exhaustion of public confidence in the balance between the costs and benefits of the present form of the welfare state. Indeed, big philanthropy's greatest opportunity for service to the nation at present may lie in helping it find its way out of this divisive, embittering, and, in human terms, tragic political impasse.

The starting point if such a task is to be undertaken must be to cast off sterile partisan formulations of the nature and origins of the present predicament. Among other things, this requires recognition that public dissatisfaction with national social policies began to be manifest more than a decade ago. The years 1950–1975 had been a period of vigorous and sustained real economic growth, which threw off huge resources available for spending in the public sector. But that untypical period came to an end in the mid-1970s. About the same time, tax-limitation statutes began to be enacted in states and localities all across the country; and in 1978 federal support for the state and local public sector turned downward. The election of 1980 simply continued and politically confirmed the decline in public willingness to put greater and greater resources into existing social programs.

That resistance grew out of at least three related trends, first, an increased cost-consciousness among taxpayers as the period of booming growth tapered off, and second, a growing sense that many costly programs were not working well and that the forces of bureaucracy and special interest politics made introducing innovations or reforms that would improve them impossible. The third had to do with the way the social services system as it had developed treated people. There developed a growing dislike for the overprofessionalization and bureaucratization of social services and indeed with the whole concept of *service*, that is, of some people "caring" for other people for pay. In many places an interest grew in developing alternative strategies that would strengthen the capacity of individuals, families, and neighborhoods to take more care of themselves and to depend less on the institutions—the "megastructures," as they have come to be called—of the modern social service state. The shift was clearly reflected in public opinion surveys and in a massive decline of public confidence in institutions.

In all these respects—taxpayer discontent, skepticism about the effectiveness of public programs, and concern about the "dehumanization" of social services and the undermining of individual and group responsibility for self- and mutual help—the American experience is roughly similar to that of other advanced societies in Europe and elsewhere.

Clearly, what is involved is not merely another episode in the old liberal-conservative debate over fiscal responsibility and compassionate government. Rather, a historic watershed has been crossed. The modern welfare state has reached its limits of administrative effectiveness and public acceptability, and a fundamental structural and conceptual overhaul is required. In this crisis, the very governability of democratic societies may be at stake because of the seemingly irreconcilable contradictions with which they are now faced, namely the unlimited nature of human wants and aspirations coupled with the limited character of the available resources and the natural tendency of people to ask more of government in services than they are willing to pay for.

The challenge to philanthropy is to help find some new and better answers to this fundamental dilemma: to help generate some fresh ideas and to test some new methods that might provide for both equity and efficiency, humaneness and effectiveness, in social programs.

But to meet this challenge they will among other things have to upend and reverse their established concept of their role in relation to government.

In the early years of the century, when the nation had reached a certain point in its economic development and was ready to move forward in its educational, medical, and cultural development, the Rockefeller and Carnegie foundations along with a few others launched the experiments that blazed the trails that government and others subsequently followed. The dramatic achievements of the period have colored the outlook, defined the approach, and shaped the definition of their highest role of most of the best big foundations ever since. Over the following decades they devoted themselves to seeking out new areas of educational, social, scientific, medical, and cultural needs and experimenting with new ways of serving them. When an experiment proved promising, they turned the matter over to government to develop on a grandly expanded scale. With the vastly greater resources available to the public sector in the 1950s, 1960s, and 1970s, and with the nation in a generally expansionist and idealistic mood, this type of foundation contribution to national development reached its apogee. The foundations saw their role as catalysts for the creation of new programs to help realize the national dream of progress and equality.

But now the era of limits and constraints has arrived, and a rethinking and redirection of approaches are necessary. National aspirations have not been abandoned, but the awareness of costs has become acute, an awareness that may become even greater in the future as energy costs resume their rise and as conventional supplies decline; as environmental protection becomes more and more expensive; and as population increases. Awareness of the limits of the willingness of the citizenry to bear the costs of social programs has also increased, along with awareness of the limited capacity of government to design and administer programs that work, whose results are commensurate with their costs, and whose unintended side effects do not nullify their other benefits.

The Robert Wood Johnson Foundation in the field of health care and the Ford Foundation in its major new effort to reexamine social welfare policy in the United States have begun to grapple with such vital and difficult issues; it is to be hoped that some others among the finest few of the big foundations that have the competence to address large and complex national problems will follow. The opportunity offered is for philanthropy to attempt to perform in the era of limits and austerity a role of comparable importance to that of the great foundations in philanthropy's golden age. But this time the task is even more difficult, namely not to help society do more with more but to enable it to do more, and better, with less, and to enable individuals to do more for themselves.

Notes

Page

7   Abraham Flexner, "Medical Education in the United
        States and Canada," *Carnegie Foundation for the Ad-
        vancement of Teaching*, Bulletin no. 4 (New York,
        1910).

7   Gunnar Myrdal, with Richard Sterner and Arnold Rose,
        *An American Dilemma: The Negro Problem and Modern
        Democracy* (New York: Harper & Row, 1944).

8   Kathleen D. McCarthy, *Noblesse Oblige: Charity and
        Cultural Philanthropy in Chicago, 1849–1929* (Chicago:
        University of Chicago Press, 1982).

Page

8   Reverend Harry C. Vrooman, "Charity, Old and New," *Arena II* (January 1895), p. 274.

9   Harry Hurt, *Texas Rich* (New York: W.W. Norton, 1981), p. 21.

9   Anthony Sampson, *The New Anatomy of Britain* (London: Hodder & Stoughton, 1971), p. 208.

15   John Steinbeck, "About Ed Ricketts," *The Log from the Sea of Cortez* (New York: The Viking Press, 1951), pp. lxiv–lxv.

15   Louis Auchincloss in *The Forbes Four Hundred* (New York: Forbes Inc., 1984), pp. 52–53.

23   *Report of the U.S. Commission on Industrial Relations* (1915), pp. 118–19, 125.

24   René A. Wormser, *Foundations, Their Power and Influence* (New York: Devin-Adair, 1968).

25   David Horowitz and David Kolodney, "The Foundations, Charity Begins at Home," *Ramparts* (April 1969).

26   U.S. Congress, House of Representatives, *Hearings Before the Committee on Ways and Means on the Subject of Tax Reform*, 91C1/ 1969, Part II, pp. 10ff.

31   John W. Nason, *Trustees and the Future of Foundations* (New York: Council on Foundations, 1977).

31   Eugene C. Struckhoff, *The Handbook for Community Foundations: Their Formation, Development and Operation*, 2 vols. (New York: Council on Foundations, 1977). This is a looseleaf book containing a collection of reprints, letters, law, and articles.

35   Lester M. Salamon and Alan J. Abramson, *The Federal Government and Nonprofit Sector: Implications of the*

Page

Reagan Budget Proposals (Washington, D.C.: The Urban Institute, May 1981).

42   Karen Rothmeyer, a distinguished journalist who is now a professor at Columbia University and was formerly on the staff of *The Wall Street Journal*, wrote a detailed article on Scaife's philanthropic activities a few years ago. In connection with its preparation she sought repeatedly to interview him but without success. Finally she encountered him in Boston, where he was attending a board meeting. As he was leaving the exclusive Union Club in that city, the following exchange occurred:

Ms. Rothmeyer: "Mr. Scaife, could you explain why you give so much money to the New Right?"

Scaife: "You f——ing Communist c——, get out of here."

68   Mary Anna Colwell, "Philanthropic Foundations and Public Policy: The Political Role of Foundations" (Ph.D. diss., University of California, Berkeley, 1980).

84   Ida M. Tarbell, *The History of the Standard Oil Company*, 2 vols. (New York: McClure, Phillips & Co., 1904).

98   Lewis Thomas, *The Lives of a Cell* (New York: The Viking Press, 1974), p. 102.

140   Alan Pifer, "Final Thoughts," *Report of the Carnegie Corporation, 1982.*

156   John R. Coleman, "Diary of a Homeless Man," *New York* (February 21, 1983).

235   George Sanders, the actor, one of Gabor's several husbands, explained their breakup, saying, "It is impossible to carry on a relationship by talking to someone under a hair dryer...."

299   On October 7, 1969, at the age of ninety-four, Mott appeared before the Senate Finance Committee in Washington to testify on behalf of private foundations. One of the news stories written about the event gives a picture of the style of this durable citizen of Michigan:

The old man spoke in a firm, sure voice and read from notes without using glasses. The opinions he expressed were brief and to the point. But the Senators seemed more interested in the man than in his testimony.

"Where are your glasses?" inquired Senator Carl D. Curtis, Republican of Nebraska. "We are amazed you can read without them."

"In my pocket," snapped Mr. Mott.

"How do you keep your youth?" asked Senator Paul J. Fannin, Republican of Arizona.

"I am absolutely dedicated to what we are trying to do in the Foundation. I don't have time to think about my age," Mr. Mott replied. "I feel I was born today. I am looking to the future. I am going ahead full steam."

His duty done, Mr. Mott rose from the witness chair to his full six-foot height. The diamond stick-pin in his mod wide gray tie flashed in the light. He remarked that it had been nice to testify, but no, the Senators hadn't bothered him. He would have a martini for lunch nonetheless, very dry with an olive. (*Washington Daily News*, October 8, 1969)

328   Warren Weaver, *Scene of Change* (New York: Charles Scribner's Sons, 1970), p. 125.

391–92   *The New York Times*, October 16, 1963.

437   For those interested in understanding these trends in more detail, a number of excellent studies are now available: Virginia A. Hodgkinson and Murray S. Weitzman, *Dimensions of the Independent Sector: A Statistical Profile* (Washington, D.C.: Independent Sec-

tor, 1984); Lester M. Salamon and Alan J. Abramson, *The Federal Government and the Nonprofit Sector: Implications of the Reagan Budget Proposals* (Washington, D.C.: The Urban Institute, May 1981); Lester M. Salamon and Alan J. Abramson, *The Federal Budget and the Nonprofit Sector* (Washington, D.C.: The Urban Institute Press, 1982); Laurence B. Lindsey, Harvard University, *A Comparison of the Costs and Potential Economic Benefits of the Treasury Proposal on Charitable Giving*, prepared for the Association of American Universities, December 1984; Charles T. Clotfelter, Duke University, *Tax Reform Proposals and Charitable Giving in 1985* (Washington, D.C.: prepared for Independent Sector, March 15, 1985); and Lester M. Salamon and Alan J. Abramson, "Nonprofits and the Federal Budget: Deeper Cuts Ahead," *Foundation News* (March–April 1985), p. 48.

A Short Sampler
of Readings

THE HISTORY OF PHILANTHROPY AND ITS DEVELOPMENT
IN THE UNITED STATES

BREMMER, ROBERT H. *American Philanthropy.* Chicago: University
of Chicago Press, 1960. A good review of the American charitable tradition and its special characteristics by a scholar who has
been called a "ruthless and sympathetic historian."

FLEXNER, ABRAHAM. *Funds and Foundations: Their Policies, Past
and Present.* New York: Harper & Bros., 1952. An opinionated
analysis of the activities of Rockefeller, Carnegie, and other early
foundations by one of the most influential figures in foundation
history.

FOSDICK, RAYMOND B. *The Story of the Rockefeller Foundation, 1913
to 1950.* New York: Harper & Bros., 1952. A literate and informative account by one of its outstanding presidents of the years

of greatness of what was once the greatest American foundation.

MCCARTHY, KATHLEEN D. *Noblesse Oblige: Charity and Cultural Philanthropy in Chicago, 1849–1929.* Chicago: University of Chicago Press, 1982. A carefully researched and well-written study that, though it has a narrow focus on one city and only certain aspects of philanthropy, illuminates the evolution of the idea of civic stewardship in American life in the late nineteenth and early twentieth centuries.

NIELSEN, WALDEMAR A. *The Big Foundations.* New York: Columbia University Press, 1972. A review of the development of the thirty-three largest American foundations and an appraisal as of the time of the Patman Hearings in 1969.

SENECA, LUCIUS ANNAEUS. *Moral Essays,* Vol. III: *De Beneficiis.* Cambridge, Mass.: Loeb Classical Library, Harvard University Press, 1964. This wealthy Roman's advice on giving and receiving benefits is more clever than profound, but it shows the sophisticated understanding of grantor-grantee relationships which already existed two thousand years ago.

The Treasury Department Report on Private Foundations. February 1965. Prepared for the Senate Finance Committee, this is a brilliant analysis and documentation of the abuses into which foundations had fallen by the 1960s.

Foundations among their other uses can serve as screens on which to project the resentments and nightmarish fears of extremists of both the Right and the Left. An example of the former is René A. Wormser, *Foundations, Their Power and Influence.* New York: Devin-Adair, 1968. Wormser served as counsel to the most incompetent of the McCarthyite investigations of the 1950s, namely that of the Reece Committee of the House of Representatives. An example of the equivalent from the other end of the political spectrum is David Horowitz and David Kolodney, "The Foundations [Charity Begins at Home]." *Ramparts* (April 1969).

WEAVER, WARREN. *U.S. Philanthropic Foundations.* New York: Harper & Row, 1967. A testy and tendentious defense of foundations by a man long associated with them, typical of what used to pass as serious analysis and appraisal of the field. It concludes with some seventeen chapters of almost uninterrupted applause by prominent beneficiaries. A notable exception is the perceptive and balanced analysis of the role of foundation grants in the field of economics by Nobel laureate George Stigler.

The two most important sources of current information about U.S. foundations:

Foundation Directory is the authoritative reference volume of the Foundation Center, based in New York City and with libraries and collections located throughout the country. Revised periodically, it gives information on the assets, trustees, staff, and programs of more than three thousand private grant-making foundations.

The Research Papers of the Commission on Private Philanthropy and Public Needs. 5 vols. Washington, D.C.: U.S. Department of Treasury, 1977. These studies commissioned by the so-called Filer Commission constitute the first substantial body of research on American foundations and the voluntary sector ever assembled. The papers are now mostly outdated, but they include a number of landmark efforts, including the studies of Martin Feldstein of Harvard modeling the probable impacts of alternative changes in tax incentives on individual giving; the analysis of Paul Ylvisaker and Jane Mavity on "The Role of Private Philanthropy in Public Affairs," and the first mapping of the size and configuration of the private nonprofit sector by Gabriel Rudney.

WEALTH, POWER, AND THE DONORS

The rich as a class have long been unloved. Aristotle in his *Rhetoric* and Plato in both *The Republic* and *The Laws* denounced them for their callousness and greed; the Bible in a well-known passage gave them relatively little chance of getting into heaven; and Karl Marx and his followers have been especially unadmiring.

In the United States a good many critical essays and studies on the rich and the superrich have been done, of which three are representative:

DOMHOFF, G. WILLIAM, and BALLARD, HOYT B., *C. Wright Mills and the Power Elite.* Boston: Beacon Press, 1968. Mills's highly controversial book first published in 1956 contended that the "power elite" in America has enormous economic and political power, that it has become a self-perpetuating class, and that its decisions are increasingly directed to immoral ends. This volume brings together the major responses, pro and con, that the original book evoked.

LUNDBERG, FERDINAND. *The Rich and the Super Rich.* New York: Bantam Books, 1969. A thoroughly researched and highly critical study, arguing that the United States now has a well-established hereditary propertied class that dominates the economy and exercises a grossly disproportionate influence over politics and the society.

VEBLEN, THORSTEIN. *The Theory of the Leisure Class,* 1899. Reprint. New York: Modern Library, 1931. A classic of economic and social literature which argues that wealthy people spend their surplus income primarily to impress other people. Some contemporary admirers of Veblen's thesis think that philanthropy may now have become the most conspicuous form of such "conspicuous consumption."

The single most influential defense of American capitalism is:

SCHUMPETER, JOSEPH A. *Capitalism, Socialism and Democracy.* New York: Harpers, 1950. This magisterial book makes the case for capitalism not only as the essential means of providing for material progress and human well-being but also for the protection of political freedom and individual liberties.

ALTRUISM, VOLUNTARISM, AND PHILANTHROPY

The social sciences have always had great difficulty accommodating the phenomenon of altruism into their theories.

BOULDING, KENNETH. *The Economy of Love and Fear.* Belmont, Calif.: Wadsworth Publishing Co., 1973. A lively and useful effort to analyze the role of "unrequited transactions" in the economy.

MAUSS, MARCEL. *The Gift: Forms and Functions of Exchange in Archaic Societies,* 1925. Reprint. Translated by Ian Cunnison. London: Cohen & West, Ltd., 1954). A classic anthropological study of exchange theory and the personal and cultural factors underlying altruistic behavior.

NIELSEN, WALDEMAR A. *The Endangered Sector.* New York: Columbia University Press, 1979. A history of the private, nonprofit element in the American pluralistic system, and an effort to define its role, analyze its problems, and suggest various changes in public policy to ensure its preservation.

O'CONNELL, BRIAN. *America's Voluntary Spirit: A Book of Readings.* New York: The Foundation Center, 1983. A valuable collection of key documents ranging from Andrew Carnegie's "Gospel of Wealth" to "True and False Philanthropy" from one of the McGuffey Readers.

PAYTON, ROBERT L. *Major Challenges to Philanthropy.* Washington, D.C.: Independent Sector, 1984. A wide-ranging inquiry into many of the philosophical issues in contemporary philanthropy by the head of the Exxon Educational Foundation.

PHELPS, EDMUND S., ed. *Altruism, Morality, and Economic Theory.* New York: Russell Sage Foundation, 1975. A number of leading economists struggle inconclusively with the contradiction between their self-interest model of human behavior and the fact that a good many people behave in ways that do not involve any apparent reward.

Among the more influential criticisms of foundation practices are the following:

BARZUN, JACQUES. "The Folklore of Philanthropy" in *The House of Intellect.* New York: Harper & Bros., 1959. An elegant and deeply felt attack on the damaging effects of both government and foundation grants in demeaning the role of teaching and undermining the loyalty of faculty to their universities.

LASKI, HAROLD J. "Foundations, Universities and Research." *Harper's Monthly Magazine* 158 (August 1928), pp. 295–303. A scathing attack on what Laski perceived as the constraining impact of foundation funding on intellectual freedom and creativity, and on the arrogance of foundation personnel.

WALSH, FRANK P. "Perilous Philanthropy." *The Independent* 83 (August 23, 1915), pp. 262–64. Senator Walsh, who headed the nation's first public inquiry into foundation activities, reflecting the mood of the Progressive era, explains why these "huge philanthropic trusts" are "a menace to the welfare of society."

Among the recent flow of speeches and articles about the nonprofit sector, two are especially knowledgeable and thoughtful:

O'CONNELL, BRIAN. "Public and Voluntary Sectors: Future Responsibilities." Speech delivered at the University of Cincinnati School of Social Work, December 12, 1984. Available from Independent Sector, Washington, D.C.

SALAMON, LESTER. "The Future of the Non Profit Sector." *Grantsmanship News* (September/December 1984). Mr. Salamon is one of the best of the younger scholars now doing research on the subject.

Index

Printed in the United States
203291BV00002B/1-24/P